AMERICAN EDUCATION

Its Men

Ideas

and

Institutions

Advisory Editor

Lawrence A. Cremin
Frederick A. P. Barnard Professor of Education
Teachers College, Columbia University

Quaker Education
in the
Colony and State
of New Jersey

Thomas Woody

ARNO PRESS & THE NEW YORK TIMES
New York ∗ *1969*

Reprint edition 1969 by Arno Press, Inc.

*

Library of Congress Catalog Card No. 76-89256

*

Reprinted from a copy in Teachers College Library

*

Manufactured in the United States of America

Editorial Note

AMERICAN EDUCATION: *Its Men, Institutions and Ideas* presents selected works of thought and scholarship that have long been out of print or otherwise unavailable. Inevitably, such works will include particular ideas and doctrines that have been outmoded or superseded by more recent research. Nevertheless, all retain their place in the literature, having influenced educational thought and practice in their own time and having provided the basis for subsequent scholarship.

Lawrence A. Cremin
Teachers College

Quaker Education
in the
Colony and State
of New Jersey

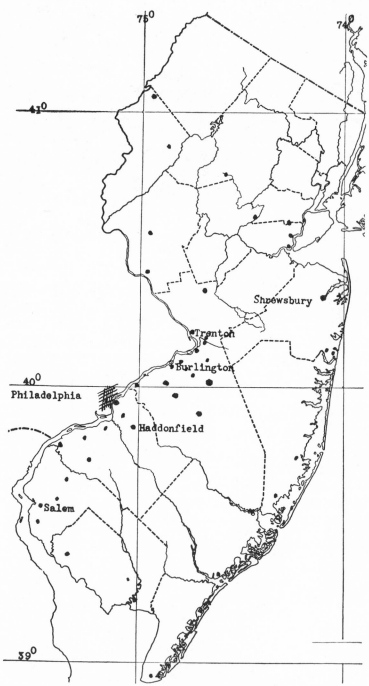

OUTLINE MAP SHOWING THE DISTRIBUTION OF IMPORTANT
EARLY QUAKER MEETINGS IN NEW JERSEY

QUAKER EDUCATION

IN THE

COLONY AND STATE OF NEW JERSEY

A Source Book

By

THOMAS WOODY

ASSISTANT PROFESSOR, HISTORY OF EDUCATION
UNIVERSITY OF PENNSYLVANIA

Published by the Author
University of Pennsylvania
PHILADELPHIA
1923

PRESS OF W. F. HUMPHREY
GENEVA, N. Y.

TO
PROFESSOR PAUL MONROE
WHO FIRST STIMULATED MY INTEREST
IN THE HISTORY OF EDUCATION
THIS BOOK
IS GRATEFULLY DEDICATED

" Neither must we cast a slight upon education, which is the first and fairest thing that the best of men ever have, and which, though liable to take wrong direction, is capable of reformation. And this work of reformation is the great business of every man while he lives."—PLATO.

QUAKER EDUCATION IN THE COLONY AND
STATE OF NEW JERSEY

CONTENTS

LIST OF ILLUSTRATIONS

PREFACE

In the following pages there is presented as full an account of the Quaker schools in New Jersey as the limitation of sources and space will permit. In many cases almost the sole source of information about the schools has been the meeting records. While the limitations of these sources are recognized, they are, perhaps, the most trustworthy of any now extant; and in many instances there are none other. They are accordingly used freely. Since the minutes of meetings and the records of old school committees are, for the most part, very difficult of access for students of education, it has seemed wise to incorporate liberal selections from the sources in the text.

Since, in the preparation of this volume the writer has read thousands of pages of manuscript records, some of which were poorly written and others badly preserved, he recognizes the inevitable fact that some points have possibly been overlooked and inaccuracies have crept in. As the presentation of a truthful statement only is aimed at, he solicits criticism of a constructive nature and correction where errors in fact may occur. In certain cases, interest would have dictated that a detailed study be made of schools but such was not practicable within the limits of this book. It is to be hoped that local historians, thoroughly familiar with the ground, having access to the records, and, being possessed of a more bountiful supply of intimate knowledge, may be able to make such detailed studies. The policy of giving full footnote references has been pursued in order to facilitate such further research; and that material now located may be consulted readily without duplication of my efforts. The voluminous character of many of the *Mss.*, and the fact that none are indexed, save occasionally for genealogical purposes, make this extremely desirable.

Though certain phases of educational development, particularly the growth of district schools out of certain Friends' institutions and the tendency towards centralization, have been traced to the present, the writer disclaims any intention of giving a view of Quaker schools of the present day. The purpose has been historical throughout. No survey of the present is attempted.

I am indebted to many librarians and custodians of records, both in this city and in various places in New Jersey. Where possible their services have been acknowledged on the proper pages of this book. To others, whom I have troubled on many occasions, it is a pleasure to acknowledge my indebtedness: Miss Linda Moore, of the Friends' Central Library, Mr. George Vaux, Custodian of Records, Mr. William Cowperthwaite at the Friends' Book Store, and Mr. Charles Bradford, now deceased, who prepared the photographs. To my colleagues, Dean John H. Minnick and Dr. E . D. Grizzell, I wish to express my appreciation of encouragement and assistance. Likewise I wish to acknowledge a great obligation to Wilhelmine Lawton Woody, whose assistance in the preparation and revision of the text has been invaluable.

Philadelphia,   THOMAS WOODY
September 29, 1922

QUAKER EDUCATION IN THE COLONY AND STATE OF NEW JERSEY

CHAPTER I

INTRODUCTION

New Jersey was settled during the last quarter of the seventeenth century. In contrast with other colonies, and notably Massachusetts, she lacked homogeneity of nationality and religion. In this she was closely akin to Pennsylvania. Among her peoples were the Dutch, Scotch, English and Swedes. As for churches, there were the Dutch Reformed, Scotch Covenanter, Quaker, Anglican, Baptist, Swedish and Moravian. This great diversity of population and religion made it inevitable that her education should be equally so.

However, the colony was not so badly divided as might seem. But two divisions were recognized: East and West Jersey. To settle disputes between Carteret and the trustees of Byllynge a line was run from Little Egg Harbor to the Delaware River at about 41° north latitude, which divided the two. To the east and north of this line the territory was retained by Carteret; on the west and south it belonged to the Quaker proprietors. This division was made in 1676. Six years later, Penn and eleven Quaker associates purchased East Jersey for the sum of £3,400. To these twelve were added other twelve "partners," mostly Scotch, who for a few years constituted the twenty-four proprietors of East Jersey. In 1702 the Proprietors withdrew from the government of the colony, retaining only property in the soil and their quitrents, and the two provinces were united under Lord Cornbury as Governor. New Jersey remained a royal province until 1776.

Little was accomplished for education in the Colonial period save through individuals and individual congregations.[1] The

---

[1] The statement made by an historian of New Jersey that "From the first New Jersey was in advance of every American state in education" is not substantiated by fact.

Concessions and Agreements of the Proprietors, Freeholders, and Inhabitants of West New Jersey in America, adopted in 1676-7, was very liberal in character, granting entire freedom of conscience, universal suffrage, voting by ballot, no imprisonment for debt, education of orphans at public expense, freedom of all from the oppression of slavery, protection of the Indians in their rights, government by ten commissioners, and an elected and paid assembly of one hundred members.[2] The colony, however, was never really governed under this system, excepting as the laws passed by the assembly, called by Governor Jennings, were in general accord with it. The section of the Concessions and Agreements, relating to education of orphans, ran as follows:

If parents die leaving child or children, and no estate, or not sufficient to maintain and bring up the said child or children, in that case the commissioners are to appoint persons to take care for the child or children, to bring them up in such manner as the commissioners shall appoint, and the charges thereof to be borne by the public stock of the province; and if none be established, then a tax to be levied by twelve men of the neighborhood, with the consent of the commissioners or the main part of them.[3]

Specific educational legislation was passed by the Quaker assembly of West New Jersey in 1682, when the Island of Matinicunk was granted to Burlington for the use of "educational purposes" forever:

And for the encouraging Learning, for the better education of youth; be it hereby enacted and agreed by the authority aforesaid that the Island called Matinicunk Island, late in the possession of Robert Stacy, with all and every the appurtenances, is hereby given, and shall be from henceforth forever hereafter, be and remain to and for the use of the Town of Burlington and to others concerned therein, within the first and second tenths, the rents, issues, and profits thereout and therefrom yearly arising, to be (by the overseers appointed or to be appointed in Burlington) employed for the maintaining of a school for the education of youth within the said town and in the first and second tenths.[4]

In East New Jersey, during the rule of the twenty-four proprietors, a law was passed (1693) which showed the influence of the New England elements in the population; responsibility for creating schools was placed on the inhabitants of the town.

Whereas the cultivation of learning and good manners tends greatly to the

---

[2] N. J. ARCHIVES, First Series, I, 241ff.
[3] *Ibid.*, 262.
[4] Leaming and Spicer: *Orig. Constitutions of N. J.*, 455.

good and benefit of mankind, which hath hitherto been much neglected within this province. Be it therefore enacted by the Governor, Council, and the Deputies in General Assembly now met and assembled and by the authority of the same that the inhabitants of any town within this province shall and may by warrant from a Justice of the Peace of that County when they think fit and convenient, meet together and make choice of three more men of the said town to make a rate for the salary and maintaining of a schoolmaster within the said town, for so long a time as they think fit: and the consent and agreement of the major part of the inhabitants of the said town shall bind and oblige the remaining part of the inhabitants of the said town, to satisfy and pay their shares and proportion of the said rate; and in case of refusal or non-payment, distress to be made upon the goods and chattels of such person or persons so refusing or not paying, by the constable of the said town by virtue of a warrant from a Justice of the Peace of that County; and the distress so taken to be sold at a public vendue and the overplus if any be after payment of the said rate and charges to be returned to the owner.[5]

How fully the right, authorized by law, was made use of is not known but, presumably, not to any great extent as a new act was passed in 1695. The Act of 1695 stated that:

Whereas there was an act made Anno Domini 1693, for the establishing of schools in each respective town of this Province, by experience it is found inconvenient, by reason of the distance of the neighborhood, the said act directing no suitable way whereby all the inhabitants may have the benefit thereof. Be it therefore enacted by the Governor, Council and Representatives in General Assembly now met and assembled, and by the authority of the same that three men be chosen yearly and every year in each respective town in this Province to appoint and agree with a schoolmaster, and the three men so chosen shall have power to nominate and appoint the most convenient place or places where the school shall be kept from time to time, that as near as may be the whole inhabitants may have the benefit thereof.[6]

During the period of the royal governors, 1702 to 1776, educational legislation was at the lowest ebb. The very illiberal attitude of the English government was indicated in the instructions given to Lord Cornbury restricting the freedom of the press:

Forasmuch as great inconvenience may arise by the liberty of printing in our said Province you (the governors) are to provide by all necessary orders that no person keep any press for printing, nor that any book, pamphlet, or other matters whatsoever be printed without your especial leave and license first obtained.[7]

---

[5]*Ibid.*, 328.
[6]*Ibid.*, 358.
[7]N. J. Archives, First Series, II, 534.

Though encouragement was given to projects of higher education, the most prominent being the establishment of the College of New Jersey (1746) and Queen's College (Rutgers) in 1766, there was no effort to provide general elementary education, and such as was afforded depended upon individual initiative. Due to the fact that colleges of that day existed primarily to train ministers, and the Quakers did not recognize collegiate training as the first requisite for ministers, they did not favor the project. Governor Belcher, according to his letters, regarded their influence at least, as detrimental. In 1748 he wrote:

But as I find upon the best enquiry hardly 60,000 souls in the whole province of New Jersey, and most of them people that live by their day labor, I am at present much discouraged about a college, not seeing where money will be found to build the house and to support the necessary officers; for the Assembly (many of them Quakers) will do nothing towards it, so that, if carried into execution, it must be by subscriptions. . .[8]

Likewise, in 1750, Belcher wrote:

When I consider the poverty of this little Province where are very few people of fortunes, and great number of Quakers among us, who you know are enemies to what they call human learning and to orthodoxy, and this sect has so much influence in the legislature that I almost despair of any help there towards the building and support of our college. . .[9]

---

[8]*Ibid.*, VII, 146. In view of this sentiment it is interesting to recall that six weeks earlier the Governor had written James Logan, a Philadelphia Friend, and in flattering terms, requested the privilege of using his name to head the list of trustees for the college. *Ibid.*, 124.

[9]*Ibid.*, 579–80; along with this statement it would only be just to mention Barclay's *Apology*, quoted on page 15 Chapter II; the actual treatment of the petitions relating to the college was as follows: Feb. 24, 1748-9, a petition was presented by a committee of the trustees of the College of New Jersey, renewing their application for assistance and encouragment of the legislature to the said undertaking. Petition was read and ordered to be read the second time. Mar. 1, 1748–9, the petition asking aid was read a second time and a vote taken; it being even, the speaker voted for reconsideration and it was so ordered. Oct. 4, 1749, a petition was made by trustees for assistance, especially that a public lottery be allowed to raise £3,000 Proc. for said College. It was ordered to have second reading. Oct. 10, 1749, the petition for a lottery was refused by vote of 17 to 4. Aside from any prejudice certain members had towards a college there must also be recalled the general atittude of bitterness between the governors and the representatives. Governor Morris had been 'at outs' with them. The first charter was given without their consent. Belcher's relations, to judge by his addresses and their replies were far from cordial.—Consult VOTES OF ASSEMBLY, 1748, and for several years following. Failure to support the government, and disloyalty to the king's government were stated explicitly or implied in his addresses. Such unpleasant relations were not conducive to a willing support of any extra-governmental activities.

New instructions were given to the governor who succeeded Belcher after 1757. These were intended to restrict education still further. Section 65 provided, in part, that,

. . .no schoolmaster be henceforth permitted to come from England and to keep school in the said Province without the license of the said Bishop of London, and that no other person now there, or that shall come from other parts, shall be admitted to keep school in that our said Province of New Jersey without your license first obtained. . .

Section 67 provided:

. . .It is our further will and pleasure that you recommend the assembly to enter upon proper methods for the erecting and maintaining of schools in order to the training up of youth to reading and to a necessary knowledge of the principles of religion.[10]

The advice of section 65 was reflected in a proclamation of the Governor in 1760, reported as follows:

New York, November 5. On the 21st Instant, his Excellency Thomas Boone, Esq., Governor of New Jersey, issued a proclamation setting forth, that whereas the education of youth is a matter of great consequence, and ought not to be entrusted but to persons of good character, and loyal principles, and professed Protestants; therefore he required all magistrates to inform themselves sufficiently of the character of the schoolmasters in that Province; to administer the oaths to them and give them, under the hands of two a certificate of approbation, by which they may obtain a license; and forbidding all persons after the 31st of December, to execute the office of schoolmaster, without such license first obtained.[11]

By way of entering "upon proper methods for the erecting and maintaining of schools. . ." the assembly, in 1761 and 1762 authorized lotteries and, during the governorship of William Franklin, incorporated the Trustees of the Free Schools of Woodbridge (1769).

On becoming independent, New Jersey adopted her fundamental constitution in 1776, in which no mention of education was made. Not until 1816, when the state school fund was begun, was there any movement to provide in a public way for state education.[12]

Thus, education being much neglected by legislators, and the government subject to frequent changes from the very outset, the

---

[10]*Ibid.*, IX, 68–69; quoted also in Clews: *Educational Legislation*, 335.
[11]*N. Y. Mercury*, Nov. 3, 1760.
[12]A phase of 19th century educational legislation to provide a state system is mentioned briefly in Chapter XIII on the Transition to State Schools.

individual communities decided school questions very much
according to their own desires. The Dutch were early cautioned
to endeavor to find out ways and means whereby they might
support a minister and schoolmaster and "for the first to procure a
comforter of the sick there." A school was established at Bergen
in 1661 or 1662,[13] and in 1672 the inhabitants were required to
pay their "share towards the support of the precentor and schoolmaster." The latter, however, was "obstinately refused."[14]
English influence developed after 1664.

The idea of town control, aside from the legislation of 1693,
mentioned above, was exemplified in the case of Newark, established in 1666 by settlers coming largely from Connecticut.
In 1676 their town records show that the "Towns Men" were
given liberty to find a "competent number of scholars and accommodations for a schoolmaster, within this town."[15] Another
entry stated:

. . .the Town hath consented that the Town's Men should perfect the
bargain with the schoolmaster for this year, upon condition that he will come
for this year, and do his faithful, honest and true endeavor, to teach the children
or servants of those as have subscribed, the reading and writing of English,
and also arithmetic if they desire it; as much as they are capable to learn and
be capable to teach them, within the compass of this year—nowise hindering
but that he may make what bargain he please with those as have not sub-
scrioed. It is voted, that the Town's Men have liberty to compleat the
bargain with the schoolmaster, they knowing the Town's mind.[16]

The settlements in West New Jersey were far more homogeneous
than those in the Eastern division. They were, for the most
part, English middle class artisans, farmers and tradesmen; and,
in religion possessed a degree of unity unknown to East Jersey
Those who came later were not in agreement with the Quakers
and, before the first of the royal governors, greatly outnumbered
them. A report of 1699, presented to the Board in England by
Mr. Dockwra, computed the freeholders of West New Jersey at
832, of which only 266 were Quakers.[17] In addition to these there
were Quakers in the vicinity of Shrewsbury in East Jersey. The

---

[13]Kilpatrick: *Dutch Schools of New Netherland*, 140; Bergen, at this time,
was a part of New Netherland rather than N. J.
[14]*Ibid.*, 206.
[15]Records of Newark, 65.
[16]*Ibid.*, 67.
[17]N. J. Archives, First Series, II, 305.

266 Quakers, just mentioned, were situated in Burlington, Salem Gloucester, and Cape May counties. Throughout all New Jersey there were established Quarterly meetings at Salem Burlington, Shrewsbury, and Haddonfield; and a yearly meeting was held at Burlington and Philadelphia. It is with the educational activities in these centers that the following pages deal.

In the words of Bancroft, "The rise of the people called Quakers marks the moment when intellectual freedom was claimed unconditionally by all peoples as an inalienable birthright." To what extent did the Quaker settlements of New Jersey claim their share of the "inalienable birthright" to intellectual freedom? This question is answered in succeeding pages so far as it is possible to judge from the manuscript records that have been preserved.

CHAPTER II

QUAKER EDUCATIONAL POLICY

Philosophy of Influential Leaders

From an examination of the works of numerous leaders in the Society it is possible to arrive at a general statement of their philosophy of education. While such general statement will be left until certain individual viewpoints have been presented, it may be well to point out that, in general, their early educational philosophy had much in common with that of other religious bodies, and other educational views, of the seventeenth, eighteenth and nineteenth centuries; again, on certain points, such as collegiate training as the requisite for ministers of the gospel, there was perfect disagreement. The movements, with which the expressions of its leaders and its own activity seem to have identified it most definitely, were Realism, Pietism, and Philanthropy; and certainly, over all there is cast the cloak of religious purpose which shrouded every system of education in Protestant countries after the Reformation.

George Fox, as early as 1667, urged Quakers to establish schools "so that young men of genius in low circumstances may be furnished with means to procure requisite education." William Penn, philanthropist, publicist, philosopher, and promoter of two colonies in North America, was also a powerful force in shaping educational policy of the Quaker settlements. Again and again, it is evident that deference is given to his guidance, while his *Reflections and Maxims*, and *Advice to his Children* came to be regarded as essential for the education of youth to life, religion and morality.

In his first words on education in the *Reflections* he states the Realist point of view:

We are in pain to make them scholars, but not men; to talk rather than to know; which is true canting. The first thing obvious to children is what is sensible; and that we make no part of their rudiments. We press their memory too soon, and puzzle, strain, and load them with words and rules to know grammar and rhetoric, and a strange tongue or two that, it is ten to one, may never be useful to them; leaving their natural genius to mechanical, and physical or natural knowledge uncultivated and neglected; which would be of exceeding use and pleasure through the whole course of their lives.

To be sure, languages are not to be despised or neglected; but things are still to be perferred.

Children had rather be making of tools and instruments of play; shaping, drawing, framing, and building, than getting some rules of propriety by heart and those also would follow with more judgment and less trouble and time.

It were happy if we studied nature more in natural things; and acted according to nature: whose rules are few, plain, and most reasonable. Let us begin where she begins, go her pace, and close always where she ends, and we cannot miss of being good naturalists.

It is a pity that books have not been composed for youth, by some curious and careful naturalists, and also mechanics, in the Latin tongue, to be used in schools, that they might learn things with words; things obvious and familiar to them, and which would make the tongue easier to be obtained by them.[1]

In this his educational theory seems to be in keeping with Realism, and so it is also in his *Advice to his Children*, wherein he emphasizes the importance of the practical duties of life:

Diligence. . .is a discreet and understanding application of ones self to business; . . . it loses not, it conquers difficulties. . . .Be busy to a purpose; for a busy man and a man of business are two different things. Lay your matters and diligence succeeds them, else pains are lost. . . .Consider well your end, suit your means to it, and diligently employ them, and you will arrive where you would be. . . .Frugality is a virtue too, and not of little use in life, the better way to be rich, for it hath less toil and temptation. . . .I would have you liberal, but not prodigal; and diligent but not drudging; I would have you frugal but not sordid.[2]

To his wife, Penn urges the necessity of providing liberally for the education of the children, which is to be of useful character:

For their learning, be liberal. Spare no cost, for by such parsimony all is

---

[1]*Reflections and Maxims*, Phila., 1901, 13-16. Compare the above with the views of other earlier and later realists, and naturalists: Montaigne—"We only toil and labor to stuff the memory and in the meantime leave the conscience and understanding unfurnished and void;" Erasmus—"Knowledge seems to be of two kinds—that of things and that of words. That of words comes first; that of things is the most important . . .;" Melanchthon—"I always endeavor to introduce you to such authors as will increase your comprehension of things while they contribute towards enlarging your language;" Rousseau—"Pedagogues, who make such an imposing display of what they teach, are paid to talk in another strain than mine, but their conduct shows they think as I do. For, after all, what do they teach their pupils? Words, words, words. Among all their boasted subjects, none are selected because they are useful . . . ."

[2]Penn: *Advice to his Children* in a volume of tracts, II, 20.

lost that is saved; but let it be useful knowledge such as is consistent with truth and godliness, not cherishing a vain conversation, or idle mind; but ingenuity mixed with industry is good for the body and the mind too. I recommend the useful parts of mathematics, as building houses, or ships, measuring, surveying, dialing, navigation; but agriculture especially is my eye. Let my children be husbandmen and housewives; it is industrious, healthy, honest and of good example[3] . . .

Penn, moreover, unquestionably regarded education as a public necessity, as he says:

Whereas, the prosperity and welfare of any people depend in great measure, upon the good education of youth, and their early instruction in the principles of true religion and virtue, and qualifying them to serve their country and themselves, by breeding them in writing and reading and learning of languages, and useful arts and sciences, suitable to their sex, age and degree; which cannot be effected in any manner or so well as by erecting public schools for the purpose. . .[4]

For his own family, due no doubt to being brought up according to the English system of tutorial education, he preferred to "have an ingenious person in the house to teach them, than send them to schools," where too many evil impressions are received.[5]

In another passage he says: "Learn, and teach your own children fair writing, and the most useful parts of mathematics, and some business when young, whatever else they are taught."[6]

Anthony Benezet and John Woolman, both mentioned elsewhere on account of their concern for the welfare of the Indians and Negroes, were prominent exponents of the educational philosophy of the Quakers. The following extracts present Benezet's point of view, regarding the need for education:

. . .Some, doubtless, are really and vitally careful, but it is generally an indulgent and partial care; was it such a watchful care as the miser has to preserve and increase his wealth, or the ambitious to gain honours, with a fervent application to God for help, I doubt not that the effects would appear. Ought not the educating and training up of the youth, both with relation to time and eternity, next to our more immediate duty to God, to be the chief concern of every one that really desires the welfare and enlargement of the borders of Zion? I have often thought that, next to preaching the Gospel, the

---

[3]Penn: *Letters to Wife and Children*; in *Tracts on Moral and Religious Subjects*, pub. 1822, 6f.
[4]FRIENDS' LIBRARY, V, 208.
[5]Penn: *Letters to Wife and Children*; in *Tracts on Moral and Religious Subjects*, (1822), 6f.
[6]Penn: *Advice to his Children*, (1901), 26.

labour that is bestowed in preventing the influx of evil, and in watching over every opportunity of instilling noble and Christian principles into the tender minds of the youth, is the greatest and most acceptable sacrifice we can offer to the great Father and Head of the family of the whole earth, and the most exalted duty a Christian mind can be engaged in. . .How many are there in the Society, of sufficient talents for educating the youth, who are so situated as that by moderate addition to their fortune, which they might easily gain by this service, might live easily, and have a mite to spare for the poor.

And I would further say, from years' experience, that it is a great mistake to think that the education of youth is toilsome and disagreeable; it is indeed not so, except to such who from a desire of gain, take upon them the care of more children than they ought or neglect to bring them into that discipline which is generally not difficult. I do not know how it is amongst you, but here, any person of tolerable morals, who can read and write, is esteemed sufficiently qualified for a schoolmaster; when, indeed, the best and wisest men are but sufficient for so weighty a charge. If the governments of this world were influenced by true wisdom, they would make the proper education of youth their first and special care. I earnestly desire that our Friends, both here and amongst you, would consider of it, and hearken inwardly to what the great and common Father would suggest in this weighty matter. Many good and necessary works are omitted, solely because custom has allowed them to be passed over as not necessary, nor binding upon us; when, if we would give ourselves time to consider them, divested from custom and prejudice, we should see them to be weighty and indispensible duties. But I fear a proposal of this kind would prove to many as great a trial of the sincerity of their love, as the instance of the young man that came to Christ. Many appear to have a love to Christ, and would sell something for his service, especially if it was to serve him in some elevated and shining sphere; but to serve Christ in a station generally so little regarded, where the labour of love, though ever so deep and sincere, is much hid, and often, when the most impartial, but the more disliked, this is hard for flesh and blood to encounter. . . .[7]

The importance of a religious education of children, is set forth by John Woolman, one-time schoolmaster of New Jersey, in the following:

Children, at an age fit for schools, are in a time of life which requires the patient attention of pious people, and if we commit them to the tuition of such whose minds, we believe are not rightly prepared to train them up in the nurture and admonition of the Lord, we are in danger of not acting the part of faithful parents toward them; for our Heavenly Father doth not require us to do evil that good may come of it; and it is needful that we deeply examine ourselves, lest we get entangled in the wisdom of this world, and through

---

[7]Letter of Anthony Benezet to Samuel Fothergill, 1758: FRIENDS' LIBRARY, IX, 220 f.; The arguments of Benezet in favor of educating the Indians and Negroes are dealt with in Chapter Nine.

wrong apprehensions, take such methods in education, as may prove a great injury to the minds of our children.

It is a lovely sight to behold innocent children, and when they are sent to such schools where their tender minds are in imminent danger of being led astray by tutors who do not live a self-denying life, or by the conversation of such children who do not live in innocence, it is a case much to be lamented.

While a pious tutor hath the charge of no more children than he can take due care of, and keeps his authority in the truth, the good spirit, in which he leads and governs, works on the minds of such who are not hardened, and his labors not only tend to bring them forward in outward learning, but to open their understandings with respect to the true Christian life; but where a person hath charge of too many, and his thoughts and time are so much employed in the outward affairs of his school, that he does not so weightily attend to the spirit and conduct of each individual, as to be enabled to administer rightly to all in due season, through such omission he not only suffers as to the state of his own mind, but the minds of the children are in danger of suffering also.

A care hath lived on in my mind that more time might be employed by parents at home, and by tutors at schools, in weightily attending to the spirit and inclinations of children, and that we may so lead, instruct and govern them, in this tender part of life, that nothing may be omitted, in our power, to help them on their way to become the children of our Father who is in Heaven.

Meditating on the situation of schools in our provinces, my mind hath at times, been affected with sorrow, and under these exercises it hath appeared to me, that if those who have large estates were faithful stewards, and laid no rent nor interest, nor other demand, higher than is consistent with universal love; and those in lower circumstances would under a moderate employ, shun unnecessary expense, even to the smallest article; and all unite in humbly seeking the Lord, he would graciously instruct us and strengthen us, to relieve the youth from various snares, in which many of them are entangled.[8]

The following restrictions on amusements, and their purpose appear in the works of Henry Tuke:

There are three rules relating to amusements, by which our conduct should be regulated.

1. To avoid all those which tend needlessly to oppress and injure any part of the animal creation. Of this class are cockfighting and horse racing; also hunting, etc., when engaged in for pleasure and diversion.

2. To abstain from such as are connected with a spirit of hazardous enterprise; by which the property and temporal happiness of individuals and families, are often made to depend on the most precarious circumstances; and the gain of one, frequently entails misery on many. Of this class are all games in which property is staked.

3. To avoid such as expose us to unnecessary temptations, with respect to

_____

[8] *Works of John Woolman*, 305–6.

our virtue, or, which dissipate the mind, so as to render a return to religious and civil duties ungrateful. Of this kind, stage entertainments are peculiarly to be avoided, with various places of public amusement, which have a tendency to corrupt the heart, or to alienate from the love and fear of God. The amusements of dancing and music, we think also come within this class. It may be alleged, that these might be practised in such a manner as not to accord with the description given. Our society, however, thinks it right to abstain from those amusements; both because of their frequent connection with places and circumstances, which are highly objectionable; and because we conceive they can scarcely be entered into without an improper employment of that time, which we are required not to waste, but to pass in fear and to redeem.

Were our minds rightly regulated, and our affections set on things above, very little which is called amusement, would be thought necessary for those who are arrived at mature age. With respect to young people, it peculiarly behooves those who have the care of them, to see that such amusements only be adopted, as may not prove injurious to their religion or virtue; but which may tend to promote their possessing a sound mind in a sound body. Were amusements thus restrained and regulated great would be the benefit arising from such restrictions; but when we see how ardently many, not only of the youth, but even of those who are considerably advanced in years, rush into dissipating and corrupting pleasures, it is not to be wondered at, that vice and irreligion should prevail to an alarming degree.[9]

The need for a "right education" was enjoined upon parents by John Griffith:

First to parents. Very much depends upon the right education of children. I therefore find it in my mind to make a few observations thereon, as it shall please the Lord to open my understanding; without whose assistance and blessing upon our labours, they prove altogether fruitless.

Exceedingly great is the trust reposed in parents and the heads of families. It is certainly their indispensible duty, as much as they can, both by precept and example, to form the tender minds of their offspring to virtue, as saith the apostle, 'And ye fathers, provoke not your children to wrath; but bring them up in the nurture and admonition of the Lord.' And, 'Train up a child in the way he should go; and when he is old, he will not depart from it.'

This care should begin very early even as soon as they are capable of distinguishing what pleases, and what displeases their parents. A self-willed, perverse disposition may soon be discovered in children, which is very earnest to have its own way, before they can judge what is best for themselves. This should constantly be subjected to those who are to judge for them. Children should never be suffered to prevail by an untoward fretful temper, not even when what they crave is suitable for them to receive, were they in a submissive disposition; that they may clearly see, which they soon will, that it is

---

[9]Tuke: *Works*, (1815) III, 150-2.

more to their benefit and comfort, to yield an entire subjection to their pro-
viders, and that nothing is to be got by a fretful self-willed temper.   This
should be done by a firm and steady hand, and it will make the work of parents
abundantly easier in the government of their children, and may prove a great
case to those concerned with them perhaps through the whole course of their
lives; since by crushing their preverseness in the first buddings, it may so die
away, as never more to gain the pre-eminence.[10]

Joseph Phipps in his *Original and Present State of Man* first tries
to get at the origin of "intemperature" in children:

Whatever were the Peculiarities attending the Fall of the First Man and
Woman, or those consequent upon it, this is certain, that their Progeny do
not come into the World in that same State of Brightness themselves were
constituted in after their Creation.   It cannot escape the Notice of those who
have had the Care of Infants, that the earliest Exertions observable in them,
evidently arise from the Powers of animal Desire, and Animal Passion; how
prone these are to increase in them and to predominate as they grow up, and
the Solicitude it requires to keep the Children out of Unruliness and Intemperature, as they advance to Youth's Estate; how much too potent their
inordinate Propensities are for the Government of the rational Faculty;
what Pains are necessary to regulate, and often but to paliate them, by a
virtuous Education, and improving Converse; and the Impossibility they
should ever be radically subdued and ruled, without the Application of a
superior Principle.[11]

Moreover, since all are concerned in salvation, it must be obtained by poor as well as rich, unlearned as well as learned:

Religion here, and Salvation hereafter, are as much the Concern and Duty
of the Illiterate and Ignorant, as of the Wise and Learned.   And as those are
by much the greater Number, religious Duty must undoubtedly consist in
something equally attainable and practicable by all; for God is no Respecter of
Persons.   It cannot lie essentially in literal Knowledge, nor in any peculiar
Mode of Education; for these are the Lot of few, in Comparison of the Whole
of Mankind.   Happiness being the End of Man's Creation, and the universal
indispensable Concern of Every Man, the effective Means of Regeneration
and Salvation must be attainable by every Man.[12]

In a later passage, he points out that the possession of learning
is "useful as a servant" but "is no part of Christianity:"

School-learning is but an human Accomplishment, and though very useful
as a Servant is no Part of Christianity,   Neither the Acquirements of the
College, nor the Formalities of human Authority, can furnish that Humility
which fitteth for God's Teaching.   Possessed of Arts and Languages, weak
People are puffed up with a conceit of Superiority, which leads from Self-

---

[10]*Life of John Griffith* in the FRIENDS' LIBRARY, V, 440–441.
[11]Phipps: *Original and Present State of Man*, II.   [12]*Ibid.*, 65.

denial and the daily Cross, into Pride and Self-sufficiency; and instead of waiting for, and depending upon the Wisdom and Power of God, into a Confidence in the Wisdom of this world, and a devotional Satisfaction in the Rote of external Forms and Ordinances.[13]

Many since the time of Phipps, arguing that the Society discouraged all learning, have forgotten the words "though very useful as a servant."

If space permitted there might be presented certain extracts from the works of other leaders such as John Banks, Thomas Scattergood, John Fry, Benjamin Holme, William Crouch, Richard Claridge, Joseph Pike, William Dewsbury, Bellers, Budd, and others, on the subject of education. The point of view of men in the Society is, however, clearly established by those already mentioned.

It is proper that some attention be given at this point to the question of higher education in relation to the preparation of ministers of the gospel.

The attitude of Friends towards higher education has often been discussed, and, it was believed by many that the Society as a whole was opposed to *all* education. Yet, the number of schools established by the Society disprove this to the mind of any candid person. There can be no doubt, however, that the acceptance of the doctrine of the *inner light* might lead logically to a general disbelief in education, and did, of course, in the case of some individuals. But the statements of the leading men of the Society, the official expressions of the various meetings, and the actual educational accomplishments, show that the development was not what it might have been. The positive development is described in the following pages.

With higher education in colleges, however, we must concern ourselves further. For information on this subject we may well turn to Barclay's *Apology*, in which he speaks "of the ministry." In the time of Barclay the chief function of colleges was the education of ministers, whether in England or America; hence, the opposition to them by the Society. In the following extract Barclay contrasts the essentials for a minister of the gospel (1) as held by his Society and (2) as held by their "adversaries:"

---

[13]*Ibid.*, 90.

As I have placed the true call of a minister in the motion of this Holy Spirit, so is the power, life, and virtue thereof, and the pure Grace of God that comes therefrom, the chief and most necessary qualification, without which he can no ways perform his duty, neither acceptably to God nor beneficially to men. Our adversaries in this case affirm that three things go to the making up of a minister, viz. 1. Natural parts, that he be not a fool; 2. Acquired parts, that he be learned in the languages, in philosophy and school divinity; 3. The Grace of God.

The two first they reckon necessary to the being of a minister, so as a man cannot be one without them; the third, they say goeth to the well-being of one but not to the being; so that a man may truly be a lawful minister without it, and ought to be heard and received as such. But we, supposing a natural capacity, that one be not an idiot, judge the Grace of God indispensably necessary to the very being of a minister, as that without which any can neither be a true nor lawful nor good minister. As for *letter-learning*, we judge it not so much necessary to the well-being of one, though accidentally sometimes in certain respects it may concur, but more frequently it is hurtful than helpful. . .[14]

Barclay then attempts to show that neither languages, philosophy, nor "school divinity" can produce this essential qualification though, as he believes they may "concur." Later he adds:

Though we make not human learning necessary, yet we are far from excluding true learning; to wit, that learning which proceedeth from the inward teachings and instructions of the Spirit. . .This is that good learning which we think necessary to a true minister. . .[15]

In another passage he states clearly that knowledge of languages is commendable and schools are necessary; but not the first qualifications for a minister's training.

. . .and therefore to answer the just desires of those that desire to read them, and for other very good reasons, as maintaining a commerce and understanding among divers nations by these common languages, and others of that kind, we judge it necessary and commendable that there be public schools for the teaching and instructing such youth as are inclinable thereunto, in the languages.[16]

On the same subject of languages William Crouch said:

They acknowledge the understanding of Languages especially of Hebrew, Greek, and Latin formerly was, and still is very useful yet they take them not therefore to be necessary to make a minister, not so profitable as that one unacquainted with them, must be styled an idiot illiterate and of no authority. They account philosophy as it is generally taught in the schools and school

[14]Barclay: *Apology* (1789), 299.
[15]*Ibid.*, 307-8.   [16]*Ibid.*, 309.

divinity from thence arising not only useless but pernicious and destructive of sound doctrine and an hindrance to the knowledge of God, and Godliness. They like not the distinguishing titles of ecclesiastic dignities as masters, licentiates, doctors, professors, etc., saying, they are only tending to swell them to a farther caprice, and to affect lording it over their fellows. They charge the protestant churches for maintaining their pastors profusely with salaries, they deny not sufficiency of food and raiment for such as preach the gospel and all things necessary and convenient for life, nay they own it to be suitable to the command of Christ.[17]

Henry Tuke, already mentioned, comments on the preparation of ministers as follows:

From our views of this important subject, there arise a few points in which we materially differ from most other professors of Christianity.

1. In not considering human learning essential to a gospel minister.

2. In believing that no individual has a right to assume the exclusive exercise of this ministry, in a congregation of Christians; but that all, both male and female, who are rightly moved thereto, may exercise this gift.

3. That this ministry being, if rightly conceived, received, and without any pecuniary expense to qualify for it, it therefore ought to be communicated freely; and no further support expected by ministers, than what is authorized by Christ, and was practiced by his apostles.

Upon each of these points it seems proper to make a few remarks. On the first very little appears necessary; for if we consider the holy scriptures, and particularly the New Testament, as any guide to us in this matter, we shall not only find, that human literature is nowhere recommended for this office; but likewise, that many of the apostles were illiterate men. It is also clear that the apostle Paul, though a man of learning, disclaimed the influence of it on his ministry, as appears from various parts of his epistles, particularly from the first and second chapters of the Epistle to the Corinthians, of which the first five verses of the second chapter appear especially worthy of notice. 'And I brethren, when I was with you, came not with excellency of speech or of wisdom declaring unto you the testimony of God; for I determined not to know anything among you, save Jesus Christ, and him crucified.'

But although we do not consider human learning as essential to a gospel minister; yet we are so far from disesteeming or slighting it's use that we wish due attention to be paid to it by the members of our society; for we believe that those who have it, and are disposed to make a right use of it, may apply it to the promotion of religion and virtue, as well as to the benefit of civil society.[18]

The statements of Barclay are authorative, and the history of education in the Society indicates the faithfulness with which he presented its viewpoint. No college of divinity has ever been

<hr>

[17]Collection of Papers of William Crouch (1712), 183.
[18]Tuke: *Works* (1815) III, 95ff.

founded by the Society; but many colleges and secondary schools have been erected that have taught the branches of higher learning. A reading of thousands of pages of meetings' records fails to reveal any effort on their part to discourage learning,[19] but rather a continued effort to extend it. A democratic religious sentiment prevailed in the Society, which made the provision of elementary education necessary above all else.

Individual opposition to both higher and lower education there was undoubtedly, within the Society. At all times, in all societies, nations and races, the notion has found expression that learning makes more clever rogues. It was to overcome this tendency on the part of some that the educational advices were frequently sent out. Commenting on this point, Edward Parrish wrote at the founding of Swarthmore College:

> The history of the Society shows that there have always been some among its members who in their opposition to an educated class, such as the clergy in other denominations, have ceased to value learning properly as the right of all, failing to see that the absence of a distinct profession, embodying the learning of the Society, and monopolizing the power which learning brings, should constitute a strong motive for the general diffusion of knowledge and the multiplication of facilities for importing it. As each individual undoubtedly has some place to occupy in the Society, and in the Community at large, there should be it would seem such a system of development that each should find his place and be qualified to fill it.
>
> It is the experience of some 'that necessity knows no law,' but where there is abundance of the good things of this life there is no excuse for neglecting the full development of the faculties of our children. In no branch of domestic expenditure is parsimony so misplaced, in nothing is it so inexcusable as in the matter of education—better that the children should grow up without a dollar to begin life with, than that they should come to manhood and womanhood without their faculties being awakened and their intellects expanded by liberal learning.[20]

THE OFFICIAL ATTITUDE TOWARD EDUCATION

Just as individual members of prominence in the Society spoke

---

[19]In 1808 the meeting for sufferings did extend counsel to those parents who placed their children at colleges and seminaries *out* of the religious Society, to give them a polished education. This was not against colleges or seminaries as such, but that they were outside the Society's control. Parents were repeatedly charged and advised against sending their children to schools of whatever grade, that were not controlled by the meetings. See Michener: *Retrospect of Early Quakerism*, 249.

[20]Parrish: *Education in the Society of Friends*, 39 and 41.

against the pursuit of common customs of the day, so the expressions of the Yearly Meetings were at first (for nearly a century) concerned mostly with prohibitions concerning books, games, language and dress, coupled with suggestions for youth's "guarded religious education." The official viewpoints of the meetings are best followed in various letters that were sent out from time to time. In 1690 London Yearly Meeting advised:

All friends concerned (so far as they are able or may be capable) to provide schoolmasters and mistresses, who are faithful friends to teach and instruct their children, and not to send them to such schools, where they are taught the corrupt ways, manners, fashions and languages of the world, and of the heathen in their authors, and names of the heathenish gods and goddesses. . .

In 1692 the London Epistle, which of course came to Friends in New Jersey, contained the following:

Being sensible how incident youth is to be corrupted, and how liable to corrupt and hurt one another by evil example and liberty, it is earnestly requested that all parents among Friends, take all Godly and Christian care in the education of their children and be good examples to them, and not to allow them in anything that may gratify a vain mind, immodest apparel or foolish garbs, or other extravagancies, tending to their hurt, and reproach of our Holy profession, and incurring God's displeasure and judgment, which stands against the pride of life and haughtiness; but sincerely to use their best endeavors to train them up in the nurture and admonition of the Lord, in Sobriety, Modesty, and plainness in apparel, language and conversation, as becometh our holy profession and Christian religion.[21]

Similar suggestions were made in the Epistle for 1700[22], and more specifically in 1703 it was recommended that:

. . .Friends of all degrees take due care to breed up their children in some useful and necessary employments that they may not spend their precious time in idleness. . . .[23]

Turning from these earlier London Epistles we find similar prohibitions in the Advices of the Yearly Meeting of Philadelphia and Burlington. After the middle of the 18th century they contain a greater amount of advice on the subject of schools, that are to be for the same purpose of securing a "guarded religious education."

Prominent among the early means for exercising control over the youth were the Youths' Meetings which were encouraged by the higher meetings. These existed for the religious and moral

[21]*Epistles of the Yr. Mtg. of London* (1818), 68.
[22]*Ibid.*, 105.   [23]*Ibid.*, 114.

education of children, and declined only toward the close of the eighteenth century when the establishment of schools entirely controlled by the Society became more common. There is no indication in the records that the Youths' Meeting served a further purpose than this. The following minute mentions the preparation of special messages to be read at Youths' Meetings in the Yearly Meeting:

And Friends we let you also know that ye Quarterly Meeting of Philadelphia having recommended to ye last Yearly Meeting that something might be drawn up concerning the Discipline and Behaviour of youth or what else might be thought needful for their instruction and fit to be read in ye youths meetings. The consideration of each of the foregoing was referred to this meeting. And this meeting having taken the same into consideration do give it as our Sence and Advice that the General Testimony Given from this Meeting in 1694 with such alteration and additions as at this present Meeting are agreed on and herewith also sent you, will be not only much conducing to answer the aforesaid about Instruction of Youth, but also for the benefit of the aged as all have due regard to the exhortation and Christian advice therein given and to the Texts of Holy Scripture therein collected and to that end we advise That the first General Testimony be kept in manuscript in a Book in Quarto in each respective quarterly and monthly meeting and be read at the beginning of the Youths' Meetings.[24]

Near the close of the century the Youths' Meetings were generally discontinued. In 1793, Burlington Quarterly appointed a large committee to consider the request of the Yearly Meeting of ministers and elders regarding Youths' Meetings.[25] A few months later the "committee on the advisability of continuing the Youths Meetings" reported they thought it advisable to discontinue them. This report was accepted and sent to the Monthly Meetings by request; upon receipt of this decision, most, if not all of the Monthly Meetings discontinued the practice of holding them. Chesterfield Monthly Meeting took such action one month later.[26]

The early advices concerning youth and their upbringing were full of prohibitions, forbidding indulgence in customs of society at that day. A few extracts concerning this phase of moral education are inserted below, as they indicate the general harmony of current puritanic ideas. Thus in 1694:

---

[24]Min. Woodbridge Mo. Mtg., Copied from the Yearly Meeting held at Burlington in 1705.
[25]*Min. Burlington Q. Mtg.*, 25/II/1793.
[26]Min. Chesterfield Mo. Mtg., 3/IX/1793.

We are willing and free for the good of all. . .to give a hint of some things that we know by our own experience that truths' testimony is against—as challenging each other to run races, wrestling, laying of wagers, pitching bars, drinking to one another, riding or going from house to house to drink rum or other strong liquors to excess, to jest or talk idly.[27]

Further admonition is offered that none should be allowed to enter into marriage without notification being given the meeting, and its assent received. The young shall not answer their parents "forwardly or crossly" but "soberly and modestly;" parents are to watch carefully to bring up children to use the plain language, avoid "ranting games," the "corrupt and vicious customs, practices and vain fashions of this wicked world," wearing plain apparel, and to keep them (children) "out of evil, vain, and loose company which greatly tends to corrupt them."[28]   In 1729, guardians and masters were advised,

that they induce them to read the Holy Scriptures,to be frequent at Meetings, and keep them from loose, wanton and vain books, and vicious company. . .and at proper time after suitable learning (Reading and writing at least) put them to some lawful employment or trade.

In 1716 it was

advised, that care be taken to prevent Friends Children, and all professing truth from going to, or being anyways concerned in plays, games, lotteries, musick, and dancings.[29]

In 1719 the meeting approved

that such be dealt with as run races either on horseback or on foot, lay wagers or use any gaming or needless and vain sports or pastime.

In 1721 the Advices of the Yearly Meeting stated that no Friends suffer romances, play books, and other vain and idle pamphlets in their houses, or families, which tend to corrupt the minds of youth; but instead that they excite them to the reading of the Holy Scriptures and other good and religious books.[30]

Not only was the reading of pernicious books striven against, but the Society also took measures to control the publication of new books.   The attitude of Friends in the eighteenth century was in favor of a censorship on books to be put out by their members.   Thus in 1709:

The care of the press being recommended to Philadelphia Monthly Meeting, a committee of eight Friends, any five of whom are desired to take care to

---

[27]Philadelphia Yearly Mtg. Advices, 25.   [28]*Ibid.*, 28.
[29]Advices of Phila. Yearly Meeting, (*Ms.*) 71.   [30]Advices, 219.

peruse all writings or manuscripts that are intended to be printed, before they go to the press, with power to correct what may not be for the service of Truth, otherwise not to suffer any to be printed.[31]

The advices contain further references of similar nature for 1718, 1719, 1722 and 1771. That of 1718, added, however,

That they take care to deal with such as disorderly persons, who shall print or publish any books or writings, which have not been approved of, by the Friends appointed by this Meeting for that service.[32]

From the above prohibitions, and especially those referring to books, we may expect a careful selection to be made of textbooks in the schools. Preference, it appears, was always given to those prepared by members, if there were any in the field, and, no matter what the source, they were judged favorably or unfavorably as they contained good "moral pieces," or not. Lindley Murray, a member of the Society, prepared a number of books which were popular in their schools.[33] The sentiments which he expressed often in the introductions, as well as the "pieces" incorporated in the texts, are evidence of the harmony of his views with those of the Society. In one book he says:

Judicious parents and tutors who feel the importance of a guarded education will find it incumbent upon them to select for their children and pupils such writings, both in prose and poetry, as are proper for their perusal; and young persons will evince their virtue and good sense, by cordially acquiescing in the judgment of those who are deeply interested in their welfare. . . .[34]

Though the minutes of local meetings bear witness to the fact that schools were often established at an early date after settlement, it did not become an urgent concern of the Yearly Meeting until near the middle of the 18th century, at which time specific suggestions begin to have more space, and the prohibitions less. That is, the program appears to be more active than passive; positive rather than negative.

The encouragement of schools was brought before the Yearly Meeting in 1746 and the following advice was agreed necessary to be sent out to the lower meetings:

We desire you in your several monthly meetings to encourage and assist each other in the settlement and support of schools for the instruction of your

---

[31]*Ms.* Advices of Philadelphia Yr. Mtg., 9.
[32]That of 1719 specified such books or writings, "tending to raise contention or occasion Breach of Unity among Brethren . . . ." *Ibid.*
[33]See pages 320ff. [34]Introduction to the *Sequel to The English Reader* (1831).

children at least to read and write, and some further useful learning to such whose circumstances will permit; and that you observe as much as possible to employ such masters and mistresses, as are concerned not only to instruct your children in their learning, but are likewise careful in the wisdom of God, and a spirit of meekness, gradually to bring them to a knowledge of their duty to . God, and one another, and we doubt not such endeavors will be blessed with success; And, on the contrary, we think there is too much cause to apprehend that some children by the evil example, and bad principles of their school- masters have been leavened with those principles which have led them to bad practices in the course of their lives. We also exhort you to bring up your children to some useful and necessary employment under the care of honest friends, that they may not spend their precious time in idleness, which is of evil example, and an inlet to vice and extravagance, and naturally leads to a familiarity, and friendship with the world and to a conformity therewith, and often into hasty, and imprudent marriages, by which they are rendered un- happy in this life and in great danger of failing to attain to eternal happiness hereafter.[35]

The above advice, though expressing the purpose of the meeting clearly enough, did not indicate so definitely how it might be realized practically. Therefore, a few years later, (1750) it was concluded that in order

. . .To enforce the consideration of the importance of training up our youth in useful learning under the tuition of religious prudent persons as schoolmasters, and giving it as their opinion as the most likely means to in- duce such persons to undertake the business will be to have some certain in- come fixed, in consideration of which they should be obliged to teach so many children on behalf of each monthly meeting, as the said meeting shall judge adequate to the salary, and that no person should receive the benefit of the salary without the appointment of said meeting. . .

This advice was sent out, and again in the year following, the meetings were urged, "as fully as their present circumstances will permit" to put it into practice. In 1753 each lower meeting was requested to appoint a committee to collect information concern- ing legacies and donations that had been made for all charitable purposes, and make a report thereon to the Yearly Meeting.[36]

It may be well at this point to state that all suggestions did not arise in the central organization. Many of the Quarterly Meetings being stirred by earlier advices, and realizing their own short comings so far as good schools were concerned, communicated with the Yearly Meeting urging that its assistance was necessary.

---

[35]*Ms.* Advices, 221.   [36]*Ibid.*, 223.

Thus Burlington in 1777 asked her Monthly Meetings to consider the educational situation and make report to the next meeting.[37] Replying thereto a few months later Burlington Monthly Meeting advised that

schools under the religious care of Friends and regularly visited will be very beneficial; and we propose it to the Quarterly to recommend the subject to the deliberate consideration of the Yearly Meeting in order that the concern may spread[38]. . .

At the same meeting the following communication was prepared for the Yearly Meeting:

The consideration of establishing of schools coming again before the meeting it is agreed that the same be recommended to the consideration of the next year's meeting in the words following: 'Dear Friends, as our minds are affected with a concern for the welfare of the rising youth, the education of whom we have sorrowfully to observe is often entrusted to improper Tutors and generally too much exposed to corrupt company, whence bad impressions are made on their tender minds, and many evil habits contracted tending to produce the disorders so frequently complained of in more advanced life—We have thought it best to propose that a matter so important in its nature and extensive in its consequences may be again taken under the solid consideration of the body, hoping benefit may arise therefrom, and perhaps some plan for the right education of our offspring formed, whereby they may generally come under the regular notice and management of Friends, agreeable to that good order for which our religious society in other respects is conspicuous.' [39]

In 1777-8 the concern of the central organization for education was still further made known, and a committee was appointed which reported in 1778. One of the signers of this report was Anthony Benezet, whose important influence we have already referred to. Essential portions of these "Observations relating to the establishment of Schools" are given below:

It is the opinion of the Committee that Friends having united with others in employing such persons for masters who have not submitted to the operation of truth, hath had a tendency to strengthen a disposition in our youth to avoid the cross, and unite with a spirit of the world . . .

The Committee finds, upon investigation, that the previous advices, particularly since 1750, have not been sufficiently followed, and 'very little has been effectually done therein.' We, therefore, think it necessary that it be recommended to the Quarterly and from thence to the Monthly and Preparative Meetings, that the former advice of collecting a fund, for the establishment and support of schools, under the care of a standing Committee appointed

---

[37]Min. Burlington Q. Mtg., 26 V, 1777.
[38]*Ibid.*, 25/VIII/1777.   [39]*Ibid.*

by the several monthly or particular meetings, should generally take place, and that it be recommended by the Yearly Meeting to Friends in each Quarter to send up the next year an account of what they have done therein.

And we also think it necessary that this weighty concern should in future become the continued care of the Yearly Meeting by an annual query, that so the matter may rest in a solid foundation, and every possible encouragement and assistance may be afforded. . .in the settlement of schools, providing masters, etc., throughout the whole extent of the Yearly Meeting.

. . .that within each meeting where the settlement of a school is necessary, a lot of ground be provided, sufficient for a garden, orchard, grass for a cow, etc., and that a suitable house, stable, etc., be erected thereon. . .Such a provision would be an encouragement for a staid person, with a family, who will be likely to remain a considerable time, perhaps his whole life in the service.

This would make it unnecessary to bargain with transient single men of doubtful character; and it would not be necessary to 'board the master from one house to another.'

The giving proper encouragement to such teachers as are capable by example and precept to promote the growth of piety and virtue; as well as due instruction in our youth, and are likely to continue in the service, would be attended with further advantages as well from the experience the teachers would necessarily gain, as the opportunity they would have of training up lame children and such, who in other respects may be incapable of supporting themselves by labor, to be educated and qualified to serve as schoolmasters; a consideration well worthy our particular care, as well from duty as interest. The benefit of the youth and the means of a comfortable living for the master may be increased by the conveniency which might be made for boarding some children, under his care, whose distant situation might otherwise impede their instruction.

And, if to what has been proposed, Friends were willing to add the promoting a subscription, towards a fund, the increase of which might be employed in paying the master's salary, if necessary, and promoting the education of the poorer Friends' children; such a fund though it might be but small in the beginning, being a fixed object, would draw the attention of Friends to contribute, whereas so long as there is no beginning made, this weighty service is neglected by many who would be glad of giving encouragement to so necessary and good a work.[40]

The advices of the committee, from which the above extracts are made, were repeated often after 1778. From the minutes of various quarterly and monthly meetings in New Jersey, and also in Pennsylvania[41] it seems that this advice was seriously regarded

---

[40]Min. Phila. Yr. Mtg., 1778, 410ff.
[41]Woody: *Early Quaker Education in Pa.*, 23f.

and resulted in the settling of schools, whereas before, only irregular efforts were to be observed.

Complying with the Yearly Meeting's suggestions, Burlington
recommended to the several monthly meetings that they appoint
committees to consider establishing schools, and also appointed a
quarterly meeting's committee to cooperate with them, "that the
important work may go forward as speedily as may be."[42] The
next year the following report was made on the status of schools
within Burlington Quarter.

We the Committee appointed by the Quarterly Meeting on the subject of
establishing of schools agreeable to the advice of the Yearly Meeting, have
several times met together with a number of the committees of the several
monthly meetings appointed on the same service and have taken that matter
under our weighty consideration. In the course of our deliberations and examination into what has been done, we find that in divers places regulations
agreeable to the Yearly Meeting's advice have taken place and that there is
reason to hope this concern will more and more increase; yet difficulties are in
the way in divers respects particularly a want of Proper Masters and Friends
still employing in some places masters who are not subject to Friends' rules.
As far as we can find there are about six schools necessary in Burlington
Monthly Meeting, five of which are provided for with masters who are Friends,
in Mount Holly about six, and only one teacher provided—in Chesterfield
about five schools and two provided with masters—At Egg-Harbor two,
neither of which are—and at Kingwood and Hardwick two schools and one
master wanting[43]. . .

In 1783, the minutes inform that "The Yearly Meeting's advice of 1778 has not in all places taken effect" and therefore it
was urged again and asked that reports be made the next year.
They then reported that

they believe the concern is kept alive, and that from some parts there is
encouragement; but from others various discouragements arise.[44]

Space will not be taken here to follow details of the process by
which many local meetings managed to measure up to the standards
suggested in 1778, as that phase of development is covered in
Chapters Three, Four, Five and Six. We may, however, cite one
instance as an example of the fulfillment of the design by a Preparative Meeting, that of Upper Springfield:

. . .We understand that Friends of the Preparative Meeting of Upper
Springfield have erected a school house on the said ground and have it in

[42]*Min. Burlington Q. Mtg.*, 30/XI/1778.
[43]*Ibid.*, 30/VIII/1779.   [44]*Ibid.*, 30/VIII/1784.

prospect to purchase ground contiguous thereto, the better to accommodate a school there intended to be kept, in pursuance of the plan recommended by the Yearly Meeting, and that they are of the mind if the title now about to be reviewed should be taken in trust for the members of the Monthly Meeting of Upper Springfield, it would be more generally satisfactory to them.[45] . . .

While the advices of 1778 succeeded generally in bringing about the establishment of more schools, there was likewise urged a greater attention to religious training in the home. Burlington urged in 1781, that they

encourage parents and those who have the guardianship of youth in the ancient practice of collecting their children and families for religious retirement, especially in the afternoon of the first days of the week, and to discourage the visiting and rambling about on that day, and mixing with unprofitable company, and associating with each other in an unseemly manner and at unseasonable times[46]. . .

LATER POLICY

Educational policy in the nineteenth century so far as a "guarded religious education" was concerned, continued without significant change. So far as the curriculum was affected, however, one may note a very liberal attitude towards the study of science; naturally, for this was in accord with the realistic point of view already noted. Let us give our attention to certain more significant expressions of the Yearly Meetings of the Orthodox and Hicksite branches of the Society.

In 1832 the Orthodox Yearly Meeting noted that a number of monthly and preparative meeting schools were not taught by members, and appointed two members, in the city of Philadelphia, who were to receive requests for teachers and also applications for positions.[47] Two years later lower meetings were asked to give specific reasons which prevented them from having well-regulated schools taught by exemplary members . . . ".[48] The answers were, in part, as follows:

In many places, one general obstruction to having schools taught by members, under the care of Monthly or Preparative Meetings, is the scattered situation of the families of Friends, and the fewness of their members, which prevent their associating together in the support of schools without the aid of

---

[45]*Ibid.*, 29/VIII/1791; See also p. 98 for a fuller account of Upper Springfield.
[46]Min. Burlington Mo. Mtg., 3/XII/1781.
[47]Yr. Mtg. Extracts (Orthodox) 1832, 5–6.   [48]*Ibid.*, 1834, 6–7.

their neighbors. Another prominent difficulty is the want of suitably qualified persons to be employed as teachers. Another cause of the low state of
education is the remissness of many parents and heads of families in a religious
concern to bring up their children and those under their care in conformity
with the simplicity of the truth and the discipline of the cross of Christ.

The great difficulty of obtaining exemplary teachers, in membership with
Friends, complained of in most of the reports, is believed to arise principally
from the circumstance that persons of suitable literary qualifications are
generally induced to pursue other kinds of business. Few children are educated
or apprenticed for the purpose of becoming teachers, and few opportunities
are furnished, within the reach of the limited abilities of many parents, for
giving their children such an education as will qualify them for this useful and
laudable calling. It is therefore obvious, that until Friends are more generally
impressed with the importance of this concern, and make provision for supplying the deficiency, and a greater number of our members are encouraged to
engage in the business of teaching school, this difficulty is not likely to be
remedied.

From the causes above mentioned, and the mixture of Friends with others in
the support of schools, the latter being frequently the great majority of a
neighborhood, the influence of Friends is diminished, and perhaps often too
easily yielded to the views of others, in the employment of teachers who are not
likely to aid concerned parents in that guarded religious care over the youth,
which the principles of Truth and our discipline require. Yet, it should be
remembered, that the local detached situation of Friends' families is not a
greater difficulty in the way of establishing well regulated schools, agreeable to
the recommendation of the Yearly Meeting than it was formerly, when those
pressing advices were so repeatedly given by the body; and it is believed that
if Friends could be stirred up to a lively zeal for the real welfare of the rising
generation, means would be found, amidst all the existing difficulties and ob-
structions, for the advancement of this righteous concern for their guarded
religious education, both at home and at school. Greater liberality would be
manifested towards well qualified teachers and towards providing suitable
school houses and furnishing them with *proper books*, maps, and other apparatus, adapted to the present improved state of education in useful learning;
and thus open the way for the improvement and stability of our primary
schools. Teachers, with families, could be accommodated with dwellings,
with whom, or with other Friends in the neighborhood of the school, the
children of those remotely situated could be boarded at a moderate rate.

If such a provision for meeting the wants of society should be found to be
too expensive for a Preparative or Monthly Meeting, it might become the
concern of the Quarterly Meeting. Thus all, or most of the advantages contemplated by the Yearly Meeting would be realized and a suitable and competent education be attained by our children, under the eye of their parents or
other concerned Friends.[49]

---

[49] *Ibid.*, 7–8.

who are members; and where it is not practicable to support a public school in the neighborhood on account of the small number of children, we should encourage their education in family schools, avoiding, as much as may be resorting to the district schools. Although it may increase the cost of education, every reasonable sacrifice should be made by Friends for the best welfare of their offspring, there being no object to which a portion of our substance can be more advantageously applied than to their select education under care of religious teachers. The subject is recommended to the continued weighty attention of Quarterly and Monthly Meetings and to Friends at large—reports of the number who are of suitable age to go to school and how they are disposed of in this respect, to be forwarded next year.[53]

From the foregoing it appears that the control of the central organization over schools became greater as the century advanced. In 1891 a committee was named to have a "fostering care over the smaller schools;" this committee reported in 1892,

That during the year they have assisted seventeen schools, one less than reported last year, eight of the nine Quarterly meetings being represented; three hundred and twenty-four children have been in attendance at these schools, one hundred and twenty-five of the children are members of our society and nineteen have one parent a member; this represents a total increase of 42 over the number reported last year and an increase of four in the number of those who are members, and a decrease of eight who have one parent a member.

It is apparent that a majority of children in attendance at these schools are not children of our members, and while it increases the responsibility upon committee, Friends, and teachers to maintain a high Christ an standard for our schools, it is gratifying to us to know that there are many in our country neighborhoods who rightly appreciate the important bearing a guarded education has upon the character of their children. In assuming the trust we do, it is earnestly hoped that our teachers may be so guided and directed as to become safe leaders to those over whom they are placed.[54]

The graph on page 30 prepared from figures given in the extracts from 1846 to 1900 shows: (I) at intervals of five years, the number of children of school age within the limits of the meetings,[55] and (II) the number of them who attended the schools of the Society.[56]

An examination of the minutes of the Yearly Meeting of Hicksite Friends for the nineteenth century reveals a very similar attitude prevailing regarding the "guarded religious education."

[53]*Ibid.*, 1853, 17–18.   [54]*Ibid.*, 1892, 25.
[55]"School age" here meant from 5 to 16 years.
[56]These figures are for the Yearly Meeting of Orthodox Friends at Philadelphia, which included the Quarterly Meetings of New Jersey.

In 1832 the meeting was brought "into exercise in relation to that part of the education of our youth," and "Friends were encouraged to promote a guarded care over them by employing exemplary teachers."[57] In 1833 a separate committee was formed to deliberate on the state of schools and to gather more information by visiting them, being charged to make such proposals as would help to promote school education.[58] The following extracts are taken from their report made in 1834:

> In many places, one general obstruction to having schools taught by members, under the care of Monthly or Preparative Meetings, is the scattered situation of the families of Friends and the fewness of their numbers, which prevent their associating together in the support of schools without the aid of their neighbors. Another prominent difficulty, is the want of suitably qualified persons to be employed as teachers. Another cause of the low state of education, is the remissness of many parents and heads of families in a religious concern to bring up their children and those under their care in conformity with the simplicity of the Truth and the discipline of the cross of Christ.
>
> The great difficulty of obtaining exemplary teachers, in membership with Friends, complained of in most of the Reports, is believed to arise principally from the circumstance, that persons of suitable literary qualifications are generally induced to pursue other kinds of business. Few children are educated or apprenticed for the purpose of becoming teachers, and few opportunities are furnished, within the reach of the limited abilities of many parents, for giving their children such an education as will qualify them for this useful and laudable calling. It is therefore obvious, that until Friends are more generally impressed with the importance of this concern, and make provision for supplying the deficiency, and a greater number of our members are encouraged to engage in the business of teaching school, this difficulty is not likely to be remedied.[59]

As was noted in the case of the Orthodox Meeting, the utility of manual labor institutions was here commented upon, but no action taken.

Though reports made after 1834 indicate some improvement made in supplying new schools, that of 1851 shows rather a small proportion of members attending the Quaker Schools. The report for 1851 stated that:

> The Committee does not yet feel prepared to make a final report, but they are united in recommending, at the present time, that Friends, in their respective neighborhoods, be encouraged to maintain schools under their own

---

[57]*Extracts Phila. Yr. Mtg.* (Hicksite) 1832, 5-6.   [58]*Ibid.*, 1833, 4.
[59]*Ibid.*, 1834, 5-10.

control, in such a manner as will make them equal, or superior, to the Public, and other schools around them. And also, that the attention of Friends, generally, and particularly those remotely situated, be especially directed to Family Schools.

The Committee, early after its organization addressed a series of interrogatories to the several Meetings composing this Yearly Meeting; and, although, in consequence of the different interpretations given to these questions, the numbers given below cannot be regarded as strictly accurate, the returns made show, however, that there are at least 4,500 children of the members of this yearly Meeting requiring school education; and most of them are, probably, sent to schools of some kind. From the reports received, it appears that of these 4,500 children, two thousand six attend Public Schools, and 998 only are educated in schools under the care of the Society. The Committee would urge the attention of Friends, generally, to this weighty subject; and, with the approbation of the Yearly Meeting, believe that further service may be required of them.[60]

In 1852 a report was made, designed to set forth the cause of the failure indicated in the report above, as also a suggestion for a satisfactory solution of the problem. The report comments on the fact that Friends are giving an amount of encouragement to the public school system "which must materially influence the prosperity of schools of Friends . . . "[61] Continuing, the report stated:

The committee believe, that in proportion as Friends cooperate with the public authorities, in their present system of education, our own schools will continue to decline, and at no distant period we may find ourselves compelled to withdraw from such cooperation, or submit to regulations adverse to the principles we profess.

During the consideration of this deeply interesting subject, various views have been presented to the committee. Many Friends believe, that if our different meetings would adopt for their own members a system of general instruction, at the common expense, it would go far to remove the evils, and meet the wants of Friends generally, throughout the Yearly Meeting.

We therefore propose that the Yearly Meeting recommend the formation in each Monthly and Preparative Meeting, as way opens, of a fund for the introduction of a Free School System, for the children of members. Each neighborhood is best qualified to judge of its own wants; and in proportion to the interest felt, will be the advance towards the establishment of the system. It is believed by many Friends, that if, in every meeting, a fund was commenced, additions would be made from time to time, by Friends interested in the subject, until in due season the fruit would be manifested by the introduction of schools, which would remove the pecuniary motive for sending our

[60]*Ibid.*, 1851, 8–9.
[61]See Chapter Thirteen on relation of Quaker to Public Schools.

children elsewhere. In this safe manner may the gratuitous plan of education be brought to the attention of Friends in their smaller meetings, and thus our members may look forward with hope to a period, more or less distant, according to circumstances, when the children of Friends shall be educated as one family; when the temptation now strongly presented to surrender the plastic mind of infancy to the forming hand of the stranger, shall measurably cease, and the necessitous shall find no obstacle to the guarded and liberal tuition of their offspring.[62]

Definite steps were taken, also, to encourage persons to prepare for the business of teaching. In 1855 the report informed that $5,250 had been spent for the furtherance of this object, and that upon receipt of another application $54 was raised by voluntary contribution in order to send young women to school.[63]

In 1873 a report was presented, stating the past interest of the Society in education and recommending the appointment of a standing committee on education, which should give assistance to schools throughout the Yearly Meeting:

From the early settlement of this part of the country Friends have been interested in the proper education of their children. School houses were built, and schools established in nearly all of the Meetings belonging to this Yearly Meeting; and, in some instances, liberally provided for; of latter years some of these houses have been occupied for public schools, not under the care of the Society, and others have been abandoned and the property gone to ruin.

We feel this condition of things should not be allowed to continue; but that Friends should be aroused to the importance of providing schools where our children may receive a guarded education under the care of the Society; that thus in early life they may be assisted in becoming acquainted with the simple truths as professed by us, and have the advantage of the moral and religious training, which has ever characterized this People.

We, therefore, recommend that Monthly and Preparative Meetings give special attention to the establishment of schools under their care; that they may become successful, they should be of such a character, that they would be sought after by Friends and others.

This can be accomplished by selecting good teachers; by making the schoolrooms attractive and comfortable, and furnishing them with the modern appliances for instruction.

The price of tuition should be moderate, but remunerative; to obtain the services of qualified teachers, liberal salaries must be paid; and these should not be made dependent exclusively upon the receipts of the schools, but should be guaranteed the teachers by the meetings which appoint them.

---

[62]Extracts Phila. Yr. Mtg. (Hicksite), 1852, 13–15.
[63]*Ibid.*, 1855, 5–6; this fund was used for educating women who expected to become teachers.

And, we further recommend, that the Yearly Meeting appoint a Committee to give attention to the subject as way opens; and that said Committee have authority to draw on the Treasurer for money to assist in aiding such schools, as in its judgment, may require help.[64]

The committee on education, appointed in accord with the foregoing suggestion, took charge of all educational work. In 1881 they broached the subject of a General Superintendent over the schools.[65]

In 1887 the report commented on the holding of teachers meetings, as follows:

The practice of former years, of holding conferences of Parents, Teachers and School Committees, at Fifteenth and Race Streets, Philadelphia, has been continued; three having been held during the past winter. There has been no evidence of any abatement of interest.

The subjects considered were:

1st. Teaching as a profession and how to prepare for it.

2nd. What are the best methods of cultivating in children a taste for the study of natural objects?

3rd. Well equipped schools, their cost and value.

4th. Methods of teaching Geography in the Primary Classes.

5th. What constitutes a suitable preparation for a course of study in Science?

6th. The necessity and means of educating the will.

7th. The first and last fifteen minutes of a school day.[66]

In 1888, the following comment was made on the establishment of the "visiting teacher:"

The main features of the work have not much varied from that of former years, excepting that in place of having several persons giving a portion of their time in delivering lectures to the Schools, as last year, it was thought best to employ an experienced teacher to devote all of his time to the interest of Friends' Schools, listen to the recitations, and confer and counsel with the teachers and School Committees, having in view the substantial improvement of all the schools.

For these duties in Sixth month last, the Committee employed Henry R. Russell, for many years principal of Deptford School, Woodbury, N. J. He at once entered upon the work, and we think has given efficient service, and has labored acceptably in the line of his appointment. Nearly all the Schools have been visited many times by him, and illustrated talks to the number of nearly two hundred have been given to the children, a portion of the School Committees and other Friends often being present. It is believed that these illustrations of scientific truths by simple experiments may be made invaluable to the pupils, by increasing their interest in the studies to which they relate,

---

[64]*Ibid.*, 1873, 9–10.   [65]*Ibid.*, 1881, 9–11.   [66]*Ibid.*, 1887, 20–23.

by inciting in them a desire for investigation, and by enlivening the ordinary routine of school work. Owing to the isolated position of many of our schools, the teachers have little if any opportunity for observing the work of others, and when the teachers are young and inexperienced, the advice and sympathetic help of a visiting teacher should strengthen and encourage them. [67]

A desire, often expressed before, was likewise renewed that,

Something should be done looking to the establishment among Friends of a training school for those of our members who contemplate teaching in order that they may understand the science and art of education, the nature of mental and moral development, and what constitutes a guarded religious education as contemplated by our discipline.[68]

A similar, progressive, note is sounded in the following extract from a pamphlet entitled *Religious Instruction in our Schools:*

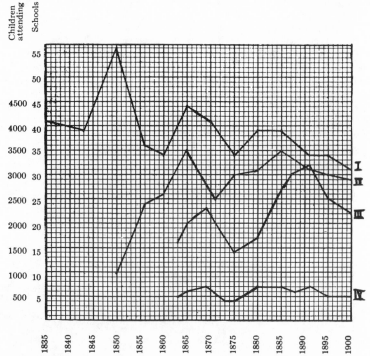

In the graph curve I shows schools reported by quarterly meetings, according to the standards set by the yearly meeting; II, the number of schools whose teachers and pupils attended mid week meeting; III, the number of children attending, indicated to the nearest hundred; and IV, the children of members attending the schools, likewise to the nearest hundred. From the figures taken from Extracts of Yearly Meeting Minutes (Hicksite) Philadelphia.

[67]*Ibid.*, 1888, 21–25.   [68]*Ibid.*

The teachers' subjects are not Mathematics, nor Latin, nor Scripture, nor Quakerism—they are boys and girls. The information imparted is, in a sense, a minor matter; the growth of the mind that assimilates it is all-important—growth in keenenss, efficiency and power. . .

To the Society at large we would put forward this view that the principles urged above are deserving of careful consideration in making any forward move. The quality of the teaching given in our schools is in a measure in the hands of Friends; they have raised admirable buildings in many places— these are a small matter compared with the character of the staff. The freedom of the teacher, which is an indispensable condition of excellence is a gift they can grant or withhold. And that we who are responsible for the term of school life may have the best chance and the best reward, we would press upon Friends the need of laying foundations and awakening interest in the days of childhood, and of turning to best account the powers of those who go forth from our schools.[69]

In connection with statements mentioned above it will be of interest to refer to the graph on page 36 which shows salient points in Quaker school history (Hicksite) during the last half of the nineteenth century. From an examination it is clear among other things, that: (1) the number of schools declined slightly during the period; (2) the number attending them, however, increased until 1891—this increase was possibly due to the improvement of schools that came with greater centralization of control; (3) the number of members' children attending, though regular, was always small compared with that of non-members.

The study of Quaker educational philosophy and practice reveals the fact that they were closely in accord. The individual views of such prominent men as Penn, Barclay, Woolman, Benezet, and others, did in fact shape educational policy in the superior meetings and these in turn influenced the local organizations. In the writing and work of these men may be seen a decided tendency to combine realistic, pietistic and philanthropic purposes in the service of education. Due to several factors, there arose a definite tendency toward greater centralization of control after 1778, which was still more strongly accentuated in the nineteenth century.

[69] *Religious Instruction in our Schools* No. 9, in a volume of pamphlets issued by the Society of Friends.

CHAPTER III

SCHOOLS OF SHREWSBURY QUARTER

Shrewsbury Quarterly Meeting was established in 1672 when it was agreed that "a men's and women's meeting for Shrewsbury and Middeltowne . . ." should be held once in six weeks, and to be every third meeting at Middletowne.[1] In 1681 it became a part of Philadelphia Yearly Meeting; since 1833 the Hicksite branch of the Quarterly Meeting of Shrewsbury has been a part of New York Yearly Meeting. In this Quarterly Meeting we are concerned with the monthy meetings of Shrewsbury, Woodbridge, or Rahway and Plainfield as it was later called, Hardwick and Randolph, and Kingwood (later Quakertown).

A meeting was established at Shrewsbury in 1669 and at Amboy in 1686. In 1686 it was agreed to hold the monthly meeting the third fifth day in every month at Benjamin Griffith's in Woodbridge.[2] Meetings were also held for Rahway Friends in 1707 in the house of William Robinson, and in 1742 at the house of Joseph Shotwell. In 1757 a meeting house was built. At Plainfield meetings were held at John Laing's until the meeting house was built in 1731. Mendham Meeting was begun in 1740 when Friends requested permission to hold a session every three months at William Schooly's; in 1758 a meeting house was erected. Other meetings with which we are concerned were at Manasquan, Squankum, Quakertown and Hardwick.

The early records reveal little of educational nature. In 1756, speaking for the region of the whole Quarter, the minutes stated that:

poor Friends' necessities are inspected and they are relieved and their children partake of learning; Friends' children are generally put out to Friends.[3]

Six years later,

some are careful in the education of their children, but many we believe,

---

[1] *Catalog of Records* at Rutherford Place, New York City.
[2] Shotwell: *Annals of our Colonial Ancestors*, 198.
[3] Min. Shrewsbury Q. Mtg., 26/I/1756.

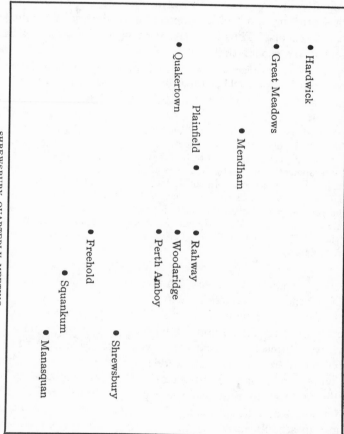

are deficient therein. In 1772 they admit further that some others, as to their subsistence and their children's learning, have been too much neglected.[4]

In 1778, receiving the urgent instructions of the Yearly Meeting at Philadelphia, a committee was appointed to "inspect the religious education and schooling of the youth,"[5] but to judge from the minutes, little was accomplished at this time beyond the stirring up of sentiment to a higher appreciation of the use of firmly established schools. Thus in 1782 a dark view of possibilities was presented in a report, that

> The situation and circumstances of friends of this meeting being such that at present we think the establishment of schools amongst us in such manner as is recommended by the Yearly Meeting is not at present likely to be accomplished.[6]

In 1784,

> The proposal of last Quarter respecting schools was revived; after some deliberation thereon it appeared to be the sense of this meeting that a committee be appointed to visit the Monthly and Preparative Meetings to advise and assist them in promoting schools in each Meeting agreeable to the advice of the Yearly Meeting as near as may be, the following Friends are appointed to the service, viz., James Haydock, Joseph Stackhouse, William Smith, John Shotwell, David Vail, William Shotwell, Jonathan Write, William Hartshorne, Thomas Tilton, George Parker, Isaac Hance, who are desired to report to next Quarter.[7]

Three years later they reported not much had been accomplished and in 1788 stated there was "no prospect for progress in establishing a school at Shrewsbury Monthly Meeting." A new committee was then appointed. It was likewise proposed that every monthly meeting should appoint its own educational committee, which was to meet with that of the Quarterly Meeting.[8] These committees were very slow about doing anything. In 1789 there was no report to make, but because of the "pressing advices" of the Yearly Meeting, they had 500 copies of the advice issued in 1778 printed and distributed. While there was no success in setting up schools according to the Yearly Meeting's standard, the minutes recorded, referring to the Negroes, that "some care is taken with respect to their education." The following report was made in 1791.

---

[4]*Ibid.*, 17/VIII/1772.
[5]*Ibid.*, 26/X/1778.   [6]*Ibid.*, 19/VIII/1782.   [7]*Ibid.*, 16/VIII/1784.
[8]*Ibid.*, 18/VIII/1788.

The school committee made a report in writing the substance of which the Clerk is directed to forward in the report to the ensuing Yearly Meeting being as followeth, to wit, 'In the Monthly Meeting of Shrewsbury a subscription is on foot and although no great progress has been made, yet the foundation appears to be permanent and their stock is accumulating by their several subscriptions being on interest. In Rahway and Plainfield subscriptions are also on foot, and considerable sums subscribed, but draw no interest on account of their not amounting to the sum agreed on to be subscribed before interest should take place. In Kingwood and Hardwick the efforts of the Committee there appointed have not been attended with success, nor does there appear a probability of anything being done in that Monthly Meeting at present, towards accomplishing this desirable purpose'—and they desiring to be released from their appointment, the consideration thereof is referred to the next Quarterly Meeting.[9]

Though the above report must have been discouraging, that of a year later, proved better: Rahway and Plainfield had subscribed a sum of £460, part of which was on interest; the school of Rahway was controlled by the preparative meeting's trustees. At Shrewsbury there was "upwards of £400 subscribed" while at Kingwood or Quakertown a "subscription is on foot and upwards of £140 subscribed." The report of 1801 stated that a school was maintained in both Rahway and Plainfield. A "girls school" was kept by a young woman, a member, at Rahway.[10] The report does not mention any school at Kingwood, Shrewsbury, Manasquan, Squankum, or Hardwick.

Two schools, male and female separate, within the Monthly Meeting of Shrewsbury, and superintended by a committee" were reported in 1809, 1810 and 1811.[11]

In 1831 there were thirty-five Friends' children in Shrewsbury Quarter "of suitable age (under sixteen years) to receive school learning," but "so distantly separated from each other, even in our different Preparative Meetings that Friends have not been able to furnish them with such schools as would be desirable."[12] A year later, "it appears impracticable at present to establish even one school among us in the manner proposed."

In 1834, a report stated:

We have been induced to believe that a small school might be supported under the care of Friends if a suitable teacher can be procured and efforts are now making, if so enabled, to carry it into effect.[13]

---

[9]*Ibid.*, 22/VIII/1791.   [10]*Ibid.*, 12/II/1801.
[11]*Ibid.*, for the appropriate dates.   [12]*Ibid.*, 17/II/1831.   [13]*Ibid.*,13/II/1834.

This was the school at Kingwood.[14]   In 1840 there was no Friends'
School reported.   There were, at that time in Shrewsbury Monthly
Meeting seven children of "suitable age for school," three of whom
were at Westtown, and the other four attended schools in the
neighborhood, not taught by Friends.   In Rahway and Plainfield
there were twenty-two children, five at Westtown, and seventeen
at schools in the neighborhood.[15]   These conditions continued.
In 1843 a minute stated that "Friends are so located as to make a
'select school' for them impossible."   The rise of district schools
was also a factor which made a meeting school difficult.   This fact
was commented upon in 1844:

". . . the preference for district schools, on account of the public money
received, amongst those not in profession with us renders it out of the
power of this meeting to establish a school that will bear its own weight."[16]

The account of these schools of the several monthly meetings is
presented in the following pages as fully as the materials preserved
will allow.

A volume of the Shrewsbury Quarterly Meeting Records (Hicksite) beginning with 1828 shows that no school was maintained
within its limits "according to the standard" of the Yearly Meeting.

Shrewsbury Monthly Meeting

Shrewsbury was settled in 1669 and the Monthly Meeting was
established at Woodbridge in 1686.   In 1672 a six weeks meeting
was established for Shrewsbury and Middletown from which developed the Monthly Meeting of Shrewsbury.   This meeting was
comprised of Shrewsbury, Squan, Squankum, and Topanemus
preparative meetings.   Not all of the earliest records have been
found but such as have been examined contain no reference to a
school under the meeting's control.   The inference is that neighborhood schools were the only kind established at this early date,
or that the only record of the church school has disappeared.

In 1757 Shrewsbury answered the fifth query:

We are not sensible of any that Suffer they are not in Want of Business.
Friends Children mostly Pertok of Larning and are mostly Placed amongst
Friends.[17]

---

[14]See page 51.   [15]*Ibid.*, 13/II/1840.   [16]*Ibid.*, 15/II/1844.
[17]Min. Shrewsbury Mo. Mtg. (Women Friends) 4/VIII/1757.

Regarding Negroes held as slaves they reported:

We know not but we are clear.

How faithfully the answers describe conditions is very difficult to say. From year to year they vary considerably. Thus in 1765, replying the fifth query, they write:

No inspection into the state of the poor hath been made, (and) one Friends' child hath been placed from among Friends.

At the same time, regarding Negroes, there is not much certainty expressed: "we believe ourselves clear."[18]

In 1778 Shrewsbury acknowledged receipt of the Yearly Meeting extracts recommending "the promoting a reformation of the religious education and schooling the youth . . ." and appointed a committee of three to join the quarterly meeting's committee on the same subject, to make an early report. Not much was done by the committee. In 1780, "The Committee on Reformation, Schooling, etc. not having done anything since last meeting—they are continued and desired to report."[19] A month later the minutes state a plan was proposed "towards a school by opening a subscription . . . ."

A report of 1791 stated:

The necessities of the poor Friends are inspected and care taken for their relief. The school education of their children in one instance neglected but has now engaged our attention and we know not of any Friends children placed from among Friends.[20]

Seven years later the records assure the reader that there were "no deficiencies respecting school learning."[21]

Though extremely little is recorded in the minutes, it is quite certain that schools were among their concerns.

Several small pamphlets of school records show that the fund for a monthly meeting school had been begun as early as 1790 and was applied to the maintenance of a school for many years. An interesting pupil's account for 1808 follows:

---

[18]Min. Shrewsbury Mo. Mtg., 5/VIII/1765.   [19]*Ibid.*, 7/II/1780.
[20]Womens' Minutes, 1/VIII/1791.   [21]*Ibid.*, 6/VIII/1798.

Peter Corlies	1 scholar			
Ciphering Book	1^s 0	Lo	1	0
Writing Book	1^s		1	
Use of Book Pens and Ink			1	
Firewood			1	
I scholar			16	

L1   0   0[22]

A deed of 28/IV/1801 transferred an acre "on the west side of road from Eatontown to the meeting house for erecting a school house and other purposes," and another of 27/IV/1802 transferred about half an acre for the same purpose. The monthly meeting school seems to have been definitely established in 1807.

The women's minutes for 1808 stated that Alice Lawrence, Hannah Wardell, Sarah Hartshorne, Sarah Parker, Rachel Solter and Elizabeth Williams were appointed in addition to those already on the school committee. In 1817 there was a school in Friends' schoolhouse at Shrewsbury taught by a person in membership, but in 1818 and after no school was mentioned.[23]

The volume of minutes 1828 to 1854, belonging to Orthodox Friends, does not show much with regard to education. The first few years are occupied with expelling Separatists. In 1829, replying to the annual query on schools they state they have none.[24] Not until 1835 is a school mentioned "kept up a part of the year by a teacher in membership, superintended by a committee of the monthly meeting."[25] The educational report, made at the same date was not very promising and the next year they reported:

There are no schools amongst us under the care of Friends. Furthermore, difficulties continue to prevail against the maintenance of a school suitable for the right improvement of our children. Several of them have been recently sent to Westtown, and others are expected to go there, yet there are a number remaining that are under the necessity of being sent to schools under the government of other societies which are a cause of exercise to us. We know of no children that are not sent to school.[26]

This condition continued until 1853. In 1851 there was no school, "by reason of indisposition"[27] and two years later they

[22]Shrewsbury, Mo. Mtg., Pupils Accounts, 1808.
[23]Min. Shrewsbury Q. Mtg., 13/II/1817.
[24]Min. of Shrewsbury Mo. Mtg., 4/II/1829.
[25]*Ibid.*, 4/II/1835.   [26]*Ibid.*, 3/II/1836.
[27]Min. Shrewsbury Q. Mtg., 13/II/1851.

reported "no school," having "no children of a suitable age to go to school belonging to our meeting."[28]

RAHWAY AND PLAINFIELD MONTHLY MEETING

This Monthly Meeting was established in 1686,[29] but until 1789 was known as Woodbridge, taking the name of an earlier settlement. It belonged to the superior meeting of Shrewsbury Quarter, where a settlement was made as early as 1669.[30]

The earliest mention of education found at Woodbridge is in connection with the receipt of the Yearly Meeting's suggestions relating to Youths' Meetings. Another feature of early education was apprentice training. In 1718 the meeting appointed two members to put out William Willis' children as apprentices, and,

one of them being a boy they are to take care that his master be obliged to give him two suits of apparel at the expiration of his time, be taught to write a legible hand and instructed in arithmetic so far as the rule of three. The other, being a girl, to be put apprentice until she arrive at the age of 18 years, obliging her master to give her at the end of her time two suits of apparel and teach her to read in the Bible.[31]

In 1779 the universal concern for education began to show itself at this meeting. At that time,

the case of schools coming under the consideration of this meeting it is referred to a committee who are desired solidly to consider thereof and report their sense to next meeting; said committee are Edward Moore, William Smith, John Shotwell, Hugh Webster and Isaac Hance.[32]

A few months later a somewhat discouraging report was made by the committee:

We the committee appointed to take under consideration the affair of schools, having several times met considered and deliberated thereon do agree to report. That notwithstanding the apparent advantages which might likely arise from such a good work if properly brought into execution, yet under the consideration of the present circumstances of the Number of the members of our Monthly Meeting and the distresses which many of them have and are still likely to be subjected to, these with other difficulties prevailing at present will in our opinion much obstruct the work. Therefore we think it best that the raising of a Fund for the establishment of a school had best be postponed for a time and hereafter taken up when it may be carried on

---

[28]This is the latest record of Orthodox Friends at Shrewsbury, examined by the writer.
[29]Shotwell, p. 198, gives 1689.
[30]Hazard: *Register of Pa.*, VII, 100, gives 1670 instead of 1669.
[31]Min. Woodbridge Mo. Mtg., 25/VI/1718.   [32]*Ibid.*, 21/IV/1779.

in a manner that may be more likely to answer the good purposes intended by the Yearly Meeting.[33]

By 1783 the committee on education was, however, better able to see the possibility of erecting a school as desired by the Yearly Meeting, and reported:

We of the committee appointed by our last Monthly Meeting to consider of the pressing advice of our Yearly Meeting, relating to the promoting of Schools having examined the extracts of the Yearly Meeting minutes on that subject, and duly weighed that interesting affair are of the judgment that the Monthly Meeting do appoint a Committee to raise subscriptions throughout the verge of said Monthly Meeting for erecting a school house and having a teacher and according to the directions of our Yearly Meeting and that said Schoolhouse should be placed at or near the town in Rahway, and that each Preparative Meeting should generously subscribe for that purpose. All which is nevertheless Submitted to the Monthly Meeting. Rahway 29 of the 11 Mo. 1783.[34]

Early in 1785 the committee on schools reported they were not able to secure "the lot of ground they had in prospect for a school house" and therefore recommended that one be built on the meeting house lot. A few months later, the minutes state:

The committee in the case of schools report it as their opinion that it may be proper to build an house one Story high 20 by 30 feet to front the road between the Meeting house and Stable, on the Meeting house lot at Rahway, and that they suppose the Expense of building would be about £30 but no subscriptions are yet gone into. The Meeting taking it into consideration agrees to refer the same under the care of the Committee until next Meeting to reconsider it if any alteration may be thought of to report the same.[35]

At the next meeting it was agreed to forward the work at once, and

Mordecai Marsh and Ambrose Copland are appointed to collect the money subscribed for the builing the school house at Rahway and pay the same to the Committee who have the care of building the house as they may have occasion for it.[36]

In 1789 proposals were made concerning the establishment of funds for permanent support of schools, as follows:

. . .agree to propose that each Preparative Meeting attend to the recommendation of the Yearly Meeting, when their circumstances will admit; in building a school house and providing suitable teachers; and likewise to raise a fund for the benefit of schools that now are, or hereafter may be established, and that in each Preparative Meeting where it is not already done, trustees be

---

[33]*Ibid.*, 15/VII/1779.   [34]*Ibid.*, 17/XII/1783.
[35]*Ibid.*, 15/VI/1785.   [36]*Ibid.*, 17/VIII/1785.

appointed to have the care and direction of schools, when any are established, and of the fund when raised, and where none are set up as well as where there are; their treasurer whom they shall appoint shall be authorized to receive donations and bequests in his own name for the benefit of schools, and the same to be accounted for by him to the trustees and by them to the Preparative Meeting and that to the trustees in each Meeting, as soon after their appointment as the Meeting may judge will best answer the good purpose intended, draw up the following form of a subscription, and promote the raising of money agreeable thereto, for the fund proposed.   We further propose that no interest shall commence agreeable to the subscription till the following sums of each Meeting is subscribed, viz.:

"Rahway	L 200	o	o
"Plainfield	200	o	o
"Mendam	50	o	o"[37]

At the close of the century the Monthly Meeting became concerned in the project of the Boarding School at Westtown, and a committee on that subject was "desired to collect what may be subscribed and forward to the treasurer of that institution."[38] The enthusiasm for schools apparently became contagious.   Early in 1801 a proposal was made that a Boarding school be established at Plainfield for the "advancement of a religious and guarded education of the youth among us . . . .", but after discussion it was dropped.[39]   The "prevailing sense" was that "there is not a sufficient degree of unity therewith to warrant its being adopted . . ."[40]

In 1812 the records stated "not enny" schools; in 1813 the monthly meeting reported:

3rd.   Two schools at Rahway taught by members in Society and superintended by committee appointed by the Preparative Meeting.[41]

The same report was produced in 1817; but in 1818 only one such school was mentioned.   This report of one school continued each year, but one, (1820), until 1826.   In 1827 the report regarding schools showed none as desired by the Yearly Meeting, and until 1875 the situation was the same.   At that time a school was established that lasted for a number of years.

In the interval during which no school was held under the monthly meeting, we gain some glimpses which indicate an interest in education, especially in education of the poor.   In 1844,

---

[37]*Ibid.*, 16/VII/1789.   [38]*Ibid.*, 17/VII/1800.
[39]*Ibid.*, 18/II/1801 and 15/I/1801.
[40]Min. Shrewsbury Q. Mtg., 12/VII/1802.   [41]*Ibid.*, 21/I/1813.

Men friends inform this Meeting they have appointed a Committee to take charge of a legacy, left in care of the Preparative Meeting for the benefit of schooling poor children—the subject being considered in this Meeting Friends propose the names of Eleanor Shotwell, Lucy H. Eddy and Elizabeth L. Browne to unite with the committee of Men Friends in the superintendency and use of said legacy.[42]

In 1850 the fifth query stated:

no poor Friends among us, nor children requiring our care in school learning—no children placed from among Friends.[43]

The following four reports made by the Monthly Meeting of Rahway and Plainfield between 1855 and 1873, fairly represent the situation so far as the number of children is concerned.

There are 21 children within our limits of suitable age to attend school, six of whom are at Westtown, 11 attend neighborhood schools, 2 receive instruction at home and 2 do not at present attend any school.

The following report was received from the Committee appointed to make inquiry relative to education which was directed to be forwarded to the Quarterly Meeting.

To Rahway and Plainfield Monthly Meeting of Friends, We the Committee appointed on that part of the Extracts relating to education report that we have 13 children within our limits of suitable age to go to school who are disposed of as follows—3 at Westtown Boarding School, 7 attend a family school taught by a member, and 3 attend a district school.

"Isaac Craft,
Henry Wood."

There are eight children within our limits of a suitable age to attend school, one of whom is at Haverford School, six at Select Schools not under care of Friends or taught by members, and one receiving instruction at home.

We also report, that there are nine children belonging to this meeting, and three recently settled within our limits and not yet received by certificate, of suitable age to attend school, 3 of whom are at Friends Boarding School at Westtown, 3 at a select school taught by one of our members, 1 at a select school not taught by a member, 2 at a district school and 3 not attending any school.

I. R. Shotwell
H. H. Bowne.[44]

In 1875 Rahway Preparative Meeting undertook to establish a school, as follows:

At Rahway Preparative Meeting held 11/II/1875 it was concluded to establish a Preparative Meeting School to be under the care of a joint committee of men and women Friends of this Meeting. The clerk was directed to inform our next Monthly Meeting thereof and request its permission to build a school room over our meeting room by adding another story thereto.[45]

The school thus proposed was advertised as follows and opened on September 6, 1875:

A select school for boys and girls under the care of the Society of Friends will be opened on the 6th of 9th month next. The school room on Irving Street near Milton Avenue is large, light and airy, and is suppled with modern apparatus and furniture.

TERMS

The ordinary studies in English, including drawing and exercises in light gymnastics, will be from $6 to $10 per quarter, according to age and advancement of pupil. The Latin or French languages will be $2 per quarter extra. Books and stationery will be furnished free of charge.[46]

FRIENDS' SELECT SCHOOL,

ON IRVING STREET, NEAR MILTON AVE., RAHWAY, N. J.

will be reopened on the 9th of 9th mo., 1878, under the charge of Ella T. Gause, a young woman of several years experience in teaching, who comes well recommended by school officials under whom she has taught. The usual English branches, with Latin, French and Drawing will be taught.

Terms from $6 to $10 per quarter; Latin or French $2 per quarter extra. The use of books, stationery, and fuel will be furnished free of charge.

For further information see circulars recently issued, or the teacher.

ELLA T. GAUSE, 170 Main St.

Or either of the school committee:

JOEL WILSON, PHEBE HARNED,
MARTHA S. SHOTWELL, GEO. A. ROBERTS
Rahway, 8th mo., 22d, 1877. au22-1m

ADVERTISEMENT OF FRIENDS' SELECT SCHOOL AT RAHWAY IN 1877.

The salary of the teacher was arranged as follows:

The committee guarantee her $200 per year, $50 of it payable at the end of each quarter. The teacher to collect the amounts due from the patrons, and pay the same to the committee out of which the committee shall pay her $75 on each quarter; it is intended that she shall receive as her entire salary $500 per year, viz.—$200 guaranteed from committee, and $300 received from the patrons of the school, provided that said amount received from the patrons shall be sufficient so to do; if not, then she is to be paid such part of the $75 per quarter as is received from patrons.[47]

It was further stated in the school regulations:

---

[45] *Ibid.*, 18/II/1875.
[46] Min. Rahway School Com., 14/VIII/1875.   [47] *Ibid.*, 16/VII/1875.

The quarter to consist of 10 weeks.

Vacations—7th day of each school week and for Monthly Meeting when held at Plainfield, also for week of Yearly Meeting, and also the customary summer vacation, from about 1st of 7th month to 1st of 9th month.

No vacation for Christmas holiday week.

School, *day session*, from nine A. M. to two P. M., with recesses according to teacher's discretion.

Absence, no deductions therefore for scholars, excepting for sickness of two weeks or more. Absences of teacher for attendance of Monthly Meeting at Plainfield to be made up at end of quarter.[48]

Patrons were apparently rather careless and steps had to be taken to deal with their shortcomings. In 1876 we find the

Question of delinquency on the part of some of the patrons of our school was considered and it was concluded that such should be informed that unless prompt payment was made their children must not be continued in school. It was also decided that notices should be prepared for the teacher to send to such as are, and shall become, deficient in this respect. Geo. A. Roberts was appointed to prepare a draft of such notice and present to our next meeting which he is to call as soon as he is ready.[49]

The report of the Monthly Meeting in 1880 stated; "There is a school at Rahway and one at Plainfield under care of committees of those meetings taught by members but not select;" in 1884 the one at Plainfield was discontinued.[50] The school at Plainfield was revived, under the meeting's care, a little later (1896), but after 1897 no school was conducted by the meeting.

In 1885 the following report was presented by the Monthly Meeting which shows there was small need for a school so far as the Society was concerned. Moreover, the school was not run at a profit.

That there are two children of suitable age to attend, one of whom is attending a public school. The other a private school not under the care of Friends.

The following is the school report for that same year:

The school for the past year ended 6 mo. 12/85, began with 22 scholars, none of them being members of our religious Society at the time of the closing of the school. One of the two who were reported as attending our school last year, has been prevented by bad health and the other is now a patron of one of our public schools.[51]

The school at Rahway was discontinued in 1886, upon presenta-

---

[48]*Ibid.*, 6/IX/1875.   [49]*Ibid.*, 20/V/1876.
[50]Min. Rahway and Plainfield Mo. Mtg., (O.) 19/II/1880 and 19/II/1885.
[51]Rahway School Com., 16/VII/1885.

tion of the following report and recommendations by the School Committee. The financial part of the report, not quoted, showed a balance in hand, after expenses were paid, of $3.68.

To Rahway Preparative Meetings of Men and Women Friends. The School Committee of said meeting herewith present their report of the affairs of Rahway Preparative Meeting School for the year ending 6 Mo. 23rd 1886. The school for the year ending 6 mo. 23rd, 1886, began with thirty scholars and closed with twenty three, none of them being members of our Society.

As there are now no Friends' Children in this meeting to be educated, and so few Friends to take charge of the school, the committee propose that the Preparative Meeting School shall be laid down, the balance on hand at the close of the school to be turned over to the Treasurer of the Monthly Meeting.[52]

Thereafter, until the close of the century, no school was conducted by the meeting, though in 1897 the monthly meeting reported two schools were taught by Friends.[53]

In 1880 a school was reported, under care of a Meeting Committee and taught by a member, but this was discontinued in 1884. It seems to have been revived by Plainfield Preparative Meeting in the nineties, but did not continue after 1896 as a school controlled by the Preparative Meeting, though taught by a member.

KINGWOOD MONTHLY MEETING[54]

The Monthly Meeting was established at Bethlehem, later Quakertown, in 1744, and was composed of Kingwood and Hardwick Preparative Meetings. Hardwick became a Monthly Meeting in 1797. A house of worship was erected there in 1746; in 1751 the meeting at Hardwick (Great Meadows) was built. The population was much scattered and difficulties were continually in the way of schools. In 1791, the Quarterly Meeting's report stated that

in Kingwood and Hardwick the efforts of the committee there appointed have not been attended with success, nor does there appear a probability of anything being done in that Monthly Meeting at present.[55]

In 1828 the meeting reported to the Quarter "No Schools estab-

---

[52]Misc. Papers of Rahway and Plainfield Mo. Mtg.

[53]Min. Rahway and Plainfield Mo. Mtg., 20/I/1897.

[54]Known as Bethlehem, Kingwood and later, Quakertown at Quakertown, New Jersey. Until 1786, Kingwood belonged to Burlington Quarter, but was then transferred to Shrewsbury Quarter. In 1832 Kingwood again changed, being placed under Bucks Quarter in Pennsylvania.

[55]See page 52.

lished amongst us at all."[56]   About 1836 a temporary school was begun, taught by a woman Friend, and attended by Friends children of that place,[57] but not under the care of either monthly or preparative meeting.   From a report of 1837 we learn that this was a mixed school, "attended by Friends' children and others of that place."[58]

SCHOOLHOUSE AT QUAKERTOWN, NEW JERSEY, NOW REMODELLED AND
OCCUPIED AS RESIDENCE

HARDWICK AND MENDHAM MONTHLY MEETING

This meeting was established in 1797, having formerly been a part of Kingwood Monthly Meeting.   It comprised the preparatives of Hardwick and Mendham, which was later called Randolph.

[56]Min. Shrewsbury Q. Mtg., 7/II/1828.   [57]*Ibid.*, 18/II/1836.
[58]*Ibid.*, 16/II/1837; the women's minutes, 1744–18–85 and the men's minutes to 1905 fail to indicate that any school was kept up by the meeting.   A map of the meeting's property likewise does not show a school.   Numerous deeds are extant concerning property that came into the control of the meeting, but none of these refer to school property.   The school referred to, then, in the following minute of 1862 was doubtless a private concern though operated by a Friend.   In 1862, while the new meeting house was being erected, it was agreed that "the men hold their monthly meeting in William Clifton's house and the women hold theirs in the school house."   Min. Quakertown Mo. Mtg., 3/V/1862.   Mr. Dalrymple, long a teacher in Quakertown tells of the school, just outside the village, which was controlled by Friends at the time he came to the place.   The dwelling shown on this page is the remodelled school house and occupies the original site.

After 1855 the meeting was laid down and its members attached to Rahway and Plainfield Monthly Meeting.[59]

In 1792 the preparative meeting at Mendham appointed Henry Brotherton and others to have care of money subscribed for a school,[60] and a year later some of Penn's works were distributed to the meeting for the use of schools. At the same time the meeting appointed a committee to look after a lot on which to build a school. The lot "below the meeting house, belonging to John Brotherton" was apparently secured for thirty pounds for this use.[61] A committee was appointed to secure funds to build a school house, which, by 1798, had collected £20. Steps were taken immediately to provide materials for the building. Rent from the school lot was also used to defray the cost of the new house. Little is given in the records concerning the life of this school, though sufficient to indicate its existence for some time. In 1811 a minute informs us that the house was repaired "so as to due to keep school in in the summer . . ."[62] In 1813 a committee was appointed to examine the school house lot, repair the fences and rent it out or sell it whichever they shall judge to be most advantageous to the meeting. It was accordingly rented, and the school discontinued. No reference appears to it later. The school house and lot were sold in 1822.

Aside from the above there was apparently little educational activity in the limits of Hardwick and Mendham Monthly Meeting. The records from 1797 to 1855 contain few educational references.

From the foregoing pages it is evident that in Shrewsbury Quarterly Meeting the various monthly meetings of Hardwick and Mendham, Kingwood, Rahway and Plainfield, and Shrewsbury did carry on some educational work, but it shrinks by comparison with other centers such as Burlington and Haddonfield. Nevertheless, educational activities in these meetings of Shrewsbury illustrate the same truths as those in the larger quarterlies, pointing to the rise of a great interest in schools controlled by the meetings after 1778, a tendency to centralize control, and, finally, the decline of schools in the latter part of the nineteenth century, due to a decrease in the number of Friends' children and the rise of public schools. Thus, Rahway, in 1885, reported two children members, neither of whom attended Friends' school. In 1886 the school was closed.

CHAPTER IV.

SCHOOLS OF BURLINGTON QUARTER

This chapter represents an effort to bring together the story of Quaker schools established within the range of Burlington Quarterly Meeting since the time of first settlement of that locality. Burlington included Burlington, Chesterfield, Mt. Holly, Upper Springfield and Little Egg Harbor monthly meetings, established in 1678, 1684, 1776, 1783, and 1715 respectively. For sake of convenience we shall trace the growth of schools which were located in the limits of these monthly meetings and conducted either under the control of the Monthly or one of its constituent particular meetings. The educational work of the monthly meetings is taken up in the order of their establishment.

Burlington Monthly Meeting

Burlington Monthly Meeting, at one time or another, was composed of Burlington, Springfield, Rancocas, North Hampton, Mansfield, Mansfield Neck,[1] and Upper Springfield preparative meetings. Some of these later had monthly meetings of their own and will therefore be dealt with more fully elsewhere.

Likewise some of these preparative meetings, such as Rancocas and Old Springfield will receive considerable space, which is justified by their educational records. In general, with these few exceptions, the work of the meeting is treated as a whole, for its influence extended to the lesser meetings. Some of the lesser meetings, as the communities grew, were made constituent parts of newly created monthly meetings and, for that reason, they recur elsewhere.

Meetings for worship were first held in Burlington in 1677, in tents and at the houses of members, until the meeting house was erected.[2] The first monthly meeting was held in 1678.

---

[1] The name of Mansfield Neck Prep. Mtg. is henceforth changed to "Lower Mansfield" because of recent survey. Min. Burlington Mo. Mtg., 1/II/1808.

[2] A minute regarding the beginning of the building occurs in 1681, and again in 1682. Min. Burlington Mo. Mtg.; Hazard: *Register of Pa.*, VII, 102.

● Stonybrook

● Trenton
● East Branch (Robins)

● Bordentown
● Chesterfield
● Mansfield Neck
● Arneytown
● Burlington ● Mansfield

● Old Springfield
● Upper Springfield
● Rancocas
● Mount
● Mt. Holly

● Vincenttown

Barnegat ●

Little Egg Harbor ●

BURLINGTON QUARTERLY MEETING

The earliest specific reference bearing on education in any way is concerned with the apprenticeship training in the carpenter's trade. In 1685 an agreement is recorded between Wm. Atkinson and Francis Collins that the latter teach Thomas Atkinson "the carpenters trade during his apprenticeship so far as he is of capacity to learn the same" and at the expiration of the time to give him fifty acres of land. In this there is no indication of any further responsibility.[3] Apprenticeship was constantly given attention by the meeting, and at a later date we find specific reference to "schooling." In 1762,

they thought it necessary to advance 10 pounds for bounding out one of her children and to enable the person taking him to give him proper schooling . . . that proper care be taken with respect to the child's education; and if any of her other children can be assisted with regard to the means of gaining sufficient learning, they are desired to look into it . . .[4]

In 1722 the Quarterly Meeting recorded:

This meeting agrees that Burlington Friends may have the use of the new meeting house to teach school in provided they can have a schoolmaster that is in unity with Friends, and when it shall be so employed the said Burlington Friends to keep it in repairs, as to windows.[5]

It would seem that in 1744 a school was being maintained near "Caleb Shreve's" as permission was then granted to hold a meeting in that school house for the winter quarter. Nevertheless we must regard these early schools as rather "unofficial," as the report from Burlington to the Quarterly Meeting in 1752 stated "the proposal about settling schools not yet entered upon."[6] Other schools were mentioned in connection with requests to hold worship in the school houses at Mansfield Neck, and Upper Springfield, in 1761.[7] Again in 1766 requests were received that permission be granted to hold meetings at three school houses, and a year later at a fourth:

1. Near Shreves Mount at the school house.
2. At the school house near William Bishop's.
3. In the school house at Mansfield Neck.
4. In school house near William Smith's.[8]

Sometimes the custom was reversed and the meeting house served as school, as this indenture shows:

[3] Min. Burlington Mo. Mtg., 4/XI/1685.   [4] *Ibid.*, 4/X/1762.
[5] Min. Burlington Q. Mtg., 26/IX/1722.   [6] *Ibid.*, 31/VIII/1752.
[7] Min. Burlington Mo. Mtg., 3/VIII/1761. [8] *Ibid.*, 3/XI/1766, and 4/V/1767.

AGREEMENT BETWEEN BURLINGTON MEETING AND THOMAS
POWELL, CONCERNING THE USE OF THE MEETING HOUSE FOR SCHOOL
PURPOSES IN 1770

Articles of agreement indented made the Twenty-seventh day of the Eighth
month in the year of our Lord One thousand seven hundred and seventy,
Between Joseph Noble, Thomas Rodman, John Hoskins, George Dillwyn,
Anthony Sykes, Caleb Carr and Benjamin Field, a committee appointed by
the Quarterly Meeting of Burlington to have the care of the Meeting House
on Broad Street in the city of Burlington of the one part—And Thomas Powell
of the said city, schoolmaster of the other part—

1st. The said committee agrees that the said Thomas Powell shall have the use and occupation of the said Meeting House for the keeping a School in from the second day of last month for and during the term of one year thereafter, and so from year to year as long as both parties please, a half year's notice to be given by either party to determine this lease.

2nd. The said Thomas Powell agrees to pay the said committee the rent or sum of Five pounds for the said one year at the expiration thereof and the same sum annually on the second day of the seventh month in every succeeding year that he shall hold the premises. And that he will repair and keep the windows in good order, and shall also keep the house with the fences and deliver up the same when he shall leave them in good tenantable repair. And that he will not apply the house to any other use than keeping a school.

3d. It is agreed that if the house shall at any time hereafter be wanted for the use of holding a Meeting it shall be immediately delivered up to such Friends of the Quarterly Meeting as may demand the same. In witness whereof the parties hereto have interchangeably set their hands and seals the day and year first above written.   Thom. Powell.

Sarah Newbold
Martha Noble

From the following memorandum, it appears that Powell was remiss about payment:

Burlington 2 Mo. 22d. 1772.

We the subscribers (part of the committee within mentioned) are of the opinion that there is a year and a halfs rent due from Thomas Powell to the 2d of last month.

                                        Caleb Carr
                                        Benja. Field
                                        Joseph Noble
                                        Geo. Dillwyn.[9]

In 1777 Burlington replied to the Yearly Meeting's suggestions on schools by appointing a committee on that service.

The case of schools is committed to the consideration of the following Friends —George Dillwyn, Peter Worrall, John Hoskins, Daniel Smith, Samuel Allinson, Solomon Ridgway, Aaron Wills, Joseph Busby, George Elkinton, Jonah Woolman, Thomas Pancoast, Thomas Enochs, David Ridgway, Cornwell Stevenson, William Ridgway, John Harvey, Peter Ellis, Isaac Bunting, Samuel Woolman and Abraham Brown and they are directed to meet at this house on the 7th day preceding our next Monthly Meeting at 9 o'clock in the morning and to report to next meeting.[10]

This committee reported a month thereafter:

[9]Burlington Prep. Mtg. Sch. Com. Records, No. 49, at 142 N. 16th Street, Phila.
[10]*Ibid.*, 7/VII/1777.

We the committee appointed to consider the subject of establishing schools for the education of youth among Friends, and the proper regulation of such schools have met and weightily attended thereto, and are unanimous in believing that the establishment of schools under the care of Friends, which should be visited and regulated in a religious manner, would be beneficial, and we hope this important matter, so much neglected in time past, will not hereafter be overlooked. And we are further of opinion that it may be useful for the Quarterly Meeting to recommend the subject to the deliberate consideration of the next Yearly Meeting, that the concern may thus spread and ripen and such advices be communicated as may tend generally to promote this good work.

Signed . . . by direction of all the committee—2nd day of 8 mo. 1777.

Peter Worrall[11]

In 1779 a more specific report was produced:

We the committee appointed on the subject of schools for the education of youth do report that we have seriously attended to the service and may inform Friends that there is a school taught by a Friend in the Meetings of Ancocas, Old Springfield, Mansfield Neck and Burlington, and another is expected, before long, to be opened in Burlington, that one appears to us necessary at Mansfield, and more may, in the compass of the Monthly Meetings, be found expedient in future, when Friends more fully break off from the employment of teachers who are not Friends . . .[12]

The encouragement of lower meetings to establish permanent funds for schooling the poor was undertaken in 1781:

The committee of schools have in the course of their attention to that concern visited two of the Preparative Meetings and proposed the raising a fund by subscription, the principal is intended to lay until it's the choice of the subscriber to discharge it, subject to an annual interest of five per cent. payable to the Trustees appointed by the Preparative Meeting for the purpose of schooling poor children, the overplus to be applied to the benefit of the school at the discretion of the Trustees. The proposal was favorably received and an encouraging beginning made in one of the Preparative Meetings, and it's intended that the same be laid before our other Preparative Meetings, as each of them have a school established under Trustees of their appointment. Upon the whole the committee has the satisfaction to find the concern of schools rest with weight on the minds of divers Friends, and are encouraged to believe it will go forward according to the recommendation of the Yearly Meeting to the advantage of the youth amongst us.[13]

The success of this step is indicated in a report made two years later:

Pursuant to our appointment we have attended the Preparative Meetings

---

[11]*Ibid.*, 4/VIII/1777.
[12]*Ibid.*, 2/VIII/1779. A minute of the Burlington School Committee in 1835 states that Burlington Preparative Meeting School was founded in 1779 . . . to be confined as far as possible to the children of Friends.
[13]*Ibid.*, 6/VIII/1781.

FRIENDS' SCHOOL AT BURLINGTON

on the subject of schools and find that each of them has established a school agreeable to the recommendation of the Yearly Meeting under the care of a committee, and has also set up a fund by subscription the interest whereof is to be applied to the schooling such children among them as may require that assistance. And the overplus of the said interest to such other uses of the school as the Trustees may from time to time judge proper. And we may just add that our friends of the Preparative Meetings mostly appear in earnest, impressed with an idea of the importance of the subject, and disposed to carry

A PAGE FROM THE ACCOUNT BOOK OF THE TREASURER OF THE
SCHOOL FUND AT MANSFIELD, IN 1794

it forward, from which we hope great advantages will result, not only to the present but to future generations.[14]

---

[14]*Ibid.*, 7/IV/1783; the Prep. Mtgs. at this date were Burlington, Old Springfield, Rancocas, and Mansfield Neck.

In 1784 property was secured by the trustees of Burlington Preparative Meeting school:

A Minute from the Preparative Meeting of Burlington was read informing that the Trustees of the School belonging to that Meeting had made a purchase of a lot of ground adjoining the Meeting House lot fronting Broad Street, and proposing that this Meeting should appoint a committee to take a title for the same in the manner which in like cases has been customary; and the Meeting apprehending that it may be safe to appoint a Committee as they desire, the following Friends are therefore named for that service: viz. John Cox, Robert Grubb, Joseph Smith, Joseph Wetherill, Robert Smith and Daniel Smith, and directed to take a title for the said lot as usual, declaring it to be in trust for the use of Friends School, belonging to the Preparative Meeting of Burlington, under the direction of the said Preparative Meeting.[15]

In 1785 they reported that a deed had been executed and a declaration of trust drawn up and signed by all the committee, stating that the said estate was vested in them

in trust for the sole use and benefit of Friends' school of Burlington under the direction and care of the Preparative Meeting of Friends held at Burlington to be appropriated by the Trustees of the said school duly appointed, or by the said Preparative Meeting as they may think best.[16]

In 1792 proposals are noted in the minutes concerning the erection of a new school house at Burlington[17] and a report made on the situation of schools at other places.

We have attended our appointment in Monthly Meeting since last quarter, and may inform that at Burlington there is no school at present, but they have a prospect of one this Fall; at Ancocus they have no school but hope to open one soon if a suitable Master can be obtained; at Springfield and Mansfield Neck they have schools which have been visited monthly. But no addition to the funds in either Meeting appears since last year.[18]

The records of some of the meetings for the maintenance of

---

[15]*Ibid.*, 6/IX/1784.   [16]*Ibid.*, 3/I/1785.

[17]This new school was on York Street, where a lot containing an acre three quarters and thirteen perches had been obtained. It was forty feet by twenty, had a door in front and one at each end, and was built of brick. Rebecca H. Roberts of Burlington gives the following list of teachers with the period of their service: Joseph Clark, 1779; Daniel Smith and his son Benjamin, 1781; Benjamin Smith, 1783; Henry Atherton, 1785; Joseph Pierce, 1790; Benjamin Tucker, 1793; John Griscom, 1794; Jos. Mifflin, 1807; Stephen Pike, 1815; James Taylor, 1826; Mayberry McVaugh, 1829; Geo. B. Deacon, 1830; George W. Taylor, 1831; Abel Busby, 1834; Benjamin H. Deacon, 1836; Jessie W. Haines, 1838; Geo. M. Glover, 1839; Adeline Glover, 1840; Mary and Martha Gummere, 1850; Louisa C. Landis, 1851; Hannah C. Parry, 1852; Charles Atherton, 1855; Nathaniel Bull, 1860; Eliza Hinchman, 1860; Martha Allen, 1861; Mary C. Stokes, 1873; and Bernice Allinson, 1875.

[18]Burlington Prep. Mtg. Sch. Com. Records, 6/VIII/1792.

schools are extremely irregular, and the usual reason offered, if any, is the lack of teachers. Thus in 1797 all meetings had a school or schools except Mansfield Neck; in 1798 their school was still vacant; later in the same year, "At Ancocas and Mansfield Neck are none at present;" in 1800 schools were in operation in all four places; in 1801 "at Burlington and Mansfield Neck schools are vacant, at the former for want of a teacher;" and in 1802 a school was again in operation at each place.[19]

In 1799 a minute was produced concerning the school property at Old Springfield which had been conveyed about 1779, soon after the first recommendation had been received regarding the establishment of schools.[20]

By 1805 the number of standard established schools had declined as only five were reported for the entire Quarterly Meeting.[21] In that year, for the purpose of getting more exact information on schools, and to stimulate lower meetings to greater activity, it was proposed that a regular annual query on schools be adopted. This was soon accomplished.[22]

In 1818 two schools, one at Burlington and one at Ancocas, were reported; in 1819, three, the two above mentioned, and a third at Lower Mansfield; in 1820, at Burlington, Rancocas, and Old Springfield; and the same report for 1822.[23]

From this point we shall trace the growth of the Preparative Meeting school of Burlington. In 1823 its trustees reported as follows:

The school has been visited monthly by some of their number, and that the good order and improvement of the children have been satisfactory.

The debts due for repairs and improvements of the school property (reported last year) have been discharged and on settling the Treasurer's account, there appears a balance in his hands of five dollars, forty-eight cents.

A set of maps has been purchased for the use of the school, the cost of which is twenty-five dollars, and which remains unpaid.

Thomas Collins, Clerk.[24]

In 1829 we learn that:

Samuel R. Gummere having informed the Trustees of his prospect of leaving

---

[19]*Ibid.*, 7/VIII/1797, 5/II/1798, 6/VIII/1798, 3/II/1800, 2/II/1801, and 1/II/1802.
[20]See page 75.   [21]Min. Burlington Q. Mtg., 26/II/1805.
[22]*Ibid.*   [23]*Ibid.*, 2/II/1818; 1/II/1819; 7/II/1820; and 4/II/1822.
[24]Min. Burlington Prep. Mtg., School Com., 1823.

the dwelling house and premises, and James Taylor's term of service having expired, it appeared desirable that a person qualified to teach the school might be obtained, who would occupy the same and take a few scholars as boarders; in order that it might be conducted more in conformity with the original design of the Preparative Meeting, and Mayberry McVaugh making application, an agreement has been entered into with him and he has now moved into the house and proposes to open the school in a few days.[25]

The report, a year later, stated:

The trustees appointed by the Preparative Meeting to have charge of the school for the past year, report that the usual monthly visits have been made by some of their number, accompanied by part of the Women's Committee. The average number of scholars has been about forty and an improvement in their learning has been noticed.[26]

In 1831 occurred another change of teachers.[27]

Mayberry McVaugh having informed the Trustees of his intention to leave the premises and give up the school on the 1st of Tenth mo. next (at which time his agreement with them expires) they have a prospect of engaging George W. Taylor to teach the school and of renting to him the dwelling-house, with the view of his accommodating a few children as boarders and scholars who are members of our Society.[28]

In 1837 the school was reported under the care of Benjamin Deacon, "a competent teacher," but the number of scholars was only 22, with an average attendance of 14. By 1840, however, the number had risen to about 40. In that year a further report was given by the trustees as to organization, and the subjects taught in the school.

That the school which at the date of last report had been closed for a short time was again opened on the 16th of last 9th month, under the care of the present teacher, George M. Glover. Many of the former scholars having been dispersed among the other schools of the place, but a small number entered at the commencement. During the autumn, however, the school attained a considerable size.

In the early part of the 4th month the school was divided in compliance with the wish of the teacher into two departments—the girls being placed in a separate room and instructed by his sister—the boys being still taught by himself—and both divisions receiving his general oversight. This arrangement combines the advantages of more thorough instruction with what is always a desirable object, the immediate management of girls by a person of their own sex—and at the same time the teacher is much relieved in his arduous duties.

---

[25]*Ibid.*, 1829.   [26]*Ibid.*, 1830.
[27]Teachers apparently are not wont to remain more than a year or two; customary elsewhere.
[28]*Ibid.*, 1831.

The two departments divide the school about equally and each contains nearly twenty pupils.

A monthly visitation has been regularly kept up both by the Trustees and the Women's Committee—the exercises of the school have been carefully observed, and the progress of the pupils inspected from time to time. The branches taught, comprise orthography, reading, writing, arithmetic, geography, grammer, history, mathematics and the elements of Natural Philosophy, Chemistry, Astronomy. Spelling is taught in part by dictation. This plan enables the teacher to economize in time and labor while it imparts to the learner a more practical knowledge of this fundamental branch of education. From successive examinations of the copy books a marked improvement is to be traced in the writing of most of the scholars. The study of arithmetic and of some of the branches of mathematics appears to be successfully pursued. In regard to the other branches taught it may be remarked that they receive their due proportion of time and attention and that the general progress in them is satisfactory. It is proper also to add that the Scriptures are read in the school daily.

The industry and order of the school afford evidence that the system of instruction and discipline is well adapted and judiciously applied—and the Trustees feel great satisfaction in recommending the Preparative Meeting School to the patronage and support of Friends.[29]

In 1842 the Yearly Meeting, by means of a questionnaire of somewhat lengthy dimensions, undertook to ascertain the exact status of education in each Preparative Meeting. The answers to these inform us that:

1st. There are 9 boys and 16 girls, members of our Meeting between the age of 5 and 16 years, 18 of whom are receiving education at schools in Burlington City—one female at Westtown Boarding School and there are 3 boys and 3 girls not at any school at present, but have been till lately—their exact ages not readily obtained—

2nd. 19 of the above children reside within the limits of the two schools in Burlington under the care of our Preparative Meeting and can conveniently attend them. The remaining 6 reside in the country and attend common schools some part of the year in their respective neighborhood.

3rd. There are two schools in our limits one for boys taught by a man and one for girls taught by a female, both members and superintended by Trustees and a committee of Women Friends appointed by the Preparative Meetings; average number of the boys school is 14 scholars, five of whom are members, the price of tuition from 4 to 5 dollars per Quarter, average of girls school 20, 10 of whom are members, price of tuition 2 to 4 dollars per quarter.

4th. We have one school house in Burlington and an annual income for house and ground rent of about $300 (in lead pencil above it was 250) appropriated to pay the Teacher and educating the poor Friends Children.

---

[29]*Ibid.*, 1840.

5th. Neither of our schools receive aid from the public school fund and of course are not under the control of the officers of the Public Schools.

6th. There are two private schools in our limits, one for boys taught by a man and one for girls taught by a female both of whom are members.   The boys school averages about 30 scholars (one of whom is a member and belongs to a neighboring Meeting).   The branches taught are reading, writing, arithmetic, grammar, geography, mathematics, history, natural philosophy, the French and Latin Languages taught in the former, the price of tuition $6–$12 per quarter.   The average number of the girls school is about 17 scholars, 3 of whom are members, the branches taught are reading, writing, arithmetic, grammar, geography, history, botany and natural philosophy.   Tuition $5 per quarter.   3 Friends children attend this school, the latter school receives a proportion of the Public School fund.

7th. There is one city Corporation school in Burlington open all the year, average number of scholars about 80.   There are also 7 private schools in Burlington that receive a portion of the public school fund monthly,—open all the year, averaging in the aggregate about 260 scholars, none of our number attend any of the above schools at present.   Some of the teachers in the above schools are respectable and even qualified.

8th. There are no schools taught in any of our Friends' families at present.[30]

In 1843 we find in the records of the school committee a letter written by the teacher, which throws light on the difficult situation in which the school found itself.

To the trustees:

Previously to my engaging in your schools it was stipulated by your subcommittee that I should receive a salary of $150 per annum for the 1st year, and that it should be continued, if the funds of the school should admit of it, if not that I should receive $100.   For the first year I received the $150, but for each of the two last years I have received only $100.

Now I am willing to submit for your consideration whether your funds are not sufficient to admit of your allowing me $150 as stipulated by your subcommittee.

I am induced to make this request partly on account of the reduced state of my school, having at present only ten scholars, two of whom expect to leave soon for Westtown School.   The decrease in my school has been caused by the establishment of the public school.

Perhaps it may be a subject worthy of the consideration of the Trustees whether or not anything can be done to increase the interest of our school.

Respectfully,
Geo. M. Glover.

8 mo. 29th 1843.[31]

In 1844 it was necessary to raise the mistress' salary also and for the same reason.

---

[30]*Ibid.*, 1842.   [31]*Ibid.*

The female teacher having been discouraged by the smallness of the school and the Trustees being desirous to secure the continuance of her services, it was resolved to make her situation worth to her $250 per annum—with the understanding however that the Trustees were not to be responsible for the collection of her bills.   The salary of the male teacher being as last year $150—in addition to his receipts for tuition.[32]

That the public schools drew away a very genuine support of the Friends schools is seen in the fact that there was a general falling off of attendance wherever the public schools opened. Those drawn away in the case of Burlington, however, were mostly outsiders, and not the members.   In 1856 there were 26 children reported of age to go to school.   These were distributed as follows: 11 taught at home, 5 at Friends school, 4 at Westtown, 3 at a school taught by a member, while 3 attended "other schools," probably the public institutions.[33]

In 1870 we are informed that:

> . . . In addition to the usual English branches and drawing, the higher mathematics and Latin and French are now taught, thus enhancing the value of the course as preparatory to a higher school.
> The number of pupils during the year has been 39—14 boys and 25 girls. Of these 10 were members and several others connected with Friends.[34]

We now turn our attention to the school at Rancocas.   In 1803 Rancocas received information that the monthly meeting expected to cast the burden of schools where it properly belonged, i. e., on the lower meetings, and that a report must be sent in giving a particular account of the state of schools.[35]   Six years later steps were taken for more permanent accommodations for the schoolmaster, apparently at the latter's suggestion.

> John Gummere having proposed to continue in our school provided a suitable house for his accommodation could be obtained; and the trustees taking the subject into consideration agree to propose to the Preparative Meeting that a lot of ground be purchased in a suitable siutation and a dwelling house be erected thereon to accomodate a schoolmaster, and they further in-

---

[32]*Ibid.*, 1844.   [33]*Ibid.*, 1856.

[34]It appears from the fact that there are no minutes of the school committee after 1870, and the Quarterly Meeting Minutes mention only three schools in place of four, that the Burlington Preparative Meeting School was discontinued at that time, though perhaps held irregularly.   Mary C. Stokes and Bernice Allinson are mentioned elsewhere as teachers in 1873 and 1875, respectively.

[35]Min. Rancocas Prep. Mtg., 1/IX/1803.

Schoolmaster's Dwelling at Rancocas

form that such a lot of land may be obtained of Samuel Ellis for 40 dollars per acre.[36]

Two months thereafter the trustees were instructed to complete the purchase of the lot and in 1810 a plan for a school-master's house was presented. The latter was completed at a cost of $930.00. As a further encouragement for teachers a barn was proposed in 1817:

Information having been received from the trustees of the school that a new barn etc. is wanted on the lot appropriated for the convenience of the school teacher—with which sentiment the meeting unites and leaves them at liberty to raise what money they may think proper by a voluntary subscription, and if there should be any surplus for it to be annexed to the school fund.[37]

In 1818 a report on the school was brought forward as follows:

The clerk, on behalf of the trustees of the school produced their report for the past year, by which it appears that in consequence of improvements done on the lot, school house etc. they have expended what money was in their hands and that there yet remains a deficiency unprovided for of $45.22; and they propose raising $100 to meet it, and to enable them to accomplish some other improvements.

They likewise report that the school has had their attention, that it is orderly conducted and scholars generally improving in their learning.[38]

In 1820 the school benefitted by two bequests, one from Howard Buzby amounting to £ 25, and the other from George Dilwyn of £20. Two years later it became necessary to erect a new house:

They also report that the house in which the school is held is so old and out of repair they that cannot indulge a reasonable hope of its being suitable for the purposes of a school another year; they therefore suggest to the Preparative Meeting the propriety of authorizing the succeeding trustees to build a new house on the lot whereon the present one stands within the ensuing year.[39]

The above proposal was approved by the Meeting, and in 1823,

They also report that a school house has been erected agreeably to the direction of the Preparative Meeting in the 2d mo. last, and that the whole expense, including the price of a new stove, etc. is $557.59; and that the funds including the price obtained for the old school house amounts to $559.23, leaving a balance in favor of the school fund of $1.64.[40]

After the division in 1827 the schools at Rancocas and Old Springfield were continued under the direct control of the new organization. In 1829 a report was produced as though nothing out of the ordinary had taken place.

[36]*Ibid.*, 28/IX/1809.   [37]*Ibid.*, 3/VII/1817.   [38]*Ibid.*, 1/I/1818.
[39]*Ibid.*, 3/I/1822.   [40]*Ibid.*, 30/I/1823.

That the school has been regularly conducted under their care since last report; Jacob Knight continued in the school as teacher until the 17th of the 4th month last. On the 18th of the same month, Susan Haines took charge of the school as teacher by agreement with the trustees and continued in the same until the 21st of 11th month last. On the 23rd of the same month Jacob Knight . . . again took charge of the school and is now . . . the teacher. It is believed the school for the past year has been satisfactorily conducted and the scholars have made encouraging progress in their learning; on an examination of the treasurer's accounts it appears there is a balance due the school fund in cash of $65.31 and in monies due $47.25. There are three schools, superintended by committees, the preparative meetings, and taught by members.[41]

The third one was probably at Lower Mansfield. Seven years later only two were reported.[42]

In 1837, the Hicksite Meeting being acquainted with the fact that Orthodox Friends were planning to erect a school, made an amicable proposal that they should join together in the support of one.

To the Preparative Meeting of Orthodox Friends (so called) held at Ancocus,

This meeting has been informed that preparations are making by you for the erection of a building on the Meeting House lot intended for a school house. We have thought this a fit occasion to address you upon the subject and let you know that in the first place it has at all times been our disposition to endeavor to make such arrangements as would be mutually satisfactory relative to a school in this place, and in such manner that we could maintain one good school in peace—instead of two of an inferior character in strife. We do not see any insuperable difficulties in the way.

If however, you should think differently, we can but express our regret and at the same time would apprize you that from motives of peace we do not propose to interfere with the progress of your building, yet we think we can see an increase of the present difficulties must be the consequence of two such rival (and, it is to be feared) hostile schools so near to each other—And that no part thereof may be justly chargeable to us, or we accused of remissness in suitable endeavors to promote good neighborhood, we have thought it right to communicate with you, and to inform that in case this is received in the same spirit in which it is dictated that our trustees of the school are fully authorized to treat with any persons you may appoint for that purpose.

The clerk of this Meeting is directed to furnish a copy of the above communication to the clerk of the meeting to which it is addressed, with a request that he should lay it before that Meeting.[43]

---

[41]Min. Rancocas Prep. Mtg., (H.), 31/XII/1829.
[42]Min. Burlington Mo. Mtg., (H.), 1/II/1836.
[43]Min. Rancocas Prep. Mtg. (H.), 26/X/1837.

In 1845 a report stated the school had been kept open about 10 months of the year. In 1851,

The trustees report that the school has been kept open about 9 months in the past year; in the summer session about 6 months; three months the winter season. The summer by a female, the winter by a male teacher. They also settled with their treasurer and find a balance . . . of $21.36.[44]

In 1855 it was agreed that the meeting house in Mansfield township be used by the district trustees for educational purposes.[45]

In 1871 the Rancocas School trustees make it evident that the operation of the district school has caused them embarrassment, because of the withdrawal of funds. Their report was as follows:

The committee appointed to have charge of the school and school property, report that on examination of the treasurer's account that there is due him $36.17.

They also report that the school has been maintained a part of the year under the care of a person in membership with us—

And a part of the time by a person not in membership—But generally to good satisfaction.

The committee or trustees believe it proper to state that the opeation of the law of this state in regard to school now deprives them from receiving any part of the State school funds . . . raised by taxation, or interest of the surplus revenue (so called).

And if the school is maintained upon the original ground of Friends' concern for the promotion of well regulated schools, it must be a pay school. Except so far as the funds under the control of the Preparative Meeting may make it otherwise.

The school house was built with funds contributed by Friends and to be exclusively under their control upon property held by them as a place for religious worship. To surrender the school house and grounds to any set of men elected by ballot as trustees or committee by the people of the school district established by law, a very small proportion of whom are Friends would be at variance with Friends testimonies upon the subject of schools, and a non-compliance with our discipline which requires all gifts to be strictly applied to the use intended by the donors.

Taking this view of the subject the Committee have declined to surrender the school house to the public under the law. And as a consequence the money which we believe equitably belongs to us is given for the support of a school under the management of trustees elected by the people as aforesaid. It would now appear that we had no consistent left us, but to submit, however unjust it may appear—We would therefore recommend that trustees for the school be appointed as heretofore and that they embrace every right opportunity for the maintenance of a school under the control of Friends.

[44]*Ibid.*, 23/I/1851.   [45]Min. Burlington Mo. Mtg., (H.), 2/II/1857.

And that they be at liberty to use any funds for that purpose which may come to their hands from the school property by gift or otherwise.[46]

In 1877 a report was made setting forth some of the difficulties met in maintaining the school:

The school has been kept open most of the terms since last report and taught by teachers in membership with Friends. Previous to school year 1877 the trustees employed Chalkley Mattack to teach the school for nine months, agreeing to pay him $35 per month. And the said Chalkley was to charge all scholars, except those sent by Friends five cents per day on behalf of the trustees, and such money so received to go into the treasury of the school.

The trustees seeing their inability to pay the said Chalkley from the funds of the treasury applied to the Yearly Meeting for assistance which resulted by contributing $100 to the school fund which was paid to the said Chalkley, as will appear more fully in the Treasurer's report.

In connection with the $100 appropriated by the Yearly Meeting: The Yearly Meeting refurnished with improved desks and benches the boys' side of the school house, the furniture of which was old, defaced, and dilapidated.

Previous to school year of 1878 the trustees thought, considering the limited funds, to contract no debts but what they could pay, and knowing the insufficiency of Friends to employ a suitable teacher for the ensuing year, thought to open the school the 1st of the 11th month for a session of 5 months and for a compensation for the yearly term of $125, or $25 per month; the use of the school house and all the teacher could make out of the school, charging at the rate of 5 cents per day. Charles Stokes, Jr., was employed to teach the school on the above conditions.

The school has been well patronized, attended by 34 scholars. only 2 of whom were Friends owing to which fact the teacher insisted that it was not practical to attend mid-week meetings.[47]

In 1880 the school at Rancocas was kept open "most of the year" by Mary Dubball "a female in membership." "She taught and managed the school to satisfaction." At the time of this report the trustees note that they have leased the school property now "to Alexander Thompson and Rebecca his wife."[48] In accordance with this the monthly meeting stated in 1883, "We have no school as queried after,"[49] but the school was later revived. In 1895, "Rancocas reports a school as queried after, but not superintended by a committee appointed by the Preparative Meeting."[50] In 1920 the monthly meeting reported:

We have one school under the care of the Monthly Meeting taught by a

---

[46]Min. Rancocas Prep. Mtg., (H.), 21/XII/1871.   [47]*Ibid.*, 27/III/1877.
[48]*Ibid.*, 22/III/1880.   [49]Min. Burlington Mo. Mtg., (H.), 5/II/1883.
[50]*Ibid.*, 15/II/1895.

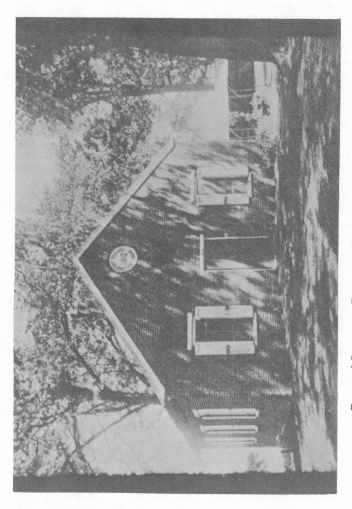

FRIENDS' SCHOOL AT RANCOCAS NOW OCCUPIED AS A DWELLING

person having one parent a member—the pupils attend mid-week meetings with the teacher. Number of pupils 6, number of members, 2.[51]

A year later steps were taken to occupy the house as a residence.

A proposition to change the Friends' School house into a dwelling house was discussed and duly criticised and united with that the (changes ?) be made and the property committee to take the matter in charge and proceed with the work at an expense not to exceed $60.00.   The year book for 1921 was received and distributed.[52]

A study of the records relating thereto seems to indicate that the official Friends' School at Old Springfield was established in 1779. "In or about that year they had two acres of ground conveyed by deeds in trust for the use of a school," and in the same year the committee informed that "there is a school taught by a Friend . . . in Old Springfield . . ."[53]

This school was still controlled by the Society in 1835, and from that time to about 1870 we can trace its history more in detail. In 1836 the meeting stated:

We have one school taught by a member and superintended by a committee appointed by the Preparative Meeting.[54]

A more complete report on the status of the school was produced soon after:

. . . The last year's committee now report they have visited the school generally every month; likewise report an addition of $200 to the funds bequeathed by William Ridgway; it now stands thus: a house and lot of two acres of land, also $522.57—$180.58 of said sum was taken to purchase land, the residue being $342.09 in obligations.   There is of interest, which has grown out of the above fund, and now at interest $107.91, making altogether now at interest $450.00 besides the land.   Also settled with the treasurer and find a balance in his hands of $76.09½ due the school.[55]

In 1873 Old Springfield was leased to the district trustees, as described in the following extract:

This indenture made this 5th day of 12th month in the year of our Lord one thousand eight hundred and seventy-three, witnesseth that we Daniel S. Zelley, Joseph Hancock, Nathan Stevenson, Clayton Zelley, and Stacy Stevenson, being a majority of a committee appointed by Old Springfield Preparative Meeting to have in charge the school house and property connected with said

---

[51]*Ibid.*, 13/II/1920.
[52]*Ibid.*, 7/I/1921. For photograph of Rancocas School as it now stands, see page 74.
[53]Min. Burlington Mo. Mtg., 4/III/1799 and 2/VIII/1779.
[54]Min. Old Springfield Prep. Mtg., (H.), 21/I/1836.
[55]*Ibid.*, 15/XII/1836.

House occupied by the school of Old Springfield Leased in 1873 to District Trustees

THE MASTER'S DWELLING, A PART OF OLD SPRINGFIELD SCHOOL PROPERTY

meeting, do lease unto the trustees elected by the legal voters of School District number thirty-nine, viz. Edwin Black, Gilbert L. Swain, and Charles G. Warner, all of the township of Springfield, county of Burlington and state of New Jersey, the school house together with the playgrounds attached thereto, adjoining aforesaid meeting property, for the term of one year (or such time as the school house is occupied and kept open as a district school) from the tenth day of eleventh month A. D. 1873 for the consideration of eight dollars (per month) cash in hand paid, to them or their successors in office, and at the expiration of said term to yield the peaceable possession thereof to the said committee, first above named, or their successors, in as good condition as when received, general wear and tear excepted, in witness whereof we have set our hands and seals the day and year above written.

	Committee	Joseph Hancock
		Daniel S. Zelley
		Clayton Zelley
		Stacy Stevenson
	District	Edwin Black
	Trustees	Gilbert L. Swain
		Charles G. Warner

(On Nov. 10th, 1874, the above lease was continued in force by general consent.)[56]

CHESTERFIELD MONTHLY MEETING

The Monthly Meeting of Chesterfield was established in 1684, and was composed, either at that date or later, of Chesterfield, Trenton, Eastbranch, Bordentown, and Stony Brook preparative meetings.

The first educational concern that we find in this monthly meeting was in connection with the placing out of children of poor parents at the expense of the meeting.[57]   It is evident however, that very early after the establishment of the meeting, a school was available, as a minute of 1693 indicates:

"It is agreed by this meeting that weekday meeting be kept every fourth day of the week at falles in the school house."[58]

But further information on schools at that date we have none. Special meetings for young people were established according to a

---

[56]Misc. Papers of Old Springfield, deposited at 15 & Race Streets, Philadelphia.   Concerning the "per month" in the above we cannot be certain: this item is written in between the lines—such a thing in the records is usually acknowledged at the end as having been written before the signatures were made.   Here such is not the case; moreover the "per month" appears in lighter ink and in slightly altered hand.

[57]Min. Chesterfield Mo. Mtg., 7/IX/1689.   [58]*Ibid.*, 7/XII/1693.

minute of 1697, which contributed to their education, but not their "school education" in which we are primarily concerned here.[59]

With the last quarter of the eighteenth century came the "educational revival" and the establishment of official Friends' schools in Chesterfield, such as we have already noted elsewhere. In 1779 the committee, previously appointed, stated:

some care is taken agreeable to the advice of the Yearly Meeting and some progress made in some places . . .[60]

In 1783 Joseph Forsythe reported for the committee that they believed subscription funds should be started at each Preparative Meeting for the purpose of buying land, building school houses, and, in answer to a query in 1786 the monthly meeting stated there were schools established as the Yearly Meeting desired. In 1787 the following form of bequest was adopted:

I give and bequeath unto A. B., Treasurer of the school called Friends school of ——— or to the treasurer of the said school for the time being duly appointed by the Trustee of said school the sum of ——— to be paid in one year after my decease and applied, by the said Trustees to and for the benefit and advancement of the said school at their discretion.[61]

In 1791 we learn, concerning Chesterfield, that

The committee appointed for the establishment of schools agreeable to the direction of the Yearly Meeting, reported there is a house at Chesterfield so far finished that a school might be kept in it, but it is not yet occupied for that purpose, neither is there any such school within this Monthly Meeting.[62]

Shortly after the production of the above report, the Preparative Meeting at Chesterfield was authorized to establish a school there:

The report of the committee on schools made in ye 8 month last being revived and the meeting taking ye same into consideration recommends the Preparative Meeting of Chesterfield and they are hereby authorized to open a school in the said house and appoint a suitable number of Friends as Trustees to take the care and oversight thereof and make rules and regulations for the government and promotion of the institution, which rules and regulations shall always be inspected by the Monthly Meeting's Committee for their approbation or disallowance and said meeting is likewise authorized to appoint a Treasurer to receive subscriptions and donations for accumulating a fund.[63]

In 1793 report was made that the fund for this school had increased to "several hundred pounds." In the same year the sum

---

[59]Quoted from Minutes of Q. Mtg., *Ibid.*, 2/VII/1697.
[60]*Ibid.*, 5/VIII/1779. [61]*Ibid.*, 6/III/1787. [62]*Ibid.*, 2/VIII/1791.
[63]*Ibid.*, 15/XII/1791.

of £ 63/19/8½ was received as their part of the quarterly meeting fund for schools.

As has been found in many other cases Chesterfield abandoned the youths' meetings about the time regular schools were established, possibly due to the fact that in a school of this nature the aims of the youths' meetings could be accomplished.[64]

In 1794 the following report on schools was made by the committee:

> We of the committee on schools having met and examined the accounts for building the school house, find a balance of £ 10/17/6 due to Joseph Forsyth for carpenter work done and the sum of £ 2/6/1½ due to John Wright, being money overpaid by him as receiver of subscriptions for said building. We also agree to report there are two schools at Chesterfield under the care of trustees one of which is taught by a woman . . .[65]

In 1801 the committee reported there were two schools under the care of Friends and visited monthly by trustees, one of them being at Chesterfield and the other at Stony Brook; they further stated a fund was established at Robins Preparative Meeting.[66]

In 1807, 1810 and 1811 schools were reported at Chesterfield and Trenton, but no statement appeared concerning Stony Brook and East Branch. In 1814, 1815 and 1816 the report returned was: "No schools agreeable to the import of this query," but there "are funds established in each preparative meeting for the promotion of schools."[67] The failure of the schools to measure up to the standards was probably due to a lack of Friends to teach them. After 1820 two schools, one at Chesterfield, the other at East Branch, were again reported as meeting the standard. In 1824, there were four of that grade:

> 3rd. The committee on schools report that there are established for the education of our youth, one school at Chesterfield, one at Trenton, one at East Branch, and one at Stony Brook, all under the care of teachers in membership with us and superintended by committees appointed by the respective Preparative Meetings.[68]

From this point we shall turn our attention to the schools at each individual preparative meeting. In some preparatives, after the separation, two schools are to be found where before there

---

[64]*Ibid.*, 3/IX/1793.   [65]*Ibid.*, 12/II/1794.
[66]Changed to East Branch by request in 1804; *Ibid.*, 3/II/1801.
[67]*Ibid.*, 8/II/1814; 7/II/1815, and 6/II/1816.   [68]*Ibid.*, 3/II/1824.

Chesterfield Friends' School

was but one. It will therefore be necessary to deal with them individually. In the case of Chesterfield the original school was continued under the direction of Hicksite Friends. In 1848 they note that it has been taught by Chalkley White and is in a flourishing condition. In 1860 two schools were reported open, but a small attendance at them.[69] In 1865 the following report was made:

> There is one school at Crosswicks under the care of a committee of Friends, comprising 30 scholars, of which 3 are members, but it is not taught by a member, nor do they attend midweek meetings.[70]

The next year the trustees were instructed to ascertain the best disposition they could make of the school house for the ensuing year, and shortly thereafter report was received that they had rented it to the public trustees for one year.[71] In 1867 they reported:

> The trustees appointed last year to have charge of the schools, report having found that nearly all the children attending were of parents not members and after consulting with the meeting it consenting, agreed to charge the trustees of school district No. 1 of Chesterfield seventy dollars ($70) a year for the use of the school house, which has been paid and have agreed to pay the same for the present year subject to the direction of the meeting trustees— the meeting trustees introducing the rules that formerly governed the school.[72]

A further report of 1868 indicated:

> The school house has been rented for the past year for seventy dollars and the school has been kept subject to the same rules and regulations that governed the school when Friends had charge of the same. The District trustees to be subject to the direction of the Meeting Trustees.[73]

In 1869 the school house was rented to the district for $100, payable quarterly, the school was operated under the rules and regulations that had prevailed when it was a Friends' school, and the District Trustees were "subject to the direction of the Meeting Trustees."[74]

In 1870 the Monthly Meeting reported:

> There is one school at Chesterfield partially under the care of Friends, but not of the description queried after.[75]

---

[69]Min. Chesterfield Prep. Mtg. (H.), 28/VI/1860.
[70]Min. of Chesterfield Mo. Mtg., (H.), 7/II/1865.
[71]Min. Chesterfield Prep. Mtg., (H.), 28/VI/1866.
[72]*Ibid.*, 23/V/1867.　　[73]*Ibid.*, 25/VI/1868.　　[74]*Ibid.*, 25/III/1869.
[75]Min. Chesterfield Mo. Mtg., (H.), 8/II/1870.

From this time onward there was no school conducted solely by this group of Friends.

Returning now to 1828 we find that a school was likewise continued by the Orthodox branch of Friends at Chesterfield. Reports, from time to time show that school funds were very plenti-

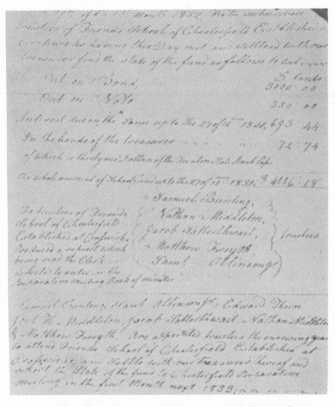

FACSIMILE OF A FINANCIAL REPORT OF THE SCHOOL AT CROSS-WICKS. THIS WAS ONE OF THE LARGEST FUNDS RECORDED FOR AN INDIVIDUAL SCHOOL IN THE EARLY NINETEENTH CENTURY

ful[76] and schools kept up, though not always taught by members. In 1842 they reported:

[76]Amounting to 3,675.44 in 1828, 3,841.97 in 1829, 4,036.26 in 1830 and 5,316.37½ in 1839. See reports for these dates in the Orthodox Preparative Meeting Minutes.

The School in Chesterfield at Crosswicks which has been continued through the year, was taught during the summer season by a female in membership—the average number of scholars about 30 of whom 22 were members. It is at present taught by a man Friend. There are 35 scholars of whom 15 are members. The Scriptures are daily read in the schools and the children attend midweek meetings with the teacher.[77]

This school was still in existence in 1850.[78]

SCHOOL AT TRENTON

A school house was mentioned at "falles" in 1693, it being proposed as a place to hold a meeting. But, following this early mention, signifying whatever it may, we know little of her school history before the nineteenth century. In 1798, replying to a request received from Trenton Preparative, the Monthly Meeting replied:

The committee appointed by the Monthly Meeting to consider the request of Trenton Preparative Meeting respecting the division of the fund for the support of a school in the Preparative Meeting of Chesterfield are of the mind that the Monthly Meeting hath no power to divide any part of the subscriptions thereof, yet we advise Friends of Chesterfield to consider them when they may open a fund for the support of a school agreeable to the direction of the yearly meeting.[79]

In 1807 the same meeting stated

There is a school at . . . Trenton, superintended by a committee of the Preparative Meeting and taught by members of the Society.[80]

Ten years later a committee for the school was named:

The following named Friends are appointed Trustees to Friends' School in this place: Joshua Newbold, Samuel Coleman, Joseph Decou, Joseph Shirm and Lewis Evans, who are desired to pay the necessary attention thereto, likewise to apply to the Trustees of Chesterfield and request them to refund the moneys that have been subscribed and paid by persons who are now members of this particular Meeting, for the benefit of the school in this place. The clerk is directed to furnish them with a copy of this minute.[81]

In the same year they record that

the Meeting united in requesting that the moneys that have been subscribed and paid to the school fund at Chesterfield by persons who now are members of this particular meeting may be transferred to the school fund in this place. The above request was directed to be sent forward to our next Monthly Meeting.[82]

[77]Min. Chesterfield Mo. Mtg., (O.), 8/II/1842.
[78]Min. Chesterfield Prep. Mtg., (O.), 5/II/1850.
[79]Min. Chesterfield Mo. Mtg., 2/X/1798.   [80]*Ibid.*, 3/II/1807.
[81]Min. Trenton Prep. Mtg., 28/II/1817.   [82]*Ibid.*, 21/VIII/1817.

A report was also returned concerning the lack of propriety in keeping school in the meeting house.

We the committee of the school of Trenton Preparative Meeting having met and considered the propriety of a school being kept in our Meeting House agree to report as there are but very few children that are members of our society at the school think it is a disadvantage and improper to keep a school in the Meeting house as this house is much dirted and the yard and fence much injured.[83]

In 1820 a new school committee was appointed, and in 1825 the meeting took up the question of alterations in "our present school room." We cannot be certain that the school continued in operation at all at this period, but may be certain at least that it did not measure up to standard. In 1831 the monthly meeting reported no schools whatever measuring up to standard.[84]

In 1841 the following minute regarding Trenton School fund is found:

Our Treasurer is directed to call on the executors of our friend Samuel Paxson (deceased) the former Treasurer of this Meeting for the school fund belonging to said Meeting and invest it in proper security for its benefit.[85]

There having been a school established by Friends at Trenton the appointment of Trustees to endeavor to encourage and promote said school coming under consideration, after deliberation thereon it was thought best to make such an appointment. Samuel Ellis Decou, John C. Haines, and Peter Decou were accordingly appointed to that service.[86]

A year later we learn that

At Trenton a school was kept for six months during the summer season, taught by a female in membership. The number of scholars was about 10, of whom three were members. During the continuance of the school the Scriptures were daily read and the scholars attended mid-week meetings.[87]

In 1843 the report for Trenton stated:

In Trenton Preparative Meeting there are 7 children who have been attending mixed schools the greater part of the year and one who has been six months at Westtown. No Friends school has been kept up during the past year.[88]

After the middle of the century no indication is found in the minutes that a school was carried on at Trenton. In 1862 the Hicksite Friends also report, "We have no fund for education."[89]

[83]*Ibid.*, 25/IX/1817.   [84]Min. Chesterfield Mo. Mtg., (O.), 8/II/1831.
[85]Min. Trenton Prep. Mtg., (O.), 15/VII/1841.
[86]Min. Stony Brook Prep. Mtg., 2/VII/1840.
[87]Min. Chesterfield Mo. Mtg., (O.), 8/II/1842.
[88]*Ibid.*, 7/II/1843.
[89]Min. Trenton Prep. Mtg., Women Friends, (H.), 16/I/1862.

EAST BRANCH SCHOOL

Let us turn now to trace the development of Robins School under the care of that Preparative Meeting. In 1800 a proposal was made concerning the establishment of a school fund, and a form agreed upon whereby subscriptions might be secured. After a few months' labor they reported that the subscriptions amounted to £ 68/15/0.[90] The school was begun without delay and reported in operation in 1801. In the same year they sought to obtain assistance, toward an increase of the funds, from Chesterfield. The result was an agreement, on the part of the latter meeting to collect subscriptions for the support of the new school.[91] In 1802 Robins received £ 6/8/6, being part of the sum derived from the sale of the old meeting house at Crosswicks, which was directed to be added to the school, according to a minute of the Monthly Meeting.[92] In 1804 the name of the meeting, and of the school also, was changed from Robins to East Branch.[93]

In 1805 the following report of the Trustees was produced:

... at a meeting of the Trustees of the school fund belonging to East Branch Preparative Meeting . . . the Trustees being all present proceeded to a settlement with Treasurer. After going through the settlement the accounts appeared to stand as follows, that is, ninety-six pounds on subscription, twenty-three pounds, ten shillings, out on bond, twenty-six pounds, fifteen shillings and nine pence in the hands of the Treasurer, two pounds, twelve shillings and nine pence interest due, not collected, and two pounds, thirteen shillings and four pence interest due on the bond the 19th of the present month, amounting in the whole to £ 151/11/10.[94] To this was added a legacy of £ 4/15/7½ in 1806.[95]

The following report, relative to a house that might serve as a dwelling for a schoolmaster, was made in 1810:

The committee appointed in the third month last to propose a plan that would do away the difficulty heretofore experienced in providing a suitable person to have the care of our meeting house, report that in their opinion it is expedient to build a dwelling house for that purpose (which might accommodate a future school master) on a lot that Samuel G. Wright has agreed to give adjoining eastwardly the one on which the Meeting House stands, with which, after due consideration, this Meeting concurs; the Trustees of the school fund are requested to pay the proper attention to the business and apply to this Meeting from time to time for further instructions as may be necessary.[96]

---

[90] Min. Robins Prep. Mtg., 24/XII/1800.   [91]*Ibid.*, 20/VIII/1801.
[92]*Ibid.*, 23/XII/1802.   [93]Min. Chesterfield Mo. Mtg., 5/VI/1804.
[94]Min. East Branch Prep. Mtg., 21/III/1805. .   [95]*Ibid.*, 19/VI/1806.
[96]*Ibid.*, 24/V/1810.

It appears from a later minute that this project may have been dropped entirely due to a disagreement about the "terms."[97]

In 1819 the trustees presented the following list of rules for the Meeting's approval:

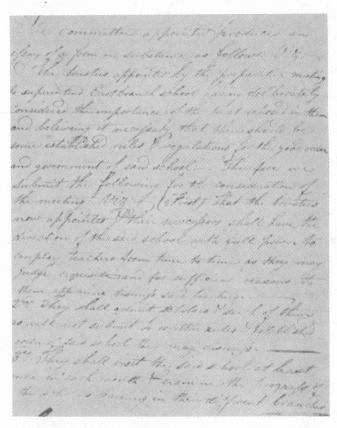

FACSIMILE OF THE RULES DRAWN UP BY THE TRUSTEES FOR THE SCHOOL AT EAST BRANCH PREPARATIVE MEETING IN 1819

The trustees appointed by the Preparative Meeting to superintend East Branch school having deliberately considered the importance of the trust reposed in them and believing it necessary that there should be some established rules and regulations for the good order and government of said school:

---

[97] *Ibid.*, 28/II/1811.

Therefore we submit the following for the consideration of the Meeting, viz., (First) That the Trustees now appointed and their successors shall have the direction of the said school with full power to employ teachers from time to time as they may judge requisite and for sufficient reasons to them appearing, dismiss said teachers.

(Second) They shall admit scholars and such of them as will not submit to written rules and established order of said school they may dismiss.

(Third) They shall visit the said school at least once in each month and examine the progress of the scholars learning in their different branches.

(Fourth) They may from time to time make such rules and regulations as they or any four of them shall judge necessary for the general benefit of the school. Provided such rules are not contrary to those now adopted and the fundamental plan of our school fund.

Edwd. Taylor, Junr.[98]

In 1824 the trustees reported:

Samuel Craft and E. Taylor Jr., attended and examined the writing and cyphering books of the scholars and heard them in most of the branches of literature in which they are engaged and the improvement of the children together with the order of the school was to us satisfactory or at least as much so as could be expected from the size of the children of school which are small at present.

Edward Taylor Jr.[99]

In 1825 it was proposed that if it could be done on "reasonable terms" a female should be secured to conduct the school six months of the summer. A few months later the committee informed that Hannah Craft had agreed to teach during the summer "at $1.75 per scholar for three months."[100]

In 1823 the following report was made, which is typical of those which concern the examination of pupils, progress, and order of the school:

. . . at which all attended and heard the pupils exercised in their various studies, examined their writing and cyphering books and we were united in believing there was a manifest improvement in several which with the order of the school appeared in a good degree satisfactory.[101]

The school at East Branch was apparently discontinued in 1833 at least as a Friends' institution. In 1833 the monthly meeting report showed that a school had been

kept up at . . . East Branch through most part of the past year and . . . now in operation . . . taught by person in membership with us and superintended

---

[98]Min. East Branch School Trustees, 29/VII/1819. [99]*Ibid.*, 4/XII/1824.
[100]*Ibid.*, 11/VI/1825. [101]*Ibid.*, 27/XII/1832.

by trustees appointed by the Preparative Meeting, and for some time past attended by about thirty scholars.[102]

In 1834 the following minute appears regarding the disposition of the East Branch School Fund:

The committee appointed to take into consideration the present situation of the school fund at East Branch Meeting and to propose what they may think necessary to be done respecting the same, having met and conferred together on the subject, do agree to report— That it appears by the last settlement with the Treasurer of said school fund that there was out on interest and remaining in the hands of subscribers which are considered safe and good, eight hundred and eighteen dollars and ninety-eight cents. Also that the Trustees of said fund did purchase half an acre of land, and built a good schoolhouse thereon in the year 1819, with interest arising on this fund, which schoolhouse and lot, together with the sum mentioned, remains in the possession of Friends; but as the Preparative Meeting of East Branch, under whose care and superintendence this fund was raised and heretofore managed, is now laid down agreeably to discipline, we believe it now becomes necessary for the Monthly Meeting to take care that the original design of this institution be complied with as nearly as present circumstances will admit of: and as there are no children within the limits of that Meeting of the description contemplated in the trust to be schooled out of the fund, and there being but two Trustees now, who have the superintendence thereof, we therefore unite in proposing that the Monthly Meeting appoint a Treasurer to take charge of the money obligations belonging to the school fund above mentioned and that Caleb Wright and Edward Taylor, the two present Trustees be continued to that service and that at least five other Friends be appointed as Trustees to unite with them in the superintendence and care of the funds, school-house, etc., aforesaid, which Treasurer and Trustees shall report to the Monthly Meeting at such times as the nature of their duties may require and in case of vacancies in either Treasurer or Trustees, they are to be supplied from the Monthly Meeting from time to time as may be necessary; and the Trustees to be appointed shall have power to apply the interest arising on the said fund money to pay for the education of children members of our religious society, whose parents are indigent, at their discretion, anywhere within the limits of our Monthly Meeting, but more especially where there are not other funds provided for similar purposes; and in case the whole interest money should not be expended for the purposes of education, then the Trustees shall be at liberty to appropriate so much thereof as may be necessary for the payment of East Branch particular Meeting's proportion of the Yearly Meeting stock and of such moneys as are directed by the Monthly Meeting to be raised for the use of the poor; and we further propose that if there should hereafter be a Preparative Meeting again established at East Branch agreeably to discipline, then the fund and other property before mentioned and now taken under the care of the Monthly Meeting shall

---

[102]Min. Chesterfield Mo. Mtg., 5/II/1833.

be returned to and placed under the superintendence of that Preparative Meeting as it was heretofore.[103]

That part of the above extract, relating to the use of a part of the funds for paying East Branch's quota of the Yearly Meeting stock, was later objected to.   In 1845 the monthly meeting stated:

The committee on the subject of East Branch school made the following report which was upon consideration approved, and the nomination of Samuel E. Decou, Peter Decou, Mark Collins, and John C. Redmond being united with, they were accordingly appointed. The clerk was directed to furnish the Trustees with a copy of this minute and the report. The committee appointed to take into consideration the situation of East Branch school fund, etc., having examined a copy of the subscription and the report of a committee adopted by the Monthly Meeting 2 mo. 4–1834, are of the opinion that the recommendations of that committee so far as relates to the purposes of education, do not exceed the limits prescribed by the original subscription . . . but we think that part which relates to paying East Branch's quota of the Yearly Meeting stock and money for the use of the poor is a violation of the trust, and we are united in recommending that no part of the money arising from that fund shall be applied hereafter for any other purpose than the promotion of education . . .[104]

After 1833 the answers to queries do not indicate a school was continued at East Branch, but the fund for educational purposes is sometimes mentioned.   In 1849 this fund amounted to $1277.-07.[105]

In 1693 William Penn purchased land in the neighborhood of Princeton, and thither came several prominent Quaker families in 1696 to form the settlement of Stony Brook, where the old meeting house still stands.[106]   Just when a school was begun it is impossible to say, but prior to the establishing of the College of New Jersey (1747), it is probable that no other school existed in the neighborhood.[107]

In 1781 Stony Brook Preparative Meeting asked leave to build a house on the Meeting's land at that place for the residence of a school master.   This request was granted by the Monthly Meeting of Chesterfield, stipulating that a schoolmaster should be employed agreeable to the direction of the Yearly Meeting.[108]   In the same year rules were drawn up for the government of the school and the

---

[103]*Ibid.*, 4/II/1834.   [104]*Ibid.*, 5/VIII/1845.   [105]*Ibid.*, 8/V/1849.
[106]Hageman, in his *History of Princeton*, gives an account of these first settlers. Vol. I, 25ff.
[107]*Ibid.*, II, 68.   [108]Min. Chesterfield Mo. Mtg., 3/V/1781.

order of the scholars.[109] Another report in 1801 indicated that a school was carried on there, "Under the care of friends and visited monthly by trustees," having a fund established for education.[110] Few documents relating to the history of this school survive, but we may gather a few facts about its existence. In 1821 we find the following:

Memorandum of an agreement between John Edgeworth and the Trustees of Stony Brook Preparative Meeting School.

The said John Edgeworth engages to teach school for the term of one quarter commencing the — day of this month at the rate of two dollars per quarter for each scholar, and such extra charge for wood as the same may cost. And the said trustees engage to pay him the sum of Twenty Dollars in aid of said school, out of the fund belonging thereto, and also engage that he shall have fifteen scholars or to pay him at the rate aforesaid for any deficiency, but they are not to be responsible for the tuition money of those who

---

[109]"The Master shall keep a particular account of employers' names, number of scholars, and time of entrance, and a particular account of all transient scholars and the time they come.

"No scholar shall be admitted into the school who will not comply with the rules and orders.

"No distinction shall be shown to the children of rich or poor, but the strictest impartiality shall be observed by the trustees and teacher to all.

"The hours of teaching shall be from eight o'clock to 12 and from 2 to 6 from the 1st day of the 4th mo. to the 1st day of the 10th mo., and from half after 8 to half after 4 from the 1st of the 10th mo. to the 1st of the 4th mo., allowing two hours at noon.

"The master shall be careful to speak the grammatical plain Scripture language and require it on all occasions, and shall give the strictest attention to prevent evil words and actions and vice of every kind. Every scholar is to behave him or herself orderly and becoming, on pain of being expelled from the school, but the master shall not dismiss any without a sufficient cause, approved by a majority of the trustees; and where any employer is dissatisfied with the master's conduct in school, he or she shall lay it before the trustees, that it may be settled in a friendly manner, as becomes people professing Christianity.

"The master shall suffer no scholar in the school who hath the itch or any other infectious distemper.

"It is expected that the master will attend our own religious fourth day meetings, accompanied by his scholars.

"In future no scholars to be admitted without the approbation of a majority of the trustees.

"The master is not to withhold correction from any when needful, but is to be careful not to strike in any improper or tender place, especially the face—"

(Rules to be observed by the scholars duplicated others already reproduced elsewhere in this work. They enjoined punctual attendance, silence in study, attention to lessons, plain language, kindly behavior one to another, and reticence about speaking of things relating to the school. Hageman: *Hist. of Princeton*, II, 68f.)

[110]Min. Chesterfield Mo. Mtg., 3/II/1801.

may send to the school. And the said John Edgeworth further agrees to teach two poor children gratis, if recommended by the said trustees.

> Joseph Olden
> Elisha Clarke
> David Clarke
> Emley Olden
> Trustees.[111]

The following direction to the treasurer also appears:

Elisha Clarke, Treasurer of Stony Brook }
   Preparative Meeting School Funds }
Please to pay John Edgeworth or order Twenty Dollars, it being so much we have agreed to allow him towards the support of his school for the quarter ending the 12th day of the present month, out of our Funds.

> Joseph Olden }
> David Clarke } Trustees
> Emley Olden }

2 month 15th–1821[112]

In 1826 Benjamin Clarke was asked to have necessary repairs made to the school house, but the report of 1827 states the school "is not under the care of this meeting." The report follows:

Trustees of the school established under the care of this Meeting report that they have examined the Treasurer's account and find in his hands a balance of four hundred and twenty six dollars and thirty-two cents, they also report that the sum of two hundred dollars of the permanent stock of the school fund has been paid off and is unappropriated; they also further report that there is a school kept in the school house but not under the care of this Meeting, towards the schooling of poor children at said school has been paid the sum of sixty-one dollars and sixty cents, out of the school fund since our last report.

> David Clarke }
> Benjamin Clarke } Trustees.[113]
> J.O. Clarke }

In 1839 the school was reported still under the care of a teacher in membership and under superintendence.[114]

In 1842 it was considered necessary to select a new treasurer for the school funds and Thomas Wright was appointed.[115]

In the same year a report on the school fund was made:

The Trustees of the school fund of Stony Brook Preparative Meeting report to said Meeting that they have settled with Emley Olden, late Treasurer,

---

[111]From a loose paper among the records of Chesterfield Mo. Mtg.
[112]*Ibid.*   [113]Stony Brook Prep. Mtg., 1/XI/1827.
[114]Min. Chesterfield Mo. Mtg., (O.)5/II/1839.
[115]Min. Stony Brook Prep. Mtg., 1/IX/1842.

and believe his accounts to be correct. We find a balance in his hands due three hundred and sixty dollars for which he has given his note payable with interest. And also that he has transferred over to Thomas Wright our present Treasurer all the bonds and other evidences of debt the property of said Meeting.[116]

The monthly meeting report for 1843 informed that:

In Stony Brook Preparative Meeting there are nine children of a suitable age to go to school, one of whom has been six months at Westtown, two attend Friends' school, three are taught in a Friends' family by his daughter and the remainder attend common schools in the neighborhood.[117]

In 1848 the School at Stony Brook was kept up "most of the year," and again in 1851 was mentioned as being established according to standard.[118]

After this date (1851) it is not clear whether the school at Stony Brook was continued under the meeting's supervision or not, but the Preparative Meeting records have many items relating to expenditures made from the school funds for purpose of sending poor children to school.[119]

Mr. Hageman in his *History of Princeton*, published in 1879, states:

The old school is closed. . . . There are probably not more than half a dozen members of this society who attend an ordinary meeting at Stony Brook on the Sabbath . . .[120]

BORDENTOWN

From an examination of the records it appears that no school was established at Bordentown. A minute dated 1870 mentions the fact that a school fund was begun there in 1808 with the intention of having a school, but, the number of members being small no such school was established. The fund was used by trustees towards paying for education of children going to other schools.[121] The monthly meeting's answers to queries, likewise, do not indicate that a school was held at that place.

MT. HOLLY MONTHLY MEETING

Mt. Holly was established as a Monthly Meeting in 1776

---

[116]*Ibid.*, 3/XI/1842.　　[117]Min. Chesterfield Mo. Mtg., 7/II/1843.
[118]*Ibid.*, 4/II/1851.
[119]Min. Stony Brook Prep. Mtg., 1862, 1866, 1873, 1875, etc.
[120]Vol. II, pp. 66ff.　　[121]Min. Bordentown Prep. Mtg., (H.), 26/X/1870.

being composed of Mt. Holly, Shreve's Mount, Old Springfield, Upper Springfield, and Vincenttown meetings. As the two Springfields are discussed elsewhere, we shall concern ourselves here with schools at Mt. Holly, the Mount, and Vincenttown preparative meetings.[122]

Immediately after being created an official meeting for business, Mt. Holly entered upon the task of establishing a school according to the proposals of the Yearly Meeting. In 1777, a minute acknowledged the receipt of their instructions, and, upon being considered, the case was recommended to each preparative meeting.[123] In 1778 more definite action was taken in the appointment of a committee:

> The subject of schools agreeable to the recommendations in the Extracts from the Yearly Meeting coming under consideration of this Meeting, the Meeting appoints Henry Burr, John West, Asa Shinn, John Gardner, Jos. Burr, and Tanton Earl to unite with a committee already appointed to consider what will be best for the better education of the youth and comes nearest to what is recommended in some observations on that subject.[124]

In 1779, the committee on schools was increased by the addition of ten members and in 1780 the report is made that "There is one school established in Mt. Holly which is under the direction of that Preparative Meeting."[125] In 1782, two schools are mentioned as "established by Friends" though not completely as recommended by the Yearly Meeting.[126] In 1783, steps were taken towards providing a building for the school:

> Mt. Holly Preparative Meeting requests the liberty of building a school house on a lot of land adjoining the grave yard, which was purchased of George West, which being considered, this Meeting grants them their request and the school is to be under the direction of Friends.[127]

A year later the minutes informed that a school house and dwelling house were prepared at Mt. Holly, but no school held at the time.[128] In 1788 a school was reported in operation at Mt. Holly and two other school houses, one of which was vacant.

In 1793, "thirty-one books" were received, "printed for the use of schools," and put into the care of the school committee. In the same year the Youths' Meetings, that had been held regularly

[122]See page 56 for location of meetings.
[123]Min. Mt. Holly Mo. Mtg., 9/VII/1777.   [124]*Ibid.*, 9/XII/1778.
[125]*Ibid.*, 9/VIII/1780.   [126]*Ibid.*, 7/VIII/1782.
[127]*Ibid.*, 5/VI/1783.   [128]*Ibid.*, 5/VIII/1784.

previously, were discontinued, in accord with a minute received from the quarterly meeting. This year was also notable for the

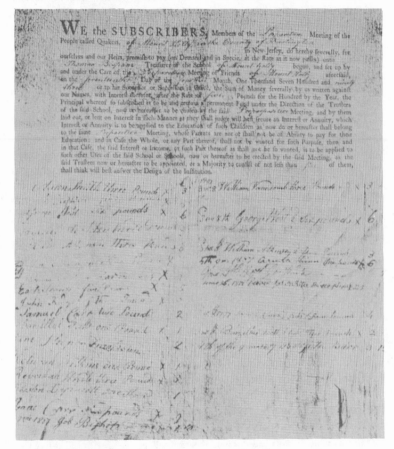

PLAN FOR RAISING SCHOOL FUND AT MT. HOLLY, 1793

beginning of a regular school fund.[129] For several years thereafter reports made state that no school is conducted "agreeable to direction," but again in 1808,

There is one school at Mt. Holly taught by a Friend and visited monthly

[129]See fascimile reproduction of the plan on this page.

by a committee of the Preparative Meeting to a good degree of satisfaction and there has been some addition to the fund since last year.[130]

After another period, 1808–1818, during which a school was reported now and then as being "according to direction" the school began a continuous existence which lasted until 1865. After 1865 it was at times taught by members but not always. In 1867 the following report was produced:

One school at Mt. Holly at present numbering 13 scholars, eight of which are members, has been taught by a person not in membership with us. The children attend mid-week meeting with their teachers.[131]

Two years later they reported: "We have no school of the kind queried after," and so the reports run thereafter. From a memorandum, among the records of Mt. Holly Preparative Meeting, we have the following report of the closing up of the school's affairs in 1881:

Since the close of the school 17 /VII/1881 our attention has been directed to a settlement of its accounts; we have paid all indebted persons, transferred to the educational committee of Philadelphia Yearly Meeting of Friends, all school books remaining on hand in full settlement of Yearly Meeting funds advanced to us by that Committee, and now transfer to the Preparative Meeting all property remaining in our hands, as follows . . . The total value (cost) was given as $231.28.[132]

THE MOUNT

The information relating to education among Quakers at the Mount is very fragmentary. Such as the writer has found seems to show there was no regularly established school there, among Friends, before 1808 or 1809, though a school of some sort existed. In 1808, "John Gardiner presented an account of the expenses of moving and repairing the school house . . . which sum the treasurer is directed to pay."[133] At the same time, a school committee and trustees were appointed.

The following friends are appointed a committee to superintend the school for one year, to meet once a month, viz. Daniel D. Smith, John Gardiner, Samuel Shinn, Richard Lawrence, Abram Merritt and Rowland Jones.

Daniel D. Smith and Abraham Merritt are appointed as trustees to receive the quota belonging to this meeting now in the hands of the Monthly Meeting, and put the same to use, as also all money that may be contributed for the use of the school.[134]

---

[130]Min. Mt. Holly Mo. Mtg., 4/II/1808.   [131]*Ibid.*, 9/II/1867.
[132]Records in the Mt. Holly Meeting House.
[133]Min. Mount Prep. Mtg., 3/XI/1808.   [134]*Ibid.*

In 1809 the meeting reported:

A school is established by this meeting near the Meeting House under the tuition of one of our members, and superintended by a committee appointed for the purpose, but no addition to the funds since last year.[135]

Another item in the same year, "Also a rod for the school house stove . . . $0.92," implies that the meeting had the details of school management and maintenance under their own charge. Whether the school continued under its direction is open to question, and there are few items on which to base our opinion. In 1820, however, we find an item, "By cash received of Joseph Smith for the Mt. School House $40," which may possibly mean that the school was rented to an individual or to local trustees.[136] Again in 1825, "By Cash received belonging to the School Fund of said Meeting, $108.60," would seem to indicate that the school fund was being used for other purposes than education, and was not being employed to maintain a school under Friends' control.[137] Certainly, if a school was operated, as begun in 1808, only few of its concerns were brought into the meetings' minutes.

VINCENTTOWN

Similarly, at Vincenttown, dependence seems to have been placed on a school "near William Bishop's," which, apparently, was not under the control of the society, *as directed by the Yearly Meeting*, though perhaps largely supported by Friends. The school house was built there before the meeting was officially held. We find in the minutes of Burlington Monthly Meeting for 1765, that "A written proposal of sundry Friends, for keeping an afternoon meeting during the summer, at a school house lately erected near William Bishop's, was now read and agreed to." This request was repeated and granted from time to time. In fact, the freedom with which the school house was made to serve for religious purposes, and the fact that we find no record of an agreement with another body for the use of it, lead us to believe it may have been wholly, or for the most part, under Friends' control.[138]

---

[135]*Ibid.*, 2/II/1809. [136]Account Book of the Mount Prep. Mtg. [137]*Ibid.*
[138]In numerous cases we have seen that houses originally built by the Society, were later occupied by other teachers or even passed to the control of the district trustees.

Upper Springfield Monthly Meeting

The Monthly Meeting of Upper Springfield was created by Burlington Quarterly in 1782 and began its sessions in the year following.   It was composed of Upper Springfield, Mansfield and Upper Freehold meetings.

As soon as the Monthly Meeting was established the question of education was brought to its attention and action taken, as the minute indicates:

The establishing of schools agreeable to the direction of the Yearly Meeting coming under consideration, Job Stockton, Tanton Earl, Robert Emley, Joseph Bullock, John Ellis, Richard Waln, Ebenezer Wright, Thomas Gaskill, Peter Ellis, Martin Gibbs, Thomas Smith, and Samuel Rockhill are appointed to that service.[139]

A report a year later, states there are two schools taught by Friends in the monthly meeting's limits, but "there is no school . . . held agreeable to the advice of the Yearly Meeting."[140]   In 1788 a step was taken to bring the school up to standard by the appointment of a standing committee with definite functions, described in the following minute:

In pursuance of a concern lately revived amongst Friends for the benefit of the rising generation with respect to their school education, as recommended down from the Yearly Meeting, it appeared to this Meeting that the school lately opened in this place be put under the care of a standing committee and thereupon this meeting appoints Tanton Earl, Clayton Newbold, John Wright, Job Stockton, Thomas Earl, Thomas Gaskill, William Newbold, Caleb Newbold, Samuel Stockton and Joseph Pancoast to that service by the name of trustees of Friends school at Upper Springfield Meeting; and the Preparative Meeting directs as follows, viz., That the said Trustees and their successors shall have the direction of said school, that they keep said school house in good repair, order the necessary expenditures when they have cash in hand for those purposes, when otherwise they are to lay before this Meeting an account of the sum wanted and the occasion, and receive our directions therein, they are from time to time and as occasion may require to employ teachers and for sufficient cause to them appearing to dismiss them and admit scholars and discharge them who may misbehave and make such rules for those and other purposes tending to the good government of the schools as they may judge necessary provided the same be not repugnant to this fundamental plan. They are to visit ye said school at least once in every month, examine the progress made by the scholars in their learning, and see that good order and decorum is preserved.   Any six of the trustees for the time being are to be

---

[139]Min. U. S. Mo. Mtg., 4/VI/1783.   [140]*Ibid.*, 4/VIII/1784.

sufficient to transact any business within their appointment. The Trustees for the time being shall appoint a Treasurer, to whom by his name donations and bequests may be made for the benefit of the school and the same accounted for by him to the Trustees, he shall pay no money out of the stock but to the order of the Trustees, said Trustees are to keep fair accounts of all such donations and bequests, a note of the terms, if particular on which given, and apply the same accordingly. They are to keep a regular account of their proceedings of their receipts and payments and the same with such regulations as they make, lay before this Preparative Meeting yearly for approbation.

Joseph Pancoast
Clerk[141]

To exercise further control over the school certain articles of agreement were fixed upon relating to the trustees and the school master. These were approved by the meeting.

1st. The master shall keep a book to enter employers' names, number of scholars and time of entrance.

2nd. Each employer subscribing for one or more scholars shall not at any time send more than double the number subscribed for.

3rd. The master shall teach spelling, reading, grammar, writing and useful arithmetic, such as is generally taught in public schools.

4th. The price of schooling shall be twelve shillings and six pence per quarter, exclusive of board, and for any branches of learning not usually taught by the quarter ye customary prices.

5th. The hours of teaching shall be from the 1st of the 4th month to the 1st of the 10th month from 8 o'clock to twelve in the forenoon and from 2 to half-past 5 in the afternoon and from the first of ye 10th month to the 1st of the 4th month, from 9 o'clock to 12 in the forenoon and from one to four in the afternoon.

6th. The teacher shall not leave the school without giving the Trustees one month warning by delivering a written note to their Treasurer, nor shall the Trustees dismiss any teacher without giving the same notice unless for a no-compliance with the rules agreed to by the Trustees and assented to by him or a manifest deficiency in the duties of his station.

7th. The teacher shall not dismiss any scholar without sufficient cause approved of by the Trustees and if any employer from dissatisfaction incline to take away a child the master is to inform the Trustees that they may attend to the case.

8th. The teacher shall suffer no scholar in the school that hath the itch or any other infectious distemper.

9th. The teacher shall be allowed four days in each quarter, beside the necessary time for attending Meetings.

10th. The teacher shall give the scholars timely knowledge when he intends to omit opening the school.

---

[141]Min. U. S. School Trustees, 20/II/1788.

11th. And 'tis further agreed that the subscribers shall furnish the school with a sufficient quantity of good wood.

N. B. The teacher shall not admit any scholars into the school after the number of twenty-five is made up without the consent of the Trustees.[142]

FACSIMILE OF RULES THREE TO SEVEN DRAWN UP FOR
UPPER SPRINGFIELD SCHOOL

Four months later the minutes inform that a definite time has been set for school visitation and another list of rules to serve to regulate the pupils in the school.

[142]*Ibid.*

1st. Fail not to be at school precisely at the hour appointed (or rather before) with your faces and hands washed and your heads combed, unless a good and satisfactory reason can be assigned to your master.

2nd. Make all your speeches to your master with due respect, observing cheerfully to perform his directions with dispatch according to your abilities. If strangers should speak to you give a modest and ready answer, turning your faces towards them.

UPPER SPRINGFIELD FRIENDS' SCHOOL

3rd. Be always silent at your studies so that your voices shall not be heard unless when you are saying your lessons or speaking to your master, hold no discourse with your school fellows during the time of study unless to ask something relating to your learning and then in a low voice.

4th. Behave yourselves at all times in a gentle, obliging manner to your school fellows, becoming virtuous children, the boys to treat the girls with that manly respect and decency which is due to their sex and the girls the boys with a becoming reserve and modesty.

5th. Never provoke one another, contending or complaining about frivolous matters but courteously use kind expressions one towards the other, observing to make some grateful return for any little kindness received, never returning injuries but learning to forgive shewing by exemplary deportment how all ought to behave and if disputes at any time arise you are to refer the matter to be decided by the master.

6th. You are carefully to observe true grammar, plainness of speech in using the singular number to a singular person and in every other respect avoid such additions in your address to others as are inconsistent with truth.

7th. Be not forward to divulge anything passed in school, nor to mock or jeer your school fellows when corrected—it is unkind and may happen to be your own case.

8th. And with regard to your conduct when out of school it is desired you may duly attend religious meetings being careful to be present precisely at the time appointed entering the place soberly and without noise, so as not to disturb the meditations of those who are met, when the meeting breaks up rise, not in an hurry, but rather think it a favor to be admitted to sit with your elderly Friends.

Do not spend your time on First Days in sports or any ways that tends to disturbance.

That you carefully avoid speaking evil of any one, treating aged persons with disrespect, making a mock of the lame, deformed or those deprived of their senses.

Do not throw sticks, stones, dirt or snow-balls at any person or dumb creature, but behave yourselves modestly, civilly and kindly to all.

Avoid all such amusements as are noisy, dirty or dangerous, and that you not only shun all indecent behavior in yourselves, but the pernicious conversation of others especially the shameful and exceedingly sinful practices of lying and swearing.[143]

A minute of 1792 stated that the promotion of a permanent fund for the use of the school was considered by the meeting and the Clerk was directed to have a plan drawn up on parchment. This was produced early in 1793, as follows:

... We the subscribers, members of the Preparative Meeting of the people called Quakers, or Friends, held at Upper Springfield, in the county of Burlington, West New Jersey, do severally for ourselves and our heirs hereby promise to pay on demand and in hard cash at the rate it now passes, unto William Newbold, Treasurer of Friends school at Upper Springfield aforesaid (begun and set up by and under the care of said Preparative Meeting on the twentieth day of the second month 1788) or to his successor or successors in office, the sums of money severally by us written against our names with interest therefore after the rate of six pounds for the hundred by the year until paid, the principal whereof so subscribed to be and remain a permanent fund under the direction of the Trustees of the school now or hereafter to be chosen by the said Preparative Meeting, and by them laid out or lent on interest in such manner as they shall judge will best secure an investment or annuity; which interest or annuity shall be applied to the education of such children as now do, or hereafter may belong to the same Meeting whose parents are not, or may not be of ability to pay for their education. And in case the whole interest or any part thereof shall not be wanted for such purpose, then and in that

---

[143]*Ibid.*, 18/VI/1788.

case, the said interest arising from the said moneys or such part thereof as may not be so wanted, shall be applied to such other uses of the said school or schools which now are or may be erected by the said Meeting as the said Trustees now, or hereafter appointed or any six of them shall think will best answer the design of the institution, which being put under our direction and care, will claim the particular attention.[144]

Among the first funds to be added to this foundation was £20/16/- 3½, a quota received from Burlington Quarterly Meeting. To this were added a number of bequests. In 1809, a minute reported the following:

I give and bequeath to my son William Newbold as Treasurer of the school called Friends School at Upper Springfield, the sum of eighty dollars in trust to be disposed of by the Trustees of said school in such way as they shall think will best secure for perpetuity an annual interest, which interest is to be applied by them towards the education of children members of our religious sect whose parents are not or may not be of ability to accomplish it with their own means, or in case such instances should not present or come to their knowledge, then in such other way as shall be most for the benefit and advancement of said school at their discretion. The Treasurer is accordingly directed to apply for and receive the same.

And information being given that Thos. Earl, late deceased, hath bequeathed for the like purpose the sum of ten pounds, equal to twenty-six dollars and sixty-seven cents, the Treasurer is directed to obtain an extract from his will relative thereto and insert it on the Minutes, and also to receive of the Executors the said legacy.[145]

In 1821 George O'Neal's bequest of ¼ acre of land for use of the school is mentioned, which was leased and its income applied to school purposes.[146] Relating to the school fund a minute of 1825 stated:

The funds of the school being now mostly in the hands of the Treasurer it is concluded to collect in what remains due from original subscribers, and put the whole out together on good and sufficient land security if a suitable person can be found to take it, and James Shreve, Isaac Horner and Caleb Newbold are appointed to assist the Treasurer in the business.[147]

This fund grew to be one of the largest found in any one meeting in New Jersey. In 1845, when the question of its disposal was raised before the Meeting for Sufferings in Philadelphia, the total value of the fund was $4500 plus one quarter acre of land.

In 1793 settlement was made of accounts connected with the

---

[144]*Ibid.*, 19/II/1793. [145]*Ibid.*, 25/XII/1809.
[146]*Ibid.*, 7/III/1821. [147]*Ibid.*, 6/V/1825.

building of the school, by which it seems that the cost was slightly over 80 pounds.[148]

In 1789 the minutes inform, concerning a school master that:

Our present school master Titus Bennett informing us that the time he engaged to teach school is nearly expired, and being willing to continue, the Trustees therefore agree with him to teach one year to commence the tenth day of the eighth month, 1789 under the same restrictions of last year, except that he is allowed the privilege of engaging thirty scholars and after that number is completed if any more should present he is to apply to us for direction therein.[149]

Titus Bennett taught until 1791, when he asked to be released apparently because there was "some expectation of entering in another place to more advantage to his interest." This request was granted, but later in the year he decided to teach if the trustees would agree to his proposition which was done. In 1793 he is again reported as teaching there and at the end of the year made a proposal to the trustees, described as follows:

. . . The time of our school master Titus Bennett being now expired he informs us of his willingness to engage for another year provided we agree to the terms of his proposals which are as follows that we the Trustees engage to give him a salary of one hundred pounds, that he will keep a fair account of all the schooling of non-subscribed scholars and such as send over their subscriptions which with such as we may yet subscribe he will allow us credit for on behalf of the salary at the former price of 12/6 per quarter (provided we make account of none but such as shall be at the time of subscribing able and likely to pay) and in case of a deficiency in making up the said salary by the profits of the school the Trustees to be accountable therefore—viz.—if the said sum should exceed £100 the Trustees to have the disposal of the overplus, which being agreed to except the overplus if any should arise which he is to have and Joseph Pancoast, Uz Guantt, Wm. Newbold and Thos. Sykes are appointed to take in subscriptions for the ensuing year as soon as may be convenient and report to our next meeting.[150]

During the year 1796 the school was vacant "some considerable time" so early in 1797 certain members were directed to write to Philadelphia for suggestions as to teachers, informing them of the local situation, and the probable salary to be paid "a suitable master."[151] A teacher by name of Tucker Earl was secured who remained for two years. In 1801,

---

[148]The pound in New Jersey and Pennsylvania was equivalent to 12s, about $2.66⅔.
[149]Min. U. S. School Trustees, 8/VI/1789.
[150]*Ibid.*, 13/XI/1793.   [151]*Ibid.*, 15/II/1797.

application by some of the employers or senders of children to our late school has been made for leave to employ a person not a member of our society (such an one now presenting whose recommendation is produced here, signed by several Friends in Evesham, setting forth that he is an orderly man and qualified teacher).

FACSIMILE OF THE CLOSED ACCOUNT OF J. TUCKER EARL, A
TEACHER AT UPPER SPRINGFIELD IN 1799

It is concluded that our present situation (as there is no apparent probability of having such an one as we are desirous of obtaining agreeable to our constitution and rules) it may be safe to admit him into the house for nine months; and in order that the business may be methodically arranged Thomas Gaskill and William Newbold are appointed to examine the house previous to his entrance and to lease it to the said teacher for that term, for the alone purpose

of teaching school in, on such terms as they may think right, and in such way
as to secure to ourselves and successors the entire and exclusive control of
said house and its appendages.[152]

In 1803 the school was revived under the charge of a member,
employed according to the following agreement :

As considerable time has elapsed since we have had a school at this place
under our care (no master presenting that appeared likely to fill the vacancy to
satisfaction) yet some of the Trustees (urged by the solicitations of divers
who wished for a school) of late turned their attention to enquire for one and
Charles Roberts, a young man lately from Westtown School being recommended
as a person qualified for the business and likely to answer our views; he was
wrote to on the subject by one of our number and encouraged to come over,
which he has accordingly done and now attending here, we have had a conference with him, heard his terms and on consideration think it safe and advisable to accede thereto and engage him for one year, to commence on or
about the 4th of 4th month, the agreement entered into being as follows:

That for a salary of three hundred and twenty dollars he is to teach the school
consisting of not more than thirty subscribed scholars, to collect the money
himself and quarterly if he chooses, and at the end of the year if there should
be any debts that he can not with a reasonable attention and exertion collect,
the Trustees are to assist him therein, and if the whole sum collected does not
amount to the said salary, the Trustees makes up the deficiency.

That the Trustees, previous to the opening of the school, are to procure a
subscription of the scholars that will be the principals in composing the school
at the price of three dollars per quarter exclusive of board, for instructing them
in spelling, reading, grammar, writing and arithmetic and for any branches
not usually taught by the quarter to charge the customary prices.   The teacher
is to keep a book to enter employers, number and name of scholars with time
of entrance and continuance at school, whether they are subscribed for or not,
and every employer subscribing for less than one scholar is not admitted to
send more than one at a time without first having the consent of a majority
of the Trustees, those subscribing for one or more, may send at one time, no
more than one in addition to the number subscribed for (and that only until
their subscription is filled) without the like consent, and non-subscribers not
to be admitted but at the discretion of the Trustees.   The hours for teaching
to be as specified on page four of this book, and the master also to be governed
by the 7th, 8th 9th and 10th articles in page five, every subscriber is to pay
at the time of subscribing, for each scholar, and proportionably for less,
thirty cents entrance money, which is to be deposited in the hands of the
teacher to procure fire-wood, ink, etc., for the use of the school and those not
subscribing or exceeding their subscriptions is to be assessed in the like proportion—and in addition to the books already belonging to the school, more is
to be purchased at our expense, if the teacher thinks it necessary, so that the

[152]*Ibid.*, 20/V/1801.

whole school may have reading books of suitable kinds.—The master is to keep a constant supply of suitable writing paper and furnish the children at a moderate price in preference to their having various kinds and qualities.[153]

After Charles Roberts had been employed for a year an attempt was made to get him for the Negro school at Philadelphia. After considerable correspondence on the subject, dwelling on the ethics of such action, it was agreed he should remain at Upper Springfield. Perhaps it was because of this difficulty that when Townsend Speakman was employed in 1806, a lengthy contract was entered into. In many points this is similar to the general rules on a previous page which were to govern trustees and teacher, but this was a particular agreement with one teacher.

In consequence of the enquiry of our committee (under appointment to seek for a teacher) and their invitation to Townsend Speakman (late from Westtown) he attended here and the following contract was entered into with him, viz.—

First.—Previous to his opening the school a subscription of such scholars as are likely to be the principals in composing it is to be had—at the price of three dollars per quarter and thirty cents entrance money, which last is to be paid at the time of subscribing,—and on or about the 9th of next month he is to commence for one year.

Second.—He is to keep a book to enter employer's names, number and name of scholars, with time of entrance and continuance at school, whether they are subscribed for or not, (and it is to be understood that non-subscribed scholars are not to be admitted, but at the discretion of the Trustees.)

Third.—He is to teach spelling, reading, grammar, writing and arithmetic, at the above price, and for any other branches not usually taught by the quarter to charge the customary prices.

Fourth.—The hours of teaching shall be from the first of 4th month to the first of 10th month from 8 to 12 o'clock in the forenoon and from 2 to 5½ o'clock in the afternoon. And from the first of 10th month to the first of 4th month from 9 to 12 in the forenoon and from 1 to 4 in the afternoon—(yet the hours may be gradually varied in proportion as the days increase in the one instance and decrease in the other; but so as to have the full quantum of time throughout the year, as above expressed.)

Fifth.—The teacher is not to dismiss any scholar without sufficient cause approved of by the Trustees and if any employer from dissatisfaction incline to take away a child the master is to inform the Trustees that they may attend to the case.

Sixth.—He shall not suffer any scholar to be in the schools that hath the itch or any other infectious distemper.

Seventh.—He is to be allowed four days in each quarter beside the necessary

---

[153] *Ibid.*, 11/III/1803.

time for attending our usual mid-week meetings which he is attend with the scholars.

Eighth.—He is to give the scholars timely notice when he intends to omit opening the school.

Ninth.—He shall not leave the school (at any time) without giving the Trustee three months warning, by delivering a written note to their Treasurer, nor shall the Trustees dismiss the teacher without giving the same notice, unless for a non-compliance with the rules agreed to by the Trustees and assented to by him, or a manifest deficiency in the duties of his station.

The teacher is to procure ink and firewood for the use of the school and charge them to the Trustees—and it is wished that he keep a constant supply of suitable writing paper and quills and furnish the children at a moderate price, in preference to their having various kinds and qualities.

And for his services in teaching the school, the teacher is to have a salary of three hundred and twenty dollars—to collect all the money himself from subscribers and others who may send—and quarterly if he chooses—but if at the end of the year there should be any debts that he cannot with a reasonable attention and exertion collect, the Trustees are to assist him therein, and if the whole sum collected does not amount to the said salary the Trustees are to make up the deficiency.[154]

The teacher of the school in 1814, probably Samuel Gummere who was employed on the same contract as Speakman (above named), seems to have been more progressive than the average.

The minutes inform that:

our teacher having proposed that the study of geography be introduced into the school, the same was on consideration approved, and as our house is not sufficiently roomy and convenient for hanging maps, etc., and more room having often been wanted especially in the winter season, it is concluded to have an addition of about ten feet put to the end of it . . . .[155]

Other improvements were also attempted according to the following minute of that date:

The adoption of a plan to secure a more regular attendance of the scholars at school has long been desired both by us and our teachers, from a belief that benefit would result to the scholars and a greater degree of reputation be gained to the school—and the subject having had our renewed attention, it is, on due deliberation, now resolved: that every scholar in their first coming after the commencement of our teacher's next year is to be entered by the teacher as a permanent scholar and continued as such (whether they attend or not) until due notice is given to the said teacher, by the person sending, that such scholar is withdrawn, such scholar may nevertheless be entered again at any future time. In cases of sickness however, or any other bodily inability to attend the time of absence is not to be charged for. Thirty cents is to be paid

---

[154] *Ibid.*, 5/V/1806.   [155] *Ibid.*, 11/IV/1814.

for every entrance of a scholar and $3 per quarter for tuition in the ordinary branches of spelling, reading, grammar, writing and arithmetic, with the usual advance on the higher branches if they are taught. And in order that all concerned may be duly informed of this regulation Michael Earl, Thomas Earl, and William Newbold are appointed for one or other of them to accompany the teacher on a visit to such, shew them the said regulation and propose their signing the same as an evidence of their assent to the same.[156]

From June 1815 to September 1819 the school was discontinued, and on the latter date, "there not appearing any probability of having one soon" a number were appointed to dispose of the "maps and gazateer" belonging to the school and pay the proceeds to the treasurer. This, however, was not accomplished, apparently, for in 1825, "having never been sold" a new committee was appointed to dispose of them.[157] At this time, though no school was being supported at Upper Springfield, the trustees of the fund did pay certain school expenses for children of members who attended elsewhere.

In 1827 an effort was made to revive the school, according to the following minute:

Some of the trustees desirous of having a school and believing that one might be made up they entered into an agreement with Louise Bennett to teach the same for a year at a salary of one hundred and eighty dollars in quarterly payments, and she accordingly commenced on the 12th of last month and the said contract being satisfactory, we confirm it as our act and take the charge of the school. It is concluded that for the present the school be limited to thirty scholars, large boys to be admitted only at the discretion of the teacher, and subject to dismissal by the Trustees if their conduct is not satisfactory.[158]

Again, seven months later,

The teacher requesting that the west room of the school house be fitted up for the reception of the maps and that they might be replaced there for the use of the school, it is concluded to have it done and Clayton Newbold and Clayton Newbold, Junior, are appointed to the service, have the room put in good repair as soon as they can, receive from Michael Earl the said maps and the gazetteer if he has the latter, and also to get from Thomas Earl such of the books, which he has in charge belonging to the school, as may appear needful.[159]

These provisions having been made the school continued till 1829 when it was closed. Trouble occurred at this time over the school property and house, and as the number of members was

---

[156] *Ibid.*
[158] *Ibid.*, 15/XII/1827.
[157] *Ibid.*, 6/V/1825.
[159] *Ibid.*, 18/VII/1828.

exceedingly small the school was not revived.   In 1843 Upper
Springfield noted:

> The treasurer of the trustees of the school fund belonging to this meeting
> informs that the said fund has accumulated to a considerable amount without
> there having been any appropriation thereof for some time past.   This Meet-
> ing, concluding that there will not probably be an opportunity of applying
> the funds according to the original designs of the donors, directs the said
> Treasurer to transmit to the Clerk of the Meeting for Sufferings, for its advice,
> a clear and suitable statement of the case and Clayton Newbold and John S.
> Curtis are appointed to assist him in making it out and to report to this meet-
> ing.[160]

In the following year the Meeting for Sufferings summarized
the case as follows:

1. Total value of school fund of Upper Springfield is $4,500 plus ¼ acre of
land.

2. The preparative Meeting is urged to keep up the usual number of trustees
in charge of the fund, and apply it to:

a. The education of children of their Meeting.

b. If there are not enough children (The number of children of school age
in 1842 was 3, one at Wilmington, one at Westtown, and one at Haverford.)
to utilize the whole income, the residue may be utilized by Burlington Quarter
to which Upper Springfield belongs.[161]

At the same time we find a proposal on the part of Upper Springfield Monthly Meeting that the Preparative Meeting of that name
be discontinued and their rights of property be vested in Mansfield
Preparative Meeting and its members for the uses and provisions
originally designed.   The Quarterly Meeting gave approval to
this step.[162]

Mansfield Preparative Meeting School was established with a
permanent fund for its support, in 1782.   At that date a large
parchment was prepared upon which to enter subscriptions, the
sum of which had, by 1815, reached £ 330.[163]

In 1783, when Upper Springfield became a monthly meeting,
Mansfield and their school became subject thereto, and the history
of the two is closely interwoven.   In 1784 the monthly meeting reported two schools taught by Friends, but not "agreeable to the

---

[160]Min. U. S. Prep. Mtg., 16/XI/1843.   [161]*Ibid.*, 22/VIII/1844.
[162]Min. Upper Springfield Mo. Mtg., 4/XII/1844.
[163]This Parchment is now in the vaults at 142 N. 16th St., Philadelphia.
It measures 2 ft. 6½ inches by 2 ft. 2¼ inches and sets forth the purpose of
the subscribers to the school fund.   The amounts subscribed varied between
£ 7 and £30.

advice of the Yearly Meeting." One of these was at Mansfield and the other at Upper Springfield. In 1804, three schools were named, the two above and an additional one of Upper Freehold "under the care of trustees and by some of their number mostly visited monthly."[164] In 1812 those at Mansfield and Upper Freehold were again named as being active, while that at Upper Springfield was vacant; the situation was the same in 1813,[165] and so continued until 1827. At that time, after a brief disturbance, the Mansfield School was resumed and continued in operation until 1845, after which it was often "not strictly speaking of this description;" i. e., up to official standard. From a number of references, the school house at Mansfield was apparently used for a time as a meeting place for religious services after the separation.

In 1831 women were added to the school committee.

It has been thought that a benefit would arise in the Woman's Preparative Meeting appointing a few of their members to meet with the Trustees of the school, to advise and assist in the government of said school when female children attend it, which proposition the Woman's Meeting has united with.[166]

In 1842 the monthly meeting reported they had twenty-one children of age for school, and that eleven had attended the Mansfield School, which was taught most of the year by members and superintended by trustees; the pupils attended mid-week meetings and heard the Scriptures read generally in the school.[167]

A year later, the educational situation was more fully shown:

From the report of the Preparative Meetings it appears we have 18 children of a suitable age to go to school, and also one school at Mansfield which is taught by a man in profession with Friends and superintended by Trustees appointed by the Preparative Meeting at that place, and which has averaged for the last 10 mos. 40, and now 45 scholars, and it appears to be well conducted and in a prosperous condition, and the Teacher and Scholars regularly attend the week-day meetings. Eight of the children have been at this school, most of them the greater part of the year, and three of them still attend it, two others attend a domestic school in their father's house taught by a member, and one of which last summer went to a Friends' School within the limits of a neighboring Meeting. Six others are not near any Friends School and have been at the common school, not taught by members, nor under the control of Friends. Most of the past year, of the remaining two, one has been last

---

[164]Min. U. S. Mo. Mtg., 8/II/1804.   [165]*Ibid.*, 3/II/1813.
[166]Min. Mansfield Preparative Meeting, (O.), 2/VI/1831.
[167]Min. U. S. Mo. Mtg., (O.), 9/II/1842.

summer at a Friends' School within the limits of our Quarterly Meeting, but is now at home and the other one is now at said school.[168]

From 1845 onward the Mansfield School was sometimes "not strictly as queried after," as in 1847, and again, apparently came under entire control of the meeting, as in 1848. In 1875 it was "up to standard" while in 1876, "no school of the description queried after" was reported. After 1876 the school was not revived, and the reports stated there was "no school of such description."[169] The following table, the figures of which are drawn from the Monthly Meeting Minutes of Orthodox Friends, throws light on the educational problem within the limits of Upper Springfield and Mansfield Meetings.

TABLE

	1851	1861	1870	1880	1890	1900
Children of School Age	23	25	18	17	9	2
Boys	12					
Girls	11					
School at Mansfield	7	1	3	3[171]		
Westtown	1	5	4	5	7	2
Common Schools	15	19[170]	8	5		
Taught at home			3	4		
Select School Philadelphia					1	
Not in School					1	

At the time of the division in the Society of Friends, 1827, the monthly meeting of the new organization reported that there were,

Two schools one at Upper Springfield and one at Upper Freehold, taught by members and superintended by Committees appointed by the Preparative Meetings.[172]

The report a year later, however, stated that:

Owing to peculiar circumstances attending this Meeting there are no schools in the immediate situation of those queried after.[173]

It was noted above that a school had been established under the care of the meeting at Upper Freehold; this school was still in operation in 1826. After the separation the Upper Freehold

---

[168]*Ibid.*, 8/II/1843.   [169]*Ibid.*, 1876 and thereafter to 1900.

[170]District school in this year was taught by a member.

[171]Quite probable that these attended the Mansfield school, though it was not controlled by the meeting.

[172]Min. U. S. Mo. Mtg., (H.), 6/II/1828.   [173]*Ibid.*, 4/II/1829.

school came under the jurisdiction of the Hicksite meeting. A minute of 1833 stated:

One school taught by a member and superintended by a committee appointed by the Preparative Meeting at Upper Freehold.[174]

In 1836 the minutes stated the Upper Freehold School was not taught by a member; and similar reports continued until 1849, when it was said to be under the tutelage of a Friend. Shortly thereafter, it passed into other hands save that the preparative meeting had oversight and control of it. In 1858, it was again according to the direction of the higher meeting:

We have one school taught by a member, under care of Committee appointed by Preparative Meeting.[175]

The number of scholars in attendance at the School was 44 in 1868, 7 of whom had one parent a member, and 2 of whom were members.[176]

The school was not mentioned after 1870.

LITTLE EGG HARBOR MONTHLY MEETING

A meeting was settled at Little Egg Harbor in 1704 and the monthly meeting, established in 1715,[177] came under the jurisdiction of Burlington Quarterly Meeting.

From all records now available it appears that schools were not well provided for among Friends at Little Egg Harbor, even late in the 18th century. In 1793 they state the "necessities of the poor have been attended to, but that of learning is yet wanting among many." A similar report was made in 1794.[178] Again in 1796, "no cause of complaint respecting the query except that of learning which is wanting among us."[179]

In 1803 the preparative meetings were directed to raise $20.00 "in the usual manner" and pay it to the treasurer for the use of the poor. It is barely possible that this was partly intended for assisting them by way of schooling. At any rate the report that

[174]*Ibid.*, 6/II/1833.   [175]*Ibid.*,3/II/1858.
[176]*Ibid.*, 5/II/1868. From items kindly transcribed from the records by Martha E. Gibbs, Columbus, N. J.
[177]Hazard: *Register of Pa.*, VII, 102.
[178]Min. Little Egg Harbor Mo. Mtg., 14/VIII/1794.
[179]*Ibid.*, 11/VIII/1796.

followed in 1806 was somewhat better, in that "some care extended towards the education of their children."

In 1808 the record of the preparative meeting indicated that something had been undertaken with reference to providing a school under its care.

Some time back Jeremiah Willits was appointed to assist the Treasurer of the school committee in collecting the moneys that belong thereto, now reports that he has attended to his appointment and has collected part, but not been able to collect it all, and requests to be released which the Meeting concurs with.[180]

No permanent success was achieved for, in 1812, the monthy meeting reported "not any (schools) under the care of committees."[181]

Again in 1818 we find that:

This Meeting appoints Simeon Haines, John Hallock, Thomas Bellanger. Nathan Bartlet, Eli Mathis and Aaron Bellanger, Trustees to have the schools and funds belonging thereto within the compass of this Preparative Meeting and the former committee is released.[182]

In 1820 three men were appointed to join the school committee of this Meeting to consider the propriety of "building a new school house at the west end of the shore."[183] Two months later they had decided "to build a new school house but not fully concluded where to set it." In 1821 the ground for the school was reported secured. In 1824,

This Meeting appoints John Hallock, David Maps, William Gifford, Nathan Bartlet, Nathan Bartlet, Junior, and Timothy Pharo as a school committee to this Preparative Meeting—Nathan Bartlet is appointed Treasurer.[184]

Regarding the financial status the committee stated in 1828:

We the committee appointed to settle with the school committee and those that have the care of the grave yard, report that they find in the hands of those for the school in cash $7.54, in notes of hand against several persons for $222.08, interest $62.76.[185]

In 1830 the following report, on schools within the limits of Little Egg Harbor, was made to the quarterly meeting:

Little Egg Harbor Preparative Meeting has a small school fund, and also a school house, in which a school is sometimes kept, under superintendence of

[180]Min. Little Egg Harbor Prep. Mtg., 7/V I/1808.
[181]Min. L. E. H. Mo. Mtg., 13/II/1812.
[182]Min. L. E. H. Prep. Mtg., 2/VII/1818.
[183]*Ibid.*, 2/III/1820.   [184]*Ibid.*, 2/IX/1824.   [185]*Ibid.*, 3/I/1828.

that meeting; but there was no school kept there at the time a part of the committee was there.

Barnegat Preparative Meeting has neither school house, school, nor a school fund, but divers of it members are interested with others, not members of our society, in a school house, in which a school is sometimes kept.[186]

A similar report was made two years later:

At Little Egg Harbor there are two schools under the direction of that Preparative Meeting, both taught by men not in membership with Friends, and visited by committees appointed by the said Meeting; at one of the schools there are 40 scholars taught, 6 of whom are members, at the other school there are 25 children taught, 9 of whom are members.

At Barnegat there are 8 children members that attend a school in the neighborhood over which the Preparative Meeting have no control.[187]

In 1840,

William Gifford also produced a bill for repairs on the school house to the amount of 26 01 ($26.01 ?) which was allowed and the treasurer is directed to discharge the same.[188]

In 1844 the monthly meeting reported no school at Barnegat Preparative Meeting but "one school at Little Egg Harbor taught by a member under the care of Friends." This school continued until 1866 but is not mentioned thereafter as a Friends' preparative meeting school. All reports beginning in 1867, and thereafter, are in effect: "We have no such school."[189]

The following table, made up from reports in the minutes of Little Egg Harbor Monthly Meeting, shows the situation regarding the number of children members and the manner in which they were distributed. Compared with other meetings it would seem that the sentiment in favor of a meeting school was never very strong here. Many meetings maintained schools until the number of children was as small as three, two and even until there were none remaining. In this instance, there is little doubt but that the

---

[186]Min. Burlington Q. Mtg., 30/XI/1830.   [187]*Ibid.*, 25/II/1834.
[188]Min. L. E. H. Prep. Mtg., 4/VI/1840.
[189]Little Egg Harbor Preparative Meeting was authorized by law in 1866, to dispose of "a certain lot of land . . . particularly mentioned and described, . . . which had been devised in 1805 by Jonathan Smith and Hannah his wife to The committee for schools for the Preparative Meeting of Friends of Little Egg Harbor, and their successors in office for the entire use of a school house and school for the Preparative Meeting of Friends of Little Egg Harbor forever." The enabling act stated they had "no longer any use for said property for the purposes of a school . . ." See LAWS OF NEW JERSEY, 1866, 560.

district schools when introduced proved themselves superior to anything the meetings had been able to provide.

TABLE

	1855	1859	1865	1870	1876	1879
Children of suitable age for school	19	17	18	17	14	16
Westtown	3		3	6	5	7
Friends School	4	4	5			
District Schools	7	7	8	7	7	4
Not attending any school	3	2				
Select School not under care of Friends		2				
Family School		2				
Instruction at home			2		2	5[190]
Select Schools				4		

We have now traced the development of schools in the Monthly meetings belonging to Burlington. The figure below indicates the number of schools maintained under the care of trustees, or committees, taught by members, and having permanent funds in many cases, between 1722 and 1895. These schools were reported as being "according to the plan of the Yearly Meeting." The abrupt decline between 1825 and 1830 is occasioned by the division of the Society of Friends in 1827, as a result of which schools suffered greatly. The number soon increased, however, in both branches of the Society. The second sharp decline in point of numbers occurred after 1866 when state support was withdrawn from Friends' schools. After 1827 only the schools of the Orthodox Friends are represented in this graph; complete figures for the Hicksite Branch are not available. Nevertheless, judging by the decline of schools in individual meetings, and the tendency in other meetings where figures are available, we may conclude that figures for the entire Hicksite Quarterly Meeting at Burlington would follow the same general tendency indicated above.

---

[190]"Instructed at home, or not attending any school."

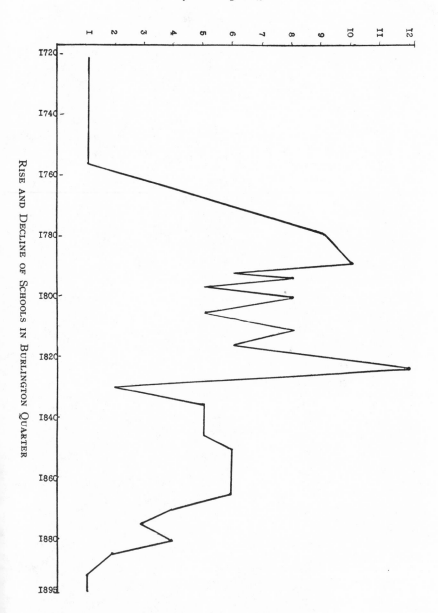

RISE AND DECLINE OF SCHOOLS IN BURLINGTON QUARTER

CHAPTER V

SCHOOLS OF SALEM QUARTER

Let us turn our attention to West Jersey, to Salem, the Colony of Fenwick, settled in 1675. It was this town that, in 1682, gave its name to the Quarterly Meeting of Friends, whose educational activities we are about to examine. Salem Quarter was composed of Salem, Greenwich, Maurice River, Woodbury, and Pilesgrove monthly meetings, established in 1676, 1770, 1804, 1785, and 1794, respectively.[1] It is to the manuscript minutes of these meetings we must turn for information concerning their educational affairs.

SALEM MONTHLY MEETING

Salem Monthly Meeting was first established in 1676 "to consider of outward business, and of such as have been convinced, and those that walk disorderly,"[2] but with the development of the community and the increase of public affairs, it came also to exercise control over the educational opportunities of the locality. It is stated in a local history that,

What appeared to be of the utmost importance to the everlasting happiness of our forefathers, and to their descendants, was undertaken, speedily to endeavor to advance the moral culture of the people, in building up meeting houses for public worship in almost every township in the county where needed, and erecting school houses for the instruction of their children.[3]

The records of the earliest days, however, are not as full as desirable and most historians content themselves with easy generalizations of the above character. Perhaps, this is not far from the truth. Certainly, after the middle of the eighteenth century, a great many references are found, giving evidence of the high esteem in which education was held.

In 1746 the Yearly Meeting directed the

[1]Bunting: *List of Records*, 89-97; also the first volume of each meeting's minutes.
[2]Michener: *Retrospect of Early Quakerism*, 44.
[3]Johnson: *First Settlement of Salem*, 168f. Raum, also, says "Fenwick's settlement at Salem opened a school soon after its establishment . . ." *Hist. of N. J.*, II, 284–5.

several Monthly Meetings to encourage and assist each other in the settlement and support of schools for the instruction of your children, at least to read and write, and some further useful learning, to such whose circumstances will permit it . . .[4]

Further directions concerned the quality of masters that were to

```
                        • Woodbury

                    • Upper Greenwich

                    • Woolwich
                • Upper Penn's Neck

                    • Piles Grove


    Salem •        • Allowaystown
                                    Great Egg Harbor  •
                • Alloways Creek

                    • Greenwich    • Maurice River

                                        • Cape May
```

SALEM QUARTERLY MEETING

be employed. These were reiterated more at length in 1750, and 1751, but not, at first, favorably received by Salem Monthly:

This meeting thinks the circumstances of our county no ways suits the proposals concerning schools in answer to the extracts from the Yearly Meeting . . .[5]

Following the more urgent suggestions of the Yearly Meeting in 1778[6] a greater interest is evident:

The extracts were read in this meeting, and the following accounts directed to be sent in the reports. The advices handed down from the Yearly Meeting with respect to the state of society having been weightily before the Meeting, several Friends gave in their names to attend several Preparative Meetings to assist them . . . also with respect to the education of our youth, which labor has been extended, in part, to general satisfaction and remains under care.[7]

In 1788 a committee on schools was named "to meet and confer together on the subject and report their sense of the state of schools amongst us . . .,"[8] but this report was not given in the minutes. A year later the committee was directed "to visit the schools that

[4]Min. Yr. Mtg., 1746, See Chapter Two.
[5]Min. Salem Mo. Mtg., 26/VI/1751.   [6]Chapter Two.
[7]Min. Salem Mo. Mtg., 26/VIII/1782.   [8]*Ibid.*, 27/VII/1788.

are under the direction of Friends, and the teachers members of
the society . . ."[9]   Accordingly, a report was made:

. . . on behalf of the committee appointed in the 5th month last to visit
the schools under the care of Friends, that they have attended to their appointment and visited such as were under the care of Friends to satisfaction.[10]

In 1791 steps were taken to establish a permanent fund, and thus
place the schools on a more permanent foundation. A committee
composed of John Wistar, Joseph Reeve, Jonas Freedland, George
Colson, John Barnes, and Isaac Pedrick,[11] reported a plan in
October, of which the following is a summary:

1. Nine trustees and a treasurer to be appointed annually, responsible to the monthly meeting.

2. Notes to be given for amount subscribed, bearing interest at
six percent.; principal not to be demanded during lifetime of
subscriber, provided he remains a member of this monthly meeting.

3. Treasurer shall make "full and clear entries of all moneys" in a
book.

4. Interest to be applied to education of "poor children, and to
no other purpose, but by direction of the monthly meeting . . ."

5. Trustees shall make report to meeting in May, annually;
new trustees to be appointed in June, annually, and all interests
paid in January.

6. On decease or removal of subscribers, the treasurer shall call
in the principal sum, invest it or put it out in safe hands at the
advice of the meeting.

7. Only by direction of the monthly meeting can the principal
be used in raising an annuity.

In accordance with the above plan, trustees continued to be
regularly elected, annually, throughout the next century, and their
reports each year shows the success with which the end in view
was reached. The following is one of the early reports, bearing
date of 1795:

The trustees of the school fund made report that they had attended to their
appointment and that there has been paid in of the interest on the notes
£ 21/14/5½, of which sum £ 12/3/6½ has been expended in schooling white
and some black children, and as they mention some part of the principal to
be paid in, they are directed to put out the same at lawful interest.   The following Friends are appointed Trustees of the Fund for the succeeding year, to

⁹*Ibid.*, 26/I/1789.   ¹⁰*Ibid.*, 31/VIII/1789.   ¹¹*Ibid.*, 25/IV/1791.

wit—William Abbott, John Redman, Richard Smith, Jonas Freeland, Joseph Bassett, William Carpenter, and John Redman is appointed Treasurer for the year ensuing.[12]

The figures subjoined, though not for regular intervals, indicate the growth of the fund and the purposes for which expended, between 1796 and 1826:[13]

TABLE

Year	Schooling poor.	Schooling Blacks	White and Black Children	Value of Fund
1796	6/8/6			
1798		16/4		
1801			14/4/10	
1804	22/3/9			
1810	27/3/9			
1813	$42.61			$663.76
1815	27.63½			703.75½
1816	37.46			771.85
1822	40.66			779.65
1823	52.75			820.26
1824	84.23			818.90
1825	99.90			862.91
1826	104.24			843.86

A report on the school fund in 1850 shows $114.95 paid in connection with a farm at Penn's Neck devised to the meeting by Elijah Ware, $24.86 for sundry school bills, and $30.00 paid to teacher of colored school in Salem.[14] Details concerning the colored school do not appear in the minutes, though there is frequently an item of $30 paid to the teacher. The funds expended for schooling the poor were not confined to Friends' children.[15]

Let us return now to the schools themselves, the situation of which was set forth in a committee report:

Salem 1791 the 7 month 25th

We the committee appointed to enquire into the state of schools within the compass of the Monthly Meeting having made inquiry and met and conferred upon the subject do agree to report that there is one school in the town of Salem, the constitution whereof is such that Friends have the chief prerogative and is under the care of seven Trustees all members of this Meeting, and is

[12]*Ibid.*, 29/VI/1795.   [13]Collected from the minutes for the above dates.
[14]*Ibid.*, (O.), 27/III/1850.   [15]*Ibid.*, 29/III/1854.

taught by a Friend. Also that there is several other establishments for schools now without teachers in several neighborhoods of Friends where they have the chief management and agreeable to their constitution, might have them under the care of Trustees Members of this Meeting and taught by members of the same if Friends would exert themselves and diligently attend all their annual and convened Meetings for the opening of or managing the affairs of said schools which we apprehend might open a way for raising and expending a fund agreeable to the advice of Superior Meetings.

John Wistar	John Barnes
Jonas Freedland	Isaac Pederick.

Though the above report indicates some progress, it does not appear that Salem Monthly was able to raise its schools to the level of excellence desired by the Yearly Meeting. In 1808, when answers are made to annual queries relating to schools, they reply: "None in this meeting exactly under that description."[16]   In fact, from 1808 to 1854, the report is to the same effect. This does not mean that there were no schools; only, that they were not successful in meeting the standard set by the superior meeting.

After the separation in 1827 the importance of "a guarded" education was again urged by the Yearly Meeting, and a committee was duly appointed to consider the possibilities. Report was soon made, however,

that having several times met and conferred together on the subject, no way has presented to obviate the difficulties Friends at present labor under.[17]

In 1831, replying to a request for information and a full report on schools, whether under the care of this meeting or otherwise, and the number of children, if any, who were without proper opportunities, a committee was appointed which produced the following report:

The following proposition offered by the Committee appointed by this Meeting on the subject of education having been considered appears to be united with and the Committee is encouraged to establish a school under the regulations therein proposed, viz.

After making inquiry into the state of this deeply interesting concern in our several neighborhoods we have to remark that as there is no select school within our limits Friends seem under the necessity of sending to such mixed schools as are contiguous in which their children are exposed to the corrupt example of those whose language and manners are not in accordance with that simplicity which our principles lead into, and altho in looking toward a remedy many difficulties have presented themselves, we are encouraged in the

---

[16]*Ibid.*, 25/I/1808.   [17]*Ibid.*, (O.), 27/X/1830.

belief that they are not altogether insurmountable and that a blessing will attend every right endeavor to remove them. Under this conviction, we propose that a school be established in the town of Salem for the instruction of girls and small boys, members of our religious Society, to be taught by a properly qualified female (also a member) and superintended by a joint committee of men and women to be annually appointed by the Monthly Meeting whose duty it shall be to visit the school once in every month and report its state to the Meeting at the expiration of each year. The said school to be located conveniently for the teacher and children to attend our weekday Meetings. The teacher's salary and all other needful expenses to be paid out of the income arising from the price of tuition to be charged on each scholar, which if found insufficient to defray the whole expenses of the school, the deficiency to be supplied from such available funds as the Meeting shall direct.[18]

The "not altogether insurmountable" difficulties were apparently overcome and the following report on schools produced in 1832. The difficulties in the way of establishing a "Select School" are obvious when we consider that in one school, six scholars, and in the other, "four only" were members of the Society.

There are within the limits of this Meeting two schools taught by members of our Religious Society. One of these is situated in the town of Salem and composed of about thirty-five scholars, six of whom are the children of Friends, the other situate in Mannington has had during the past year the average number of twenty-five scholars, of whom four only are Friends' children. The former is a private establishment conducted by two young women. The latter is under the direction of Trustees who are members of but not appointed by the Monthly Meeting. The house and property is also held by members of society. These two schools are so located as to be within the reach of most of our members, yet there are a few families so remote that they derive no benefit from them, two of which are so peculiarly situated that no provision has yet been made for them. We also report that after making a more particular enquiry into the state of our members in respect to the probability of carrying into effect the plan for a select school submitted to the Monthly Meeting in the 8th month last, have the discouraging prospect that from the many existing difficulties which have presented themselves no way yet presents to carry the said plan into operation.

Clayton Wistar
Hannah Smart.[19]

In 1833 four schools were reported: two primary schools, composed of a small proportion of Friends' children; and two "family schools" of "recent origin." These were so located as to accommodate most of the members, but some had to attend "mixed"

---

[18]*Ibid.*, 31/VIII/1831.　　　[19]*Ibid.*, 1/II/1832.

neighborhood schools, or send their children away to Friends' Boarding Schools. A year later, "two mixed schools" and three "family schools" all taught by members were reported. In 1837 the school committee reported:

. . . that there are three schools within our limits composed of Friends' children and others promiscuously, and taught by members of our Society. One of these schools is superintended by a committee of Friends, but they are not any of them under the care of the Preparative or Monthly Meeting. It also appears that there are forty-öne children within our limits of suitable age to go to school, all of whom have partaken within the past year of the benefits of literary instruction. And we may further remark that altho we hope the guarded religious education of our youth is a subject of increasing interest with a number of our members, yet we trust it will be readily admitted that a more general as well as faithful discharge of fireside instruction would prove beneficial to the children and comforting to parents and caretakers.[20]

In the same year (1837) the committee reported:

that it would be a proper step for the Meeting to take for reasons assigned in a statement which they have laid before the Meeting. After deliberation it appears the judgment of this Meeting to open a school which shall be free for all classes of children without distinction of color, and the Trustees of the school fund are requested to have the oversight thereof and make such rules for the government of it as they may think necessary. And are authorized to appropriate so much of the fund in their hands as they may think proper. And directed to furnish this Meeting with information of the state of the school in their Annual Report.[21]

In 1839 this school was reported as established "under care of Trustees belonging to the preparative meeting, though not subject to its appointment."[22] It continued, apparently, for a few years only, due largely to the fact that there were but a few Friend's children to attend it. After 1855 the only answer found, to the query regarding schools was: "we have no school of that description."

Though the irregular classification of children, found in the reports, makes concise tabulation impossible, the following table will suffice to show (1) the rapid decline in number of children members, "fit to attend school" and (2) the manner in which a great part of them scattered in "mixed," "family," and district or common schools.[23]

---

[20]*Ibid.*, 2/I/1837.   [21]*Ibid.*, 27/IX/1837.   [22]*Ibid.*, 30/X/1839.
[23]Figures collected from reports in Minutes of Salem Mo. Mtg. from 1840–1900.

TABLE

	1840	1850	1855	1860	1865	1870	1875	1880	1885	1890	1900
Number of children of suitable age for school	26	26	31	28	28	11	7	5	5	6	4
Number at Westtown		1	10	7	11	3	1	3	1	4	1
Number taught in Family Schools		6	3								
At Haverford					3						
Select School at Philadelphia					2						
Common Schools					12	6	6	2		2	3
Not in School									1		
Number taught in Schools by members	10		9						2		
Number taught by Friends in families	2			5		1					
Number taught in mixed schools	14	19	9	16		1					
Not accounted for									1		

From a minute of 1890 it appears that negotiations were entered into by the Trustees of Friends School Property and the Public Board of Education, whereby the latter secured the location for a public school. The following extract describes the manner in which this was accomplished:

The surviving trustees of the school house lot on Walnut Street report: That the Board of Education of the City of Salem, who have leased a portion of the lot for the use of the public school since 1850 desiring to erect a more commodious building thereon, and considering it essential that the title should be vested in themselves, commenced legal proceedings under an act passed in 1889 for the condemnation of property wanted for public school purposes, and for which a price could not be agreed upon with the owners. They made application to the court and have three commissioners appointed to assess the value of the land and the damages arising by reason of its being taken.

Having been informed that the Board, or some members of it, entertain the belief that the property did not legally belong to the Society of Friends, we thought it best to employ counsel to defend our rights, and through his efforts and our own, succeeded in establishing our title, and an amicable agreement was reached by which the commissioners were to award us 1,500 dollars as the value of the land; which sum, though much less than its real value, we agreed to accept, partly in consideration of the fact that the lease, by virtue of which they have held possession of the property did not expire for nine years:—and partly because we considered that the lot if acquired by the Board of Education and used for the purposes of a Public School would be more nearly devoted to the purpose for which it was originally purchased by the "Salem Free School Society" in 1783, than if occupied in any other way.

The above named sum has been paid over by the Treasurer of the Board of Education to the trustees who propose investing it for the use of the Preparative Meeting, to which Meeting, the property would seem to belong, according to papers relating to its history which are in our possession.

Signed   Richard Wistar
Casper W. Thompson
Josiah Wistar
Trustees.[24]

In addition to efforts to provide education in Salem, the Monthly Meeting, from the first, paid at the direction of the Yearly Meeting a considerable amount towards the support of Westtown Boarding School. An early record of this support is found in 1797, and is continuous thereafter:

The Friends appointed to receive subscriptions to the Boarding School reported that they had received of the subscriptions, £ 54/17/9, which is directed to be paid to the Clerk of this Meeting to be forwarded to the Treasurer of the Committee appointed by the Yearly Meeting for that service. And that there is on the subscription £ 21/10/ unpaid. The subscription papers is directed to be lodged with the Clerk, to be kept with the papers of this Meeting. The Clerk is directed to report to this Meeting when completed.[25]

From an early date, 1696, the Yearly Meeting of Friends had directed their influence against the trade in Negroes, giving it attention in all their meetings, and, after 1758, provided for disownment of those who persisted in the practice after they had received admonition to discontinue it. In this movement for their freedom and education Salem Meeting took a prominent part. In 1756 they reported "none imported" but "those that have them are not all so careful to train them up in the principles of the Christian religion as they ought."[26] To remedy this lack, about 1778 religious meetings were established at stated periods, especially for them, and a plan was set on foot to raise a fund to provide them an education.[27]

---

[24]*Ibid.*, 2/VII/1890. [25]*Ibid.*, 25/IX/1797. [26]*Ibid.*, 25/X/1756.
[27]*Ibid.*, 29/VI/1778. See Chapter Nine.

[Friends' School at Salem, New Jersey, now occupied by an industrial concern

After the division of the Society in 1827, it became necessary to duplicate educational efforts and much energy was dissipated, due to the fact that the smaller body often did not have enough children located so as to attend one school; and for a period of a few years, one branch or the other was usually without a permanent fund. As a general rule, however, it was not long before the "Separatists," "Hicksites," or "other branch," as they were called, had schools on a permanent basis, similar to the original meeting; and, in some instances the old school properties and funds passed into the hands of the new organization, while the original exerted itself to establish new funds and acquire new property. In any case, similar educational ideals and practices prevailed in both branches.

In 1828, in answer to the annual query, the new meeting at Salem replied "None of the description queried after,"[28] but nine months later,

Jonathan Woodnutt, treasurer of the school fund, informed this meeting that he has received an obligation of $300 of the school fund monies, and that there is $27.83 interest due on it at this time.[29]

In 1832 seven members were appointed trustees of the school fund[30] and continued to report regularly thereafter, indicating in their reports that the children of Friends, both rich and poor, were provided with opportunities for schooling.

Six years later, a special committee reported on the building of a school house, which should accommodate boys and girls:

The committee, . . . after a free expression of sentiment were united in the opinion that it would tend to the benefit of the members of this Monthly Meeting and also the surrounding neighborhood to establish a school within its borders; to attain this object the committee recommends to the Monthly Meeting a propriety in erecting a brick building on the lot belonging to Friends, across the street, opposite this house, of suitable dimensions—the lower, or basement story to be occupied by a boys school room and the upper story for the girls, all of which the committee believes is attainable at the present time; which they submit to the Meeting for its consideration and judgment in this important concern.

Signed on behalf of the committee by

> Benjamin Griscom
> Joseph Bassett, Jr.
> George M. Ward
> Ann. D. C. Thompson
> Rebecca Nicholson
> Maria Elliott.[31]

---

[28]Min. Mo. Mtg., of Salem (H.) 30/I/1828.
[29]*Ibid.*, 29/X/1828.   [30]*Ibid.*, 1/II/1832.   [31]*Ibid.*, 30/V/1838.

A further report, three months later, estimated the cost at $1000, "already subscribed" and asked the appointment of a building committee of three to have the work begun immediately, "so the school for boys may begin this winter." In September, Caleb Lippincott, George M. Ward, Jesse Bond, Thomas Shourds, Clement Acton, and Elisha Bassett were named as a committee "to employ teachers" for the school and visit it at stated periods, at least once in every month and attend to such other concerns as may be necessary in relation thereto." In the following year, 1839, two schools were reported, and in 1843,

> The committee appointed to have the oversight of the school under the direction of this Meeting report the school has been frequently visited by some of the Committee and they are united in reporting that it continues to be conducted in a manner creditable to the Society.
> The Boys school has averaged 40⅓ scholars and the Girls 29 scholars.[32]

Reports from 1840 to 1850 show the average attendance was about 40, most of whom made "satisfactory improvement in the several branches of useful learning." But in 1851, according to the committee's report, "the school has only averaged about 25 in consequence of the opening of the Free School in the 9th month last."[33] In consequence of the small number attending, the usual rent of $12 was not exacted from the teacher, Noah Leeds. He was, however, allowed to pay the bills for "whitewashing and cleaning the schoolroom," and $2 for tuition to Charles P. Smith.

In the course of a few years the schools (two) of the meeting more than regained their former size, furnishing education to one hundred children in 1857, 81% of whom were outsiders.[34] By 1865, the number of schools reported, increased to three, having in a "male department," whole number 110, 28 Friends' children, and an average attendance of 60; and in a "female department," whole number 106, members 22 professors 32, other denominations 52, and an average attendance of 67.[35] In the same year proposals were discussed for making an addition to the school building and in 1866 it was agreed to raise money for the school house by subscription.

The year 1866 marks a turning point in the history of Friends'

[32]*Ibid.*, 2/VIII/1843.
[34]*Ibid.*, 25/II/1857.
[33]*Ibid.*, 30/IV/1851.
[35]*Ibid.*, 1/II/1865.

schools in New Jersey. Thereafter, according to the law, section 12 of the Act of 1846 was repealed, which had permitted church schools to receive assistance from the public school fund. The enrollment at this time was very heavy, but it declined perceptibly when the law went into effect. The following figures describe the decline.

TABLE

Year	No. of pupils enrolled	Remarks
1850	39	
1851	25	
1857	100	Girls and boys
1865	216	" " "
1867	249	Male, female and primary departments
1869	256	" " " "
1872	126	" " " "
1873	96	
1874	73	
1875	35	"one school"
1876	47	two schools
1877	51	one school, 19 members attending
1880	42	one school
1881	53	two schools
1886	65	one school with four teachers
1892	72	" " " " "
1900	47	one school; three teachers; two pupils members, and 13 had one parent a member.

In 1866 Salem Meeting responded to a request from Woodbury Monthly Meeting that they send a committee to Camden, on the tenth of December, "to consult and decide upon what measures shall be taken to reestablish Friends in their just rights of the public school fund, which an act of the last legislature deprived them of . . ."[36] This passed, without appreciable effect, and in 1872 the Friends trustees were petitioned by the district to lease their property for a public school. The Friends' school at that time had an en-

---

[36] *Ibid.*, 31/X/1866; see also Chapter Thirteen.

rollment of 126 and "way did not open for leasing the house and grounds for a public school and the applicants were so notified."[37]

In 1873 proposals were made for grading the school, and this was accomplished, judging by the report in February 1874. Two years later a new set of rules were drawn up for controlling the school, and it continued under these until it was discontinued, under Friends supervision, in 1905. In that year,

Rebecca T. Wistar, on behalf of the Friends appointed to visit Margaret Ross on account of her application at last meeting, reports they offered her the use of the school house for the ensuing year, free of any charge for rent, but she must pay the city for water tax, and repair all damage to the property caused by her occupancy, reasonable wear and tear excepted, and she is at liberty to conduct it as a private school, which offer she agrees to accept. The Meeting accepts the report and the committee is released.[38]

Thus, the school continued as a private institution until recently when the building was occupied by an industrial concern.[39]

GREENWICH MONTHLY MEETING

Greenwich Monthly Meeting was so established about 1770, consisting of two preparative meetings, Alloway's Creek and Greenwich; later Maurice River and Cape May were added. From 1694 it had existed as a preparative meeting under Salem Monthly.[40]

Upon being created a Monthly Meeting it became necessary for the new organization to give official attention to educational affairs. But though reports were regular, we find that no great progress was made. In 1790, "agreeable to the advices of the Yearly Meeting" a committee was appointed to consider education and report what "may appear most expedient for the occasion."[41] Apparently the only conclusion arrived at was "to offer the proposals to the next preparative meeting, and lend them assistance as they may be enabled to do."[42] For the next thirty years there appear numerous items regarding small amounts raised and expended for the poor; and, in 1793, "one dozen of Penn's *Reflections and Maxims*, designed for the use in schools," were received and "directed to be divided in the usual proportion."

[37]*Ibid.*, 26/VI/1872.   [38]*Ibid.*, 31/V/1905.   [39]See page 127.
[40]Bunting: *List of Records*, 91; Michener: *Retrospect of Early Quakerism*, 45-6.
[41]Min. Greenwich Mo. Mtg., 30/VI/1790.   [42]*Ibid.*, 2/II/1791.

In 1821 the meeting's fund for educating the poor was augmented by the following provision in legacy:

Fifthly, I give and bequeath to John G. Mason and Joseph Thompson, aforesaid, one tenth of my estate (notwithstanding the said one-tenth which I give them in trust) shall be paid over to the Treasurer of Greenwich Monthly Meeting for to be applied either to charitable purposes, or more particularly the interest thereof to the schooling of poor children. The Monthly Meeting of Greenwich of which Joseph Thompson is a member is desired to receive said donation and apply it, or the interest thereof, as they may think will be most conducive to the welfare of the poor in the neighborhood of Greenwich or Alloways Creek. The above legacy which is one hundred and nineteen dollars and 46 cents, was paid . . . to . . . Treasurer "subject to the direction of this Meeting."[43]

The regularly recurring answers to the fifth query, of which the following is typical, indicate that a constant care for the poor and their education was maintained:

Poor Friends' necessities are inspected and relief afforded them, and when there are children of that description they freely partake of learning. No Friends' children placed from among Friends since last year.[44]

In 1828, regarding schools, it is reported, "We have one of the description . . .," but in February 1831 it was "at present vacant." Later in the year (December) the committee reported:

We have one school under the care of the Preparative Meeting taught by a member, another taught by two females, members of society, though not under care of the Meeting. Neither of which are select. The average number of scholars in each about twenty-five, five of the pupils attending the former and four the latter are children of Friends.

Benjamin Sheppard
John E. Sheppard
Mary Sheppard
Ann H. Bacon.[45]

A similar report was produced in 1835:

The committee appointed on the subject of Education produced a written report, as follows:

That the number of children of a suitable age to go to school remains about the same as mentioned in the report of last year, and likewise the state of our schools. We have one family school amongst us taught by a member, and a school under the care of a committee appointed by the Preparative Meeting has been kept about half the past year—also kept by a member, though not select, the average number of pupils about twenty-five, of which number from

---

[43]*Ibid.*, 28/III/1821.
[44]Min. Greenwich Mo. Mtg., (O.) 29/I/1829.   [45]*Ibid.*, 29/XII/1831.

five to eight only are members. There are, also four of our members at the several boarding schools.

Although we believe there is an increased care felt by our members to give their children what may be termed a suitable literary education, yet if a greater concern was felt to instruct them, not only in the principles of the Christian religion, and the precious testimonies given us to bear as a religious society, but to endeavor, through watchfulness of their own conduct, to evince to them, that their chiefest concern was to lay up Heavenly treasure, we think a great advantage would arise.

Joseph Miller
Grace Lippincott.[46]

In a later report of the same year it is brought out that though only four or five of the 25 attending are members, there are some families "so located as to be out of reach of the school." This probably explains, in part at least, the irregular existence of the school throughout the 19th century. In 1850 "there is one school under the care of a teacher in membership;" in 1856, "we have no school of that description;" 1860, "we have none of the description queried after;" 1870, "there is no school of the description;" 1875, "there is one school of the description queried after;" 1881, "no school of the description;" 1885, "there is one school of the description queried after;" 1890, no school of that kind; and similarly in 1893.[47]

The following table gives the essential facts concerning the number of children of school age, in Greenwich Monthly Meeting and the widely variant schools they attended.[48]

TABLE

	1851	1853	1856	1860	1865	1870	1875	1881	1885	1890	1893
Children of age to attend school	7	14	14	12	7	9	13	14	11	10	7
At a Prep., Mo. or Yr. Meeting School	1	9				1	5	7		2	
Instructed at home	4				5[49]	3[49]	2	1		2	1
At schools not taught by members	2							1			
Family Schools			4	8	5[49]	2[49]				4	

[46] *Ibid.*, 29/I/1835.   [47] From answers given to the annual queries.

[48] Gathered from reports in the minutes of the Mo. Mtg. for the dates mentioned.

[49] At home or in family schools.

Neighborhood School	1								
Westtown Boarding School	2	2	2	3	3	6	4	3	2
Haverford	1						1		
Select School—Phila.	1								1
Boarding School taught by a member	1								
Public School	1			2		1		2	1
Germantown Friends School				1					
Situation Unknown					3				
Not in School								2	2
Cornell University									1

Following the separation of 1827, the existence of standard established schools conducted by the new organization at Greenwich seems to have been quite as precarious as that we have just reviewed. In 1828 a school was reported, under the care of Greenwich Preparative Meeting; in 1829, none; 1835, no schools; 1840, "one school of that description;" 1848, "two of the description queried after;" 1856, one of the description queried after, the children of which attend mid-week meetings; 1862, one school; in 1866 the school at Alloway's Creek is mentioned; but after 1868 no schools are reported.[50]

Though there is not much evidence on the subject, it appears from certain entries in the women's minutes that they took part in the management of schools, as is often found in other localities:

This meeting is united in appointing Sarah S. Bacon to take the place of Elizabeth Reeve in visiting the school.

Also in the appointment of Mary M. Sheppard and Margaret Miller to that service.[51]

Alloway's Creek Preparative Meeting became, with Greenwich Preparative, a part of Greenwich Monthly Meeting in 1770.

As early as 1761, Joshua Thompson, a member of the Society, advertised "on behalf of myself and neighbors" for

a schoolmaster . . . wanted in the township of Elsinborough, in Salem County, and Western Division of New Jersey; one that can come well recommended, may meet with good encouragement, by the inhabitants of said township . . .[52]

In 1784 we find reference to a legacy left to the Meeting by Wil-

---

[50]See Min. Mo. Mtg. of Greenwich (H.), 1828–1868.
[51]Min. of Greenwich Prep. Mtg. of Women Friends (H.), 22/VI/1836.
[52]*Pa. Gazette*, No. 1721, December 17, 1761.

liam Booth, to be kept out at interest for the use of the poor, and a part of this probably was used to provide them an education.[53] So far as can be learned from minutes of the meeting, however, there does not seem to have been much done towards establishing a standard school, until 1845, when,

Rachel Hancock, Mary Bradway, Sarah F. Powell, and Rebecca Bradway (were) appointed to join men Friends as Trustees to a school now about being established under the care of Friends, to visit said school monthly and report yearly to this Meeting.[54]

The school was reported to be under "competent female teachers." Some attempt was made, at the same time, to establish a library and in July, the Committee on Education and Libraries reported they had collected a few books and the library was ready for their reception. Rebecca C. Bradway was appointed librarian for the month.[55] A list of the books in 1860 shows that the little library contained over 125 volumes—some duplicates—most of them dealing with Friends and their history, but others such as *Farmers Instruction, Young Chemist, Parley's Columbus, Life in the Insect World*, and *Ocean Work*, indicate a realistic trend.[56]

The school appears to have grown rapidly, and provided an education mostly for those who were not members. In 1866 they reported:

One school of the description queried after under the care of Alloway's Creek Preparative Meeting, 83 children attended last year; 2 of which are members, and 8 professors with Friends.[57]

After 1869 the school was permanently discontinued, having been in operation under the care of a committee since 1845. In that year we find the following minute, which gives the immediate cause for its discontinuance:

The committee appointed 22/V/1845 to have the care of the Preparative Meeting school house report that in consequence of a law passed by the Legislature of the state depriving them of any share of the Public school fund they have been obliged to discontinue said school, and there being no prospect of the house being wanted in the future for school purposes, they propose to the Meeting that it be sold and removed from the premises.[58]

---

[53]Min. Alloway's Creek Prep. Mtg., 22/IV/1784.
[54]Min. Alloway's Creek Prep. Mtg. of Women Friends (H.), 22/V/1845.
[55]*Ibid.*, 24/VII/1845.
[56]*Ibid.*, 27/XII/1860: see also Chapter Eleven.
[57]Min. Greenwich Mo. Mtg. of Friends, 1/III/1866.
[58]Min. Alloway's Creek Prep. Mtg., Women Friends, (H.), 18/II/1869.

MAURICE RIVER MONTHLY MEETING

Maurice River, established as a Monthly Meeting in 1804, was discontinued after 1855, and its lower meetings, Maurice River and Cape May preparatives, were attached to Greenwich, already discussed. Though admitted so late to the official position of a monthly meeting, there was a considerable settlement at Maurice River in the early 18th century—so considerable at least as to necessitate the appointment of a constable by the Quarter Sessions Court at Salem, in 1720.[59]

A thorough examination of the source of material, relating to the Meeting, fails to reveal any evidence of a school under the care of Friends before its establishment as a monthly meeting; and throughout the next 51 years, at the end of which it was discontinued, it appears dependence was placed upon schools in the neighborhood supported and attended by other denominations. Aside from this failure to establish exclusive schools, the meeting pursued a course very similar to others.

In 1807, it made record:

Care is taken concerning the poor; their children partake of learning and none are placed from among Friends.[60]

At the same Meeting, replying to the 3rd annual query, they say there are:

. . . two schools taught by Friends but not particularly under the care of this Meeting.[61]

The report of 1810 confirms the above statement. In 1811 they inform that:

Friends generally endeavor to bring up those under their direction in plainness, and to encourage the reading of the Scriptures and to restrain them from reading pernicious books and corrupt conversation.[62]

From a report of 1812 it may be inferred that the responsibility for schooling children was individual as "there are none amongst us but appear able to . . . school their own children."[63] From this date to 1823 there is no indication that a school was established; and the Women's minutes, which cover the period to 1854, fail to reveal the existence of any. It seems clear, however, that in the

---

[59]Elmer: *Hist. Cumberland County*, 73.
[60]Min. Maurice River Mo. Mtg., 30/I/1807.
[61]*Ibid.*   [62]*Ibid.*, 4/I/1811.   [63]*Ibid.*, 31/I/1812.

case of poor families, the meeting gave attention to the school learning of the children.[64]

Though no records are to be found of an exclusive meeting school there is evidence that some interest was taken in education and that they cooperated with the educational Committee of the Yearly Meeting. The following notice of the appointment of a committee by the women's branch is representative:

A minute from the Yearly Meeting's committee on the subject of education (concerning a meeting to be held 13/XII/1844) was received and read requesting some information respecting schools and education among us. Elizabeth Jones, Prudence Murphy and Rebecca Sharp are appointed to take the subject into consideration and obtain such information as is desired.[65]

So far as evidence from records available is concerned, there was likewise no school established under the care of Friends' meeting at Cape May.

WOODBURY MONTHLY MEETING

The first meeting at Woodbury was held at the home of John Wood in 1696, but removed soon after to a newly built meeting house. Woodbury was established as a separate monthly meeting in 1785, being made up of Woodbury and Upper Greenwich preparative meetings.[66]

Shortly after being created a monthly meeting, Woodbury, acting under the influence of the recommendations of the Yearly Meeting of Philadelphia, began to plan the establishment of a permanent school fund.[67]

---

[64]Min. Maurice River Mo. Mtg., Women Friends, (H.), 31/I/1835.

[65]*Ibid.*, 3/II/1844.

[66]Bunting: *List of Records*, 94; Michener: *Retrospect of Early Quakerism*, 46–7.

[67]Some progress towards permanency of school foundations had been made earlier in 1770 when James Cooper made a Declaration of Trust to Woodbury Preparative Meeting: "That is to say for the benefit, use and behoof of the poor people of the said Quakers . . . for a place to erect and maintain a meeting house and school house for the use and service of the said people." Deptford Free School on Delaware Street was built in 1774, being established and forever to be controlled "by the Society of Friends." Those of other persuasions were admitted, however, on agreement to pay and submit to the rules of the school. Jeremiah Paul seems to have been the first teacher. The "Cooper School Fund" is mentioned in 1873 as consisting of $2300 and 17 shares of turnpike stock; likewise plans for the Woodbury Free School had been drawn up in 1773. Parchment containing these regulations is in Gloucester Historical Society's Library at Woodbury, N. J.

The following extract is from the first page of the Minutes and Ptroceedings relatingo the School Fund:

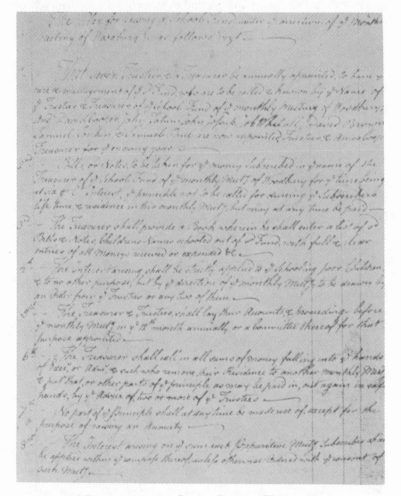

PLAN FOR RAISING SCHOOL FUND AT WOODBURY

The Yearly Meeting having for many years past frequently recommended to ye Quarterly and Monthly Meetings the establishing of permanent Funds for the support of schools,—the schooling of the children of poor Friends, children of Blacks, etc., and in the year 1789 renewed this advice in a very

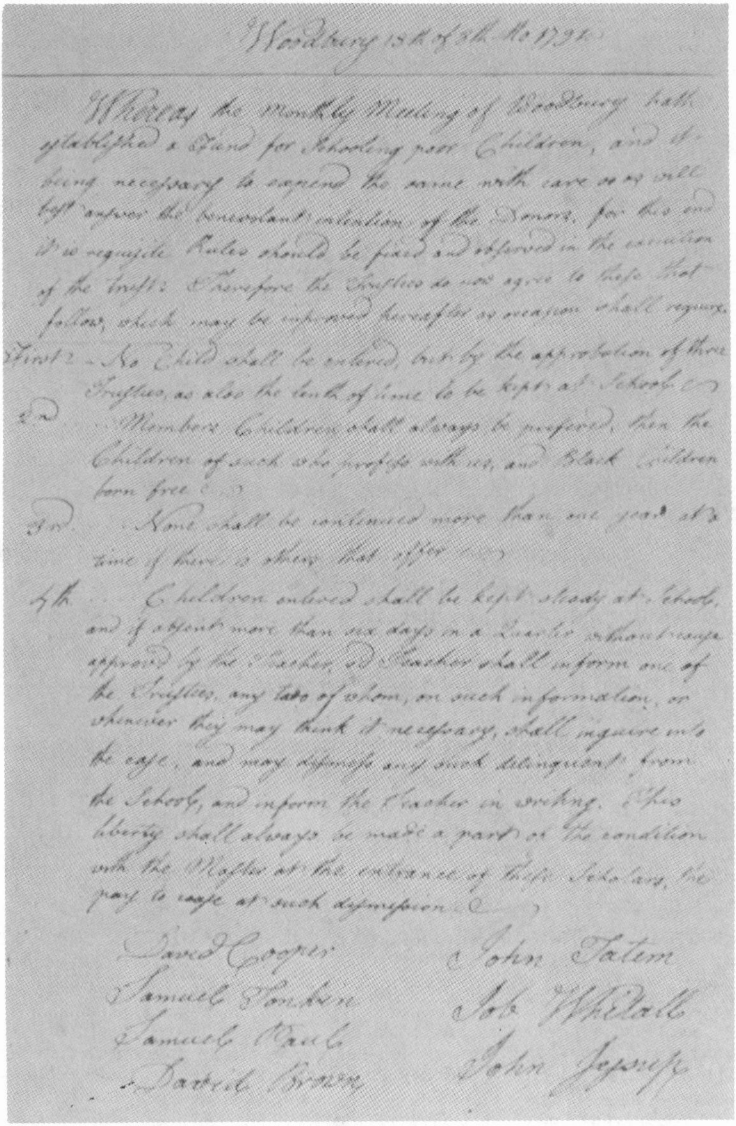

Woodbury 13th of 8th Mo 1792

Whereas the Monthly Meeting of Woodbury hath established a Fund for Schooling poor Children, and it being necessary to expend the same with care so as will best answer the benevolent intention of the Donors, for this end it is requisite Rules should be fixed and observed in the execution of the trust. Therefore the Trustees do now agree to these that follow, which may be improved hereafter as occasion shall require.

First. No Child shall be entered, but by the approbation of three Trustees, as also the length of time to be kept at School.

2nd Members Children shall always be prefered, then the Children of such who profess with us, and Black Children born free.

3rd None shall be continued more than one year at a time if there is others that offer.

4th Children entered shall be kept steady at School, and if absent more than six days in a Quarter without cause approved by the Teacher, sd Teacher shall inform one of the Trustees, any two of whom, on such information, or whenever they may think it necessary, shall inquire into the case, and may dismiss any such delinquent from the School, and inform the Teacher in writing. This liberty shall always be made a part of the condition with the Master at the entrance of these Scholars, the pay to cease at such dismission.

David Cooper — John Tatem
Samuel Tonkin — Job Whitall
Samuel Paul — John Jessup
David Brown

Rules to govern Trustees of Woodbury School Fund

pressing manner which induced this Quarterly Meeting to appoint a committee to consider ye subject, who in ye 5th month, 1790 reported a plan to fulfill in part ye desire of ye Yearly Meeting, which being approved was recommended to the Monthly Meetings to carry into execution.[68]

The fund is still in existence and, according to present members, is used for educational purposes in the two preparative meetings.

Several interesting items, concerning the schools at Woodbury, may be gathered from the Diary of Samuel Mickle, an illustrious citizen of the place.[69]   A few years after the establishment of the school fund he informs that in 1799 "the two schools in Woodbury have subscribed $40 each (to the fire company) besides fire buckets . . ." and that there is "surveyed an additional piece of ground to enlarge our school yard . . ."[70]   In 1802, he notes: "School visitation.   Upwards of 50 scholars of whom 42 are writers;" six years later, there were "60 scholars of whom 49 are writers;" in 1813, "Visited Deptford Free School 52 scholars of whom 45 are writers viz. 40 boys and 5 girls;" in 1816, he reports, "went to Females' School; 51 girls of whom about 1 doz. writers" and "at 1st day Boys School 40 attended, 47 absent;" 1819 he records, "Deptford school not visited today by one trustee!", by which it appears school responsibilities did not lie heavily on the shoulders of some.[71] Throughout the *Diary* are found items indicating that friends and relatives came to his home to board while attending school in Woodbury.

Samuel Mickle was also active in the Woodbury Library Company, established in 1794 and the First Day School Association which he notes was established March 3, 1816.[72]

The School Fund Plan entered upon 1790–91, was remarkably successful; by 1811, it had risen to almost $1900 and in 1815 passed $2000.[73]   In 1840 the income from it was larger than necessary for the ordinary school charges, partly due to support derived

---

[68]Min. and Proceedings of Woodbury Mo. Mtg. School Fund, 1790. At present in care of Warner Underwood, Woodbury, New Jersey.

[69]See Stewart, Frank H., *Notes on Old Gloucester County*, 155ff. *Diary* covers period from 1792 to 1829.   Samuel Mickle was an industrious member of the Friends Meeting, Woodbury Fire Company, Abolition Society, Gloucester County Bible Society, the Library Company, and·concerned in the Deptford Free School.

[70]Stewart: *Notes on Old Gloucester*, 164 and 178.

[71]*Ibid.*, pp. 174, 185, 194, 203, and 210.   [72]*Ibid.*, 202.

[73]Min. Woodbury Mo. Mtg., 24/XII/1811, and 7/XII/1815.

WOODBURY FRIENDS' SCHOOL

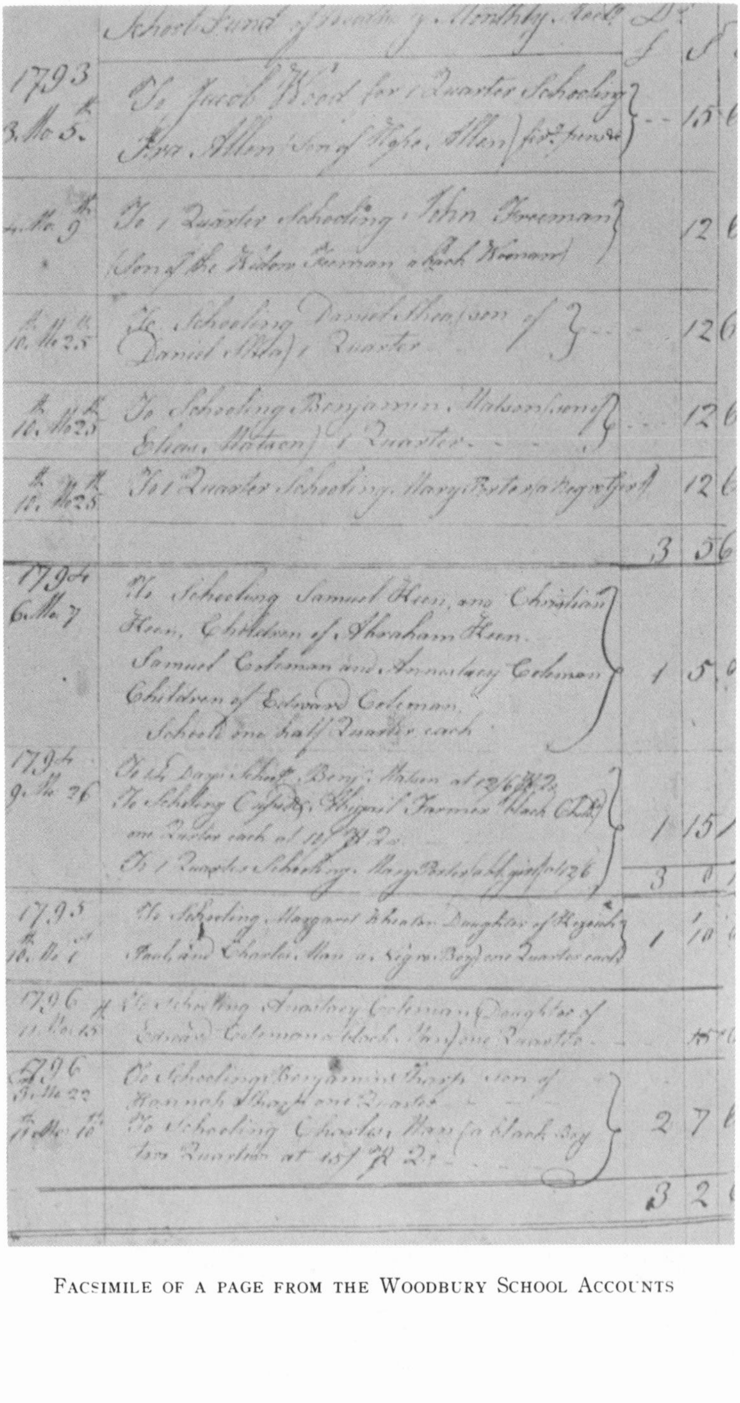

FACSIMILE OF A PAGE FROM THE WOODBURY SCHOOL ACCOUNTS

from public school money, and it was accordingly resolved to dispose of a part of it as set forth in the following minute:

HICKSITE FRIENDS' SCHOOL AT WOODBURY, NEW JERSEY

Whereas the constitution of the school fund belonging to Woodbury Monthly Meeting directs that the interest ensuing from said furd be strictly applied to the education of poor children, unless otherwise directed by the Monthly Meeting; and whereas the manner in which the public school fund is appropriated, and several other causes, it does not appear necessary to use all the interest as was contemplated by the donors; a proposition was made at last meeting to apply so much of the interest or rent of said fund for the purpose of building a comfortable school room for the education of female children on the lot belonging to Woodbury Preparative Meeting . . . referred for further consideration; and the subject now claiming the consideration it was agreed that Friends of Woodbury Preparative Meeting be at liberty to make use of so much of their proportion of said fund as shall be necessary to accomplish said purpose.[74]

In 1855 a minute from the monthly meeting raised the question of dividing the School Fund income between the preparative

---

[74]*Ibid.*, (H.), 30/III/1840.

meetings of Woodbury and Upper Greenwich (Mickleton). Upon examination it was pointed out that when the fund was established by the monthly meeting in 1790-91, Woodbury Preparative had subscribed £ 271 and Upper Greenwich £ 38; since then the proportionate share had been applied to schooling the children of those meetings. It being proposed that both share equally, permission was asked of Woodbury that it might be accomplished. To this Woodbury assented and the expenditures thereafter made accordingly.[75]

After 1887, when the "female school on Delaware Street" was rented to the district trustees,the meeting pursued the policy of paying for the education of Friends children, and applying the remainder to the preparative meeting fund. The decision is recorded as follows:

> as it appears that the funds received for school purposes are accumulating, it is the united judgment of this Meeting that the school expenses of the children of our members should be paid from the funds, and the balance, if any, should be set over to the Preparative Meeting fund, to an amount not exceeding 45% of the whole income for any one year.[76]

The school continued especially strong in point of numbers, (though not many were members of the Society) till the last quarter of the 19th century. In 1867 the whole number attending was 65, of whom three were members and nine had one parent a member. The teacher was not a member but usually attended the midweek meetings with part of the pupils. "Good order" was maintained, "and the lessons recited with animation and interest."[77] Ten years later, however, the success seems to have been somewhat more in doubt, and it was agreed that the " . . . trustees should not be authorized to guarantee the teacher any fixed salary as heretofore . . ." Some laxity, too had apparently crept into attendance upon religious meetings and it was now stipulated specifically " . . . with the understanding that all the children accompany their teacher to our mid-week meetings."[78]

In harmony with the usual practice in the early schools of Friends, girls were admitted, and women were employed as teachers. In his *Diary*, Samuel Mickle writes: "Elizabeth Cowperthwaite

---

[75]Min. Woodbury Prep. Mtg., (H.), 21/II/1856.   [76]*Ibid.*, 20/IX/1888.
[77]*Ibid.*, 21/II/1867; also 23/VI/1859.   [78]*Ibid.*, 23/V/1878.

Rules for the observance of the Committee & Teacher

1. After engaging a Teacher the Committee are to give her three months notice, should they wish a change, and they expect the same from her, unless sickness, or some unexpected circumstance render it inconvenient.

2. No Boys are to be kept in the School, nor admitted after seven years of age.

The price of tuition is to be 3 Dollars for the highest branches, — $ 2.50 for those who write and cypher, and $ 2 for the rudiments.

3. The Teacher is to make no change in the studies taught in the School, nor in the Books used therein without the consent of the Committee.

4. A short and appropriate portion from the Holy Scriptures, is to be read daily by the Teacher, either at the opening or closing of the School, and the pupils are to read therein, at least once in the week

5. It is recommended, that the committee meet every three months, and appoint two Friends of each sex to inspect the order of the School & the improvement of the Scholars, and report thereon at the next meeting.

6. The Teacher is desired in the government of the School so to unite firmness in discipline with gentleness of manner, as to ensure to her that respect which is needful to a well ordered School.

WOODBURY'S RULES FOR COMMITTEE AND TEACHER

Rules, for the obser[...]on of the Schola[...]
in Friends Female Scho[...]dbury
The School is to commenc[...] the three months of
Spring and Autumn, at half past eight in the morning and half past one in the afternoon closing at
twelve and half past four — In Summer, at
eight and two, closing at five. In Winter, at
nine and one, closing at twelve and four.

2 Each scholar capable of reading in the Scripture, should commit a small portion thereof to
memory every week, to be recited at such seasons, as the Teacher may [...]

[...] The children are to avoid any other noise,
when learning their lessons; and no conversation to be allowed, nor any child suffered to leave
her seat without permission from the Teacher

4 The Scholars are required to obey their Teacher
always treating her with the respect due to her station. If however any should [...] obedience, the circumstance should be represented to the visiting committee for their decision thereon —

5 The Parents and Guardians are expected when they
enter a pupil, to pay for their time whether present
or not, unless kept at home by serious indisposition
in which case they are at liberty to send another child in her place

6 The children are affectionately desired to endea-
vour at all times to live [...] and harmony with
each other, remembering the injunction of our
Holy Redeemer to do unto others as we would
wish them to do unto us.

RULES FOR WOODBURY FRIENDS' FEMALE SCHOOL

finished school keeping in Woodbury yesterday,"[79] and in 1813, "5 girls" are named as "writers" in the Deptford Free School.[80]

In 1830,

The subject respecting the appointment of trustees for the Female School was revived and the former committee reappointed, Josiah Stokes, Seth Matlock, James Davis and William Cooper.[81]

A report of 1858 gives the status of the school as follows:

The school has been open forty-four weeks during the year.

Whole number of pupils attending school, Seventy, of which sixteen are members of Friends Meeting.

Amount of public money received by the Treasurer for tuition—$100.

Amount of Monthly Meeting fund expended $34.62.

Average price of tuition per quarter about $3.20.

There has been expended for repairs and improvements on the school house and lot, the sum of $66.85.

Samuel Ogden
Samuel Lippincott
on behalf of trustees.[82]

Special mention is made of the fact that in 1861,

at the close of the session (of 44 weeks) the scholars passed through an examination of their principal studies, which was creditable to both teacher and pupils, evincing it was not a labored display for the day only, but that there had been considerable effort that they should be, and were understood.[83]

In 1873 the school was made free for all children of the members, while before, only the poor had shared education without cost:

After deliberate consideration of the subject it was the judgment of this meeting that the trustees of Friends Female School on Delaware Street be directed to permit all the children of our members to receive their schooling free, and to use so much of the school fund, belonging to this Preparative Meeting as may be necessary for that purpose.[84]

After the public schools developed, the patronage of the Friends school declined rapidly. We noted that in 1858 the attendance was 70. In 1861 there were 45, an average attendance of 26, and 17 members; 1864, average attendance 32—members 11; 1870, whole number during the year 45; 1875, 21 in attendance, of whom 4 were members; 1880, number in attendance 19; 1882, 19 attended of whom one was a member; a few years later the school was discontinued.

---

[79]Stewart: *Notes on Old Gloucester*, 184.   [80]*Ibid.*, 194.
[81]Min. Woodbury Prep. Mtg., (H.), 21/I/1830.   [82]*Ibid.*, 27/V/1858.
[83]*Ibid.*, 25/VII/1861.   [84]*Ibid.*, 23/I/1873.

A minute of 1875 seems to indicate that an effort was made to enable the school to cope more successfully with holding patrons:

... The Meeting was united in authorizing the trustees of our school on Delaware Street to make such changes, and procure such books as may seem necessary to enable the teacher to conduct the school with more system and to draw on the treasurer for such amount as may be required for this purpose.[85]

In spite of all efforts the school continued to decline and in 1884 we find that:

The school for the present season is not under the care of the Preparative Meeting, the teacher not being in membership with us, and the children do not attend our mid-week meeting.[86]

In 1885 report is made that the "property is in good condition and there has been no school kept there during the past year."[87]

In 1887 the trustees of the public school in Woodbury made application to rent the "female school" property, and it was done. In 1889 the committee,

... having charge of Preparative Meeting Property reports the property in usual condition, with school house on Delaware Street rented as last year (for $25), and this meeting unites in continuing the same committee to have charge of the property the ensuing year . . .[88]

Upper Greenwich Monthly Meeting

Upper Greenwich, so called to distinguish it from Greenwich on the Cohansey, existed as a meeting as early as 1740. It was a branch of Haddonfield Monthly and Quarterly Meetings until 1785, when it was attached to Woodbury Monthly Meeting, being subject to Salem Quarterly. As a member of that Meeting, Upper Greenwich evinced an educational interest by subscribing £ 38 to the school fund, which exercised an extensive influence on education in the vicinity of the two meetings until the public schools were established to provide education for all at state expense.[89]

Early in the nineteenth century the meeting undertook to establish a school under its exclusive care, but *for the neighborhood*.[90] Their progress is described as follows:

The period of time having now arrived for the building of a new school

---

[85]*Ibid.*, 23/XII/1875.   [86]*Ibid.*, 24/IV/1884.
[87]*Ibid.*, 23/IV/1885.   [88]*Ibid.*, 25/IV/1889.
[89]*Ms. History of Upper Greenwich Meeting* by Wm. Haines—shown the writer by William Borden, Mickleton, N. J.
[90]Michener: *Retrospect*, 47.

house, (1808) to supply the place of two old ones, which had been chiefly managed by the society; one of which was located in [Clomell ?] on lands of Isaac Cooper and the other on the north side of [?] Creek on what is called the Quaker Road, on lands of Solomon Lippincott. The subject claiming the attention of Friends resulted in a purchase at a mere nominal sum, of a lot of ground adjoining the Meeting House lot of 2 a 10 p. of Samuel Tonkin and Samuel Mickle, each the one-half part thereof by deeds dated the 10th day of the 3rd month, 1808. And in the 1st month 1809 it was concluded to proceed to the building of a school house thereon, size 27 by 33 feet of brick, and one story high. The committee on building was Samuel Tonkin, Samuel Mickle, Wm. Allen, Wm. Pine, and George Mickle who obtained on subscription for the purpose the sum of $363.25 which appears to have been sufficient to complete the house. The bricks were burned on the farm of Wm. Pine, (now Edward Cooper's) and the house well furnished, the lower floor being doubled. A large tin plate wood stove occupied a place near the middle of the house little smoke from which escaped thru a long pipe to a chimney in the south end. This old stove held its place for about 50 years and was in good keeping when it was forced (necessary ?) to abandon it. The new school house was reported finished the 4th of 1st month, 1810, and Samuel Paul, Thomas Clark, Josiah Stokes, Wm. Beckett and Wm. Haines were appointed the first trustees who agreed with George Mickle as teacher and opened a school on the 8th of the same month. In the 5th month, of the same year, there appears to have been a committee of women Friends joining the men in the selection of teachers, a regular record of teachers has been kept, with the time taught by them up to the present year 1873. viz. 167 quarters, being an average nearly of three quarters per year.[91]

The economic situation of the school was further enhanced by the will of Samuel Tonkin in 1819, which amounted to $200.[92] Later, the public funds were a valuable assistance, though not for a long period of time. In 1854 we find an entry of $155.00 "Public School money received during the year" and "wholly used for the purposes of education."[93]

Due to the zealous care of its supporters, this little school had a most happy career, there being almost no interruption from 1809 to 1874. The records of the school committee do not tell us much of its internal life, but are sufficient proof of its permanent character. Their meetings, so far as record of them remains were concerned with financial statements, selection of teachers, and, usually, give a brief statement of the school affairs; one typical report of 1861 is given herewith:

---

[91]*Ms. Hist. of Upper Greenwich Mtg.*   [92]*Ibid.*
[93]Upper Greenwich Prep. Mtg. Book for use of schools, 1854.

The trustees of Upper Greenwich School report that the school has been open for most of the year, has been taught by persons in membership with us with a good degree of satisfaction, and they have visited it during the winter season, once each month, and given such advice as they deemed necessary. During the summer term the school has been under the care of a committee of Women Friends who have given it attention.

	Wm. Haines	Edwin Craft
3rd Mo. 21, 1861.	Edward Cooper	Amos J. Peaslee
	Charles Heritage.[94]	

A list (almost complete) of the teachers in the school is preserved. The first teacher was George Mickle, who taught but a short time, which , indeed was customary. The greatest exceptions, prior to 1865 were William Mickle who taught 1812–16 and again in 1820; and Benjamin Heritage who taught, almost continuously from 1855 to 1865. Most of the teachers appear but one or two years.[95] Women were employed as teachers from the first (1810). As a general rule the men opened the school in November and continued for five or six months; women opened school in April and taught three or four months. The length of the school term reported was usually about three "quarters."

In 1874 the school was reorganized at a meeting held October 26 in the school house, it being agreed to

maintain a school on the mutual plan viz. each employer to pay his or her equal proportion of actual expenses and to carry out this object a board of five managers was appointed with power to act in the premises as best calculated to maintain a school of high grade.[96]

To further this object:

The trustees of the school are authorized to purchase desks, blackboards, and books, which are to be held as other property belonging to the Preparative Meeting, but they are allowed to loan them temporarily to a new select school about to be opened in the neighborhood for the instruction of Friends children and others and report to a future meeting.[97]

The above experiment, however, had but a brief existence. In 1876 we find the following instructions:

The trustees of the school property appointed in 3rd month last were directed to notify the trustees appointed by the district that at the expiration of the ensuing school year, commencing 9 month 1st, the management would again be resumed by the Preparative Meeting. The same trustees are also authoriz-

---

[94]*Ibid.*   [95]*Ibid.*, 1809–1865.
[96]Min. Upper Greenwich School, 1874–84.
[97]Min. Upper Greenwich Prep. Mtg., (H.), 22/X/1874.

ed to organize a select school during the coming winter to be under the care of the Preparative Meeting.[98]

Under the hands of the preparative meeting the school seems to have prospered again. In 1880, under a committee of men and women, it was reported open 9½ months, "to a good degree of satisfaction," at a cost of $660.35, a half of which was assessed on patrons, and the rest made up from the school fund.[99] In 1884, it was open eight months, kept by a member, "an efficient teacher," visited by a committee and cost $445.56. The attendance was small, but in 1889 the report was somewhat more hopeful.

The school has been kept open about 9 months during the year and taught by a member among Friends who has given good satisfaction. The teacher and pupils have generally attended mid-week meetings. The attendance of the school has been somewhat increased since last report. The school has been visited at times by the trustees. The visiting teacher of Friend Schools within the limits of Philadelphia Yearly Meeting has frequently attended the school and given illustrated and other interesting lectures encouraging teacher, pupils and patrons in school work.[100]

In 1896 the school was placed under the care of a committee appointed by the monthly meeting, and, according to the following minute of that date, was run in close connection with the Educational Committee of the Yearly Meeting.

It is gratifying that our school is one among the 32 reported, under the committees appointed by the Preparative or Monthly Meetings, belonging to the Yearly Meeting. That we have children among us to attend school places us under obligations to be ever watchful that we give them the best opportunities that we can command.

Three members of the Yearly Meeting's Committee on Education visited the school in second month last. They manifested much interest in our situation and gave encouragement. One of our committee gave an instructive talk to the children on nature history subjects . . .[101]

From this time on the school declined until in 1908 at the opening of school there were but 10 pupils in attendance, which later increased to 14. This was the last year it was kept open.[102] In 1910 it was agreed to rent the school property to the District year by year, for $15.[103]

---

[98]*Ibid.*, 24/VIII/1876.   [99]*Ibid.*, 27/V/1880.
[100]*Ibid.*, 20/VI/1889.   [101]*Ibid.*, 25/VI/1896.
[102]Min. Upper Greenwich School, 27/VII/1908.
[103]Min. Upper Greenwich School, 6/VIII/1910; William Borden, Mickleton, N. J., informs me the custom continues at present.

PILESGROVE MONTHLY MEETING

Pilesgrove Monthly Meeting, established as such in 1794 when it was set off from Salem, was composed of Pilesgrove, Mullica Hill and Upper Penn's Neck preparative meetings.[104]

From the beginning of the monthly meeting we find evidence that efforts were made to establish schools on a permanent basis. In 1794, John Barnes, Samuel Ogden, Elihu Pedrick, Benjamin Moore, and Isaac Eldridge were appointed trustees of the school fund and Jacob Davis the treasurer.[105]   And, on the same day, there was presented a constitution for the control of school money, as follows:

First, That five trustees and a treasurer be annually appointed to have the care and management of the said fund, who are to be called and known by the name of the trustees and treasurer of the school fund of the Monthly Meeting of Pilesgrove, who are already appointed for the ensuing year.

Second, Bills and notes to be taken for the money subscribed in the name of the treasurer of the School Fund of the Monthly Meeting of Pilesgrove for the time being at 6% interest.   The principal not to be called for during the subscriber's lifetime and residence in this Monthly Meeting, but may be at any time paid.

Third, The Treasurer shall provide a book wherein he shall enter a list of said bills or notes, children's names schooled out of the said fund, with full and clear entries of all moneys received or expended, etc.

Fourth, The interest arising shall be strictly applied to the schooling of poor children and to no other purpose but by direction of the Monthly Meeting, to be drawn by an order from the trustees or a majority of them who are enjoined to meet every three months or oftener as they may find occasion.

Fifth, The treasurer and trustees shall lay their accounts and proceedings before the Monthly Meeting in the 5th month annually, or a committee appointed for that purpose and the appointment of trustees and treasurer shall be in the 6th month following and the interest always paid in the first month yearly.

Sixth, The treasurer shall call in all sums falling into the hands of executors or administrators, and such who remove their residence to another Monthly Meeting and put that or other parts of the principal as may be paid in, out again in safe hands by the advice and direction of the trustees or a majority of them.

Seventh, No part of the principal shall at any time be made use of except by direction of the Monthly Meeting, for the purpose of raising an annuity.[106]

[104]Records in Meeting House (H.) Woodstown, New Jersey; see also Michener: *Retrospect of Early Quakerism*, 47–8, and Bunting: *List of Records*, 96–7.
[105]Min. Pilesgr̃ ve Mo. Mtg., 20/XI/1794.   [106]*Ibid.*

In 1807 they reported one school within limits of Pilesgrove, which was being taught by a member and superintended by a committee.[107]   In 1819, after the operations of the year there was a balance of the fund amounting to $341.32.[108]   There was no interruption in the school under the meeting's care until the separation on 1827, at which time a reorganization was necessary.

BACON ACADEMY, WOODSTOWN, N. J.
LATER OCCUPIED BY THE WOODSTOWN HIGH SCHOOL

After the separation no regular school was kept by Orthodox Friends.   They report that "Poor Friends necessities are inspected and relief afforded; their children partake of learning and no children, who are under our direction, placed from among Friends . . .," but, at the same time, in answer to the third annual query, they reply "not any" or "none."[109]   Consequently, those who "partook of learning" probably did so in a mixed neighborhood school.

The greatest educational activity, thereafter, in Woodstown was in the more numerous Hicksite branch of Friends, but for a

---

[107]*Ibid.*, 22/I/1807.   [108]*Ibid.*, 27/V/1819.
[109]*Ibid.*, (O.), 30/I/1829 and 29/I/1830.

BACON ACADEMY,

WOODSTOWN, SALEM CO., N. J.

H. A. Mattison, A. B., = = Principal.

This Institution is under the supervision of a committee appointed by Pilesgrove Monthly Meeting of Friends, is located in Woodstown, Salem Co., N. J. The village is pleasant, quiet, and healthy, and in every respect well suited to a school of the highest order.

The Academic year will be divided into four quarters of twelve weeks each, commencing on the first second day in the ninth month. Young ladies and gentlemen may here receive a thorough education in all branches commonly taught in our highest Seminaries.

Attention will be paid to the moral, social, and physical education of the pupils, and no student will be permitted to remain in the school, who refuses to comply with the rules of morality and good order, or whose influence may be deemed prejudicial to the welfare of others.

Pupils are received at any time during the quarter, and expenses graduated accordingly. No deduction made for absence, except in case of sickness.

A Teachers' Class will be formed if desirable, in which the members will be taught by lectures, and otherwise, the elements of correct school discipline, and the best mode of teaching particular branches.

Teachers of experience are engaged, and nothing will be left undone to make the School a good one.

Good Board can be procured in the Village.

COURSE OF STUDY.

Besides a complete system of English and Commercial Studies, the coarse of instruction will comprise, the Languages and Ornamentals usually taught in Seminaries. Particular attention paid to Composition and Declamation.

TERMS OF TUITION.

$2,50—$3,00—$3,50—$4,00—$5,00—$6,00 per quarter, according to studies pursued.

For further particulars inquire of

JAMES WOOLMAN, ⎫
WM. CAWLEY. ⎪
JOSEPH ENGLE, ⎬ *Trustees*
ABRAHAM WOOLMAN, ⎪
JOSIAH DAVIS, ⎭

AN ANNOUNCEMENT OF BACON ACADEMY

few years they, too, reported no schools that met the Yearly Meeting's standard. In 1837, "one of the description queried after" was reported,[110] and in 1844, "There are two of (that) description . . ."[111]

At this time the school prospect became much brighter for Pilesgrove, due to the generosity of David Bacon. Section thirteen of his will provided:

Thirteenth, To Pilesgrove Monthly Meeting I give and devise the sum of $600 to be placed at interest and the interest used in supporting indigent members of the Meeting and I do further give and devise to the aforesaid Monthly Meeting of Pilesgrove, all the residue or remaining part of my estate after paying the before mentioned debts and legacies, of wh'ch residue or remaining part, so much as may be necessary for the purpose shall be used in purchasing a lot and erecting thereon a good substantial frame building, two stories high and of suitable dimensions for a school, which building shall be used for a school house and be under the direction and control of the aforesaid Monthly Meeting. And the balance or remaining part of said residue, after paying for said lot and completing the beforementioned school house, shall be placed at interest and the interest used for paying the school bills of orphan and poor children of all classes and keeping said house in good repair.[112]

The "residue" or "remaining part," mentioned above, proved to be a considerable legacy for that day and the result was the founding of Bacon Academy,[113]certain facts concerning which are presented in the following minute:

We the undersigned trustees appointed . . . to receive and apply a residue bequeathed to the Monthly Meeting of Pilesgrove by David Bacon . . . for the purpose of building a school house etc., report, that the trustees have received from the executors of said deceased the sum of $5356.40½ being in full of said bequest—and further that said trustees all met and after free interchange of sentiment seven out of nine of trustees were united in believing that a house to receive day scholars together with boarding scholars if desired, would be more in compliance with the wish of the testator than one calculated only to receive boarding scholars, within the compass of the Monthly Meeting or elsewhere. . . . the trustees therefore devised a plan and appointed David E. Pancoast and Chalkley Lippincott to superintend the building of said house, and the undersigned also report—that since last Monthly Meeting they have examined the accounts of the building committee with the vouchers accompanying them and believe the account to be correct as presented at last meeting, and that they have acted in accordance with the will of a majority of the trustees

[110]*Ibid.*, (H.), 31/I/1837.   [111]*Ibid.*, 30/IV/1844.
[112]Extract from Bacon's will, in a packet of papers relating to the Bacon estate, Mtg. House (H.) at Woodstown, New Jersey.
[113]See p. 153.

and that the cost of the building, fencing, etc., is $2,471.88 together with the cost of the lot amounts to $3,110.88 leaving a balance of $2,400.00 . . .[114]

In 1850, the following report of the trustees shows the status of the school:

The following report of the state of the school under the care of this Meeting was produced by two of the trustees, and directed to be minuted viz., two of the description queried after—one for boys and the other for girls.

The boys school for the last year was open 8 months at an average of 30 pupils, taught 5 months by a member of Friends, the balance by a professor.

The girls' school open about 10 months, with an average of about 45 pupils, five months of the time taught by a person in membership; the balance by a professor with Friends.

The branches taught were Reading, Writing, Arithmetic, Geography, Grammar, Botany, Philosophy, Natural History, Physiology, and the mathematical branches.

James Woolman
David C. Pancoast.

4th Mo. 30th, 1850.   Trustees.[115]

The report, a year later, shows a very large increase in the enrollment. In the boys' department there were 73 scholars; and the number in the girls' department was 65. This report makes clear also that reading, writing, arithmetic, grammar, geography, botany, physiology, philosophy, history and drawing were taught the girls.[116]

It was customary that both men and women should exercise a control over education. In 1852,

Mary Ann Davis, Hannah L. Robins, Mary W. Barton, Mary Davis, Hannah B. Smith, Mary A. Davis, Ann F. Robins, and Amy B. Matson (were) reappointed as a committee to superintend the Bacon School.[117]

In 1854 an attempt was made to make the school distinctly co-educational, whereas before the male and female departments had been separate. The two departments were united "for the past year" and placed under the superintendance of a woman principal with suitable teachers to assist her. The school was kept open ten months and attended by 53 boys and 49 girls.[118]

In 1866 Pilesgrove appointed a committee to attend a meeting called by a minute from Woodbury to deliberate on measures necessary respecting the school law just passed. In January the

---

[114]Min. Pilesgrove Mo. Mtg., 26/IV/1842.
[115]*Ibid.*, 30/IV/1850.   [116]*Ibid.*, 29/IV/1851.
[117]Min. Pilesgrove Prep. Mtg., Women Friends, 27/V/1852.
[118]*Ibid.*, 20/IV/1854.

next year, they reported that there had been a general agreement to send a memorial to the legislature requesting the reenactment of section 12 of the School Law.[119]

In the year that section 12 was repealed, the District Trustees applied to the trustees of Bacon School,

to rent (it) and allow it to receive its proportion of public money and our meeting still have the entire control of the school. This, "after free expression thereon"

met with approval,[120] and the arrangement was apparently continued for six years. During this period the attendance was about the same as previously, but the number of members attending in 1868 were but 40, out of a total attendance of 136. "The children (did) not regularly attend mid-week meetings."[121]

In 1872 the school was again placed under the sole care of the meeting.

The committee appointed at last meeting on the subject of the Bacon School and funds, report that having all met but one, and taken the matter into consideration they were united in recommending that the school house be no longer rented for the use of the district and that a school be established under the care of trustees appointed by the Monthly Meeting; and they further recommend that the entire income from the Bacon Fund be devoted to the maintenance of the Bacon School; which being deliberately considered by mens' and womens' meetings conjointly, the first propositions were united with and in regard to the last it was thought best that application be made to the representative committee or Meeting for sufferings for its advice or assistance.[122]

Regarding the division of the funds of Bacon Academy and their use for that at Mullica Hill, it was directed by the Representative Committee that the money be "annually apportioned amongst all pay schools under the care of Friends within the limits of the Monthly meeting."[123] To this suggestion both men and women agreed.

After the change of mangement in 1872 the school was continued as a Friends' institution, and, though suffering some financial stringency in 1892[124] and 1896,[125] was kept up according to the usual standards. In 1897 the following report was made:

The school has been in session 10 months with Albert T. Yarnell as principal, Margaret R. Caley, Assistant, and Rachel L. Moore in charge of the Kinder-

---

[119]Min. Pilesgrove Mo. Mtg., 1/I/1867.
[120]*Ibid.*, 25/IX/1866.   [121]*Ibid.*, 25/II/1868.   [122]*Ibid.*, 28/V/1872.
[123]*Ibid.*, 30/X/1877.   [124]*Ibid.*, 29/XI/1892.   [125]*Ibid.*, 1/XII/1896.

THE BOARDING HOUSE WHERE CHILDREN LIVED WHILE ATTENDING ELDRIDGE'S HILL SCHOOL, NEAR WOODSTOWN, N. J.

garten Department, all members but one. There have been 60 pupils . . . during the year, 21 of whom were members, 25 with one parent a member, and 14 not members.

A full course of the different branches taught in the Higher schools has been given and six of the pupils have completed the required work in a satisfactory manner. Appropriate commencement exercises were given by the graduates

ELDRIDGE'S HILL BOARDING SCHOOL AS IT LOOKED IN 1922. THIS SCHOOL, TAUGHT BY ALLEN FLITCRAFT, DREW STUDENTS FROM MANY SURROUNDING STATES

on the 9th of the 6th month in the Friends' Meeting House. A large gathering of Friends and patrons of the school were present, it being the first formal graduation from the school of which we have any record.[126]

After 1905 the school served as the Woodstown High School. It was recently torn down.

Besides the schools under the preparative and monthly meetings there were a number of private boarding schools in New Jersey under the care of Quaker masters. Most famous of these independent institutions were those at Camden, Burlington, Crosswicks, Moorestown, Salem, Bridgeboro, Woodbury, and Eldridge's Hill near Woodstown. The buildings occupied by the latter are still standing, but are falling into decay.[127] Here in 1855 were

---

[126]*Ibid.*, 29/VI/1897.   [127]See pages 158 and 159.

taught the common branches, and also navigation, surveying, Latin, practical astronomy, and book keeping.[128]

No complete records for Woolwich Preparative Meeting, held at Mullica Hill, have been found. From those available a few facts of their educational history can be gleaned. As early as 1797 Friends at Mullica Hill were granted permission "to hold a religious first day meeting in the school house . . . in every week during the space of four months (on trial) to begin the eleventh hour."[129] It is possible that the school house was in the hands of Friends, but this is not certain. Four years later, 1801, the "Meeting of Woolwich" was established at Mullica Hill.[130]

In 1862 the meeting recorded that inquiries were received from the superior meeting regarding families, children and schools, and a committe was appointed to collect the information but this report was not brought to the meeting at the time named. Again in 1875 a committee was named to furnish educational information and this report was produced:

The . . . report that they had forwarded the desired information to the Yearly Meeting's committee; the number of children being members is 26, and those having one parent a member is five; and further that we have no school, and circumstances are such that we do not desire aid for that purpose at this time.[131]

In 1876 a proposal was made that a school be established and a committee of 12 men and women was named and asked to report to the next meeting.[132] In September

The committee appointed at last meeting concerning a school to be under the care of this Meeting, report that they have succeeded so far as to employ a teacher by the name of Anna R. Sylvester for the consideration of $100 for 3 months; also, rented a room for $18 per quarter which was accepted and the committee are continued to carry out such other matters concerning the school they may think necessary for its promotion.[133]

Five years later, a report was made which dealt with the school up to 1881.

The committee in charge of the school under the care of this Meeting present the following report:

[128]*Woodstown Almanac*, 1910, p. 23.
[129]Min. Pilesgrove Mo. Mtg., 21/IX/1797.   [130]*Ibid.*, 1801.
[131]Min. Woolwich Prep. Mtg., 25/VIII/1875.
[132]Min. Woolwich Prep. Mtg., Women Friends, 28/VIII/1876.
[133]Min. Woolwich Prep. Mtg., 20/IX/1876.

The school was first opened on the 25/IX/1876 with Anna R. Sylvester as teacher and was kept open three entire (terms ?) of sixty days each.

The school was reopened about the first of the 11th month 1877 in charge of Caroline Gibbons and was continued ninety days.

The school was again reopened in the fall of 1878 in charge of our first teacher, Anna R. Sylvester, and we believe was kept open two terms of 60 days each. The school was reopened in the fall of 1879 under the care of R. Anna Kester and was continued two terms of 60 days each.

The school was resumed in fall of 1880 under the care of our first teacher, and is yet in session. The teachers have all been members of the Society of Friends, and with the scholars have always attended our midweek meetings. The number of pupils in attendance has varied from six to 26 with an average attendance of about 20 . . . Signed by Thos. Barton, Anna E. Borton, Caroline Gaunt, Asa Engle, on behalf of the Committee.[134]

So far as information is available, it appears that Woolwich School was supported (1) by subscriptions, (2) by money received from Pilesgrove Monthly Meeting[135] and (3) by money advanced for the use of the school by the Educational Committee of the Yearly Meeting to pay for books, furniture, buildings, and salaries.[136]

The school was in operation but a short time. In 1883,

Asa Engle and Samuel Gaunt (were) appointed to join a like committee of women Friends to dispose of part of the School appurtenances belonging to this Meeting, in such a way as they think best.[137]

Later, in the same year, the treasurer of the school reported that he had returned to Friends Book Store in Philadelphia all books formerly used by the school (148 in number), that the house had been leased and the furniture removed; and that there was a balance of $4.37 in his hands.

Upper Penn's Neck was established as a meeting in 1796, and a meeting house was built about the same year. Moreover, it is evident that steps were taken for establishing a school immediately, though materials for its later history are not available. A volume of minutes, 1796–1867, however makes brief but definite references to a school.[138]

In 1797 we find the following notes regarding the school and its property.

Be it remembered that the hereafter described instruments of writing be-

---

[134]*Ibid.*, 23/III/1881.   [135]*Ibid.*, 26/IV/1881.   [136]*Ibid.*, 15/IV/1880.
[137]*Ibid.*, 21/III/1883.   [138]Min. Upper Penn's Neck Prep. Mtg.

longing to Upper Penn's Neck Preparative Meeting and School Society is lodged in the hands of Isaac Ward by direction of the Meeting.

The first is the concessions of the School Society dated the 17th day of the 2nd. mo. 1787.

The second is the School Society quit claim to Friends for the lot of ground and is dated the 6th day of the 7th month 1796.

The sixth is a deed from Isaac (peddrick) (elsewhere written "Pedrick") and wife Hannah to Elihu peddrick and other in said deed named for a lot of ground for the use of the School Society and burying ground and is dated the 12th day of the 7th month 1796.

The Seventh is a declaration of trust from the said Elihu Peddrick and others in said declaration (named) of said lot being for the use of the School Society and a burying ground dated the 12th day of the 7th month 1796.[139]   (These parchment deeds and instruments of trust are at 15th & Race Sts., Phila., Pa.)

In 1855 the school house under Friends care was turned over to the public:

This Meeting being informed of the state of our school house, it wanting repairs and Friends not feel willing to do it, it being the judgment of this meeting to give it up to the public or the school committee for the benefit of the public; they are to move it off the ground belonging to Friends.[140]

[139]*Ibid.*, 18/X/1797.
[140]*Ibid.*, 25/IV/1855.

CHAPTER VI

SCHOOLS OF HADDONFIELD QUARTER

In this chapter is presented material relating to the early history of schools in Haddonfield, Chester, Medford, Evesham, Great Egg Harbor and Cape May monthly meetings, together with their various preparative meetings, all of which made up the Haddonfield Quarter. As 'the Haddonfield Quarterly Meeting was not established until 1794, by division of the Gloucester and Salem Quarterly, the history of some of its component meetings antedate it by as much as a hundred years. We shall deal with the various monthly meetings comprising it in the order of their establishment: Haddonfield, 1695; Great Egg Harbor and Cape May about 1726; Evesham, 1760; Medford, 1794; and Chester, 1803.[1]

HADDONFIELD MONTHLY MEETING

This meeting, formerly Gloucester, was, from 1695 "held at Newton in the house of Thomas Shackle" until 1721 when the meeting house was erected at Haddonfield.[2] Concerning early schools there is now little information, but it seems unsafe to assume, for that reason that schools were lacking. Prowell says land was at once set aside in 1682 for a meeting house and school and that Thomas Sharp, the surveyor, was the first teacher. The school house stood near the old Newton Meeting House, opposite the present Champion School.[3] In 1729 a school house was mentioned in the vicinity of Newton Meeting and proposals made to hold meetings there for a period of four months.[4] Haddonfield had a school as early as 1715 at the home of Jonathan Bolton, and in 1720 a school was established near the meeting which has been maintained ever since.[5]

But, though certainly some localities were early supplied with schools, it was not always the case. It was to remedy this situ-

---

[1]Records of the several meetings; also Michener: *Retrospect*, 117–118.
[2]Hazard: *Register of Pa.*, VII, 102.   [3]*Hist. Camden Co.*, 308–9.
[4]Min. Haddonfield Mo. Mtg., 10/IX/1729.   [5]*Hist. Camden Co.*, 309.

ation that the Yearly Meeting began to urge the establishment of schools about the middle of the eighteenth century. Early in 1751 Haddonfield mentioned receipt of the proposals for schools and asked that a concensus of opinion be returned to the next quarterly meeting. In 9/VII/1751,

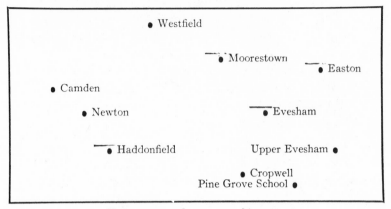

HADDONFIELD QUARTERLY MEETING
Great Egg Harbor and Cape May not shown

The proposals relating to schools having been duly weighed and considered the Meeting is unanimously of opinion that it will not assist the purposes thereby intended by reason of Friends living at a distance from each other, but rather conclude that Friends being careful to employ such persons as are therein mentioned for School Masters might be equally beneficial.[6]

The above sets forth the most frequently mentioned difficulty in the way of schools, and indicates that they will continue with the same kind of schools as before, with greater attention paid to the selection of members for teachers.

One of the first agencies used to educate the youth, that is, for religious education, was the Youths' Meeting. About the end of the eighteenth century the popularity of these declined and in some meetings they were discontinued. In many, their discontinuance was discussed, though not accomplished. Haddonfield, in 1776, reported:

This meeting having several times considered that of our Youths' Meetings not being so well attended as could be desired, now agrees to appoint a com-

[6]*Ibid.*, 9/VII/1751.

mittee to take this matter into consideration whether there may not be some alteration that may be likely to occasion them to be better attended, otherwise to be laid down, and report their sense to next meeting . . .[7]

Four months later, after several postponements, it was agreed to continue the Youths' Meetings, and attempt to improve their attendance.

It was at this time that a greater interest in education, on the part of the superior meetings, became evident. This interest, and the resultant frequent urging, brought the question home to the lower meetings, and, as a consequence many schools of more permanent character were established.

In June, 1778, an epistle relating to schools was received from the Yearly Meeting; and in 1779 it was

recommended to the weighty consideration of the several preparative meetings and said meetings desired to report their circumstances respecting schools to next meeting to be further deliberated thereon.[8]

Accordingly, this report was made:

The subject of schools now coming under consideration report was made from Woodbury that they had a school settled upon an extensive plan, since the year 1774; and from Haddonfield that they had adopted a similar plan in the year 1776, and had made some progress so as to procure a convenient lot, etc., which care appears to be satisfactory to this Meeting. And Friends of Upper Greenwich report that Friends are settled so wide one from another that they have no prospect at present of doing anything respecting the establishing of a school upon the plan laid down by the Committee of the Yearly Meeting; the subject is notwithstanding recommended to their further care and attention to proceed therein as way may open.[9]

In 1781 there were three schools reported: at Woodbury, Haddonfield, "heretofore mentioned" and "one other now kept under the care of Friends." The "one other" was probably at Upper Greenwich.[10]

A few years later the practice of visiting the schools was begun, and a report on them regularly made to the superior meetings:

The following Friends are appointed a standing committee to visit the schools that are taught by Friends within the compass of their Preparative Meetings, and to make report of their service in the 9th month annually, to wit: Joshua Evans, John Gill, John Gaunt, Isaac Ballinger, David Cooper, Aaron Hewes, William White, David Brown, Samuel Paul.[11]

---

[7]*Ibid.*, 8/IV/1776. [8]*Ibid.*, 8/II/1779. [9]*Ibid.*, 23/III/1779.
[10]*Ibid.*, 10/IX/1781. [11]*Ibid.*, 10/V/1784.

The report of 1788 shows that considerable progress had been made in establishing schools:

Report was also made that the committee appointed to visit the schools taught by members, had attended to the service, and had in the course of the year visited six different schools, so kept, and had endeavored to afford such advice and assistance for the promotion of learning and virtue, as they were enabled, to a good degree of satisfaction.[12]

The report a year later states that "some appeared to be kept in a satisfactory manner, others not so fully as could be desired."[13]

In 1790, a committee of the quarterly meeting drew up a plan to guide its lower meetings in the establishment of funds for educational purposes. As this was the basis of the funds in Haddonfield, Woodbury, and many other meetings, herein discussed, the full report of the committee is quoted herewith:

We the committee appointed at last Meeting to take under our consideration the subject of providing Funds for the better support of schools, and schooling poor children agreeable to the recommendation of the Yearly Meeting, having met agreeable to appointment, and taken the same under our weighty consideration, are of the mind, that there would be a use arise from funds being raised in the respective Monthly Meetings to be kept out at interest, and the income of interest applied under the care of judicious trustees for the schooling of poor white and black children, as well as that funds so established under the care and direction of the Monthly Meetings of business, would be laying a permanent foundation for funds, that might in time become much enlarged by donations from humane and benevolent persons, whereby Monthly Meetings might have it in their power more extensively to promote and encourage this weighty and important service: We therefore propose that it be recommended:

1st. That each Monthly Meeting appoint one friend for Treasurer and five or more for Trustees, to be styled the treasurer and Trustees of the School Fund.

2nd. That the members who are in circumstances generally execute to the treasurer and his successor for the time being, notes or other engagements for the payment of a sum of money, with interest annually at the rate of six per cent.

3rd. If any friend would choose to advance his subscription or discharge his note . . . at the end of any one year, the treasurer shall receive and place the same out at interest to such persons, and on such security, as shall be approved by three or more of the trustees.

4th. The treasurer shall provide a book and make a fair entry of the subscribers names and contributions, that the amount of the fund may at any time be ascertained and shall keep a regular account of the receipt of the interest money and of his disbursements thereof to the trustees without whose

[12]*Ibid.*, 8/IX/1788.   [13]*Ibid.*, 14/IX/1789.

orders, or order of two of them, no money shall be applied; and once in the year the trustees shall exhibit to the Monthly Meeting a clear and distinct account of the application of the interest for the approbation of the Meeting, as well as to enable it to send forward an account to the Quarter to be from thence transmitted in the report to the Yearly Meeting as occasion may require.

5th. The interest money arising on the fund, or so much thereof as will be necessary, shall be applied by the trustees from time to time for the schooling of the children of poor Friends, and those of the black people, whose condition gives them a claim to this benefit agreeable to the advices which have been or may be, sent down from the Yearly Meeting, in as equitable a manner as may be at the different schools within the compass of the Monthly Meeting, that all parts may receive a proportionable share of the benefit, and in case the fund shall become so enlarged, as that the interest thereof will be more than sufficient to school the children of poor friends, and those of the blacks aforesaid, the Monthly Meetings may divide such overplus to be applied to the schooling of other poor children, the enlarging the teachers salaries, or such other purposes for the promotion of schools as to any such meeting may appear expedient.

6th. As the fund so raised will be the property of the members of the Monthly Meeting for the time being, for the purposes aforesaid the meeting shall have authority to make a new choice of their treasurer, and annually appoint trustees to have the management thereof.

7th. If it shall appear to be the sense of any of the Monthly Meetings, that it will be more consisent with their situation and circumstances, or be more likely to answer the design in view, in going into the subscription or raising of funds in their preparative meetings, such meetings are left at liberty to proceed in either way as to them may appear best.   Signed in behalf of the committee.

Salem, 5th month 17, 1790 by

Thomas Redman.[14]

In accordance with the above plans the committee reported, 1791:

A fund is established in this meeting the income whereof to be applied to the care of poor white and black children and some attention paid to the schooling such children, and that care has been extended to the schools taught by Friends by a committee of this meeting.[15]

To this fund, besides the regular subscriptions, many bequests were added, a few of which are named:

1. £ 20, bequeathed by Ann Tomlinson, and applied by the meeting to this fund.[16]

2. £ 50, from Sarah Hopkins, "for the purpose of educating poor children."[17]

---

[14]*Ibid.*, 13/XII/1790.   [15]*Ibid.*, 12/IX/1791.
[16]*Ibid.*, 10/I/1791.   [17]*Ibid.*, 8/V/1797.

3. £ 50 from Joseph Sloan, for "schooling poor children of any color."[18]

4. $1,000.00 from Samuel Nicholson, "for the purpose of promoting the guarded education of the children of its members in schools under the care of Friends."[19]

Seven years after the fund was reported established the principal of it amounted to £ 239/18;[20] and in 1800 it had increased to £ 687/8.[21]

The following items indicate how the fund was expended:

1. £ 36/8/4 expended for books and for schooling poor children.[22]

2. For schooling poor white and black children, expended $155.-75.[23]

3. Schooled 18 children the past year, most of them for 2 quarters; none of those schooled at expense of this fund were Friends' children.[24]

4. $198.30 paid for education of children, none of whom were "members of our society."[25]

5. Spent for dwelling for teacher and fencing it in, etc., $1781.41.[26]

The existence of such a fund had a salutory effect on schools. In 1794, they report "one large school has been kept up at Haddonfield, and a number of black children have partaken of school learning with other poor children . . ."; and three years later four schools were reported in the monthly meeting.[27]

A report of 1803 gives us a clearer idea of the size of the school and the number of studies included.

We the committee appointed in the fourth month last to superintend the school at Haddonfield, agree to report—That we have paid attention to the appointment, and have procured a well-qualified teacher, being a member of the Society; the school is at present large, consisting of about 80 scholars, and an assistant teacher is employed. Upon the whole we are of the mind that the school has increased in solidity and is growing in reputation, as a Seminary for useful learning, wherein the English Grammar, the Mathematics,

[18]*Ibid.*, 14/X/1799.   [19]*Ibid.*, 3/XI/1880.   [20]*Ibid.*, 12/III/1798.
[21]*Ibid.*, 13/I/1800.   [22]*Ibid.*, 14/II/1803.   [23]*Ibid.*, 14/II/1814.
[24]*Ibid.*, 13/II/1837.   [25]*Ibid.*, 8/II/1841.   [26]*Ibid.*, 12/II/1855.
[27]*Ibid.*, 8/IX/1794 and 11/IX/1797.

THE

ART OF SPELLING

FACILITATED.

BEING

A SYSTEM OF PRONUNCIATION

OF THE

ENGLISH LANGUAGE.

FOR THE

USE OF SCHOOLS;

AS WELL AS OF FOREIGNERS, AND OTHERS,
WHO WOULD WISH TO BECOME
ACQUAINTED,

With the practice of the difficult accentuation
and orthoepy of our Language.

———

'TIS EDUCATION, FORMS THE COMMON MIND.
POPE.

———

By STEPHEN M. DAY,

MASTER OF FRIENDS' SCHOOL AT HADDONFIELD

———

PHILADELPHIA:
PRINTED FOR BENJAMIN JOHNSON,
NO. 31, *MARKET-STREET.*

....
[J. RAKESTRAW, PRINTER.]
....

1804.

DAY'S "ART OF SPELLING FACILITATED"

The Combination of the Consonants and Vowels, into simple Sylables.

Ba	be	bi	bo	bu	by	ge	he	je	ke	le	me
ca	co	cu	ce*	ci*	cy*	ne ˙	pe	re	se	te	ve
da	de	di	do	du	dy	we	ye	ze	bi	ci	di
fa	fe	fi	fo	fu	fy	fi	gi	hi	ji	ki	li
ga	go	gu	ge*	gi*	gy*	mi	ni	pi	ri	si	ti
ha	he	hi	ho	hu	hy	vi	wi	zi	bo	co	do
ja	je	ji	jo	ju	jy	fo	jo	ko	lo	mo	no

ka	ke	ki	ko	ku	ky	ro	so	to	vo	wo	yo
la	le	li	lo	lu	ly	zo	bu	cu	du	fu	gu
ma	me	mi	mo	mu	my	hu	ju	ku	lu	mu	nu
na	ne	ni	no	nu	ny	pu	ru	su	tu	vu	by
pa	pe	pi	po	pu	py	cy	dy	fy	gy	hy	jy
ra	re	ri	ro	ru	ry	ky	ly	my	ny	py	ry
sa	se	si	so	su	sy	sy	ty	vy	zy	ab	ac

ta	te	ti	to	tu	ty	ad	af	ag	aj	ak	al
va	ve	vi	vo	vu	vy	am	an	ap	ar	at	av
wa	we	wi	wo	ya	ye	ax	az	eb	ec	ed	ef
yo	za	ze	zi	zo	zu	eg	ej	ek	el	em	en
zy	ba	ca	da	fa	ga	ep	er	es	et	ev	ex
ha	ja	ka	la	ma	na	ez	ib	ic	id	if	ig
pa	ra	sa	ta	va	wa	ik	il	im	in	ip	ir
ya	za	be	ce	de	fe	is	it	iv	ix	iz	ob

prescription may startle at innovation, but such should remember that improvements are gradual and progressive; and that in letters as in policy, the way to prevent the catastrophe of violent revolutions, is to obviate the necessity of them, by the exercise of docility, and a sound judgement, that can distinguish between rash innovation and real improvements.

*c and g soft.

THE METHOD OF INSTRUCTION IN THE "ART OF SPELLING FACILITATED," BY S. M. DAY

Geography and the Latin and French languages are, or may be taught.   Signed in behalf of the committee 2nd month 17th 1803.

By Thomas Redman.[28]

In 1808 two schools were reported,

established for the education of youth within our limits, under the care of teachers in membership, one superintended by a committee of the Monthly, the other by one of the Preparative Meeting.[29]

During the temporary disturbance in 1828 the answer to the third annual query states "there is one school . . ." but, soon after, 1830, "there are two schools . . ."[30]   These are the same mentioned in 1808.   From this time on the number of schools reported increases.   In 1836 there was presented a full report on Education, as the Yearly Meeting demanded:

. . . report that there are four schools superintended by committees either of the monthly or preparative meetings, three of which are taught by persons

---

[28]*Ibid.*, 14/III/1803; Concerning the teachers of the school at this time, some information has been gathered.   Stephen Munson Day was born in 1776 at Morristown, New Jersey and in early life showed a marked interest in science and languages, as well as religion.   He was educated, it is said, to the profession of law, and received a diploma, but never entered the bar.   Soon after 1801 Day became an assistant in the Academy at Burlington and shortly removed to Haddonfield where he became a teacher in the Friends School. He appears to have had unusual abilities as a teacher, securing good results, "however obtuse the faculties of his pupils."   Tradition has it that Day taught Latin, Greek, and Hebrew at the Haddonfield School.

Day was the author of a number of small books for the use of schools, but probably not widely used.   In 1804 "The Art of Spelling Facilitated" was published and also, as an appendix to the same, "Lessons in Reading."   These reading lessons were scriptural in character.   Another text "The Pronouncing Spelling Book" was published in 1811, in which Day is described as preceptor of the Boarding School at Haddonfield.   Other literary activities were undertaken.   In 1804 *The Evening Fireside* a periodical publication was launched but Day retired from the editorship of it, out of deference to his friends.   An assault was also made against the drink traffic in a booklet called "Serious Thoughts on the Traffic in Distilled Spiritous Liquors, and on the Customary Use of that Article as a Common Drink."   In addition to these interests Day was also inclined to an experimental study of agriculture.   His death occurred in 1812.

E. Littell, publisher and proprietor of *Littell's Living Age* was once a student at Haddonfield School.   Concerning Day he wrote: "I dwell with much pleasure upon the memory of my preceptor—my patient, gentle and wise friend—Stephen Munson Day."

Other teachers, near the close of the eighteenth century and early part of the nineteenth, were John Redman, who taught Latin, and M. Guerrier, a French noble, friend and associate of Louis Phillipe Duke of Orleans; the latter taught French for a time.—The writer is indebted to Mr. James Pennypacker, Haddonfield, N. J., for the privilege of examining some of Day's textbooks.

[29]*Ibid.*, IV/1808.   [30]*Ibid.*, 8/III/1830.

LESSONS IN READING:

BEING

SELECT PASSAGES

FROM THE

SCRIPTURES;

CHIEFLY

FROM THE PROPHECIES OF ISAIAH.

TO SERVE

AS AN EASY INTRODUCTION TO READING.

PRINTED FOR BENJAMIN JOHNSON, No. 31,
MARKET-STREET.

1804.

A POPULAR TEXT BY S. M. DAY

in membership with us and one by a person not a member.   The schools have all been visited and there appears a care for the religious as well as the literary education therein.   The Holy Scriptures are frequently read and the teachers as well as the scholars of two of the schools attend our midweek meetings. Their deportment as well as their advancement in their studies are generally satisfactory.   The following is a statement of our members at different schools to wit:

> 2 at the University in Philadelphia
> 1 at Haverford
> 3 at Franklin Park
> 5 at Westtown
> 2 at Frankford
> 5 at the one not taught by a member
> 17 at Friends Schools taught by members
> <u>17</u> at Common schools
> 52

And it appears that there are 29 of our members of a suitable age who are not at school at present, most of whom have received education during a part of the past year at Friends' schools, although it would be desirable to establish select schools for the education of the youth agreeably to the advice of the Yearly Meeting, but the members are so scattered that way does not yet open to accomplish so desirable an object, but it appears that there are no Friends children but what are receiving a competency of education to fit them for business.

Signed on behalf of the committee, 2 mo. 8th, 1836.

> Thomas Evans
> Richard W. Sheppard[31]

About the middle of the century the committee experienced some difficulty in keeping the school open.   One of the chief difficulties seems to have been the obtaining of suitable teachers.[32] Furthermore, it would seem from reports as to the distribution of Friends' children,[33] that when schools were open they were almostly entirely attended by non-members.   Nevertheless, plans were made to improve the school.   The school house was repaired and furnished with new desks and proposals made "to erect a dwelling house for the teacher on the school house lot."[34] $1781.41 of the school fund was used for this purpose.

With these improvements the school continued much as before, with the exception that the number attending was usually less than in the early years of its existence.   In 1858 the report stated "the

---

[31]*Ibid.*, 8/II/1836.   [32]*Ibid.*, 12/II/1849; 11/II/1850; 14/III/1835.
[33]*Ibid.*, 9/II/1852.   [34]*Ibid.*, 12/IX/1853.

average number of scholars last winter was forty; at present there are 27 on the list."[35]   The number of Friends' children attending became even less, but it was resolved that " . . . We believe the influence of the school is salutary in the neighborhood."[36]

In 1866–7 attendance sank to an unprecedented extent, and in addition, the income from public funds was withdrawn by the law which repealed section 12 of the Act of 1846, but a firmer determination is evident to run the school for its service in the moral education of the community.   The situation is described more exactly in the following report:

That the school has been visited by the trustees at the usual times, Joseph Jones having withdrawn as teacher, Samuel B. Redman was appointed to succeed him who entered upon his duties in the 9th month last.   As there are at present no arrangements for boarding scholars, the number in attendance has been smaller than usual.   The order of the school and deportment of the scholars have been generally satisfactory.   Number on the list at present 19. Average attendance for the past three months, 14½.   We believe a school of this character, if rightly conducted may be of great service to the youth in our neighborhood and desire that the original concern of the Monthly Meeting in establishing it may be kept in view, which we believe, not only had relation to the literary improvement of those placed under our care, but also to their moral and religious advancement, so far as a qualification therefor may be experienced.   We feel that the present day is no time to relax our efforts in these respects, but rather calls for increased earnestness to discharge our duty fully and faithfully to the children under our supervision.   The Holy Scriptures are read at the opening of the school, but a very few of the scholars attend mid-week meeting being excused therefrom, at the request of their parents or guardians.[37]

The report for 1868, a digest of which appears below, shows the extent to which the children of members were scattered and that the Haddonfield School was made up mostly of non-members:

> 53 of suitable age for school
> 5 at Westtown
> 6 Friends Select at Philadelphia
> 4 at Friends schools taught by members
> 4 at schools not under care of Friends, though taught by member
> 22 at common district schools
> 12 at family schools.[38]

In the same year we learn that,

---

[35]*Ibid.*, 8/II/1858.   [36]*Ibid.*, 13/II/1865.
[37]*Ibid.*, 6/II/1867.   [38]*Ibid.*, 5/II/1868.

John Broadle having been engaged as teacher, entered upon his duties last 9th month.   The committee have authorized the admission of girls in addition to boys as scholars and have found it satisfactory.

Thus the school continued to the end of the nineteenth century. The following report shows its status in 1895, when the division into primary and secondary departments was made:

The school has been kept open with the regular vacations since last report. It was closed 5th month 30th, 1894, about two weeks earlier than usual on account of the ill health of the teacher Mary M. Smith who had held the position very satisfactorily for two years.

Early in the 9th month the school reopened with Lydia B. Kite as teacher, under whose care the children are attentive and deferential.   The average attendance for the year has been about 20, at this date there are 19 pupils on the roll, the greater portion of whom are of a primary grade.   It is thought that a school composed of primary and secondary classes, carefully and thoroughly taught will best meet the needs of its patrons.

Good order has been maintained and the children have made satisfactory progress in their studies.   They continue to attend our midweek meetings, where they conduct themselves with propriety. When the town water was introduced into the dwelling a pipe was placed in the school room which is found to be very convenient.   In conclusion the committee would urge all Friends to take an active interest in the school and to manifest the same by occasional visits to it during its sessions.   Elizabeth Bacon
                                                              Joseph G. Evans.[39]

The report of 1868 showed that few Friends' children were attending the monthly meeting school, but this situation changed to some extent.   In 1870, 9 out of 38 attending were Friends; 1875, there were 7 out of 19; 1880, there were three out of 25; 1890, 14 members were in attendance; and in 1895 there were nine.[40]

The Haddonfield school is still in existence and conducts three departments: Kindergarten, Primary and Grammar.

There is an annual enrollment of about 80, 25 per cent of whom are usually members.

Along with other monthly meetings of the Philadelphia Yearly, Haddonfield contributed to the establishment and support of Westtown Boarding School in Pennsylvania.   In 1797 they recorded that Haddonfield Preparative Meeting paid in £ 39/18/9 and Newton £ 15.[41]

---

[39]*Ibid.*, 6/II/1895.   [40]Reports in minutes for above dates.
[41]*Ibid.*, 11/IX/1797.

The attitude of Haddonfield Meeting was always favorable to the Negroes, and they made successful efforts to secure their freedom and education. As early as 1760,

... appeared and declared that he did not know the purchasing of a negro was a breach of our discipline or he should not have done it ... in confirmaiton thereof he hath set his hand to this minute in the meeting.[42]

Those who held slaves were repeatedly visited by members who urged manumission, and stubborn refusals were followed by disownment. Religious meetings especially for the Negroes were commonly held, and, with the establishment of special funds in 1790 an increasing attention was paid to their school education, placing them on a plane of equality with other poor in the neighborhood who depended on charitable agencies for their education.[43]

Besides the "large school" at Haddonfield under the monthly meeting there were others in the Western and Eastern districts; each of these were under the preparative meeting and were overseen by special committees.[44]

The school property deed in the Eastern District Delaware Township, went back to 1787, and the school was in almost continuous existence until 1874, a part of the time being rented to the District Trustees for $20 per year. In 1874 it was recommended that the property be sold, and the proceeds used to educate Friends' children, since the district school provided education for all others.[45] From the report of 1880, however, it appears that the trustees continued to rent it to the District:

The committee having care of the Eastern District School property, report: balance on hand at last settlement 29/XII/1874, $280.79. Received rent for dwelling $125.00; received rent for school house $100.00—whole amount $505.79.[46]

We have already noted[47] that Friends Meeting was held in 1729 in a school house near James Cooper's. This was undoubtedly one of the six schools reported by Haddonfield in 1788.[48] Of its early history however, little has been ascertained. At the separation

---

[42]*Ibid.*, 14/IV/1760.   [43]See Chapter Nine.
[44]Min. Haddonfield Prep. Mtg., 7/V/1835 and 4/VI/1835.
[45]*Ibid.*, 4/II/1874.   [46]*Ibid.*, 1/I/1880.   [47]page 167.
[48]On June 23, 1804, the grandchildren of Jacob Cooper deeded lots 156 and 157 on which to build a school house and house for a master. The "Academy was built on this lot but no master's house was erected."—From Cooper's *Sketch of Camden*, 54.

in 1828 the Orthodox Friends retained the meeting house, while the new organization found shelter in Hatch's School (private) "in the upper part of Camden."[49]

In 1848, it is evident that a school was being maintained by the new meeting, as they reported:

HOUSE FORMERLY OCCUPIED BY FRIENDS' SCHOOL, CAMDEN, NEW JERSEY

. . . We have (been) giving attention during the past year to our school and until the 1st of fourth month last it was attended by an average number of 30 scholars and taught by a male teacher, a member of our society and we believe he gave general satisfaction to his employers; since that time we have employed a female who now has charge of it and appears to be well qualified for the station.[50]

A year later Wm. Folwell was directed to insure the school house for $400, which was done;[51] likewise a bill for printing circulars for the school was presented and paid.   In 1850 a temporary school was provided by allowing "John Willits' daughter" to have "the upper room in the meeting house for a school room, provided there can be a sufficient number of scholars raised."[52]   A school was

[49]H. M. Cooper: *Hist. Sketch of Newton Mtg.*
[50]Newton (Camden) Prep. Mtg., 8/VI/1848.
[51]*Ibid.*, 4/I/1849.   [52]*Ibid.*, 3/X/1850.

probably continued under these irregular conditions until about 1874, when, . . .

. . . Isaac C. Martindale, Asahel Troth, and Charles B. Coles were appointed to unite with a similar committee of women Friends to take into consideration the advisability of establishing a school under the care of the Preparative Meeting.[53]

PRESENT FRIENDS' SCHOOL, GAMDEN, NEW JERSEY

This committee acted at once and decided a regularly controlled school should be established in the old school house which had been let out to another:

Committee appointed to take into consideration the establishment of a school reported that it was their opinion that such a school could be maintained. Meeting received report favorably and decided to establish a school at earliest possible time and the committee were continued as trustees for the ensuing year.

This Meeting having been informed that the school house is at present occupied by another person it was decided that said person be notified to vacate said school house on or before the 14th of 9th month next. Francis Boggs was

[53]*Ibid.*, 1/I/1874.

appointed to notify said occupant of this action of the Meeting and the clerk directed to furnish him with a copy of above minute for that purpose.[54]

A year later a minute informed that the school had been in operation:

> . . . The school was opened 9th month 7th 1874; for the term ending 1st mo. 31st the whole number of pupils in attendance has been 28, the average attendance being 23; of the whole number of pupils 6 are children of members, 4 have 1 parent a member, other pupils 18; with the teacher (who is a member) they regularly attend midweek meeting. The receipts for tuition were $381.-56.[55]

In 1875 the committee reported an attendance of 37 and an average attendance of 22; in 1881 the whole number enrolled had increased to 44, though the average attendance was but 23. Seven of those attending were members of Friends, while seven others had one parent a member, and thirty were outsiders. In 1887 there were 68 pupils and an average attendance of 47. The minutes show that assistance was' received from Philadelphia Yearly Meeting's Committee on Education. Most of the funds, however, were repaid.[56]

In 1895 it was decided to encourage the attendance of Friends children at the school by reducing "the regular rate in all classes" to one-half.[57] At this time application was also made for assistance from the "Committee on Education and Disposition of the Samuel Jeanes Fund." Money was thus received and expended for educational purposes by Howard Cooper who acted as treasurer.[58]

The Camden School which was reorganized, as above noted, in 1874 has continued to the present day. It now has an enrollment of 80 pupils, about a tenth of whom are members, and employs 7 teachers. The school is organized into Kindergarten, Primary, and Intermediate grades.[59]

GREAT EGG HARBOR AND CAPE MAY MONTHLY MEETING

Great Egg Harbor and Cape May Monthly Meeting was established in 1726 and discontinued by their request in 1843.[60]

Upon comparing the educational activity of this monthly meeting with that of others in New Jersey we find it very slight. The

---

[54]*Ibid.*, 29/I/1874.   [55]*Ibid.*, 25/II/1875.   [56]*Ibid.*, 3/III/1887.
[57]*Ibid.*, 26/VI/1895.   [58]Min. Haddonfield Mo. Mtg., 8/VII/1896.
[59]*School Bulletin*, 1922–23.
[60]See two volumes of Records at 302 Arch Street, Phila.

first mention of a concern regarding education was upon the receipt of the "observations on the education of youth" from the Yearly Meeting in 1778.[61]   Nine years later,

> . . . the request of our Yearly Meeting respecting the education of youth, schools, etc., coming under consideration of this Meeting it appears necessary the Quarterly Meeting should be informed that we apprehend we are not in a capacity at present to erect schools amongst us, as is directed by the Yearly Meeting . . .[62]

In 1795 they acknowledged receipt of proposals concerning subscriptions for the "relief of the Ingen Natives," and in 1797 they directed the preparative meetings to take up subscriptions for the Westtown Boarding School.[63]   In 1807 they reported:

> We have one school taught by a friend in membership and superintended by a committee within the compass of this Meeting.[64]

The school had a very irregular history so far as teachers were concerned, so far as we may judge by reading the answers to the school query from year to year.   In 1814 they replied to this query: "Not any of the description queried after among us," and in 1816 "one school taught by a member and under the care of a committee appointed by the Preparative Meeting."   In 1817, "not any school of the description queried after."[65]   Thus it went from year to year.   From 1818 to 1843, at which time the monthly meeting was discontinued, there was a school or schools in charge of a committee and taught by a member in the following years: 1822; 1826, two schools; 1827, 1833, 1834, 1838; 1839, two schools; 1840, 1841 and 1842.   It is possible, that, judging by similar situations in other meetings, a school was conducted in the other years, looked after to some extent by a committee, but not visited regularly, due to the fact that teachers were not members.

EVESHAM MONTHLY MEETING

This meeting was established in 1760 by Haddonfield Quarterly Meeting, and continued to 1884 when part of its members were attached to Medford and Chester monthly meetings.[66]   During this period of over a century, Evesham fostered several schools within its limits.

---

[61]Min. Great Egg Harbor and Cape May Mo. Mtg., 7/XII/1778.
[62]*Ibid.*, 3/IX/1787.   [63]*Ibid.*, 1/V/1797.   [64]*Ibid.*, 6/IV/1807.
[65]*Ibid.*, 7/III/1814; 4/III/1816; 3/III/1817.   [66]Records of the Meeting.

In 1761 the Preparative Meeting of Evesham requested permission "to hold a meeting for worship in Bradock's School house"
and this was often repeated and granted.[67]   In 1774,

> Friends appointed reported they had attended the school house meeting to
> good satisfaction and that they apprehended an enlargement of their meeting
> place was necessary; therefore . . . members thereof are at liberty to make an
> addition or build a new house if they see meet.[68]

In 1778, the meeting began to take official notice of the schools,
in harmony with instructions received from the Yearly Meeting:

> And Josiah Roberts, John Hunt, John Roberts, Isaac Borton, John Collins,
> Joshua Hunt, and Job Collins, are appointed to take the case of schools
> weightily under their care, agreeable to the direction of the said extracts.[69]

The next year steps were taken to secure a lot for the school:

> The committee on the care of schools reported that they had a prospect of
> purchasing a lott of ground suitable for the purpose, part of John Evans, and
> part of Benjamin Haines, which was approved of and they are directed to
> proceed to obtain a title to them, or any three they may appoint in trust, and
> to forward subscriptions to pay for the same and other services toward
> completing the school.[70]

In 1779 the report of the committee on schools stated the situation as follows:

> We the committee appointed by the Monthly Meeting of Evesham for the
> regulating of schools, have many times met and attended to that service,
> and agree to report that we think it needful there should be first established a
> school at each particular Meeting, belonging to our Monthly Meeting and
> we have succeeded as far as that a school is opened at Chester Meeting some-
> what agreeable to Friends' advice, though we have not a prospect of procuring
> a suitable lot of ground at that place as yet.   At Lower Evesham we have a
> prospect of procuring a lot of ground convenient for that service, but not a
> teacher.   At Upper Evesham we have little or no prospect of getting a suitable
> lott of ground; also a teacher at that place is wanting.   We think that a
> more general convincement of the necessity of such schools and due attention
> to so good a work is much wanting, and very much obstructs the works going
> forward.
>
> The former advice of collecting a fund is not as yet complied with; Friends
> in divers places are not yet disengaged from former contracts with teachers

---

[67]Min. Evesham Mo. Mtg., 9/IV/1761.
[68]*Ibid.*, 7/IV/1774.   [69]*Ibid.*, 10/XII/1778.
[70]*Ibid.*, 6/V/1779.   It appears, from deeds and papers at 15th & Race
Streets, that a deed was made 4/XII/1779 by Benjamin Haines and wife and
John Evans and wife to trustees for land in Evesham to accommodate a
public s.hool under the care of the Evesham Monthly Meeting and for no other
purpose.   Not being used for this purpose the land reverted to former owners.

not of our society and some yet continue to contract with such to teach their children.

Signed by Lawrence Webster.[71]

In 1781 it was agreed that, to forward schools, it would be advantageous to place the schools, already established, under the care of preparative meetings, and from this time onward, there are reports returned by these meetings.[72] Still they maintain "there is room for further weighty labor in that respect."

In 1783 the following report was directed to be acted upon. It shows clearly the guiding influence of the Yearly Meeting:

We the select committee for the establishment of proper schools do report that we have divers times met and maturely considered the same and are united in judgment that the most likely way to advance this momentous concern appears to us, agreeable to the advice of the Yearly Meeting, to procure a lot of ground sufficient for a school house, dwelling house, orchard, etc. for a teacher, and his family in proper places so as to take in as large a circle of Friends as may be likely to send to such a school, in order that our schools may be of annual duration; which may be one essential step to induce well qualified teachers to undertake the task. And then, as way may open, to move forward in building such houses, and making the habitation of those teachers as easy and comfortable as convenient. And, as soon as it can be done, to open a subscription for those schools, the capital of which to remain on a moderate interest, first for the schooling of Friends children who may not be in circumstances to pay therefor and the surplus of such interest to be applied to make up the deficiency in the common rate of education, whereby a sufficient support may be secured for the teacher and his family; and also to such other uses as the trustees may think most likely to advance the institution which we have thought should be under the care of the respective Preparative Meetings in the verge of which it lies, and such trustees as they may annually appoint to oversee and direct the same.[73]

A few months later the minutes of Evesham Preparative Meeting recorded the establishment of the school under their care:

In pursuance of a concern lately received amongst Friends for the benefit of the rising generation with respect to their school education as recommended down by the Yearly Meeting, divers Friends contiguous to this meeting have opened a school at the Meeting house, until a school house can be built, on a lot of ground which has lately been procured for that purpose, as well as to build a house for the residence of a teacher; and it being apprehended necessary that the said school shall be under the care of a standing committee, the following Friends (to wit) William Rogers, Edward Domell, Thomas Ballinger, Jr., Joshua Lippincott, Noah Haines, Caleb Austin, and Samuel Allinson are appointed to that service by the name of Trustees of Friends School near

[71]*Ibid.*, 9/IX/1779.   [72]*Ibid.*, 8/III/1781.   [73]*Ibid.*, 8/VIII/1783.

The Master's Dwelling at Evesham

Evesham Meeting House and it is unanimously concluded that the said trustees and their successors, shall have the direction of the said school; that they keep the school house, and dwelling house for the teacher, when built, in good repair; make provision for the comfortable support of said teacher and family, order what may be necessary for these purposes, when there is cash in hand, when otherwise they are to lay before this meeting an account of the sum wanted, and the occasion, and receive our advice therein; They are, from time to time, as occasion may require, to employ a teacher or teachers, and for sufficient cause to them appearing to dismiss them, admit scholars, and discharge those who may misbehave; and make such rules for these and other purposes tending to the good government of the school as they may judge necessary, provided the same do consist with this fundamental plan.　They are to visit said school on the fifth day preceding the first second day in every month, examine the progress made by the scholars in their learning, and see that good order and decorum is preserved.　The trustees for the time being, shall appoint a treasurer to whom by his proper name, donations and bequests may be made for the benefit of the school, and the same shall be accounted for by him to the trustees; he shall pay no monies out of the stock but to the order of the trustees, or any three of them; and any three of the trustees are also sufficient to transact any other business within their appointment.　The trustees are also to keep fair accounts of all such donations and bequests, and a note of the terms if particular, on which given, and apply the same accordingly. They are to keep a regular account of their proceedings, of their receipts and payments, and the same with such regulations as they make, lay before this Preparative Meeting in the 8th month annually, for the sense of Friends thereon, at which time the trustees are always to be renewed.　The trustees are desired to transcribe this minute as the foundation of their proceedings.[74]

In 1784 the monthly meeting records note that a school at Moorestown has been discontinued; that another is likely to be established in Chester near Job Cowperthwaite's; and that the above named school at Evesham is established.[75]　In 1785 a lot was reported secured for a school in Cropwell.[76]　Two years later, a standing committee was named and a plan, similar to the one used by Evesham was adopted for the control of the school.[77]

In 1786 the report sets forth that plans are in progress for schools at six points:

We may further report that since last accounts there has been a lot procured by Friends near Wm. Matlack's, and a commodious school house erected

---

[74]Min. Evesham Prep. Mtg., 6/XI/1783.
[75]Min. Evesham Mo. Mtg., 10/IX/1784.
[76]Min. Evesham Prep. Mtg., 7/IV/1785; Woodward, in the *History of Burlington County*, says that Cropwell dates back to 1760 when the meeting was established.
[77]*Ibid.*, 7/XII/1787.

thereon; (2) another school house near Chester Meeting; (3) a lot procured near Evesham Meeting, and a dwelling house for a teacher erected thereon; (4) another lot and house erected near Samuel Allinson's; (5) also a lot for

ARTICLES OF AGREEMENT FOR TEACHERS, TRUSTEES AND EMPLOYEES IN EVESHAM MONTHLY MEETING. RULES BY THE LOWER MEETINGS WERE MADE IN ACCORD WITH THESE.

that and other purposes adjoining meeting house lot at Upper Evesham; (6) also seeking to get ground near Abraham Engle's convenient for school house, but not fully completed.[78]

[78]Min. Evesham Mo. Mtg., 11/VIII/1786.

The chief difficulties in the way of maintaining these schools were those of getting teachers, set forth in the following minute:

We may further add that at present there are several vacant school houses at which a competent number of scholars may be procured, were there but teachers well qualified to undertake therein—the lack of which we apprehend is one principal reason why the work is so much impeded.[79]

In 1790 Evesham adopted a plan for raising school funds, similar to that already mentioned in the case of Haddonfield, and also used at Upper Evesham, based upon the plan offered by the quarterly meeting.

In 1792, for the better control of the schools by committees, and the better order of the school itself, two sets of rules were produced, read, and agreed to and a new committee appointed by the Monthly Meeting.[80]

In the same year, on account of the room, where the Evesham school was held (in the Meeting House), being very inconvenient for that purpose, a lot of ground was procured near the meeting house whereon a house was to be built, and a number were named to secure a deed for the property.[81] A minute also indicates that the school formerly proposed near Samuel Evan's was called the Pine Grove School. This school was in 1795 placed under the care of Upper Evesham Monthly and Cropwell Preparative meetings.[82]

In 1800 the following report was produced for the Monthly Meeting:

We the committee . . . inform that there are six schools[83]taught by Friends,

---

[79]*Ibid.*, 7/IX/1787.

[80]*Ibid.*, 6/I/1792; Minutes of Trustees of Evesham School, at 302 Arch Street, Philadelphia.

[81]Min. Evesham Prep. Mtg., 9/II/1792.

[82]*Ibid.*, 8/XI/1792; and Min. Evesham Mo. Mtg., 11/XII/1795.

[83]The following table gives a list of school properties in Chester and Evesham Monthly Meetings given in Min. Evesham Mo. Mtg., 10/V/1799.

Chester

Date Conveyed	By	To whom	Purpose
	Jacob Hollinshead	John Warrington	School lot at
15/V/1782	Joshua Roberts	Joshua Hunt	Moorestown
	Jonas Cottell	Hugh Cowperthwait	
	John Collins	Robert French	
		Edmond Hollinshead	
		William Roberts	
31/VIII/1784	Job Cowperthwait	Joshua Roberts	School lot near
	Ann Cowperthwait	John Collins	William
		Hugh Cowperthwait	Matlack's
		Reuben Matlack	
		Thos. Thorne	

three of which are under the direction of the several Preparative Meetings, all of which have been visited by some of our number; and we find there is but one kept up through the year; that the others are kept up during the winter season, and that the school house at Moorestown has been vacant a considerable time for want of a teacher.   And we are united in believing that it would have a tendency to promote the design in view, to encourage such of our young men as are qualified for the undertaking to engage in the service of teaching, that it might render them more useful to society in other respects and be a benefit to themselves.

Isaac Snowden.[84]

Early in 1801, Evesham Preparative stated:

Levi Ballinger informed that there was a lot of ground procured of Uriah Barton in order to erect a school house and for the use of a school, by the Friends, adjacent thereto to be under the care of the Preparative Meeting.[85]

A committee was appointed to take a deed for the property and ten months later, a minute indicated a school was in operation called "Lower Evesham School."   Trustees for the school were at this time appointed.[86]   In 1802 the school was taught by Elijah Weaver.

27/VII/1791	Samuel Shute	Samuel Lippincott Thos. Lippincott Henry Warrington Wm. Roberts Joseph Matlack	School lot in Chester
		Evesham	
3/XII/1797	John Evans Benjamin Haines	Enoch Evans Caleb Austin Robert Engle	School lot near Evesham Mtg.
3/III/1792	John Evans	Gabriel Davis Levi Ballinger Joshua Sharp	School lot near Evesham Meeting.
16/IX/1789	Abraham Engle	John Barton John Engle Wm. Wilkins Stacy Haines John Haines	School lot near Engle's Mill.

In the minutes for 11/II/1803 other items of property for schools are mentioned:

"25/III/1801, Uriah Barton and Mary Barton, to Levi Ballinger, Job Borton, Joshua Sharp, Joseph Haines, John Barton, Isaac Ballinger, a lot for the use of a school to be under the care of Friends.

1/I/1802, William Wilkins and Sarah Wilkins to Bethuel Moore, Cyrus Moore, Joshua Mason and John Engle, for the use of a school and othe purposes of Friends.

Again, 11/XII/1812, property is conveyed by Wm. (Hewlings?) and Lydia Hewlings to Wm. Haines, Abram Haines, John Haines, John Jessup and Job Collins, for the use of a school to be under Evesham Preparative Meeting."

[84]Min. Evesham Mo. Mtg., 7/III/1800.
[85]Min. Evesham Pep. Mtg., 5/ I/1801.   [86]*Ibid.*, 10/XII/1801.

In 1801 we find the following interesting comment on girls' schools:

And we likewise think Girls Schools would be necessary where men teachers discontinue in summer, and a female as usher in steady schools, at times, who might teach needlework and obviate the necessity of girls' going from such schools, to others, to learn that art.

And we belive it would remedy much inconvenience, if boys and girls were not allowed to play together in times of relaxation from business, but each have proper bounds allotted them. Caleb Atkinson

Levi Ballinger.[87]

From a report of 1802 it appears little success had been met with in establishing homes for schoolmasters as "there is but one house erected for that purpose" though there were five good school houses under the care of the preparative meetings.[88]

After the separation in 1827 the number of schools controlled by the Orthodox Friends decreased. In 1835 we have the following report:

We have visited our schools both for summer and winter and find nearly all the children of our members have the opportunity of attending Friends' schools.

We have within the compass of this Monthly Meeting 57 children of an age to go to school, only 2 of which have been at schools not taught by members, 3 have been at Westtown, and the remaining 52 at our schools under the care of the Preparative Meetings.

We have one school at Easton, one at Evesham, during the year; also at Evesham a small school for girls during the winter season, all which are taught by members and visited by committees of the Preparative Meetings. The Scriptures have been daily read in them during the past year, and we are encouraged to believe there is an increasing concern with Friends to promote the guarded religious education of the youth, and encourage ther instruction in the scriptures and the doctrines of Friends.

Job Haines, Joseph Borton, Bathsheba Roberts, and Patience Engle.[89]

Only in rare cases is there a continuous record extant of an individual school, which covers any considerable period of time. In the instance of Evesham School we have a record of the school trustees from 1785 to 1840 from which some details of its history may be obtained. Some extracts from their proceedings are here included as they give the best picture of the school obtainable at this date.

In 1796 they report:

---

[87]Min. Evesham Mo. Mtg., 10/IV/1801.
[88]*Ibid.*, 5/III/1802.   [89]*Ibid.*, 9/I/1835.

We heard the scholars go through their several exercises to our satisfaction—and at the close of the school, the rules of said school were read and divers remarks made to the children, according to what is mentioned in said rules for their further improvement, as we find some improvement made in said school by the scholars since last month.[90]

In 1797,

Four of the trustees present and examined the writing books, where some improvement was observed.[91]

That trustees showed some regard for the feelings of a beginning teacher is evident from the following:

25/IV/1810 Ambrose Chapman opened school for one year and next day being visitation day the trustees adjourned by request of the teacher for one week.

In 1814,

1 month 27 day 1814 Being visitation day and all the trustees were present and examining several branches of larning and wher satfied with the improvement. No. of scholars 62.

In 1817,

At a visitation the 3 mo/27/1817, Three of the trustees heard the children gowe through the Several branches of Learning to Satisfaction. Schollers 33.

At a Visitation 7 mo. 22 two of the trustees present heard the Children read and spell to satisfaction.

The following is the final report of the Trustees relating to the school in 1840.

We the trustees appointed to the care of Evesham School report that the school has been taught by Henry Haines about 2 months, by Mary Ann Lippincott about 4½ months, and is at present taught by Jacob Roberts; the average number of scholars about 23. The school has been visited monthly by some of the trustees, and we believe was conducted in an orderly manner by the above named teachers; and the scholars have conducted orderly as far as appears. There are $300 school fund at interest at the control of the Preparative Meeting; and the Separatists continue to keep in their hands $212, exclusive of interest. After receiving the rent of the frame school house and lot and the interest on the $300 we believe there will sufficient to clear the school of debt.

Signed on behalf of the trustees,

> John Needles Jr.
> Mary R. Jessup

The above report was read in Preparative Meeting and the following named Friends were appointed trustees for the ensuing year: Benjamin M. Haines, William Jessup, David Darnell, Clayton Collins, John Needles Jr., Mary

[90]Min. Evesham School Trustees, 1796, p. 9. [91]*Ibid.*, 16/XI/1797.

Jessup, Ann Darnell, Anner Haines, Sarah Ann Troth, Kezia Haines, and Lydia Needles—Jacob Lishman is continued treasurer. 1 mo. 23rd 1840, three of the trustees attended at the school; 32 scholars present. John Needles Jr. is continued clerk of the trustees.

The tenure of teachers was, almost without exception, of brief duration. In 1798 the trustees report states the school has been kept open "the most part of the year under the tuition of several teachers."[92] In 1834, "the school has been taught . . . about 2 months by Benjamin M. Haines, and about 7 months by Hannah Gillingham, and at present by William R. Lippincott."[93]

———

[92]*Ibid.*, 9/VIII/1798.
[93]*Ibid.*, 2/I/1834; The following is a list of teachers mentioned from 1796 to 1840:

1796	school was concluded from under the care of James Griffiths.
18/IX/1796	school opened under Wm. Wood.
16/XI/1797	school opened under care of John Jones.
9/IV/1798	opened under care of Abigail Jones.
	(3/V/1798 school was visited by 1 trustee and several Women Friends, who were well satisfied.)
27/XI/1798	again opened under John Jones.
15/IV/1799	school opened under James Heminway
	school at this time had about 22 scholars, 29/VIII/1799, 27/XI/1799 were 43 scholars.
	Hemingway seems to have been employed from 1799–1805.
V/ /1805	Ellin Atkinson opened school and continued 3 months.
	Hemingway again taught in 1806.
18/X/1807	Benjamin Lippincott opened school.
25/IV/1808	Jesse Williams opened school to 9/III/1810.
25/IV/1810	Ambrose Chapman (part of year in 1812).
31/XII/1812	Josiah Evans "Taught remainder of the·year."
1814	both Evans and Chapman taught and 5 months under the tuition of a female.
2/I/1817	Edward Bullock
5/X/1818	Joshua Stevenson commenced teaching.
25/VIII/1820	Joshua Stevenson "adjourned the school."
24/IV/1820	Elizabeth Borton opened school.
X/1820	Elizabeth Borton closed school.
2/II/1820	John Thornton opened school.
3/I/1822	Ellis Comfort mentioned as having taught for some months past.
2/I/1823	2 months by Jacob Lishman; 7 mos. by Abigail G. Bedford; 2 mos. by Wm. W. Burr.
11/XI/1825	Benjamin Buckman opened school.
25/III/1826	Benjamin Buckman closed school.
27/XI/1826	David Hunt opened school.
Between 25/III and 27/XI Rebecca Engle taught for 6 months.	
23/IV/1827	Joshua Haines opened school.
26/XI/1827	Benjamin Buckman opened school.
23/IV/1829	Amy Haines opened school.
30/XII/1830	Ann Sykes 7 mos. of past year.

The items in trustees' reports, dealing with the number of pupils attending, show that attendance fluctuated between great extremes; but that, in general, attendance in mid-winter was largest, falling away in summer months. Some reports for summer months, however, show record breaking attendance. Below is given the record of attendance over a few years.[94]

3/I/1833	Mary H. Cooper 6 mos. of past year. and four months by Benjamin Haines.

The 30th of 3rd month Summer School opened this week under the tuition of Hannah Gillingham. Present 3 men and four women. Number of scholars 22.

2/I/1834	William R. Lippincott.
31/XII/1835	"There is one lately commenced by Rebecca Glover."
27/XII/1836	" . . . school held at the brick house taught by Henry Haines." (At this time there were two schools one in a brick house and another in the frame house.)
XII/1837	Phebe Williams taught summer school.
3/I/1839	Samuel Haines, 3 mos. past Amy Borton, 7 months past.
26/XII/1839	Mary Ann Lippincott for 4½ months past.
2/I/1840	Jacob Roberts at present teacher.

[94]Collected from reports of the school trustees, 1799–1811

Date	Pupils	Date	Pupils
29/VIII/1799	22	3/V/	21
3/X/	27	2/VIII/	20
31/X/	27	30/VIII/	22
27/XI	43	29/XI/	28
2/I/1800	39	3/I/1805	30
30/I/	43	28/II/	39
27/II/	32	3/X/	26
3/IV/	24	31/X/	25
28/VIII/	28	28/XI/	25
1/I/1801	26	2/I/1806	48
29/I/	42	23/I/	50
26/II/	36	23/V/	19
2/IV/	25	25/I/1810	46
30/VII/	29	22/II/	51
3/IX/	33	3/V/	77
1/X/	36	24/V/	74
3/XII/	39	21/VI/	62
31/XII/	40	26/VII/	62
28/I/1802	50	23/VIII/	62
30/IX/	29	20/IX/	47
28/X/	30	25/X/	38
30/XII/	35	22/XI/	30
1/IX/1803	23	27/XII/	43
29/IX/	28	24/I/1811	70
3/XI/	23	21/II/	57
29/XII/1804	33	21/III/	47
2/II/1804	43	25/IV/	55
1/III/	35	23/V/	60
27/III/	27	1/VIII/	47
		22/VIII/	51

Up to the middle of the nineteenth century children at Evesham, almost without exception, attended Friends' schools. After that time (1) the number of members of age for school declined until by the end of the century there were but few of age to attend school, (2) the number at district schools tended to increase, and consequently (3) the preparative meetings' schools were discontinued. The following table[95] sets forth the facts concerning this decline and the dispersion of children into different schools.

TABLE

Children—how situated	1855	1860	1865	1870	1875	1880	1885	1890	1895	1900
Of age for schooling	34	36	35	21	12	12	19	16	11	9
At Prep. Mtg. schools	31	25	19	4						
At Westtown	3	9	6	7	2	2		7	3	4
District Schools		2	7	8	8	1	11	6	1	1
Deaf & Dumb Inst. Phila.				1	1					
Select Sch. taught by member				1		2				
Not attending				1						1
Select school not taught by member					1				1	
Friends' Select School, Phila.					2		1			
Family Schools under Friends						6				
Not accounted for						1				
At schools under care of Friends							7		6	
Moorestown Friends' Academy								2		3
Boarding School not under Friends								1		

Returning now to 1827, we find that at the separation a part of the school funds, amounting to $212.00 was in the hands of the "Separatists," and some schools were continued under their care. In 1848, we learn from the women's minutes that:

> The trustees of Evesham Lower School produced a report that there had been a school taught six months by Abigail Eldridge and visited by the Committee. The Meeting unites with continuing the same committee with the addition of Deborah Warrick's name.[96]

Again in 1859,

> The situation of center school house claiming the attention of this meeting, Pemberton Borton, William D. Rogers and John H. Dudley are appointed

---

[95]Compiled from the Min. Evesham Mo. Mtg. for the dates mentioned.
[96]Min. Evesham Prep. Mtg., Women Friends, (H.), 28/XI/1848.

to take charge of it and do as in their opinion may seem best and report to this meeting when prepared.[97]

By 1864 the "Lower Evesham School" had become defunct:

There has been no school taught since last report, and there is no prospect of any; We therefore recommend the sale of the property.

There is a balance in the treasurer's hands of eight dollars and ninety-five cents . . . which was satisfactory to the meeting, and after a free expression of sentiment it was the judgment of this meeting to authorize the trustees of said school property to offer it at public or private sale and transfer the proceeds thereof to the treasurer of said meeting for its use, and report when prepared.[98]

In the answers to questions, sent in to the Educational Committee of the Yearly Meeting in 1875 we have a statement of the causes for the discontinuance of schools at that place.

The Friend appointed at last Meeting to frame answers to the questions produced the following which was read, united with and Wm. D. Rogers appointed to forward them to the Clerk of the Educational Committee.

1. We have no school under the care of our Meeting.

2. There are 10 children of suitable age to attend school, that are members of our meeting; 8 that have one parent a member.

3. The children are so isolated that they could not attend any one school, and not sufficient members to support one, there being a good public school in the immediate vicinity of the Meeting; therefore, any assistance that the Committee would be likely to give would not support a school.

4. There is no school under the care of our Monthly Meeting.[99]

EASTON SCHOOL

Easton Preparative Meeting was not established until 1810. The first minute bears the date 26/IV/1810, but, though the Easton School was already in operation its trustees' reports were presented to the older meeting at Evesham. On 23/I/1812 their report was first brought before the Easton Preparative Meeting.

Easton School dates back to the very beginning of the century. In 1801,

Bethewel Moar (More ?) informed that William Wilkins was disposed to convey a lot of ground for the use of a school and other purposes, to be wholly under the care and direction of this Preparative Meeting, the following Friends to take a title for the said lot and to execute a declaration of trust: Bethewel Moar. Joshua Mason, Cyrus Moar, and John Engle . . .[100]

[97]Min. Evesham Prep. Mtg., (H.), 1/XI/1859.
[98]*Ibid.*, 26/I/1864.   [99]*Ibid.*, 27/VII/1875.
[100]Min. Evesham Prep. Mtg., 8/X/1801.

In 1803,

This meeting was informed that Friends have built an house suitable for a school house on a lot of ground deeded by William Wilkins for that purpose, to be known by the name of Easton school house and request that trustees be appointed, which was united with and . . . appointed: William Wilkins, John Engle, Samuel Roberts, Bethewel More and Stephen Morris; and Wm.

QUAKER SCHOOL AT EASTON MEETING

Wilkins is appointed treasurer, who are to report their care in the 8th month next, the day of visitation to be the second day following each monthly meeting.[101]

The above named trustees made report on the school, in the year following:

We the trustees of Easton School agree to report that we have generally attended to our appointment and visited the school monthly.

We believe there was a good degree of order and decorum preserved in the school during its continuance which was six months in the year.

(Signed for the trustees by Samuel Roberts)[102]

---

[101]*Ibid.*, 8/IX/1803.　　　　　[102]*Ibid.*, 9/VIII/1804.

In 1806 a lot was secured for the benefit of Easton School, being deeded by William Wilkins and Sarah Wilkins to Joseph Haines,

THE DEBIT SIDE OF THE EASTON SCHOOL ACCOUNTS IN 1831

Obadiah Engle, John Engle and John Borton for that "and other religious purposes of Friends and no other use whatsoever."[103]

[103]Min. Evesham Mo. Mtg., 5/II/1808; for other property see also a deed at 15 & Race Streets (packet of Papers in Haddonfield Box) dated 15/IV/1847, giving land for use of Easton School.

Besides the regular means of support—subscriptions—the school benefitted in two ways considerably: In 1825 Obadiah Engle ac-

THE CREDIT SIDE OF THE EASTON SCHOOL ACCOUNT BOOK IN 1831

knowledge receipt of $500, being the payment of a legacy; and after 1836, there are frequent items of money received from the state school fund.[104]

---

[104]Easton School Treasurer's Account Book.

The following is a typical report of the Easton Trustees in the early part of the century:

> The trustees of Easton School agree to report that we have mostly attended to our appointment and visited the school monthly to general satisfaction, during its continuance, which was about 6 months. Josiah Evans, teacher. N. B. There has been a school in said school house *three months* taught by Elizabeth Conrow and visited by women trustees.[105]

By mid-century a few changes are to be noticed: a longer school term; women teaching longer terms; and men teaching shorter terms. The following is typical for this later period:

> The trustees of Easton school report that there has been a school taught in said house about 9 months of the past year—about three months of the time taught by male teachers, and visited by men trustees to general satisfaction.
>
> Also six months taught by a female and visited monthly by Women trustees to general satisfaction.

The amount of the fund at interest is	$735.00
Interest due not paid	21.00
Balance on Hand	12.66
	———
Making in all—	768.66

Signed on behalf of the trustees.

Nathan Roberts, Benjamin Roberts.[106]

In the early part of the century male teachers are usually recorded as teaching about 6 months of the year; the women, usually a three months term. In the middle of the century women teach six months and more; while male teachers are employed often for not more than three months. In 1850 the school report stated the school had been taught for eleven months, 3 months by a male, and 8 months by a female teacher.[107] In 1872 the school was carried on for 9 months, 4 months by a male and the rest by a female teacher.[108]

---

[105]Min. Easton Prep. Mtg., 23/I/1812.

[106]*Ibid.*, 27/I/1842.   [107]*Ibid.*, 26/XII/1850.

[108]*Ibid.*, 25/I/1872; The following is a list of teachers mentioned at Easton School, 1813–1870, gathered from minutes of Easton Prep. Mtg., and Account Book of Treasurer of Easton School.

Date	Name
21/I/1813	Josiah Evans
	Samuel C. Atkinson
	Elizabeth Conrow
27/I/1814	Allen Moore
26/I/1815	Charles Moore
25/I/1816	Job Roberts
21/I/1819	Aron Quicksal 8 mo.

Between 1872 and 1878 the preparative meeting minutes make no mention of a school being kept. In 1878 a financial statement was rendered, but there is no indication that a school had been operated by the meeting. The amount of the school fund, however, was $1081.22.[109]

21/I/1819	Rhoda Collins 3 mo.
27/I/1820	Beaulah Matlack 3 mo.
22/I/1824	Cornwall Stephenson and Charles Moor
23/VI/1824	Charles Moore
5/I/1825	Mary E. Haines
21/III/1825	Joseph E. Haines
28/X/1825	Abigail Borton
26/I/1826	Abigail Borton 6 mos.
1826	Henry Worrington (The Remainder.)
13/IX/1827	Henry D. Worrington (Warrington?)
18/I/1828	Jacob Buckman & his wife Elizabeth
31/IV/1828	Benjamin Roberts
28/III/1829	Camel (Cornwall?) Stevenson
15/IX/1830	Lucy Page
25/I/1832	Martha Warrington
31/III/1834	Sarah Ann Engle
29/VIII/1834	Barclay Haines
1836	Henry W. Lippincott
1836	Julianna Powell
1840	Samuel R. Wilkins
1840	Abigail Eldridge
1842	Edith Buzby
1842	Clayton Brown
1843	Rachel Eldridge
1944	Nathan L. Engle
1846	Ann Prickett
1846	Ezra Engle
1847	Julianna Powell
1848	Jacob Roberts
1849	Joseph H. Borton
1849	Hannah B. Lishman
1851	Mark H. Buzby
1852	Lucy Ann Burr
1854	Robert B. Engle
1855	Anna Estlack (Eastlack?)
1856	A. S. Haines
1858	Mary L. Buzby
1859	Clayton L. Brown
1861	Sarah Eastlack
1861	Samuel L. Moore
1862	Wm. B. Endicott
1863	Rebecca W. Kite
1865	Susanna H. Engle
1870	Henry H. Wilkins
1870	E. E. Roberts

[109] *Ibid.*, 24/I/1878.

MEDFORD MONTHLY MEETING

In 1760, upon request of Friends situated at Upper Evesham, it was permitted by the Evesham Meeting that a meeting for worship be held "at the school house near Robert Braddock's." This was an indulged meeting until 1774, when they requested advice concerning the "enlargement of their meeting place." Upon advice of Evesham it was enlarged, and the Preparative Meeting of Upper Evesham created in 1784. Ten years later the Monthly Meeting of Upper Evesham was created, composed of the preparative just mentioned and that at Cropwell. Since 1850 the Monthly Meeting has been called Medford.[110]

Several years before the creation of the Preparative Meeting at Upper Evesham some efforts had been made to secure land for a school but "little or no prospect of getting (it)" was reported, and also that "a teacher at that place is wanting."[111]

In spite of these obstacles, however, "schools" were established, and in 1783,

> The following Friends were appointed to have the oversight of the schools kept by Friends within this Preparative Meeting, to wit: Joshua Owen, Joseph Wilcox, John Haines, and Jobe Collins, who are desired to attend to that service, and report their care therein to a future Meeting.[112]

In 1786 a committee was at work to secure a lot for the school, and, after several months service, reported they had purchased 4 acres of ground of Cornelius Bramin, adjoining the meeting house lot, paying for the same £ 12 per acre.[113] This lot having been secured, a school was conducted under superintendance of a committee, though "not kept to so much satisfaction as could be desired, yet we believe there is encouragement for further labor;" the committee further deprecates the "want of the masters and employers more fully uniting with (it) in that necessary work."[114] However, a year later, they find "the school in reasonable good order in the general, and some considerable improvement in school learning."

In 1792, in accord with suggestions made previously by higher

---

[110]Record of the several meetings; also, Michener: *Retrospect of Early Quakerism*, Hazard: *Register of Pa.*, VII, 101–2 and Bunting: *List of Records*, 84f.
[111]Min. Evesham Mo. Mtg., 9/IX/1779.
[112]Min. U. E. Prep. Mtg., 4/VI/1783.
[113]*Ibid.*, 3/V/1786.   [114]*Ibid.*, 9/I/1788 and 9/IV/1788.

meetings, the following plan is recorded for unifying the funds for school support in Upper Evesham:

We the committee appointed to consider of a plan for a uniformity on the right settlement of schools in proper places, and raising funds therefore, do report that we have all met, maturely deliberated on the subject and are generally of the mind that it may be best. *First.* that the Monthly Meeting should have a standing committee under that concern which should be renewed annually at, or soon after the receipt of the extracts, who should visit the schools approbated and established by the respective preparative meetings and advise and assist in establishing them in proper places, when called upon, and make a clear report to the Monthly Meeting which precedes the Quarterly Meeting in the 9th month annually, of the general state of schools, each of which schools should by a minute of the Preparative Meeting have a competent number of Friends appointed as trustees and a treasurer with powers given them as in the following essay of a minute, to wit:

At a Preparative Meeting at Upper Evesham, First month, fifth, 1791, It appearing necessary that the school house and school at Upper Evesham wholly belonging to Friends should be under the care of a standing committee, the following Friends viz.: John Haines, Job (Prikitt ?), Job Collins, Laurence Webster, and Joseph Wilcox, are appointed to that service, by the name of Trustees of Friends School at Upper Evesham and Barzillai Braddock, is also appointed Treasurer to the said school, to whom, by his proper name or name of office, donations may be made by last will or otherwise, for the benefit of said school, and the same shall be accounted for by him to the trustees. He shall keep fair accounts, and a note of the terms of such donations, if particular, in order that they may be applied accordingly and shall pay no money out of the stock without the approbation of the trustees.

And it is agreed that the trustees for the time being shall have the care of the said school, keep the buildings, which are, or may be provided for schools or residence of the teachers, in good repair; make provision for the comfortable support of said teachers, order the necessary expenditures when they have cash in hand for these purposes and if difficulties occur, respecting the raising of more when wanted, or in any other matter, they are to lay the same before this meeting and receive our advice thereon; they are to employ teachers who are always to be approved members of our Society, and for sufficient cause dismiss them; admit scholars and discharge those who may misbehave; and make such rules for these and other purposes tending to the good government of the school as they may judge necessary, provided the same be not repugnant to this fundamental plan, or the minutes of our Yearly Meeting. They are to visit the said school on the first fourth day following the Monthly Meeting in each month at the usual school hour, examine the progress made by the scholars in their learning, and see that good order and decorum is preserved. The number of trustees is to be 5 and any three of them may transact any business within their appointment. They are to keep regular minutes of their proceedings . . . or a short statement thereof, with such regulations as they make, lay before this Preparative Meeting in the eighth month annually, for our sense thereon, when a fresh appointment of trustees and treasurer is always to be made for the ensuing year.

Second, that a subscription should be opened in the Preparative Meeting for each of these schools . . . in substance as follows:

We the subscribers, in religious membership with the people called Quakers, do hereby severally, for ourselves and our heirs, promise to pay on demand and in hard cash as it now passeth current,unto Barzillai Braddock, Treasurer of Friends School at Upper Evesham . . . or to his successor in that office for the time being, the sum of money by us respectively written against and with our names, with interest therefor at the rate of six pounds for the hundred by the year, the principal sum to be and remain a durable fund under the direction of the trustees of said school—now or hereafter and be appointed by the said preparative meeting and by them, when paid in, to be laid out, or lent on interest, in such manner as they shall judge will best secure an interest or annuity and the interest or annuity thereof is to be applied to the education of such children as now do, or hereafter shall belong to the said meeting, or within the compass of said school, whose parents are, or shall be in low circumstances, and to the education of such black children as shall by said trustees be thought to have a claim to this benefit. And in case the whole shall not be wanted for the purpose, then in that case the interest of the said monies so unexpended may be applied to the schooling of other poor children, or to such other uses of the said school, now, or schools which hereafter may be approved by the said meeting at or near that place, as the said trustees for the time being, or the major part of them shall think will best answer and advance the design and benefit of the institution . . . and it is agreed that the sum subscribed shall not be called for from the subscriber whilst the interest is duly paid, but may be paid when he or she pleaseth.

Which subscription should be freely entered into by the members generally within the limits of the said school, and by any other Friends who are free thereto, according to their respective circumstances. Thus, and by donations from benevolent persons in their last wills, our Funds may, in time, become sufficient to induce well qualified teachers to undertake the trust of educating our youth and give all necessary instruction to the children of Friends in low circumstances and of the black people.

Third, and it is advised that Friends of ability may be liberal in their subscriptions, not only to the particular school within whose limits they reside, but to such others within their Monthly Meeting where Friends may not be of ability to raise the necessary funds for supporting and advancing this good work.

Signed on behalf and desire of the committee, 11th month, 22d, 1790, by
William Rogers.[115]

In 1792 a special Committee was appointed to superintend the "school taught by Isaac Andrews" near Joshua Peacock's, and

---

[115]*Ibid.*, 4/IV/1792.

reported "to a good degree of satisfaction." This, with "the school kept in the back apartment of this house" were the two schools of the meeting.[116] The school "near Joshua Peacock's" is later called the "Northampton School."[117] In 1794 the following report concerning it was produced:

The trustees appointed last year to have the care of Friends School in the township of Northampton . . . produced the following report from the minutes of their proceedings to wit: . . . have mostly attended thereto monthly until said school was discontinued, which was in the 5th month last and do report that said school was well conducted in the general, and a good degree of decorum observed and also considerable improvement in school learning, particularly in reading and writing, yet more attention to this weighty trust . . . is needful.[118]

In 1794 the "school at Upper Evesham was conducted in a good degree orderly," while that at Northampton was not visited as the teacher was not in membership. But in 1800 they note "some improvement was perceivable—the Rules of the School being several times read and remarks made thereon for their instruction."[119]

In 1801, a report made by the monthly meeting, recorded "four schools within the compass of this meeting, three of which have small funds raised for the schooling of poor children." These four were in Cropwell and Upper Evesham Preparative Meetings.[120] In 1802 the following report was made:

We the committee . . . have visited three of the schools that are . . . under friends care . . . but the school in North Hampton being occupied by one not professing with us in religious membership, we therefore did not attend. We also find the principal sum of the fund for the schools within the compass of Upper Evesham Preparative Meeting amounts to £ 30/10/1, and the principal sum subscribed to the Cropwell school amounts to £ 105, and interest unexpended 18/3/9. The schooling of several poor children has been paid for out of the said funds since last year.[121]

A year later, all four schools were under the care of the meeting's teachers and "purty well conducted."[122]

The following report on Northampton appeared in 1805:

We the trustees have . . . attended thereto every month while taught by Jesse Bond, he having left it last spring in order to obtain further instruction

---

[116]*Ibid.*, 4/I/1792 and 8/VIII/1792.   [117]*Ibid.*, 7/XI/1792.
[118]*Ibid.*, 6/VIII/1794.   [119]*Ibid.*, 9/VIII/1797; 6/VIII/1800.
[120]Min. U. E. Mo. Mtg., 7/III/1801.   [121]*Ibid.*, 6/III/1802.
[122]*Ibid.*, 12/III/1803.

himself and returned in the fall, since which time we have had the satisfaction of observing a considerable improvement both in school learning and the order of the school in general.[123]

In 1805 the preparative meeting recorded that a lot of 3 acres had been purchased at Brotherton for the purpose of establishing a school and burying ground. A committee was appointed to have charge of the title to the said property.[124] This was to be called Hartford School. In 1806 the committee reported they had taken title to the property for Hartford school, but little is heard of it afterwards. In the same year the meeting was informed that 1½ acres had been purchased near Fostertown and a school house built thereon; a committee to take title for the same, and a committee to superintend the school, were appointed.[125] This was known as the "Northern School," which, with the Northampton and Upper Evesham schools, made a total of three belonging to the preparative meeting, and possibly a fourth—the Hartford School.[126]

In 1809 the following report was made on the Northern School:

The trustees of the Northern School . . . report that we have endeavored to attend to our appointment, but owing to the difficulty of procuring a suitable teacher, the school has been vacant nearly half of the year very much to the loss of the children of the neighborhood when it has been occupied by a teacher we have most of us visited monthly and to a good degree of satisfaction.[127]

In 1814 the question of establishing a Boarding School for boys above the age to go to Westtown, was discussed by the Monthly Meeting:

It being proposed for the consideration of this meeting the propriety of es-tablishing a Boarding School within the compass of our Yearly Meeting and under its care and direction for completing the education of lads of riper age than those admissable at Westtown, that institution affording ample provision for females, while the education of the other sex after the age of 15 is not suffi-ciently provided for within the pale of our society. After deliberate considera-tion the meeting united in forwarding the subject to our ensuing Quarterly Meeting in order that if there united with the same may be forwarded to our ensuing Yearly Meeting for its consideration.[128]

In 1827 the preparative meeting made the following report on schools.

---

[123]Min. U. E. Prep. Mtg., 6/III/1805.   [124]*Ibid.*, 6/XI/1805.
[125]*Ibid.*, 8/I/1806.   [126]*Ibid.*, 5/III/1806.   [127]*Ibid.*, 8/II/1809.
[128]Min. U. E. Mo. Mtg., 12/II/1814.

The trustees appointed to the care of the school at Medford, report—that it has been kept up nearly all the past year; the average number of scholars has been sufficient for the encouragement of the teachers, part of the time taught by a male and part by a female, all in membership with us. While taught by the latter it was under the care of a committee of Women Friends—and when by the males, most of us generally visited it monthly, and have had the satisfaction of perceiving a considerable advancement in school learning. The order maintained, and general deportment of the scholars, has been satisfactory.

The trustees last appointed to the care and oversight of Hampton School report that most of us have paid attention thereto (but not always monthly). The school has been kept up about half the year but taught by a person not in membership with us; the general order of the school in a good degree satisfactory, and a progressing in school learning perceivable.

We . . . report that it has been kept up about 8 months of the year, the fore part of the time by a master, and in the summer season by a female teacher, both members of our society, and, although we have to acknowledge our frequent neglect in a punctual attention to our appointment, yet believe the school has been kept to a good degree of satisfaction. The latter part of the time it has been vacant for want of a teacher.

At an annual Meeting of the trustees of the several schools under care of said meeting, the accounts of the Treasurer of the school fund were settled up to 1/II/1827, by which it appears there has been expended during the past year for schooling poor children $52.13. The whole principal sum now is $1130.09. Interest unexpended, which is now due, $117.57.[129]

In 1829 the three schools, Medford, Northern and Hampton, were reported again in good condition; and in 1834 likewise, with the exception that it was proposed that Hampton be discontinued because there was a new school in the vicinity. In its place a new Friends' School was planned.[130] A few months later, the following report on the new school was submitted:

We the undersigned inform that we have procured a lot of ground of David Haines, at the Cross Roads near his residence, whereon we have erected a convenient frame school house, and established a school therein, which we propose to denominate the Eastern School, and request the meeting to appoint trustees to superintend it on its behalf; it being our intention to support this school as a Friends school in lieu of Hampton school—which we submit to the meeting.

Joshua Stokes   Joseph Haines
David Haines   John Collins
Job Ballinger.[131]

---

[129]Min. U. E. Prep. Mtg., 1/II/1827.
[130]*Ibid.*, 29/I/1829, and 30/I/1834.
[131]*Ibid.*, 29/V/1834.

A report of 1841 shows that these schools were still controlled by the preparative meeting.[132]

After the separation (1827) attention to schools was urged upon monthly meetings more strongly than ever before. Replying to a request for a full report Upper Evesham stated in 1830:

We the committee . . . do find that with respect to the situation and state of our schools there are 5 within our limits, all under the control of Friends, and superintended by 5 trustees to each of them, appointed annually by the Preparative Meeting and who report thereto; and all of them except one, taught by members of our Society; three of them, being within the limits of Upper Evesham Preparative Meeting have a fund of about $800 belonging in common stock, and appropriated where most wanted, to the assistance of the children of such Friends as may need it; and when there is a surplus, it is by the united assent of all the trustees made use of in paying for such other scholars as they may think proper, as there is often a difficulty in making up at all times in the year, a number sufficient to employ a teacher. The school in the Eastern District of said meeting has very few Friends children within its limits, and the Trustees have often been induced to employ teachers that were not Friends, owing to the great difficulty of finding qualified teachers of our own society. Within Cropwell Preparative Meeting the school at Pine Grove has a small fund in the possession of Friends and appropriated as occasion may require, exclusively for the benefit of those within its limits. There is also a fund for the benefit of Cropwell school, and, until of late, it was applied in the same way; but said fund is now in the hands of the former treasurer, who has gone off with the Separatists, and who declines settling with the committee appointed for that purpose.

There is but one family of Friends who have children, within the limits of our Monthly Meeting but what are within a reasonable distance of one of the five schools, and that family is out of reach of all, but in circumstances that will enable them to place their children amongst Friends to obtain their learning, whenever they wish so to do. The important part of the recommendation of the Yearly Meeting respecting a religious education has particularly claimed our attention, and we feel the necessity of endeavoring to impress on the minds of parents and heads of families the responsible situation in which we are placed, and the very important charge with which we are entrusted; that we may endeavor to be good examples, which is said to go before precept—and that we may experience a qualification to watch over the tender openings of their youthful minds in very early life, and as they unfold to impress on them the truths of our Holy Religion and the necessity of conforming to the simplicity of our religious profession, for which our worthy predecessors suffered so much, especially in their testimony on account of their plain language, and nonconformity to the compliments and customs of the world; believing that as there is a willingness wrought in the minds of Friends to bear the cross and live

[132]*Ibid.*, 28/I/1841.

more in conformity with our discipline, it will prove as a hedge about us and preserve us from many hurtful things.

And we do feel desirous that a more frequent and diligent perusal of the Holy Scriptures may be put in practice especially on the first day of the week; and believe that as Friends are engaged to seek for strength and opportunity to sit down together in their families and have them read, they will afford comfort and consolation to the minds of those who are sincerely desirous of being benefitted thereby.

Signed by

> Josiah Reeve
> Joseph Evans(Evens?)
> Lydia Stokes
> Rebecca C. Evans.[133]

A summary of the report returned in 1835 shows the following schools.

1. School at Medford open during the year.
2. Eastern School open nearly all time since house was built in the spring, and taught by members.
3. Northern school open 9 months and during summer taught by a member.
4. Pine Grove open ½ year, most of time taught by person not in membership.
5. Cropwell, 9 months, by members.
6. Young men and women members have alleviated the distress by enlisting as teachers in winter and summer.
7. Some attend mid-week meetings.[134]

In a period of thirty years, about 1840 to 1870, the number of Friends children of suitable age for schooling decreased by more than half, and consequently the incentive for maintaining schools was less strong. Moreover, of those, suitable for school, a much smaller proportion attended Friends' schools in 1870 than in 1842, and a considerable number patronized the district schools. The table shows how children were placed among schools in this period.

TABLE

Distribution of children in schools.

	1842	*1851*	*1855*	*1860*	*1865*	*1870*
Children of age for school	86	86	77	56	46	41
Westtown	7	14	9	10	10	3
Schools under Friends Care	45	45	40	36	18	13
Family School	6	5	9	4		

---

[133]Min. U. E. Mo. Mtg., 6/XI/1830.   [134]*Ibid.*, 7/III/1835.

Schools not under care of
Friends	17				
Not at School	8	6	1		1
Not accounted for	3				
Public Schools		16	4	4	10	11
Boarding school not under					
Friends' care			1		
Private Schools taught by					
Friends			13		
Taught at home				2	8	13

Besides the schools controlled by Upper Evesham Preparative Meeting there were two, the Cropwell and Pine Grove schools, that were under Cropwell Preparative Meeting.

In 1785 John Haines, Thomas Hollingshead, Enoch Evans, Thomas Lippincott, Isaac Borton and Samuel Burroughs were named to take a declaration of trust for the school lot which had been secured.   Two years later a standing committee for the school was appointed and a plan for raising funds adopted.   A report of the school committee was received in 1788.[135]   The records, by which the existence of the schools at Pine Grove and Cropwell can be traced, are very attenuated; but their regularity assures us they were constantly kept up.   Brief notices, such as the following, appear regularly:

The minutes of the school being produced and read to some satisfaction, the following Friends are appointed trustees, to wit: Samuel Lippincott, Amos Ashead, Joseph Rogers, Thomas Lippincott, John Haines Jr. and Joseph Rogers is reappointed Treasurer for the year ensuing.[136]

In 1814 steps were taken for better accommodation of the Cropwell School:

At Cropwell Preparative Meeting held 22/IX/1814 the trustees of Cropwell school reported that they have procured a lot of ground adjoining the same on which the meeting house stands, and Samuel Lippincott being willing to execute a deed of conveyance to Friends for the benefit of said school.   Joseph Evans, Benjamin Haines, Joshua Lippincott, Joshua Haines, and John Roberts are appointed to take the same in trust on behalf of the meeting, and report when the same is completed—said trustees wishing for the better accommodation of school children to have the privilege of removing the fences on the south side so as to include the school within the meeting house lot; which

[135]Min. Evesham Prep. Mtg., 7/IV/1785; 7/XII/1787; 7/II/1788.
[136]Min. Cropwell Prep. Mtg., 31/VII/1795.

tne Meeting is taking into consideration, is united with; the said trustees to beat the necessary expense of moving the fence to the situation it's now in if any disadvantage by granting aforesaid privilege should arise to the Meeting hereafter, which they acceeded to.[137]

In 1829 the two schools were still continued, though it appears from the following that some trouble in school finances arose at the division:

THE PINE GROVE SCHOOL

The trustees of Cropwell school made report in writing which was read and the following Friends appointed trustees for the ensuing year, to wit: Isaac Brown, Joseph Evans, Isaac Stokes, Samuel Haines, Jacob Roberts—who are requested to make report of their care thereto in the 1st month next.

Joseph Evans appointed treasurer of the school fund for the ensuing year who is directed to call on the former treasurer and request the books and papers and such balance of the Fund as may appear in his hands, upon a settlement with him by the trustees.

Pine Grove school made a verbal report stating that it had been kept up all the year and taught by Joshua Haines and in their attention to it had found

[137]*Ibid.*, 22/IX/1814.

it orderly conducted, etc. The following Friends appointed trustees for the ensuing year, Jacob Evans Sr., John Evans, Jacob Evans Jr., Thomas Evans and Isaac Darnell. Jacob Evans Sr. reappointed treasurer.[138]

Several minutes appear, indicating that further efforts were made to restore the funds of Cropwell School as late as 1833. The two schools continued in existence very probably to about 1870 when superseded by the public school.

CROPWELL SCHOOL HOUSE

Though a school at Pine Grove existed earlier it was not so named definitely until 1792. Previously it was referred to as the school near Samuel Evans'. In that year trustees were appointed, and a treasurer, to control its affairs.[139] By a minute of 1795 it was agreed to transfer it to another meeting:

We the committee appointed by the Monthly Meeting to take into consideration . . . Pine Grove School, . . . report . . . it would be for the benefit and advantage of said school to be placed under the care of Upper Evesham Monthly Meeting and Cropwell Preparative Meeting with the privilege for

[138]*Ibid.*, 22/I/1829.   [139]Min. Evesham Prep. Mtg., 8/XI/1792.

the Preparative Meeting to appoint such Friends as trustees out of the two other Preparative Meetings as they may think suitable that are employers in said school.

John Roberts
Laurence Webster[140]

In the same year property was secured on which a school house was to be erected, and a committee appointed to have charge of it, which brought in brief reports from time to time. In 1822 a minute of the meeting recorded a gift from Joel Evans:

Item. I give and bequeath to the treasurer and trustees of Pine Grove school for the time being and their successors in office forever the sum of $100 to be paid to them by my executors in two years after my decease, the principal sum to be by them kept at interest and the interest arising therefrom to be appropriated to the schooling of poor children within the limits of said school, under the same regulations as the like fund of Cropwell school now established.[141]

After the separation came about, in 1827, difficulties arose in Upper Evesham over the control of schools. Thus, in 1828 the new meeting stated:

Two of the trustees appointed last year to have the care of Hampton School produced a written report, which being read, appeared, in a degree satisfactory. The other two schools have been generally under the care of our opposing Friends so that there can be no particular account given thereof.

The treasurer of the school funds and the settlement of his accounts is wholly confined within the power at this time of our opposing friends, the treasurer being one of their number.

The following Friends are appointed to have the care of schools the ensuing year and make report thereof to our Preparative Meeting in the second month to be held next year: For Medford School, Joshua Sharp, George Craft, Edward Bolton, and Isaac Haines; Northern School, Charles Wilkins, and Josiah Thorn; Hampton School, Benjamin Davis and Geo. Roberts.[142]

Three months later, the monthly meeting reported regarding schools: "none are immediately under our control."[143]

The committee of the preparative meeting, appointed in 1828, produced the following report a year later, and a new committee was appointed:

The trustees appointed the thirty-first of the first month 1828 to have the care and oversight of the several schools, reported they had not been unmindful

---

[140]Min. Evesham Mo. Mtg., 11/XII/1795.
[141]Min. Cropwell Prep. Mtg., 21/III/1822.
[142]Min. U. E. Prep. Mtg., (H.), 31/I/1828.
[143]Min. U. E. Mo. Mtg., (H.), 7/III/1828.

of their appointment, but, owing to the unsettled state of society no opening appeared for their services.[144]

As it was impossible to retain control, or a share in the control of the old schools, the meeting agreed to appoint

Joshua Sharp to succeed . . . as treasurer . . . authorizing him to receive the said books, etc., belonging to this meeting relative to the school funds thereof, and the interest arising on the said funds; and if the books and papers be not obtained, he is requested to collect the interest now due and to grow due annually from such of the said subscribers and others as are willing to pay him and to give them credit for the same in a book to be by him provided out of the money received and to pay out the interest money so by him received agreeably to the directions of the trustees appointed annually by this meeting to superintend the schools under its care, and to settle his accounts with them previous to the Preparative Meeting in the 2nd month annually in order that they may report the state thereof to this Meeting yearly.[145]

In a report of 1830 it appears that Henry Smith was engaged to keep school in the old Medford School house, but this not being permitted,

. . . we soon procured another house where school has been kept up since, taught by the same friend and most of the time it has been large.

There has been no opportunity for the service of the trustees, at the other schools, and, on enquiring into the situation of the School Fund that was created some years ago, . . . it appears that the following named friends with others, did subscribe to the said fund, to wit: Benjamin Davis, . . . $33.33; George Roberts $16.67 and John Stokes $4.00; which altogether making $54 principal . . . we have appropriated $9.00 of the said interest towards schooling poor children . . .

Signed on behalf of the trustees, 28/II/1830

Benjamin Davis
George Craft.[146]

By 1833, the school referred to above, that was begun in 1830, was provided with permanent quarters.

Benjamin Davis informed this Meeting that he had purchased a lot of ground on the easterly side of the street in Medford, containing about ¾ of an acre, part of the property late of James Reily deceased, upon which lot there has since been a new school house built by himself and other friends. He now proposes that this Meeting appoint two or three Friends as trustees to whom he will convey a portion of the title of said lot in such manner as that they shall hold the title in common with himself in trust for the use of a school to belong to this Meeting and be under its care, and superintended by such trustees as this Meeting may from time to time appoint; and the Meeting may be at

---

[144]Min. U. E. Prep. Mtg., (H.), 30/I/1829.
[145]*Ibid.*, 1/V/1829.   [146]*Ibid.*, 26/II/1830.

liberty to make such other use of said property or lot . . . that will not in any wise at any time interfere with the school. On consideration of the subject, this Meeting agrees to accept the proposal and appoint Wm. Braddock, Wm. Stokes, and Job Braddock to receive the conveyance from Benjamin Davis for such individual portion of the said premises, and then to execute a declaration acknowledging that they receive the said title and hold it in trust for the use and purposes aforesaid in the usual form, and after it is accomplished to report to this Meeting in writing and lodge the papers with such Friends as this Meeting may appoint to receive them for safe keeping.[147]

MEDFORD FRIENDS' SCHOOL

Though another report of the same year names committees for two schools, one at Upper Evesham and one at Cropwell, the latter probably did not last long, for the monthly meeting's answer to the query on schools only declares the existence of one in 1830 and in subsequent years. Moreover, the preparative meeting thereafter received the reports of the committee of the one school. In 1844 the following was received.

The trustees appointed in the third month last to have the care of the school report that the school has been kept open nearly all the year past and taught by members. The school has not been quite so large as it has been at some

147*Ibid.*, 29/XI/1833; This was reported accomplished on 3/X/1834.

previous years. We have several times visited the school and have witnessed some improvement in the education of children and that we have received our proportion of the school money from the township and apportioned it among the scholars as we thought most advisable.   Wm. Stokes

Barclay Stokes.[148]

In 1868 the average attendance was given as "about forty, members none." The latter part of the answer is significant. Taken in connection with the withdrawal of public funds from support of the private schools it explains the closing of the school. In 1872 there was "no school of the description queried after,"[149] and it appears from a lack of information of a positive charcter in the minutes that there was no Friends' School held between 1869 and 1882. In the latter year,

The subject of establishing a school under the care of the Preparative Meeting was introduced some months since, by a committee appointed by the Yearly Meeting's Educational Committee, it was again brought before us, and the following named friends are appointed to join men friends and take the subject under consideration, Rebecca Hollinshead, and Hannah L. Braddock.[150]

Three months later the committee reported that they had agreed to establish a school under the preparative meeting, and in August, that,

Men Friends have informed that they have appointed three trustees to attend to our school, and this Meeting unites that women friends appoint three to join men friends in acting as a committee: Rebecca Cowperthwait, Elizabeth L. Braddock, and Hannah L. Braddock are appointed to that service the following year.[151]

From the time of its reestablishment to 1886 regular reports of the school committees were returned to the preparative meeting. In that year it was agreed to leave "the school to the care of the Yearly Meeting's Committee, with the view of its becoming larger and more self-sustaining."[152] The school was still in operation in 1890, under a local committee working in conjunction with the Educational Committee of the Yearly Meeting.

CHESTER MONTHLY MEETING

In 1803 it was proposed that there be a division made in the

[148]*Ibid.*, 28/III/1844.   [149]Min. Medford Mo. Mfg., (H.), 30/III/1882.
[150]Min. U. E. Prep. Mtg:, Women Friends, (H.), 30/III/1882.
[151]*Ibid.*, 3/VIII/1882.   [152]*Ibid.*, 1/IV/1886.

Evesham Monthly Meeting, thereby creating a new one at Chester, made up of the Preparatives of Chester and Westfield.[153]   A preparative meeting had been held at Chester since an early date, a meeting house being erected in 1721[154] to take the place of an old log house, used for religious purposes, which had been destroyed by fire.   But of education among Chester Friends at the beginning of the eighteenth century little is known.   It is not until the last quarter of that century that educational affairs began to occupy any considerable place in their records.

THE CHESTER "BRICK SCHOOL"

In 1779 the Monthly Meeting of Evesham, to which Chester belonged, noted that a school was opened at Chester but not yet any prospect of procuring a lot of ground for the purpose.[155] Ground, "two acres, three roods and twenty-three perches," was purchased in 1781 "to be applied to such use or uses as the body of Friends belonging to the above named meeting shall think proper."[156]

153Min. Evesham Monthly Meeting, 1803.
154Hazard: *Register of Pa.*, VII, 102.
155Min. Evesham Mo. Mtg., 9/IX/1779.
156Purdy: *Moorestown, Old and New*, 129.

It was on this lot that the original stone building was erected for a school. It was completed and occupied for school purposes in 1785 and in 1786,

The following Friends (were) appointed to have the care and oversight of Friends School in Moorestown and inspect into the good order and improvement thereof, viz., Jacob Hollinshead, John Collins, Joshua Hunt, Robert French, John Roberts and Samuel Roberts, Jun., and report to this Meeting in the 8th month next or sooner as occasion may require.[157]

WESTFIELD FRIENDS' SCHOOL

The "Brick School" near Wm. Matlack's was opened near the same time. In 1785,

The following Friends were appointed to have the care and oversight of Friends school near William Matlack's to inspect into the good order and improvement thereof, viz., Samuel Roberts (?), Jonas Cattell, Joseph Roberts, and Reuben Matlack and report to this Meeting in the 8th month next or sooner as occasion may require.[158]

Five years later, plans were drawn up and adopted for raising permanent funds for the school. This plan was practically the

---

[157]Min. Chester Prep. Mtg., 6/XII/1786.
[158]Min. Chester Prep. Mtg., 6/XII/1785.

same as that proposed by Evesham Monthly Meeting and recommended to the several lower meetings, which appears elsewhere in this volume.[159] In 1791 the minutes mention three schools held within the limits of Chester Preparative: Moorestown School, Brick School, and the school taught by Abraham Warrington. The last named was possibly the "lower school" of Chester mentioned later.[160] In 1801 it was agreed that "the lower school being in the compass of Westfield Preparative Meeting in future it will come under that Meeting's care."[161]

In 1826 two legacies were recorded for the benefit of the school fund, the first by Ann Edwards and the second by Samuel Shute.

I give the sum of $50 unto the treasurer of the school fund (pertaining to Friends at Moorestown), or to his successor in office to be placed out at interest and disposed of at the discretion of the trustees of said school for the education of necessitous children within its limits.

Item. I order and direct my executors to pay to Josiah Roberts, treasurer of Chester School of Friends, or to his successor in office, the sum of $500.00 to be put out at interest on good security, the proceeds whereof to be applied at the discretion of the trustees of said school for the time being, for the education of Friends children and others in lowish circumstances, residing within the limits of the same.[162]

In 1828 the following report on schools was produced:

Short statements relative to the three schools under the care of the Preparative Meetings were received by which it appears that they have been kept up the greater part of the past year being taught by teachers in membership and visited monthly by part of the trustees appointed in said meetings. The order and improvements in that at Westfield not being satisfactory—that of the other two being mostly satisfactory.[163]

A month later it is recorded that Hicksite Friends at Westfield had assumed "entire control" of the school at that place.[164] In 1829 the minutes explain the school situation as follows:

Information being received from the Preparative Meetings respecting the situation of the three schools within our limits it appears that Moorestown school has been kept up the past year by teachers in membership with us and visited monthly by trustees; the order and literary improvement therein being in good degree satisfactory; That the Brick School has been taught about two months since last year by a teacher in membership with us and visited monthly by trustees, the order and improvement being satisfactory.

[159]*Ibid.*, 10/XII/1790; see page 167f. [160]*Ibid.*, 2/VIII/1791.
[161]*Ibid.*, 4/VIII/1801. [162]*Ibid.*, 23/II/1826.
[163]Min. Chester Mo. Mtg., 12/II/1828. [164]*Ibid.*, 11/III/1828.

In the 4th month last some of those persons who have separated themselves from our religious society took possession of the school house, removed the lock from the door, applied another and employed a person favorable to their views to open a school therein, since which they retain the possession thereof and that in consequence of Friends being deprived of their school house at Westfield there has been a school taught in a private dwelling about two months and visited by trustees, the deportment and improvement of the scholars being satisfactory.[165]

To meet the necessity arising out of the loss of the "Brick School" the trustees were authorized to "use their endeavors to support that school in as convenient a place as circumstances will admit."[166] This was possible since the "fund, consisting of about 500 dollars principal money, and also the maps and class books . . ." were retained by the original organization.[167] The school was, for a time, held at Joseph Roberts'.[168] On the whole, the effect of the separation was to stimulate attention to the work of education rather than otherwise, and the three main schools continued their existence in spite of material obstacles. In 1835 the meeting stated:

The committee on education . . . report that on solid deliberation way opened to visit some of our families tending to encourage and strengthen in a more faithful discharge of parental duty, by endeavoring to cultivate the minds of our beloved youth for the reception of the good seed.

There are three schools within our limits taught by members and superintended by trustees which the committee visited, and observed a commendable degree of decorum and literary improvement.

The number of members attending is 30. These with the aid of two small family schools taught by members, which 5 of our children attend, and 6 others now at Westtown afford an opportunity to nearly all the families to procure an education according to the views of the Yearly Meeting.[169]

In the same year (1835),

they united with the Proposal to build a house for the accommodation of that school (the Brick School) inasmuch as the Separatists, now known by the name of Hicksites, still retain possession of the house originally built for that purpose.[170]

Again in 1850,

Reports from the three schools under the care of the Preparative Meetings were produced and read; by which it appears that the Moorestown school has

---

[165]*Ibid.*, 10/IX/1829.   [166]Min. Chester Prep. Mtg., 29/I/1829.
[167]Min. Chester Mo. Mtg., 14/XII/1830.
[168]Min. Chester Prep. Mtg., 3/XII/1830.
[169]Min. Chester Mo. Mtg., 10/II/1835.
[170]Min. Chester Prep. Mtg., 26/II/1835.

been kept open about 10 months of the past year; the Brick school seven; (and) Westfield nine months. Having all been taught by teachers in membership. The order and literary improvement of the scholars being generally satisfactory.[171]

By 1870 the school at Westfield had become defunct, no reports on it being made thereafter to the monthly meeting.[172]

In 1860,

Statement of two of the schools under the care of the Preparative Meeting at Chester were received and read, by which it appears that the Moorestown School has been kept open the past year, the Brick School about three months, both taught by members and visited monthly by trustees, the order and improvement has been satisfactory.[173]

A similar report was presented in 1865 and 1870.

In 1874,

The trustees of the Brick School report that the school has been kept open about four months of the past year, taught by a member of our society and visited monthly by some of our number; the order and improvement of scholars have been satisfactory.[174]

After this the records state it has "not been kept open the past year"—but a report was made each year on the Brick School Fund, which was a few years later put to use in the new institution, the Academy.

In January 1879,

The Trustees of Moorestown School report that the School was continued from the time of their appointment until near the end of the 5th month last, by a teacher in membership, and visited monthly by some of their number. The order and improvement was satisfactory. After the vacation of the school the house was altered and enlarged in order to provide for a school to be under the care of the Monthly Meeting.[175]

This new school was the Moorestown Academy, concerning the establishment of which a committee reported in 1878. The committee on improving the schools reported:

That we nearly all met in company with the trustees of the different school funds and examined the trust under which they are held. A portion of them is limited in its application to the education of those in necessitous circum-

---

[171]Min. Chester Mo. Mtg., 12/II/1850.
[172]The latest report in the Men's Minutes on the Westfield School of Orthodox Friends, appeared in 1857, but the women's minutes indicate its continuance to 1870.
[173]Min. Chester Mo. Mtg., 14/II/1860.
[174]Min. Chester Prep. Mtg., 31/XII/1874.   [175]*Ibid.*, 30/I/1879.

ELEMENTARY SCHOOL BUILDING, MOORESTOWN, NEW JERSEY

HIGH SCHOOL BUILDING, MOORESTOWN, NEW JERSEY

stances and a portion is not so limited, but while designed for school uses may be applied as the Monthly Meeting shall direct.

The committee have given the subject . . . careful consideration and concluded to recommend to the Monthly Meeting to alter the present school building at Moorestown by the addition of a story to be built of brick, with a tin roof, the outside walls to be rough cast, the height of the present room to be increased by lowering the joists about two feet, and new and larger windows to be put in.   The whole expense of these changes, it is thought will not exceed $1000.   They propose that the cost be defrayed as the Monthly Meeting may direct out of such of the school funds as may safely be applied to that purpose with the approbation of the Preparative Meetings under whose care the funds are placed.[176]

Shortly thereafter, as a result of the problem of establishing a higher grade school being put before the two preparative meetings at Chester and Westfield, the following reports presenting their views, were received.

From Westfield Preparative:

On considering the report of the committee of the Monthly Meeting on the school funds this Meeting unites with the proposal to increase the school accommodations at Moorestown so as to establish there a school of higher grade for the benefit of the children of the Monthly Meeting, and to pay to such persons as the Monthly Meeting may appoint to receive it, the sum of $500 from our funds to aid in building the proposed school house at Moorestown; we also agree to assist in maintaining the school so long as the funds are not needed within the compass of this Meeting.[177]

By Chester Preparative we are informed that the proposals were received and considered and were referred back to the monthly meeting for action.   The school house was prepared for use at once, the cost reported at its completion and furnishing being $2492.22.   Of this the two Preparatives contributed $500 each at the outset.

In August a school committee of men and women was appointed, a new principal and assistant were secured, and the following rules adopted for the government of the school:

1. The school year shall consist of 2 terms of 20 weeks each, commencing the 1st 2nd day in the 9th month of each year; there shall be an interval of one week in the 4th month at the time of holding our Yearly Meeting.

2. The teacher shall not dismiss any scholar from the school without first consulting the committee; parents having cause for dissatisfaction are requested to inform the committee thereof.

---

[176]Min. Chester Mo. Mtg., 9/IV/1878.   [177]*Ibid.*, 14/V/1878.

3. Parents and guardians are requested to encourage those under their care to use the plain Scripture language in addressing one another, also to dress them in a simple manner becoming our Christian profession.

4. The teacher shall not leave the school without giving the committee three months notice of his intention in writing; nor shall the committee dismiss any teacher without giving him a like notice except for non-compliance with the rules of the school or manifest deficiency in the duties of his station.

5. The scholars shall assemble punctually at the hour appointed and before entering upon the duties of the day, after suitable pause the teacher shall read a portion of the Holy Scripture.

6. It is expected that the teacher will bring with him to our weekday meeting as many of the scholars as may be practicable.[178]

The following brief report on the first year's activities was made in 1879.

The committee appointed to the care of the school under the direction of this meeting report that it was opened on the 1st 2nd day of the 9th month last and continued to the 13th of last month, a term of 40 weeks.

It was taught by male and female teachers in membership and has been visited frequently by sub-committees appointed monthly for the purpose.

There were at one time 73 children in attendance and the average of the year was 58, whose literary progress was satisfactory . . .[179]

In 1882 this school was under the leadership of a graduate of Haverford College. The attendance was considerably larger, a total of 102 being enrolled. This made it necessary to employ three persons throughout the year, and a part of the time, four. At this date, the report mentions also an "introductory department."[180] Three years later we read the school had been regularly visited, inspection made of books, health, time of recitations, and time spent in attendance. A "light room (had) been prepared in the basement for a play room in bad weather, and provision made for evening lectures, and lantern slide lectures." On this subject the report said:

. . . Several instructive lectures on scientific subjects were delivered in the school building during the past year by interesting Friends, to which, not only the scholars, but their parents and others were invited; these were illustrated by views thrown on a screen and were valuable aids to the instruction imparted by the teachers. The philosophical and other apparatus belonging to the school has also been freely used in illustrating the studies . . .[181]

In 1890,

---

[178]*Ibid.*, 13/VIII/1878.   [179]*Ibid.*, 15/VIII/1879.   [180]*Ibid.*, 4/VII/1882.
[181]*Ibid.*, 7/VII/1885.

. . . arrrangements were made for the children to be supplied at the midday recess during part of the year, with a warm lunch, mostly soups, at a moderate cost to them. This was served in the basement of the school building and it is thought to have added to the comfort and health of those who partook of it. The cost of supplying tables and dishes was paid by interested friends of the school. . . .[182]

About the same time a graded school was established, concerning the success of which, and the difficulties involved, a report was made in 1894:

Some years since the Monthly Meeting reached the conclusion that something more than an elementary school was needed at Moorestown and accordingly a graded school was established. The various committees appointed from year to year have striven with varied success to carry the Monthly Meeting's concern to a satisfactory issue. To maintain a successful graded school requires the services of 5 to 7 teachers; and to enable a school with a corps of this size to be financially successful calls for an attendance of about 100 pupils; it is hoped that nearly this number of children will be secured to the school the ensuing year. The need of a good graded school for our members has steadily increased because of the growing number of families of young children within our limits, until now we have approaching 70 children of all ages not yet in attendance at Westtown.[183]

Chester Monthly Meeting of Orthodox Friends offers a contrast, in general, to the history of others during the last half of the nineteenth century. The number of children "of age for school" increased rather than diminished after 1850; likewise the proportion attending their own schools increased. In 1851 about 25% of Friends' children attended schools of the meeting; in 1895 about 50% attended such schools. The increase was due, among other things, to the fact that the school's trustees responded to the need for a better school by concentrating the resources of three smaller ones, and thus were enabled to compete successfully with other institutions. After establishing the Monthly Meeting School in 1878 the total enrollment was increased as also the number of their own members who attended. The following table gives the essential facts concerning the distribution of children during this period.

---

[182]*Ibid.*, 8/VII/1890.
[183]*Ibid.*, 3/VII/1894.

TABLE

Schools	*Distribution of Children*									
	1851	*1855*	*1860*	*1865*	*1870*	*1875*	*1880*	*1885*	*1890*	*1895*
Of school age	29	33	49	45	35	42	38	52	43	45
At Westtown	4	2	6	11	7	6	7	21	16	11
Private School not taught by Friends	1	1								3
District School	1	1				5	1	2		
Boarding School of a Friend	1		6	6	6	1	1			
Prep. Mtg. Schools	7	16	10	12	12	21	22[184]	27	23	23
Taught at home	12	2	9	6		3		1		1
Not at school	3									
Family Schools		11		5	3					
Select School Phila.			1		1	3	1	1	2	4
Schools not under care of Friends[185]			17	5	4	2	5		2	
Haverford					2	1				
Univ. of Pa.							1			
Not accounted for										3

In recent years a further step in cooperation has been taken by the union of the "Moorestown Academy" and the "Friends High School." The success of this experiment, during the limited time of its trial, has justified the hopes of its advocates and proven a credit to the liberal mindedness which made the union possible.

We turn now from the schools established in Chester to that within in the bounds of Westfield Preparative Meeting. This meeting was held from time to time under Evesham Monthly Meeting until 1801 when a meeting house being erected, liberty to hold a preparative meeting there was granted.[186] The school under control of Friends at Westfield, however, began at an earlier date. In 1790 the Monthly Meeting at Evesham received the report of its committee on the settlement of schools with permanent funds, and copies of the proposals were sent to each Preparative Meeting.[187]

---

[184]After 1878 the resources of the two old Prep. Mtg. Schools were united to establish the "Moorestown Academy" which was a Monthly Meeting School.
[185]Some of these were probably at District schools.
[186]Min. Evesham Mo. Mtg. [187]*Ibid.*, 1790.

In the following year, Chester Preparative, to which those settled at Westfield belonged, noted the existence of three schools, two at Moorestown, and one other "the school taught by Abraham Warrington."[188]   This was the "lower school" of Chester, as it is subsequently referred to.   In 1801, when the Preparative Meeting at Westfield was established, we find: "The Lower School, being in the compass of Westfield Preparative Meeting, in future it will come under that Meeting's care."[189]   Accordingly a month later the school and school house at Westfield, formerly called Lower Chester, was placed under the following committee named by the new meeting: Abraham Warrington, William Evans, Henry Warrington, William Burrough, and Joseph Stokes.   Joseph Matlack was appointed treasurer, to receive all donations made by will or otherwise to the school.[190]

In 1818 Benjamin Hallowell, being 19 years of age, became master of the Westfield school, which he states was in charge of a committee of men and women Friends.   At that time the school was large, sometimes running as high as eighty scholars.   When large, an assistant was employed by the master seemingly at his own charge.   In Hallowell's case the debt was paid by giving his assistant, Charles Lippincott, instruction in surveying.[191]

The division of the Society in 1827 caused a duplication of educational efforts which resulted in great dissipation of energy. The control of the original school "fund of about 600 dollars, school house, lot, class books and maps" were taken over by the Hicksite Friends, but a new school was "taught at a private dwelling about two months and visited by most of their number (trustees); average number of scholars about 22.   Their deportment and literary improvement satisfactory."[192]

A month later a committee of three was named to have charge of erecting a new school house, and in November they reported the school house completed and proposed to hold meetings in it also.[193]   The school was kept regularly, but the number attending was generally small, and the length of term variable.   The following reports were produced in 1833, 1836, and 1840.

. . . it appears there has been a school kept about eight months the past

---

[188]Min. Chester Prep. Mtg., 2/VIII/1791.   [189]*Ibid.*, 4/VIII/1801.
[190]From a *Ms.* in hands of Mrs. H. C. Parrish, Riverton, N. J., which was kindly loaned to the writer.
[191]Hallowell: *Autobiography*, 41f.   [192]Min. Westfield Prep. Mtg., 5/II/1829.
[193]*Ibid.*, 5/XI/1829.

year. The order and improvement of the scholars have been to general satisfaction. And they are continued to give further attention thereto the ensuing year, with Edward Taylor added to their number.[194]

We the trustees of Westfield School agree to report that school has been taught about three months the past year and observe the order and literary improvements of the scholars to good satisfaction, their number averag (ing) 34.[195]

The trustees of Westfield School agree to report that there has been one taught 8 mos. of the past year, by male and female teachers in membership. We think the order and literary improvement of the children has been satis- actory.[196]

In 1850 the school was kept for about nine months, and in 1857, "about 7 months." The number in average attendance at the last date was about 26.[197] This is the last report on the school appearing in the men's minutes, but the women's minutes indicate the school continued to 1870—perhaps not continuously but at least in certain years. In 1865 it was kept for 10 months, taught by members, and visited monthly. In 1870 it was open 8 months, and taught 5 months by a member of the Society.[198] In 1878 the resources of the Orthodox schools of the Westfield and Chester preparative meetings were drawn upon to establish the "Moorestown Academy" under the direction of the monthly meeting.

From 1828 until the charges just mentioned took place, education in Friends' institutions at Moorestown was cared for by the two meetings separately. The development of schools of Orthodox Friends has already been traced.

Two years before the separation three schools had been reported, and, thereafter, there were three, and sometimes four under the care of the Hicksite Meeting. A report on the "Chester Brick School" was recorded in 1828 and one on the "Moorestown School" in 1829:

The Trustees of the brick school produced a written report which was satisfactory to the meeting . . . that a school has been taught about three months by a female teacher and four months by a male teacher in member- ship with us since our appointment and visited monthly and generally by the greater part of our number. The order and literary advancement of the scholars mostly satisfactory, average number of scholars about 30.[199]

---

[194]*Ibid.*, 7/II/1833.   [195]*Ibid.*, 4/II/1836.
[196]*Ibid.*, 6/II/1840.   [197]*Ibid.*, 8/I/1857.
[198]Min. Westfield Prep. Mtg., Women Friends, 9/II/1865 and 10/II/1870.
[199]Min. Chester Prep. Mtg., 24/I/1828.

The trustees of Moorestown school . . . report . . . a school has been kept up the past year and taught by a member of the Orthodox party and visited monthly by the greater part of our members, the order and literary improvement of the scholars in a good degree satisfactory, the average number about 40.[200]

In 1834 a committee of five men and five women was appointed by the other branch of Friends to have charge of "Moorestown School."[201] As a general rule a new committee was appointed each year throughout this period. From this book a number of interesting facts about the school may be gleaned. From the repeated items paid for washing, scrubbing, whitewashing, brooms, brushes, and buckets, it appears that considerable thought was taken for school sanitation. The poor were generally schooled under the regular teacher at the expense of the trustees. As for the contract between teacher and trustees it varied. Generally, it seems, the latter guaranteed a certain number of scholars. Thus in 1840 Silas Walton was paid 12.44½ by the trustees on account of the deficient number of scholars. The treasurer made a financial report each year.

A typical report on the three schools under the control of the meetings was made in 1835 as follows:

By reports from the Preparative Meeting it appears that the three schools under our care have been kept up the greater part of the past year, taught by teachers in membership with friends, and visited monthly (except 1 mo. at Westfield) by trustees appointed in the Preparative Meeting, the order and improvement observed generally satisfactory.[202]

Similar reports of the three schools were made each year until 1857. In that year four schools were reported, two at Moorestown and two at Westfield Preparative Meeting, "kept open the greater part of the year, visited monthly and taught by members."[203] In 1860 these four schools had an average attendance of 151 scholars. The teachers in two of them in that year were members of Friends, while in the other two members taught but a part of the year. Ten years later the following report was made:

By the reports from the Preparative Meeting it appears there are four schools under their care, Chester reports two, one of which has been open two months,

---

[200]*Ibid.*, 22/I/1829.
[201]Moorestown School Book, 1834-1854, p. 1; this book is in possession of Mrs. H. Herr, 601 East Main Street, Moorestown, N. J.
[202]Min. Chester Mo. Mtg., (H.), 5/II/1835.   [203]*Ibid.*, 5/III/1857.

taught by a member, number in attendance about 30 and that the house is leased for the winter for a district school; the other has been kept open 8 months, taught by members, except three months, whole number of scholars 61, of whom nine are members and 2 where 1 parent is a member. And Westfield 2, one of which has been kept about five months, average number of scholars 65, the other during the year, average number of scholars 18, number of Friends' children 6, number of which one parent is a member one, and that they have been visited monthly by some of the committee, the winter session taught by male teachers in membership with us, the summer session by a female not a member.[204]

The school reported above as being "leased for the winter for a district school" was reported on more fully in 1871.

The committee appointed to have the care of Chester Brick School . . . report the school is organized under the state school law, but has been visited by a part of the committee several times during the year. It has been taught four months by William Paul and five months by Elizabeth M. Roberts, members of Friends. The improvement of the scholars has been mostly satisfactory. The average number 23. Forty have attended during the year, eight of whom had both parents members and two but one parent a member. . . [205]

Thus the transition was made easily from the Meeting to State control. The report of 1872 shows that the school had been visited by Friends' School Committee but that said Committee was then discontinued:

The committee having the care of Chester Brick School report that it has been organized under the State School Law and is under the care of trustees appointed by the district which trustees are Friends and have visited the school a number of times. The school has been kept open nine months during the year and taught by members. The order and improvement of the scholars satisfactory, average attendance 25 of whom 8 are members. The school having gone from under the care of the meeting, the committee are discontinued.[206]

After the report of 1870, quoted above, only two schools were reported conducted by the meetings at Chester and Westfield. But though the number was decreased the strength of the two remaining increased markedly during the latter part of the century. In 1872 the following report on Westfield was made:

Westfield Preparative Meeting reports having had one school under its care the past year, held in two sessions of 4½ months each, the winter session was taught by a male and the summer by a female; both members; average

[204]*Ibid.*, 9/II/1870.
[205]Min. Chester Prep. Mtg., 26/I/1871.   [206]*Ibid.*, 25/I/1872.

number in attendance in winter 19, in summer 8, number of Friends children 5, number of which one parent is a member 5. The school was visited monthly (with one exception) by some of the trustees.

The order and improvement of the scholars generally satisfactory. They with their teachers attended midweek meetings. The winter term was partly free to the patrons, the summer entirely so.[207]

In 1881 there were 121 scholars attending both schools; whole number of teachers employed, five. In 1882 there were 137 attending; and six teachers. Further increase is to be noted in the reports of 1890:

Westfield Preparative Meeting reports that the school has been kept open 10 months of the past year, taught by two female teachers, both in membership with Friends. It has been visited monthly by some of the committee; the order and improvement of the school is satisfactory. The teachers and pupils attend mid-week meetings. Whole number of pupils, 33, average attendance 26.[208]

The school at Moorestown had, by this time, been expanded, and had kindergarten and "High School" departments.[209]

Chester Preparative Meeting made the following report. The school under its care has been kept open 9½ months of the past year. The fall term commenced on the 2nd of ninth month, with 6 teachers in the High School and 3 in the Kindergarten, 4 of these teachers are members, with Friends. The children of the High School attend midweek meetings with their teachers. when the weather is favorable.

Whole number of scholars enrolled in the high school	117
Average attendance	91
Whole number enrolled in Kindergarten	33
Average attendance, about	28[210]

We have now completed a survey of the schools established under the care of monthly and preparative meetings of Haddonfield. The chart (Number I) below shows the number of schools under the care of that quarterly meeting of Hicksite Friends from the time of separation. Though the number of schools declined, they were larger in point of numbers and number of teachers employed. Thus in three schools in 1900 fourteen teachers were engaged, caring for an enrollment of 186. In the five schools of 1865, five teachers were employed. Chart II shows the number of schools

---

[207]Min. Chester Mo. Mtg., 8/II/1872.   [208]*Ibid.*, 6/II/1890.

[209]The High School classes were added in 1880, and a new building was provided for their accommodation. This Friends' High School was united in 1920 with Moorestown Friends' Academy.

[210]*Ibid.*, 6/III/1890.

according to standards, reported in the Orthodox Friends Quarterly Meeting. In the two schools reported in 1910 there were sixteen teachers employed.[211]

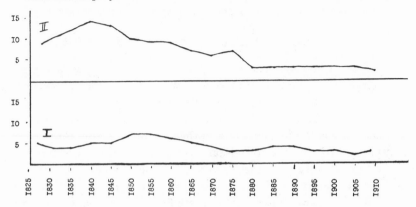

THE SCHOOLS OF HADDONFIELD QUARTERLY MEETING

---

[211]The lines are drawn according to reports in the quarterly meeting minutes for the years mentioned.

CHAPTER VII

CARE AND EDUCATION OF THE POOR

The seventeenth and eighteenth centuries witnessed many attempts to alleviate the suffering of the poor by philanthropic projects; and most prominent in the minds of philanthropists was the belief that the "laborious poor" should be given an education such as would lift them up from their degraded status. By many philanthropists the provision of education was considered a Christian duty to the less favored of society. The outcome was the establishment of institution's and systems of schools, both by individuals and united action, the influence of which was felt not only in European countries but in the American colonies as well. Thus they became a factor in our educational development.

Most prominent among the movements referred to were these: the creation of an organization in England known as the S. P. C. K.[1] in 1698, which within ten years had established almost ninety schools in and near London, attended by 3,402 children;[2] the Society for the Propagation of the Gospel in Foreign Parts, a branch of the S. P. C. K., created in 1701, which operated in the Colonies until 1783;[3] the Sunday School Movement which was widely extended by Robert Raikes after 1780, and introduced into the United States in 1786; the Lancasterian system of schools, begun in 1798 by Joseph Lancaster in Southwark, London, which was soon brought to America and applied not only to elementary but also to secondary institutions; and the *Franckesche Stiftungen*, which developed as a result of the labors of Francke at Halle in 1695, combining decidedly realistic, pietistic and philanthropic tendencies. Many other schools might be mentioned which contributed to the advance of the philanthropic movement, as:

---

[1] Society for the Promotion of Christian Knowledge.
[2] Allen, W. O. B., and McClure, E., *Hist. of S. P. C. K.*
[3] Kemp. W. S., *Support of Schools in Colonial N. Y., by the S. P. G.*

"Ragged Schools," "Circulating Schools," and "Infant Schools" both in France and Great Britain.[4]

It is not to be assumed, however, that the enthusiasm for education of the poor was universal. The views of the opponents of charity education for the poor are in part set forth in Mandeville's *Essay on Charity Schools*, in which he says:

. . .it is manifest that in a free nation, where slaves are not allowed of, the surest wealth consists in a multitude of laborious poor; for besides that they are the never-failing nursery of fleets and armies without them there could be no enjoyment, and no product of any country could be valuable. To make the Society happy, and people easy under the meanest circumstances, it is requisite that great numbers of them should be ignorant, as well as poor. Knowledge both enlarges and multiplies our desires, and the fewer things a man wishes for, the more easily his necessities may be supplied.

The welfare and felicity, therefore, of every state and kingdom require that the knowledge of the working poor should be confined within the verge of their occupations and never extended (as to things visible) beyond their own calling. The more a shepherd, a ploughman, or any other peasant knows of the world, and the things that are foreign to his work or employment, the less fit will he be to go through the fatigues and hardships of it with cheerfulness and content.[5]

In the establishment of schools the agencies mentioned above were actuated, in general, by a desire to (1) relieve the poverty-stricken condition of the masses by promoting schools, a function not then recognized as necessary by governments, (2) improve standards of conduct by a diffusion of moral and religious instruction, and (3) in some cases to actually provide food, clothing and shelter. The constitution of one Ragged School Association stated:

It is the object of this association to reclaim the neglected and destitute children of Edinburgh, by offering them the benefits of a good common and Christian education, and by training them to habits of regular industry, so as to enable them to earn an honest livelihood, and fit them for the duties of life.[6]

But the end of a religious, moral, and practical education was not always pursued on liberal lines as might be assumed under the three heads above named. It was an age filled with sectarian

---

[4]For general accounts, see Cubberley: *Hist. of Education*, 449 ff., and 614ff.; Graves: *Hist. of Education*, II, Ch. 19 and III, Ch. 3; Monroe: *Textbook in the Hist. of Education*, 722 ff.

[5]Mandeville: *Essay on Charity and Charity Schools*, 179.

[6]Quoted in Cubberley: *Readings*, 516 from Guthrie, Thomas, *Seedtime and Harvest of Ragged Schools*, Appendix II.

bitterness as well as the sentiments of liberal philanthropy. Thus, the success of the Lancasterian schools acted as a stimulus in causing the creation of the "National Society for Promoting the Education of the Poor in the Principles of the Established Church" in 1811. In the schools of this society the primary purpose was religious instruction with a sectarian bias, as is indicated in the following:

> To the end the chief design of this school, which is for the education of Poor children in the Rules and Principles of the Christian Religion as professed and taught in the Church of England, may be the better promoted; the master shall make it his chief business to instruct the children in the principles thereof, as they are laid down in the Church Catechism; which he shall first teach them to pronounce distinctly and plainly; and then, in order to practice, shall explain it to the meanest capacity, by the help of *The Whole Duty of Man*, or some good exposition approved of by the Minister.[7]

This prevalent conception of education, (whether for poor or rich), that it must be guarded against the heresies of other denominations, was also accepted in Quaker schools, and a "guarded religious education of our members" repeatedly urged; likewise efforts were made to secure only members for teachers, but these met with frequent failure.[8]

From the foregoing statement, concerning the prevalence of philanthropic projects for education, and that which follows, it will be evident that a care for the support and education of the poor, on the part of Friends, was part of a wide-spread movement, found among dissenters and orthodox churchmen alike. But of the two it would seem that the closer alliance was between Puritanism, Pietism, and Philanthropy. The sentiments of the dissenting bodies, though differing in many points, were in agreement in this, that religion must be stripped of formality and hark back to the essence of "pure religion" as defined by James:

> Pure religion and undefiled before God and the Father is this, to visit the fatherless and widows in their affliction and to keep himself unspotted from the world.[9]

Likewise the statement to the righteous indicated that the essence of true religion lay in service:

---

[7] Quoted in Cubberley, *Readings*, 380.
[8] Chapter on Organization and Control of Education.
[9] James, I, 27.

I was a stranger and ye took me in; naked and ye clothed me; sick and in prison and ye visited me. . .[10]

Philanthropy in education raised substantial monuments to this interpretation of religion.

From this point let us turn to an examination of the attitude of Friends as individuals towards education of the poor; the official viewpoint of the meetings established; and the actual attempts of local meetings to incorporate in their activities, provision for such care and education.

INDIVIDUAL VIEWS ON THE CARE AND EDUCATION OF THE POOR

Ideas of philanthropy in education appear among Quakers throughout the latter half of the 17th century and occupied an important place in their writings during the 18th and 19th. Social service is probably their most prominent characteristic at the present day. The idea of social service through a system of education was advocated by John Bellers in his *Proposals for Raising a College of Industry*, which was to prove of "Profit for the Rich, a plentiful living for the poor, a good education for youth" and an "advantage to the government by the increase of the people and their riches." The plan for this communistic college was published in 1696.[11] Likewise Thomas Budd, a citizen of New Jersey, in 1685 presented proposals in *Good order established in Pennsylvania and New Jersey*, whereby prosperity and a contented society were to be secured by the establishment of a system of industrial and literary education for all its members. The philanthropic social purpose was also dominant in the mind of Lancaster, whose cheap system for educating the poor made public men credulous concerning the possibilities of education for the masses.

---

[10]Matthew, XXV, 35-36.
[11]A letter of the 27/VII/1718 to the Quarterly Meeting of London contained a point of view common to the earlier *Proposals for Raising a College of Industry*. In the epistle to the Quarterly Meeting, he wrote: "So it is also recommended by that great Apostle James, when he wrote, that pure religion and undefiled before God and the Father, is to visit (or relieve) the Fatherless and the widows in their afflictions, and to keep unspotted from the world.

"Therefore a virtuous education that may keep the YOUTH unspotted from the World, and a sufficient provision for the Imployment of the able POOR with a charitable subsistence for the Disabled, is one of the most Essential visible Parts of the true Apostolick Christian Religion.

Another influential spokesman on behalf of the poor was John Woolman, who, on several occasions, conducted a school at Mt. Holly, New Jersey. In *A Plea for the Poor* he stood not only for the extension of charitable assistance by the rich to the poor, but argued against the injustice of the economic system which produced them:

The word *right*, is commonly used relative to our possessions. We say, a *right* of propriety to such a dividend of a province; or a clear indisputable right to the land within such certain bounds. Thus, this word is continued as a remembrancer of the original intent of dividing the land by boundaries, and implies, that it was designed to be equitably or rightly divided,—to be divided according to righteousness. In this, that is, in equity and righteousness, consists the strength of our claims. If we trace an unrighteous claim, and find gifts or grants proved by sufficient seals and witnesses; this gives not the claimant a *right;* for that which is opposite to righteousness, is wrong, and the nature of it must be changed before it can be *right*.

Suppose twenty free men, professed followers of Christ, discovered an island unknown to all other people, and that they with their wives, independent of all others, took possession of it; and, dividing it equally, made improvements, and multiplied. Suppose these first possessors, being generally influenced by true love, did, with paternal regard look over the increasing condition of the inhabitants, and near the end of their lives, gave such directions concerning their respective possessions, as best suited the convenience of the whole, and tended to preserve love and harmony; and that their successors in the continued increase of people, generally followed their pious examples, and pursued means the most effectual to keep oppression out of their island:— but that one of these first settlers, from a fond attachment to one of his numerous sons, no more deserving than the rest, gives the chief of his lands to him; and by an instrument sufficiently witnessed, strongly expresses his mind and will.

Suppose this son, being landlord to his brethren and nephews, demands such a portion of the fruits of the earth, as may supply him and his family and some others; and that these others, thus supplied out of his store, are employed in adorning his building with curious engravings and paintings, preparing carriages to ride in, vessels for his house, delicious meats, fine-wrought apparel and furniture, all suiting that distinction lately arisen between him and the other inhabitants: and that, having the absolute disposal of these numerous improvements, his power so increaseth, that in all conferences relative to the public affairs of the island, these plain, honest men who are zealous for equitable establishments, find great difficulty in proceeding agreeably to their righteous inclinations, while he stands in opposition to them.

Suppose he, from a fondness for one of his sons, joined with a desire to continue this grandeur under his own name, confirms chief of his possessions to him; and thus, for many ages, over near a twentieth part of this island, there is one great landlord, and the rest, poor oppressed people; to some of whom, from the manner of their education, joined with a notion of the greatness of their predecessors, labour is disagreeable; who therefore, by artful applications to the weakness, unguardedness, and corruptions of others, in striving to get a living out of them, increase the difficulties amongst them; while the inhabitants of other parts, who guard against oppression, and, with one consent, train up their children in frugality and useful labour, live more harmoniously.

If we trace the claim of the ninth or tenth of these great landlords, down to the first possessor, and find the claim supported throughout by instruments strongly drawn and witnessed; after all, we could not admit a belief into our hearts, that he had a *right* to so great a portion of land, after such a numerous increase of inhabitants.

The first possessor of that twentieth part, held no more, we suppose, than an equitable portion; but when the Lord, who first gave these twenty men possession of this island, unknown to all others, gave being to numerous people, who inhabited this twentieth part, whose natures required the fruits thereof for their sustenance,—this great claimer of the soil could not have a *right* to the whole, to dispose of it in gratifying his irregular desires: but they, as creatures of the Most High God, possessor of heaven and earth, had a *right* to part of what this great claimer held though they had no instruments to confirm their *right*.

Thus, oppression in the extreme, appears terrible: but oppression, in more refined appearances, remains to be oppression; and where the smallest degree of it is cherished, it grows stronger and more extensive: that to labour for a perfect redemption from this spirit of oppression, is the great business of the whole family of Christ Jesus, in this world.[12]

Elsewhere, he says:

"To educate children in the way of true piety and virtue, is a duty incumbent on all who have them;" and in another passage, "all we possess are the gifts of God to us; now in distributing it to others, we act as his stewards; and it becomes our station, to act agreeably to that Divine Wisdom which he graciously gives to his servants."[13]

The renunciation of wealth and fastidious tastes would release much for a better support of education:

Were we thoroughly weaned from the love of wealth, and fully brought out of all superfluities in living;—employments about vanities being finished, and labour wanted only for things consistent with a humble, self-denying life, there would, on a reasonable estimate, be so much to spare on the education of our children,—that a plain, humble man, with a family like himself, might be furnished with a living, for teaching and overseeing so small a number of

---

[12]Woolman's *Works*, 348–351. [13]*Ibid.*, 353 and 335.

children, that he might properly and seasonably administer to each individual, and gently lead them on, as the gospel spirit opened the way, without giving countenance to pride or evil inclinations among them.[14]

Thomas Budd, a resident of the Colony of New Jersey, interested in its welfare and progress, had also a word to say regarding education of the poor in his *Good Order established in Pennsylvania and New Jersey*, published at Philadelphia in 1685.

And to the end that the children of the poor people, and the children of Indians may have the like good learning with the children of the rich people, let them be maintained free of charge to their parents, out of the profits of the school, arising by the work of the scholars, by which the poor and the Indians as well as the rich, will have their children taught, and the remainder of the profits, if any be to be disposed of in the building of the schoolhouses and improvements on the thousand acres of land, which belongs to the school.

George Fox, whose suggestions were most highly regarded in the Society, writes that "it came upon me to write to Friends throughout the nation about putting out poor children to trades."[15] This idea was considerably elaborated in a plan whereby the quarterly meetings should oversee the apprenticing of their poor; moreover it was consistently followed in practice. The purpose of such apprenticeship Fox stated in these words:

This will be the way for the preserving of many that are poor among you, and it will be the way of making up poor families.

One of the most thorough-going philanthropists was Anthony Benezet, whose writings on the subject by no means measure up to his actual service in the education of the poor, both white and black. In a letter to Samuel Fothergill, 1758, he observes:[16]

There are others whom God has so blessed with substance, that they have nothing to do but to spend the income of it; yea, time hangs heavily on their hands, and proves even a snare to themselves and others. And there are some who, though they have already a large affluence of wealth, yet are toiling hard to add thereto, without knowing wherefore they thus toil, and whether a wise man or a fool shall possess it after them. Many persons in these different situations are doubtless, in the main, honest souls, who, though they find no call to the ministry, yet think themselves willing, with one of old, to follow Christ wheresoever he goes. Why, then, do they stand so long idle, when so large a field lies before them? What account will many of these be able to give of their time, when every word, and consequently, every inch of time, must expect to be called into judgment? What more beneficial employ, and more fruitful of comfort and joy in the end, than time spent in an honest

---

[14]*Ibid.*, 352.   [15]Friends Library, I, 129.   [16]*Ibid.*, IX, 220–2.

labour for the proper educating these innocent souls, which the Almighty has clothed with flesh and blood, and by Divine help, to be so enabled to watch over them, as to frustrate the wiles and devices of the grand adversary, that these youth might truly answer the end of their creation?

Continuing, he suggests the propriety of Friends giving their wealth, "taking more especial care to make the poor and helpless the first objects of such a care."

If a number of such Friends, in their different allotments, would, as it were, shake hands with the world and all its enticing prospects, seeking and expecting nothing from it but bread and trouble, and would freely dedicate themselves to the care of the youth, not limiting themselves to the narrow views of fleshly ties, nor even to religious denominations, but looking upon themselves as fathers and brothers of all that want their help, taking more especial care to make the poor and helpless the first objects of such a care, not solely of necessity, but of a willing mind, what a blessing might they be, not only to our youth in particular, but also to mankind in general. And indeed it seems to me that our principles, which, in the present corrupt state of the world, seem to prohibit our meddling with offices, etc., naturally point out to us as a people, rather than others, to serve God and our country in the education of the youth. I will acknowledge that it is a situation which does not appear so desirable as some others, nor so likely to procure riches, ease, or worldly honour. But alas! alas! what have we to do with these things? Shall we desire to be great and rich, when our Saviour has so plainly declared it a situation so very dangerous; and that his predominant choice is of the poor of this world? Is it now a time, or was it ever a time for the believer, who eyes and relies upon the promise—is it a time for such to seek for money, or olive yards, or oxen, etc.? And although by engaging in the education of the youth we should be deprived of some of those things so desirable to nature, which we might better enjoy and accumulate in the way of trade, and thereby look upon ourselves under affliction, yet may we not hope that it will be termed for righteousness' sake, and therefore should not we have thereat to rejoice and be exceeding glad, and even leap for joy?

Penn's views on this subject are stated briefly in his *Reflections and Maxims*.

It is a reproach to religion and government to suffer so much poverty and excess.

Were the superfluities of a nation valued, and made a perpetual tax or benevolence, there would be more almshouses than poor, schools than scholars, and enough to spare for government besides.

More recent expression on the subject of education for the poor is set forth in Dymond's *Essays on the Principles of Morality*, first published about 1828. In his reference to their education it is made clear that his thought had gone far in advance of current practice; that he looked forward to a time when there would be equal educational advantages for the poor.[17]

It is in this country, at least, left to the voluntary benevolence of individuals, and this consideration may apologize for a brief reference to it here.

It is not long since it was a question whether the poor should be educated or not. That time is past, and it may be hoped the time will soon be passed when it shall be a question, To what extent?—that the time will soon arrive when it will be agreed that no limit needs to be assigned to the education of the poor, but that which is assigned by their own necessities, or which ought to be assigned to the education of all men. There appears no more reason for excluding a poor man from the field of knowledge, than for preventing him from using his eyes. The mental and the visual powers were alike given to be employed. A man should, indeed, shut his eyes from seeing evil, but whatever reason there is for letting him see all that is beautiful, and excellent, and innocent in nature and in art, there is the same for enabling his mind to expatiate in the fields of knowledge.

The objections which are urged against this extended education, are of the same kind as those which were urged against any education. They insist upon the probability of abuse. It *was* said, They who can write may forge; they who can read may read what is pernicious. The answer was, or it might have been—They who can hear, may hear profaneness and learn it; they who can see, may see bad examples and follow them:—but are we therefore to stop our ears and put out our eyes?—It is *now* said, that if you give extended education to the poor, you will elevate them above their stations; that a critic would not drive a wheelbarrow, and that a philosopher would not shoe horses, or weave cloth. But these consequences are without the limits of possibility; because the question for a poor man is, whether he shall perform such offices or starve: and surely it will not be pretended that hungry men would rather criticise than eat. Science and literature would not solicit a poor man from his labor more irresistibly than ease and pleasure do now; yet in spite of these solicitations what is the fact? That the poor man works for his bread. This is the inevitable result.

In another passage he urges the extension of education on the rational grounds of social necessity—the avoidance of radical change by the creation of an enlightened public opinion.[18]

There are some collateral advantages of an extended education of the people, which are of much importance. It has been observed that if the French had been an educated people, many of the atrocities of their Revolution would never have happened, and I believe it. Furious mobs are composed, not of enlightened but of unenlightened men—of men in whom the passions are dominant over the judgment, because the judgment had not been exercised,

---

[17]Dymond: *Essays*, 277–8.   [18]*Ibid.*, 279–80.

and informed, and habituated to direct the conduct. A factious declaimer can much less easily influence a number of men who acquired at school the rudiments of knowledge, and who have subsequently devoted their leisure to a Mechanics' Institute, than a multitude who cannot write or read, and who have never practised reasoning and considerate thought. And as the education of a people prevents political evil, it effects political good. Despotic rulers well know that knowledge is inimical to their power. This simple fact is a sufficient reason, to a good and wise man, to approve knowledge and extend it. The attention to public institutions and public measures which is inseparable from an educated population, is a great good. We all know that the human heart is such, that the possession of power is commonly attended with a desire to increase it, even in opposition to the general weal. It is acknowledged that a check is needed, and no check is either so efficient or so safe as that of a watchful and intelligent public mind; so watchful, that it is prompt to discover and to expose what is amiss; so intelligent, that it is able to form rational judgments respecting the nature and the means of amendment. In all public institutions there exists, and it is happy that there does exist, a sort of *vis inertiae* which habitually resists change. This, which is beneficial as a general tendency, is often injurious from its excess; the state of public institutions almost throughout the world, bears sufficient testimony to the truth, that they need alteration and amendment faster than they receive it— that the internal resistance of change is greater than is good for man. Unhappily, the ordinary way in which a people have endeavored to amend their institutions, has been by some mode of violence. If you ask when a nation acquired a greater degree of freedom, you are referred to some era of revolution and probably of blood. These are not proper, certainly they are not Christian, remedies for the disease. It is becoming an undisputed proposition, that no bad institution can permanently stand against the distinct opinion of a people. This opinion is likely to be universal, and to be intelligent only amongst an enlightened community. Now that reformation of public institutions which results from public opinion, is the very best in kind, and is likely to be the best in its mode:—in its kind, because public opinion is the *proper measure* of the needed alteration; and in its mode, because alterations which result from such a cause, are likely to be temperately made.

OFFICIAL ACTION BY MEETINGS

The sentiments of individual members regarding philanthropy were early crystallized in letters and minutes of the Yearly Meetings at London, and at Burlington and Philadelphia. These yearly epistles doubtless served a valuable purpose in keeping all meetings, of high and low degree, awake to the important need, throughout the eighteenth and nineteenth centuries.

In 1695, while referring to education generally, and the need for qualified schools and schoolmasters, the epistle states specifically "that care be taken, that poor Friends' children may freely partake of such education, in order to apprenticeship."[19]

Especially is attention to the poor urged upon those who are possessed of material wealth.

It is further desired that such among Friends as are endowed with plenty of outward substance, be timely and tenderly advised to do good therewith in their day; that the tokens of your charity may commend your memorial, and be good precedents to generations to come.[20]

More specifically the monthly and quarterly meetings were advised in 1709:

And, where Friends want ability in the world their Monthly and Quarterly Meetings are desired to assist them; that the children of the poor may have due help of education, instruction, and necessary learning; and that children (both of rich and poor) may be early provided with industrious employments, that they may not grow up in idleness, looseness, and vice. . . [21]

The "advices" of London increased in number and urgency as the problem of caring for poor became greater, at the close of the eighteenth and beginning of the nineteenth century. A similar tendency may also be seen in the advices of the Burlington and Philadelphia Meeting. The result was the establishment of many more schools and upon a more permanent basis, as is shown more clearly in the following pages of this chapter.

In 1721 that meeting stated:

It is the advice of this meeting, that all poor friends among us may be taken due care of and that none of them be sent elsewhere for relief, according to Friends' ancient care and practice.[22]

Among the queries listed in 1743 there was one relating to the poor and their education, which follows:

Are the poor taken care of and are their children put to school and apprenticed out, after sufficiently learned, to friends; and do Friends put their own children out to Friends as much as may be?[23]

The statement of the above query was changed a little from time to time, but its purport remained the same. The form of that in 1755 was pretty closely adhered to:

Are poor Friends' necessities duly inspected, they relieved or assisted in such business as they are capable of. Do their children freely partake of

---

[19]*Epistles from Yearly Meeting in London*, 90.
[20]*Ibid.*, 93.   [21]*Ibid.*, 134.
[22]*Christian and Brotherly Advices (Ms.)*, 206.   [23]*Ibid.*

learning to fit them for business and are they, and other Friends' children placed amongst Friends?[24]

In 1753 the Yearly Meeting entered into an investigation concerning legacies and funds given for charitable purposes. This action was in accord with proposals made as early as 1746 for the establishment of schools.

. . .on consideration of the proposals concerning the reviving and continuing the consideration of the settling of schools in the country, etc. It is unanimously agreed that the several Quarterly Meetings be desired to appoint friends from each Quarter to be a committee to inspect and examine the accounts of all monies which have been given to charitable uses and the said committees are desired to meet together at the time of our next general spring meeting and bring with them a clear and perfect account of all legacies, donations, or other estate which have been heretofore given, and of the uses to which the monies arising therefrom are applied in order that proper measures may be taken to see that the intentions of such charitable persons are complied with and fully answered.[25]

The interest in more specific plans for education, though it became marked about the middle of the century, did not immediately produce great results. Not until the period following 1778 did all meetings seriously consider the question of establishing schools under the society's control. This development in practical philanthropy as evidenced in several meetings is touched upon in the following pages.

CARE FOR THE POOR WITHIN THE MEETINGS

It has already been shown that the superior meetings gave repeated advices concerning the care and education of the poor; and, from a reading of records in the several localities of New Jersey, it is evident that efforts were made in all meetings to follow them. One of the means, adopted at an early date by the society for ascertaining local conditions, was the formal query. The query relating to the poor was stated as follows:

Are the poor taken care of and are their children put to school and apprenticed out (after sufficient learning) to Friends? And do Friends put their own children out to Friends, as much as may be?[26]

In 1755 the Yearly Meeting formulated the query as follows:

---

[24]*Ibid.*, 208.   [25]*Ibid.*, 222–23.
[26]See the records of any quarterly meeting or Michener's *Retrospect*, 256.

Are poor Friends necessities duly inspected and they relieved or assisted in such business as they are capable of? Do their children freely partake of learning to fit them for business and are they and other Friends' children placed among Friends?[27]

"The poor ye have with you always" seems to have been universally true in the early Quaker meetings. References to them and measures for their financial relief, appear in the earliest records and run throughout. Some are presented here, but not all. The history of one meeting's activities in this regard is very much like that of another.

In 1678, at Burlington,

It was agreed that a collection be made once a month for ye relief of ye poor and such other necessary uses as may occur; the persons appointed to receive it are John Woolstone and William Peeche to be collected the first day before ye monthly meeting.[28]

In 1738, a report was made on the division of a sum of money for the use of the poor.

The said friend Caleb Raper, also gave account there was interest money now in hand amounting to the sum of £14 which is ordered to be distributed to the several Monthly Meetings to be given to the poor as the said respective Meetings shall see occasion to wit: To Burlington £ 8/5/0, to Chesterfield, £ 4/15/0; to Eggharbor £ 1/0/0, which makes up the said sum of £ 14 which said Caleb Raper is to deliver and make report to next meeting.[29]

In 1757 they answered the fifth query as follows:

We are careful with regard to the poor among us, but not all so much so as could be desired, in placing their children among friends.[30]

Individual cases of children were settled as thought advisable. In 1762 they reported that the case of a poor widow's children

has been cared for; and her children are likely to gain sufficient learning.[31]

Again in 1767,

Application was made by a Friend of Mt. Holly Meeting for some assistance on behalf of the poor belonging to that Meeting. (6 Friends) are appointed to make enquiry in the case and direct the necessary assistance to be given and report to next meeting.[32]

Support of the poor was not only cared for by the local members, but from a central fund or "stock" to which the lower meetings contributed. Thus in 1771 Burlington Monthly directed that

---

[27]The last part of the query relates to apprenticeship which was then generally necessary: see Chapter Eight on Apprentice Education.

[28]Min. Burlington Mo. Mtg., 18/VI/1678.   [29]*Ibid.*, 4/X/1738.

[30]*Ibid.*, 1/VIII/1757.   [31]*Ibid.*, 1/XI/1762.   [32]*Ibid.*, 2/II/1767.

fifty pounds be raised for this Yearly Meeting stock. Also in
1773, the treasurer informed the meeting that the fund for the
poor was nearly spent; 50 pounds for the use of the poor was
proposed, agreed to, and Friends appointed to collect it along with
the collection for the Yearly Meeting.[33]

The exercise of this care for the poor was vested in a committee
which usually collected, and distributed the funds, where needed
in the several preparative meetings. In 1800,

> The Meeting being informed that the money for the poor was nearly ex-
> pended it was thought necessary to raise the sum of £ 50. The Preparative
> Meetings were directed to collect their proportions and forward them to the
> Treasurer, to examine whose accounts, Nathaniel Coleman, Jonathan Hilyard,
> Wm. Ridgway (of Springfield) and Joseph Brown were appointed.[34]

In 1781 Burlington Monthly Meeting mentioned they had begun to promote a fund in each preparative meeting for the purpose
of "schooling poor children" and other advancement of the concern
for schools. A few months later, a committee of the quarterly
meeting made the following report which states the *first purpose*
of the funds to be "the education of Friends' children whose
parents may not be of ability to pay both for their schooling and
for food and raiment."

> A report from the committee on schools which was omitted at last Quarter
> was now read and is as follows:
> We the committee appointed to promote the establishment of schools within
> this quarter have in the course of the year met several times and labored in
> that service; and having at this time considered the subject with deliberation
> we are united in judgment that a more solid attention to the advice and
> recommendations of the Yearly Meeting sent down in the year 1778 appears
> necessary.
> We have the satisfaction of finding that divers schools have been lately
> opened in several of our Monthly Meetings, under the care of trustees ap-
> pointed and annually to be renewed by Preparative Meetings, being regularly
> visited by them monthly; and every year the said trustees are to lay before the
> preparative meetings who appointed them, an account of their proceedings for
> their inspection, consideration and advice. We also found that in one of our
> Monthly Meetings subscriptions are set on foot for the raising of a fund,
> the principal of which is to remain untouched, and only the interest applied,
> First to the education of Friends children whose parents may not be of ability
> to pay both for their schooling, and for food and rayment; and secondly when
> an overplus is raised it is proposed to be laid out by the trustees for supplying

---

[33]*Ibid.*, 7/VI/1773. [34]*Ibid.*, 6/I/1800.

the deficiencies of the school master's salary, or reward, or to such other uses as may appear to them most conducive to the right advancement of this momentous concern. Signed by unanimous desire of the committee, met at Burlington this 25th day of the 8th month, 1781, by Samuel Allinson.[55]

The following are typical answers to the fifth query, made by Burlington Quarterly Meeting:

5th. As far as appears attention is given to the necessities of the poor— Two instances observed of Friends' children not being placed with Friends, but are under care. (1788).

5th. The necessities of the poor are inspected and relief afforded, and the tuition of their children mostly provided for—(No Friends' children are placed from among Friends) (1805).

5th. The necessities of poor friends are inspected and relief afforded, and provision is made for the school education of their children; one child is reported to have been placed out from among friends. (1825).

5th. The necessities of poor friends are inspected and relief afforded—and provision is made for their children freely to partake of learning to fit them for business, one instance is noticed of a friend's child being placed from among friends during the past year. (1830).

The necessities of poor friends are inspected and relief afforded. And care is taken that their children may freely partake of learning: One child placed from among friends since last year. (1835-Hicksite Meeting).

A more famous example of the philanthropic movement in New Jersey, and one which has lasted to the present day, was the Friendly Institution, founded at Burlington in 1796. Its purpose was

to seek out and relieve the necessities of such poor and needy persons, within this city and neighborhood, who may not come under the particular care of the Overseers of the poor, or be fully attended to by them. . .

The founders were all Friends and among them was John Griscom, later notable as an exponent of Pestalozzianism in America. Griscom was then schoolmaster in Burlington. Soon after its founding the "Institution" became non-sectarian, and was granted a charter in 1837. Though having as its purpose "to relieve the necessities of poor and needy persons," this was interpreted to include giving assistance through education. One of the first legacies, left to the Friendly Institution in 1797, was to be "applied in the tuition of poor black children;" accordingly

---

[35]Min. Burlington Q. Mtg., 26/XI/1781.

they "agreed to take charge of finding worthy objects of said charity."[36]

In 1845 it was proposed that assistance be given "to young women who may wish to qualify themselves for teachers in their neighborhoods and have not the means to do so."[37]

Chesterfield provided early for the poor. The minutes record that:

At our monthly meeting at Francis Devenport's house in Chesterfield, agreed that Andrew Smith have a coat given him, Wm. Watson to take ye care for providing cloth, buttons and thread and to be paid by this meeting.[38]

Two years later,

Samuel Andrews acquainted this meeting that he had spoken to Isaac Horner about John Horner's children whose answer was that after he had clothed ye children, which was done, he would keep ye children without charge to ye estate.[39]

In 1797, £25 was raised for the use of the poor; and, year after year, similar amounts are mentioned. In 1826 the preparatives were directed to raise $150 for the poor and pay it to the monthly meeting Treasurer. The activities of the lower meetings were under the supervision of the higher. Thus, in 1827, it came to attention that Trenton Preparative suffered from "a want of funds for the education of poor children" and a committee on the subject reported as follows:

The committee appointed to enquire into and endeavor to ascertain the cause of the deficiency of Friends of Trenton Preparative Meeting not schooling poor children as expressed in their answer to the query in the 2nd month last, having most of them met and deliberately attended to the subject, do agree to inform that we are not prepared to make a full report on the occasion on account of our not being furnished with such official information from the Preparative Meeting as we thought requisite.

Later, the deficiency was reported to be the result of negligence of that particular meeting.

We the committee appointed to attend Trenton Preparative Meeting and enquire into the cause of the deficiency of the funds of that Meeting to school poor children, as reported in their answer to the query in the second month last, do agree to report that we attended that Preparative Meeting and had a

---

[36]An interesting account may be found in *The One Hundredth Anniversary of the Friendly Institution*, published at Burlington, 1896.
[37]Min. Burlington Mo. Mtg., Women Friends, (H) 2/VI/1845.
[38]Min. Chesterfield Mo. Mtg., 1/X/1687.   [39]*Ibid.*, 6/XII/1689.

free conference with the members present on the subject, and upon deliberate consideration it is our united judgment that the deficiency mentioned has principally arisen from a want of due attention within that Meeting to the raising by subscription a sufficient stock for the purpose of a school fund in years past, when some of the other branches of our Monthly Meeting was engaged in attending to that subject and from some dependence being placed on their drawing supplies from other sources for those purposes. Signed 6–8 mo.—1827. Samuel Craft, Geo. Thorn, David Clarke, and Samuel Bunting.[40]

Stony Brook Preparative Meeting recorded in 1835 that its quota of $60.00 for the poor had been sent to the monthly meeting, and regarding its own poor, stated:

The necessities of the poor are attended to and relief afforded them and provision made for their children to freely partake of learning and to fit them for business and no breach appears in placing out children.[41]

In 1862, Thomas Wright was directed

to pay ———— the sum of $50 for the purpose of sending her children to West-town Boarding school for six months; in 1866 to pay $100 for the purpose of sending his child to school; in 1873 to pay to ————, ————, and ————, $110.00 apiece for educational and charitable purposes; and later, $267 was divided between the same for educational and charitable purposes.[42]

In 1793 Upper Springfield received a report from Mansfield that a Friend was in needy circumstances and, accordingly six members were named to attend to his situation and others that might be necessary. The answers to the fifth query were usually as follows:

The necessities of the poor are duly inspected and relief afforded, the children of such partake of learning freely, one instance of a child being placed from amongst Friends.[43]

In probably half of the answers they stated no child placed from among friends. One of the preparatives of this meeting specified its care for the education of the poor as follows:

The following friends are appointed to inform the parents of some poor children within the compass of this meeting, that they may have the privilege of sending them to our school one month free of cost, to wit,—Thos. Earl, Joseph Willits, John Warren and Thos. Lawrie.[44]

Similar action was taken in 1793 when a request from a poor member was received:

[40]*Ibid.*, 5/VI/1827 and 7/VIII/1827.
[41]Min. Stony Brook Prep. Mtg., 2/II/1837.
[42]*Ibid.*, 23/I/1862; 22/III/1866; 18/XII/1873; and 18/II/1875.
[43]Min. U. S. Mo. Mtg., 7/II/1816.
[44]Min. U. S. Prep. Mtg., 20/X/1790.

Peter Shinn informed the Meeting that having sent his son to this school several months and he apprehends himself not fully of ability to pay therefore, which, being considered, the meeting agrees to pay for the same and directs the Treasurer to call on the school master for his account and discharge it.[45]

In like manner, 1810,

Information was received that Joseph Morris, a member of our Meeting being in low circumstances has several children of an age proper for having school instruction. William Newbold is authorized to inform him that the Trustees will pay the price for two that he may send to a school kept at said William Newbold's for three or more months as the said school may continue to be kept, and the said W. Newbold as our Treasurer is authorized to pay the charge of the same when the account may be exhibited.[46]

This policy appears to have continued without change throughout the century.

The following report was made in Mt. Holly in 1781:

The committee who have the oversight of the poor reported they had several times met and there was wanting twelve pounds to discharge the debts; after consideration the Meeting agrees to raise the sum of twenty-five pounds, for the use of the poor, and the Preparative Meetings are desired to collect it in the usual proportion, and pay to the Treasurer.[47]

In 1793 a plan of subscription for a fund was drawn up,[48] said fund "to be applied to the education of such children as now do or hereafter shall belong to the same preparative meeting whose parents are not or shall not be of ability to pay for their education."

It appears by a minute of the same year, that the care of the schools and the poor was given into the hands of the same committee.

The former committee is released and the following Friends are appointed to have the care of Friends' schools within the compass of this Monthly Meeting and also to inspect the necessities of the poor, and administer relief as they may see occasion, Joseph Powel, Joseph Ridgway, George West, Aaron Smith, Job Jones, Thomas Bispham, Daniel D. Smith, Josiah Gaskill, Richard Lawrence and Abraham Brown.[49]

These three extracts indicate how the school fund was used for the poor.

Received of Anthony Sharp, treasurer of the School fund forty-three dollars

[45]*Ibid.*, 20/III/1793.
[46]Min. U. S. Prep. Mtg., School Trustees, 19/XII/1810.
[47]Min. Mt. Holly Mo. Mtg., 7/III/1781.   [48]Facsimile p. 95.
[49]Min. Mt. Holly Mo. Mtg., 7/II/1793.

and three cents, . . .interest of the school fund, as per contract with the trustees for schooling poor children.

Mary Reeve to Edward Bullock Dr.

To quarter tuition, Stacy		$3.00
" Rachel		2.50
" Mary		2.50
Quills and ink		.15
		$8.15

Received. . .of James Hulme, Treasurer of Mt. Holly Friends' School Fund forty-three dollars and three cents for the education of indigent children for the past year.[50]

Little Egg Harbor Meeting, so far as available records show, provided an exception to the general rule of establishing permanent funds to educate the poor. They reported "the necessities of the poor has been attended to, but that of learning is yet wanting among many," in 1793, and for a number of years thereafter. At the same time, however, money was raised on occasion "for the use of the poor." In 1806, and thereafter, the situation with regard to learning was somewhat improved, but not as satisfactory as in other meetings.[51] The report for that year stated:

The necessities of the poor has been attended to and some care extended towards the education of their children. No Friends' children placed from amongst Friends.[52]

Haddonfield, in 1790, mentioned the receipt of the quarterly meeting's proposals for raising funds to school poor children. A fund was established and their poor educated in a school which has come down to the present day. In 1822 they expended $122.43 on the education of poor children.[53]

Upper Evesham Preparative Meeting reported on their school fund in 1804 as follows:

The principal of the school fund is £ 113/16/1, and in the last year the sum of 6 pounds and 7 pence hath been appropriated to the schooling of poor children and other purposes and the interest calculated on the above fund to the first of the present month which remains unexpended is £ 24.7.8¾ out of which about six pounds is directed to be paid.[54]

The situation in South New Jersey seems to have been similar

---

[50]School Fund Records of Mt. Holly Prep. Mtg., 25/III/1830; 28/V/1837; and 24/X/1844.
[51]Min. L. E. H. Mo. Mtg., 8/VIII/1793 and 14/VII/1803.
[52]*Ibid.*, 13/II/1806. [53]Min. Haddonfield Mo. Mtg., 11/II/1822.
[54]Min. Upper Evesham Prep. Mtg., 7/III/1804.

to that in Haddonfield and Burlington Quarterly Meetings. In 1756 Salem Monthly reported:

The poor are taken care of as necessity calls for it, and their children partake of learning and they and other Friends' children placed amongst Friends generally.[55]

The answers to this query were substantially the same thereafter, and individual reports deal with the amounts spent for "poor education." From the minutes of 1800 the following report is taken:

The committee appointed to inspect into the necessities of the poor reported they had in the course of their service expended of the moneys raised for that service £ 12/17/8—and from the moneys arising from the sales of the effects of a Friend lately deceased £ 9/10 and that there is remaining from said sale £ 16/8/7½ which is directed to be paid to the Treasurer of this Meeting and their service is approved.[56]

The table below shows amounts expended for the "poor's necessities," and probably includes sums paid for schooling.[57]

Throughout the period from 1828 to 1853—excepting one year— a total of $965.96 was expended upon the schooling of the poor exclusively. The largest amount spent in any one year was $117.71 in 1853; the smallest, $3.66 in 1849. The average yearly expenditure was $48.29 plus.[58]

Care was also given in the cases of defectives, as is shown by a few entries in the minutes, one of which is quoted below:

The trustees of the school fund inform that agreeably to the direction of this Meeting. . . .has been placed at the Pennsylvania Institution for educating the deaf and dumb and continued there 4½ years. Upon consideration Friends are now satisfied he should be removed.[59]

In Greenwich, in 1792 £ 5/8/2½ was received from the several preparative meetings to meet the expenses of the poor.[60] The

---

[55]Min. Salem Mo. Mtg., 25/I/1756. [56]*Ibid.*, 25/VIII/1800.

[57]

Year	Amount
1816	$123.91
1820	215.48
1823	136.07
1828	65.33
1829	14.13½
1830	3.20
1832	11.59
1835	164.95

[58]Compiled from reports in the Minutes of Salem Mo. Mtg. These figures are for Orthodox Friends.

[59]*Ibid.*, 30/IX/1829. [60]Min. Greenwich Mo. Mtg., 1/II/1792.

general answer to the query on the poor was (prior to the middle of the 19th century) that "Poor Friends' necessities" were provided for and "their children freely partake of learning." In

BEGINNING OF FIRST-DAY FREE SCHOOLS AT WOODBURY, N. J. IN 1816

1844 they reported "There are none of our members who need pecuniary aid and no Friends' child placed among us."[61]

---

[61]*Ibid.*,1/II/1844.

Woodbury Monthly Meeting, soon after its establishment, entered into a plan for raising a fund to "be strictly applied to ye schooling poor children." A facsimile of the rules for regulating the execution of the trusts is shown on page 139. Likewise the plans for Woodbury Free School, in 1773, provided for the education of poor children. It should be observed that at Woodbury, as elsewhere, no opprobrium was attached to charity education by offering it in a separate school. The poor attended the same school as those whose parents were able to pay, and the trustees of the fund settled the bill with the master according to an agreement made concerning them. On page 142 is reproduced a page of the school fund expenditures for charity education. Such expenditures were authorized first for members, second to those who "professed" with Friends, and then "Black children born free."

Sunday schools were mentioned in a previous page as one of the numerous agencies created for the purpose of diffusing moral teaching and practical rudiments of an education. Though not appearing to have been generally introduced among Friends early in the nineteenth century, some are found. Woodbury, in 1816, drew up a constitution for the promotion of "First Day Free Schools"[62] and adopted rules for the government of the same.[63]

The type of instruction given in this school is indicated in the rules to regulate the order of teaching.

The following items from records of Rahway and Plainfield Monthly Meeting in the Shrewsbury Quarter indicate that the support and education of the poor occupied their attention as we have noticed elsewhere.

Paid John Webster $10.18 for George Clark for Schooling and Doctoring a daughter of John Mooner, by order of the committee for the Poor.

To Cash paid Richard Harthorne toward the Westtown School Costs.

To Cash paid John Brown toward paying Samuel Wooly for keeping Denis Hurley's children.

To Cash paid Elijah Shotwell for schooling for a poor child, $16.

To Cash paid E. Shotwell for Quarter Schooling for I. Clark.

To cash paid Caleb Mekeel[?] for schooling Nathan King's grandchildren $6.50.[64]

---

[62]Page 252.   [63]Page 254.

[64]Account Book of Rahway and Plainfield Mo. Mtg.; 25/XII/1804; 15/I/1805; 19/XI/1812; 6/II/1814; 28/XII/1816; and 17/VIII/1817.

It is evident from a study of the records that Quakers in New Jersey took a prominent part in philanthropic education during

THE ORDER OF TEACHING IN WOODBURY SUNDAY SCHOOLS

the eighteenth and nineteenth centuries both by promoting the idea and, in a more practical way, in the meetings. The works of such Quaker philanthropists as Woolman, Benezet, Bellers, Budd and Dymond make it clear that they considered education a necessity for society, a privilege which the poor should share with the rich; and, so far as practice is concerned it is found that local and central meetings continually exerted themselves to provide "that the children of the poor may have due help of education, instruction and necessary learning," and that both rich and poor be "provided with industrious employments." For this purpose special funds were established by the superior meetings and provision made for the admission of poor children to schools at the expense of the school committee. In the nineteenth century "First Day" schools began to be established as a new means of providing education for the poor.

CHAPTER VIII

APPRENTICESHIP EDUCATION

The term apprenticeship, originating from *apprendre*, to learn' began during the Middle Ages to signify a contract between a master, teacher, or craftsman, and an apprentice or learner. The master agreed to teach the "art" or "mystery" to the apprentice and the latter agreed to serve the former during the period of his contract. Such apprenticeship was common to the learned professions, the trades or crafts, and those who were studying for the Master's degree in the Liberal Arts.

In the latter part of the fourteenth century apprenticeships were mentioned in the statutes of Richard II, and in the sixteenth, in the fifth year of Elizabeth, was passed the famous Statute of Apprentices which remained in force about two hundred and fifty years. This "Act touching divers Orders for artificers, laborers, servants of husbandrie, and apprentices," provided, among other things that:

. . .every person being an householder and four and twenty years old at the least, dwelling or inhabiting. . .in any city or town corporate, and using and exercising any art, mystery, or manual occupation there, shall and may, after the Feast of St. John Baptist next coming, during the time that he shall so dwell or inhabit in any such city or town corporate and use and exercise any such mystery, art or manual occupation, have and retain the son of any Freeman not occupying husbandry nor being a laborer, and inhabiting in the same or in any other city or town that now is or hereafter shall be and continue incorporate, to serve and be bound as an apprentice after the custom and the order of the City of London for seven years at the least, so as the term and years of such apprentice do not expire or determine afore such apprentice shall be of the age of four and twenty years at the least.[1]

It was further provided that none could exercise any art, mystery or manual occupation until he had first served an apprenticeship of seven years.[2] Those persons who refused to become apprentices might be imprisoned until they complied with the law,[3] but none except minors could be thus compelled. Unmarried women, be-

---

[1]5ELIZABETH c.4, Art.xix—See vol. IV, STAT. OF THE REALM.
[2]*Ibid.*, Art. xxiv.   [3]*Ibid.*, Art. xxviii.

tween the ages of twelve and forty years could be compelled by authority of "two Justices of Peace, the Mayor, or other head officer . . . and two aldermen, or two other discreet burgesses . . . to be retained or serve by the year or by the week or day, for such wages and in such reasonable sort and manner as they shall think meet . . .," subject to imprisonment as indicated above.[4] Provision was made for the apprehension of fleeing indentured servants.

The colonists who first came to New Jersey were not hampered by any specific laws regarding apprenticeship. All "putting out of children" referred to in the earliest meetings may be regarded as adherence to custom followed in England, enjoined both by the law, their leaders, and the official advices of superior meetings.

On the other hand, apprenticeship was implied. Although there were as yet no apprenticeship laws, provision was made for the care of orphaned children who had no estate. The "Concessions and Agreements," drawn up in 1676, provided that if a person died intestate, leaving a wife and children, the administrator should give security "to secure two parts of the estate for the children." If there were children left orphan, and no estate sufficient to maintain and bring them up the commissioners were empowered "to appoint persons to take care for the child or children to bring them up in such manner as the commissioners shall appoint, and the charges thereof to be bourne by the public stock of the Province."[5] A law to the same effect was passed in West Jersey in 1681.[6]

In 1682 the Quaker assembly of West Jersey provided by law that:

For the prevention of differences betwixt masters and servants be it hereby enacted by authority aforesaid, that all servants within this Province, who are to have reference to the custom of their country for their service at the expiration thereof, either by covenant, or to whom it shall become due, instead of other covenant shall be as follows, (viz.) Ten bushels of corn, necessary apparel, two horses, and one ox.

And further that all servants above the age of one and twenty years, transported or to be transported into this province without indentures or other agreements, shall serve four years, to commence from the time the ship shall

---

[4]*Ibid.*, Art. xvii.
[5]Leaming and Spicer: *Orig. Constitutions*, 403.   [6]*Ibid.*, 430–3

be entered in the said province; and that all other servants, under the age of one and twenty years, transported or to be transported into this province, without indentures, shall within three months next after his or her arrival, be brought to the court within that jurisdiction where he or she shall reside, which court shall appoint how long time such servant shall serve.[7]

In 1683 provision was made by law for "preventing servants running away from their masters, and other vagabonds," by directing all magistrates and officers to "take special notice of all suspicious travellers and require their pass or certificates, under the hand and seal of the magistrate. . .or public notary of the place of their last abode, to satisfy of the clearness of his, or her, or their coming away. . ." and for want of the same to take them into custody.[8]

When Cornbury took charge of the Province of New Jersey (1702) he was instructed by the Court of St. James, to,

Indeavor, with the assistance of the Council, to provide for the raising of stocks, and building of public workhouses, in convenient places, for the employing of poor and indigent people.[9]

In 1774 an act for the settlement and relief of the poor, based essentially on English practice, was passed by New Jersey. By this law a person possesseed of any "freehold estate of the value of fifty pounds" gained the right of settlement in any place where the estate might be. One, not a freeholder, must gain his right of residence by serving an apprenticeship of at least one year in the city, borough, township, or precinct; such a right of settlement could not be obtained by a servant, procured bought or hired from jails or workhouses, for, as the law notes, "inconveniences have arisen therefrom."

Regarding the apprenticeship of the poor it was provided by article eighteen:

. . .That it shall and may be lawful for the overseers of the poor, or any two of them, with the assistance and approbation of two Justices of the Peace of any county, city or town corporate of this colony, and they are hereby enjoined and commanded to put forth and bind out any poor child or children, who have no parents or whose parents shall apply to the said overseer or overseers for relief, or the child or children of any poor parents whatsoever, who shall bring up their said children in sloth, idleness and ignorance, and upon advice and direction, given by the said overseer or overseers, shall, for three months after such advice and direction, refuse or neglect to put forth and bind out such poor child or children for such a number of years as the said justices and overseers, in their discretion shall think proper, for a male person till they shall arrive at twenty-one years of age, and for a female, till they arrive at eighteen years of age, and no longer; and the said justices or any

[7]*Ibid.*, 447.   [8]*Ibid.*, 477.   [9]*Ibid.*, 642.

two of them, amongst the common covenants in the indenture and indentures, made and agreed upon between the parties, shall always insert the following clause: 'that every such master and mistress, to whom such poor child or children shall be bound out as aforesaid, shall cause every such child or children to be taught and instructed to read and write'. . .[10]

Apprenticeship was dealt with again by legislation of 1798, and 1799. That of 1799 provided specifically that children of any beggar, vagrant, vagabond, common drunkard, or common prostitute, or of any person, who shall not provide for such child. . .should be bound out to any person willing to take such child, till the age of twenty-one years, if a male, or eighteen years, if a female, or for a less time.[11]

The laws above named, respecting apprenticeship were amended frequently during the nineteenth century; in 1820, provision was made that the age given in the indenture should not be taken as "conclusive," and that the "true age of such infant may be inquired into and given in evidence in any court . . ."; in 1844, and 1854, it was amended so that an indenture to a number of masters, or a firm, might be valid. Other supplements were made in 1859, 1862, 1864, 1871, and 1875, which effected changes of detail, such as permitting houses of refuge to bind out children, requiring signature of mother, if living (1871), and permitting residents of the state to enter into indentures with those outside the same.[12]

From the foregoing it is evident that such care as may be found in the Society of Friends for the apprenticeship of their children is only compliance with the English law. The desire that they be educated in a religious fashion dictated that children be apprenticed to Friends, or those who would be zealous to give them a "guarded, religious education."

George Fox, in 1669, sent forth the following letter to Friends "throughout the nation," concerning "putting out poor children to trades."

My dear Friends:
Let every quarterly meeting make enquiry through all the monthly and other meetings to know all Friends who are widows, or others, that have children fit to put out apprentices, so that you may set forth four in a year in

---

[10]Patterson: *Laws of New Jersey*, 31; That these provisions were generally incorporated appears in old township books. Stewart, in his *Notes on Old Gloucester County* pp. 58–9, describes the indentures found in the back of an old township book of Great Egg Harbor, near the close of the eighteenth century.
[11]*Ibid.*, 411.   [12]LAWS OF N. J., for the respective years.

each county, or more, if there be occasion.   This apprentice, when out of his time, may help his father or mother to support the family that is decayed, and in so doing all may come to live comfortably.   This being done in your quarterly meetings, you will have a knowledge through the county in the monthly and particular meetings, of masters fit for them, and of such trades as their parents or you desire, or the children most inclinable to.   Thus being placed out to Friends, they may be trained up in truth, and by this means you may preserve Friends' children, and enable them to be a strength and help to their families, and nursers and preservers of their relations in their ancient days.   Thus also, things being ordered in the wisdom of God, you will take off a continual maintenance, and free yourselves from much cumber.   For in the country ye know, ye may set forth an apprentice for a little to several trades, as bricklayers, masons, carpenters, wheelwrights, plough wrights, taylors, tanners, curriers, blacksmiths, shoemakers, nailers, butchers, weavers of linen and woolen, stuffs and serges, etc.   And you may do well to have a stock in your quarterly meetings for that purpose.   All that is given by any friends at their decease, except it be given for some particular use, person or meeting, may be brought to the public stock for that purpose.   This will be a way for preserving of many that are poor among you; and it will be a way of making up poor families.   In several counties it is practiced already.   Some quarterly meetings set forth two apprentices; and sometimes the children of others that are laid on the parish.   You may bind them for fewer or more years, according to their capacities.   In all things the wisdom of God will teach you; by which ye may help the children of poor friends that they may come to support their families. . .

London,   G. F.
The first of the eleventh month, 1669.[13]

The above advice of Fox found favor in the meetings, and, being in harmony with laws already mentioned its rapid spread was to be expected.   In all meeting advices on the subject of apprenticeship there was an emphasis on the moral influence that might be secured by placing the apprentice under the care of one of their own members.   The following is representative of advices on apprenticeship of the Philadelphia Yearly Meeting:

Advised, that Friends be carefull not to put their children apprentice to such as are not Friends, whereby they are often led away, through evil examples, but as much as in them lies to bring up their children and all under their care in the fear and nurture of the Lord, that none may be blameworthy in a thing so greatly necessary.[14]

The minutes of meetings in New Jersey contain many cases in which the meeting assisted in putting young members out as apprentices, thus keeping in harmony with the injunctions of

[13]Fox: *Journal*, 424–5.   [14]*Ms.* Advices, p. 27.

leaders and within the laws of the colony. The following extracts deal with individual cases.

In 1685 the following agreement was made between two members of Burlington Monthly Meeting:

> In pursuance of an agreement made with William Atkinson at a monthly meeting of Friends at Burlington the eleventh month, 1685, I, the within named Francis Collins, do hereby further promise and engage with inbounden Thomas Atkinson to teach him the carpenters trade during his said apprenticeship so far as he is of capacity to learn the same, and at the expiration of said term to give said Thomas fifty acres of land. Witness my hand this twenty-first day of the twelfth month, 1685. Francis Collins.
> Witnesses, James Budd, George Hutchinson.[15]

Those who had oversight of the poor, sometimes a standing committee on that subject, frequently took charge of placing out the children of those who were unable to educate them, paying a sum of money, at times, to enable the master to give them a school education. In 1762, Burlington Meeting recorded:

> A friend from the committee appointed to consider the case of a poor widow wanting assistance reported they thought it necessary to advance ten pounds for bounding out one of her children and to enable the person taking him to give him proper schooling, on consideration of which the meeting doth agree to the proposal. . .that proper care be taken with respect to the child's education and if any of her other children can be assisted with regard to the means of gaining sufficient learning, they are desired to look into it. . . [16]

Nevertheless the minutes assure us the meetings were not all able, or perhaps zealous, to look after apprenticeship carefully. In 1775 the minutes of Burlington Quarterly, speaking of the situation in the several lower meetings, informed that:

> Fifth, this query nearly complied with in respect to the poor, but some omissions mentioned in placing out of Friends' children among Friends.[17]

Likewise in 1784 Upper Springfield Monthly stated the fifth query was complied with—i. e. poor cared for—"except one instance of a youth being placed from among Friends, of which some care has been taken."[18] Two were reported "placed from among Friends" in 1795; two, likewise, in 1803 and so on. These cases, which were brought up for treatment by the meeting, might be added to indefinitely if space allowed, and it were necessary, for

---

[15]Min. Burlington Mo. Mtg., 4/XI/1685.   [16]*Ibid.*, 4/X/1762.
[17]Min. Burlington Q. Mtg., 28/VIII/1775.
[18]Min. U. S. Mo. Mtg., 4/VIII/1784.

the problems of one meeting were very similar to those of another.[19] The preparative meetings had the most intimate concern with these cases, and made answer relating thereto in their replies to the fifth query. Upon a difficult situation arising a committee was named in the monthly or preparative meetings as the case warranted.

Apprenticeship of the youth to a desirable trade often necessitated his leaving home and going to the city. In such cases, the meetings prepared the usual certificates,[20] in order that he be received by Friends in his new home. The following are examples:

John Hoskins. . .requested our certificate on behalf of his son Caleb to be directed to the Monthly Meeting of Philadelphia he being put apprentice to a Friend of that meeting. Joseph Wetherill and John Cox are appointed to prepare one.[21]

Thomas Schoolfield, apprentice to John Welding at Trentown brought a certificate from Buckingham Monthly Meeting to this meeting, recommending him to the care of Friends in his minority, which was read and approved.[22]

Request was made to this meeting by one of the overseers of Pilesgrove for a certificate for Anthony Sharp, young lad who has gone apprentice to Philadelphia. Therefore this meeting appoints Preston Carpenter and John Reeve to take an opportunity with him before a certificate is granted.

[19]*Ibid.*, 5/VIII/1795; and 9/II/1803.

[20]The use of certificates was a regular rule in the Society of Friends numerous directions for their issuance and use being given by the London Yearly Meeting. Likewise Philadelphia advised concerning them repeatedly after its establishment. Their use was necessary for all members who desired to remove to another meeting; ministers who travelled about preaching, and of course, the apprentices who went to a distant town. In the case of the last named it was not so much because the law required it (after 1774) but because it was demanded by the meeting. See *Ms.* Christian and Brotherly Advices of (Philadelphia Yearly Meeting, pp. 25ff. and 301ff.) On the subject of certificates the discipline of 1744 stated: "When apprentices or persons under age, are under a necessity of going from one place to another, their parents or guardians, masters or mistresses, should apply for certificates for them, recommending them to the care and oversight of the monthly meeting whereto they remove." (Reincorporated in *Rules of Discipline*....(1834), p. 30).

The giving of certificates was provided by the law of 1774: "That if any person or persons shall think proper to remove out of any one city into another, there to inhabit and reside, and shall at the same time procure, bring and deliver, to the overseers of the poor of every such city. . .a certificate under the hands and seals of the overseers of the poor, or any two of them, of his, her, or their last legal settlement, attested by two or more credible witnesses, etc., etc., then, and in such case it shall be lawful for every such person and persons, with their families upon delivery of such certificate as aforesaid, to continue, abide and remain in any such city. . ." (See Patterson: *Laws of N. J.*, 28-9.)

[21]Min. Burlington Mo. Mtg., 3/XII/1787.

[22]Min. Chesterfield Mo. Mtg., 1/IV/1749.

Preston Carpenter requested a certificate for his son, Thomas Carpenter who is put an apprentice to Philadelphia, to a merchant, a Friend of that city, therefore this meeting appoints Bartholomew Wyatt to prepare one and bring to next meeting.[23]

Request was made for a certificate for Isaac Hause, (Hanse?) a minor placed apprentice with a Friend of Pilesgrove Monthly Meeting. Jonas Friedland and David Smith are appointed to make the needful enquiry prepare one and bring to next meeting.[24]

Upon some occasions it was necessary that the meeting take charge of the direction of financial affairs—i. e., to settle affairs among themselves without assistance of law if possible—. The following is a case in point, which involved the disposal of children as apprentices:

Friends that were appointed to speak with widow Nicholson gave testimony that according to Friends' desire, they have spoken to her, but have received little that was of any satisfaction. So this day Friends having her before the meeting advised her and proposed to her to put forth four of her children and she and the youngest of her children might have house room and firing freely for one year with Matthew Grange; and to call in her creditors and give them satisfaction out of her goods. And also to resign up the plantation that is engaged to James Marshall unto him.[25]

Fewer cases of apprenticing of girls were recorded, yet this custom was frequently followed. In 1717, at Chesterfield,

Jacob Doughty, one of the executors of the last will of Anne Beck, deceased, applied to this meeting for their advice concerning the putting out the daughter of the said Anne Beck as an apprentice to Margaret Howell, at Philadelphia and this meeting advises to make as good terms as can be for the child, and if nothing appear upon enquiry but it may be well, this meeting advises to put the child out accordingly.[26]

Woodbridge Meeting, in 1718, dealt as follows with the girls and boys of William Willis:

Benjamin Wade and John Willis were appointed by this meeting for the service aforesaid of putting out the said William Willis' children apprentice. (He being here and consenting thereinto) One of which children being a boy they are to take care that his master be obliged to give him two suits of apparel att the expiration of his time, be taught to wright a legible hand, and instructed in arithmetick so farr as the rule of three. The other being a girl, to be put apprentice until she arrives to the age of eighteen years, obliging her master to give her at the end of her time two suits of apparell and teach her to read in the Bible.[27]

[23]Min. Salem Mo. Mtg., 24/VI/1771.   [24]*Ibid.*, 27/VI/1796.
[25]Min. Chesterfield Mo. Mtg., 7/IX/1689.   [26]*Ibid.*, 4/II/1717.
[27]Min. Woodbridge Mo. Mtg., 25/VI/1718.

The case of the son of William Willis well illustrates the persistence with which meetings sometimes strove to get children placed in Friends' families. This case occupied about two years. In 1719 the meeting stated that "no place as yet presenting the child is ordered to go to John Shotwell's house until a place does present."[28] A few months later, "This meeting appoints John Laing and Benjamin Smith to speak to Thomas Cawood and his wife to see whether they may be willing to take William Willis his child until the age of twenty-one, and if so, upon what terms, and make report to the next meeting."[29]

This was not successful and,

in the sixth month (1720) an agreement by order of the meeting was made with Daniel Shottwell for the taking apprentice Nathaniel Willis, son of William Willis. while he come of age; the meeting being to pay him sixteen pounds at several payments with the child, that is to say, five pounds in the sixth month next, five pounds in the sixth month 1722 and the residue in the sixth month 1723.[30]

If the father or guardian did not take steps to apprentice the child at the proper age (at thirteen or fourteen years) or failed to ask the meeting's assistance for so doing, the latter took the case into its own hands. Thus, in 1773, Woodbridge Meeting was

Informed that a son of Abraham Thorn, a lame lad, is arrived to a proper age to be put out apprentice and said Abraham Thorn not taking proper care to put him out the meeting appoints John Webster. . .John Haydock to look a place for him and on what terms and report to next monthly meeting.[31]

A breach of the rule that children should be "placed among Friends" brought the individual so offending under the eye of the overseer. The following random selection illustrates the point:

The overseers of Pilesgrove informed this meeting that they had visited the Friends that had bound children under their care from amongst Friends to learn trades, and that one of them, viz., Thomas Barber, said that he knew it to be contrary to Friends' rules but did not think of it at that time and was sorry it happened so, but that he had obligated the master to let his son go to meeting on First days and other days of the week when his business would admit. The other, George Colson, (being brother to the child) said he was unacquainted with the rules of Friends on that account and was sorry he had disobliged his friends, but was not sorry if his brother should do well that he had placed him to the man he had—and that he had desired the master to restrain his brother from speaking evil words and other bad practices. Therefore this

---

[28]*Ibid.*, 21/III/1719.   [29]*Ibid.*, 17/VII/1719.
[30]*Ibid.*, 15/IV/1721.   [31]*Ibid.*, 19/V/1773.

meeting continues the said friends and lets them know it is a breach of our discipline and that Friends expect they will attend this meeting and make Friends satisfaction and appoints Mark Reeve to accompany the said overseers in that service.[32]

If at marriage either of the contracting parties had children by an earlier union, the meeting gave special attention to see that their rights were properly safeguarded.   In 1761, Salem recorded:

To this meeting came Thomas Copperthwaite and Mary Willis the first time and declared their intentions of marriage with each other. . .are appointed to enquire into his life and conversation and clearness in relation to marriage and Charles Fogg to join them to see that the rights and property of the said Mary Willis' children by her former husband be taken care of and report to next meeting.[33]

Another example of the same concern for children occurred in the case of Benjamin Griscom and Rebecca Thompson, who "declared their intention of marriage" and Friends were at once appointed "to see that the rights of her former husband's children are attended to . . ."[34]

---

[32]Min. Salem Mo. Mtg., 24/IX/1759.
[33]*Ibid.*, 29/VI/1761.   [34]*Ibid.*, 20/VIII/1811.

CHAPTER IX

EDUCATION OF "INFERIOR RACES"

Christianity has proclaimed in the most solemn and exalted terms the absolute equality of all men. There is neither Greek nor Jew, circumcision nor uncircumcision, Barbarian, Scythian, bond nor free: but Christ is all and in all. The precepts Christianity delivers, might have been expected to soften the feelings and tame the pride of the stronger race. It must however, be admitted that in all or nearly all the countries, where white men and black men dwell together, Christianity though it has brought from without not only devoted missionaries but such a band of noble and self-sacrificing women as went after the war to the Southern states to teach the newly liberated negroes, has failed to impress the lessons of human equality and brotherhood upon the whites established in the country. Their sense of scornful superiority resists its precepts.[1]

Thus wrote Lord Bryce, and there are exceedingly few exceptions. Upon examination of the principles and practices of the Society of Friends, however, it appears that they, as a small part of a superior white race, did recognize the principle of brotherly equality and sought to practice it. In the pursuit of this liberal policy they were guided by the vision of their great leaders.

In the letters of Fox there is a clear indication that the religious welfare of the Indians and Negroes was as near his heart as that of the white brethren. In one instance he points out that Christ's death offered "propitiation not only for the sins of Christians, bus for the sins of the whole world."[2] In another, writing to Friendt in the ministry, who had gone to America, he charged them:

Let your light shine among the Indians, the Blacks, and the Whites; that ye may answer the truth in them, and bring them to the standard and ensign, that God hath set up, Christ Jesus. . . .And, Friends, be not negligent but keep up your Negroes' meetings and your family meetings; and have meetings with the Indian kings, and their councils and subjects everywhere, and with others. Bring them all to the baptizing and circumcising Spirit, by which they may know God and serve and worship him.[3]

Woolman in his *Considerations on the Keeping of Negroes*, like-

---

[1] Bryce, *The Relations of the Advanced and Backward Races of Mankind*, 40–1.
[2] Woody: *Early Quaker Education in Pennsylvania*, 234.
[3] Letter dated 11/X/1690, in Fox's *Journal*, 642.

wise bespoke equal rights for that despised and much wronged part of humanity. In all cases his arguments are based upon the supposition of equality from the Christian viewpoint:

The color of a man avails nothing in matters of right and equity. Consider color in relation tó treaties; by such, disputes betwixt nations are sometimes settled. And should the Father of us all so dispose things, that treaties with black men should sometimes be necessary, how then would it appear among the princes and ambassadors, to insist on the prerogative of the white color?

Whence is it that men, who believe in a righteous omnipotent Being, to whom all nations stand equally related, and are equally accountable,—remain so easy in it; but for that the ideas of negroes and slaves are so interwoven in the mind that they do not discuss this matter with that candour and freedom of thought which the case justly calls for?. . .[4]

If those who were spoiled and wronged, should at length make slaves of their oppressors, and continue slavery to their posterity, it would look rigorous to candid men, but to act that part toward a people, when neither they nor their fathers have injured us, hath something in it extraordinary, and requires our serious attention.[5]

He also sees in the institution of slavery a source of ill effects in the education of children of the slave owning class.

It appears by experience that whére children are educated in fulness, ease and idleness, evil habits are more prevalent, than is common amongst such who are prudently employed in the necessary affairs of life; and if children are not only educated in the way of so great temptation, but have also the opportunity of lording it over their fellow creatures, and being masters of men in their childhood, how can we hope otherwise than that their tender minds will be possessed with thoughts too high for them, which by continuance, gaining strength, will prove, like a slow current, gradually separating them from (or keeping from acquaintance with) that humility and meekness in which alone lasting happiness can be enjoyed.[6]

Woolman incorporated his belief in practice. Upon a certain occasion a request came to him to write the will of one who expected to dispose of slaves, among other things.

I told the man that I believed the practice of continuing slavery to this people was not right. . .and had a scruple in my mind against doing writings of that kind. . .and desired to be excused from going to write the will.[7]

Anthony Benezet, a teacher of long experience both in schools for white children, and that established for Negroes in Philadelphia,

---

[4]Woolman's *Journal*, (1837), 229–30.   [5]*Ibid.*, 239–40.
[6]Woolman's *Works* (Philadelphia, 1806) p. 224.
[7]*Ibid.*, 44. In 1774 the Yearly Meeting Advices followed the principle of John Woolman saying that none ought to act as executors or administrators to such estates where slaves were bequeathed.

was an indefatigable protagonist of their cause. In laboring to promote it he wrote voluminously: brief tracts, articles in newspapers, and also more pretentious publications served to spread abroad his contention that human slavery was utterly incompatible with the most elementary Christian principles. By his vigorous campaign he was able to stir up the Society, of which he was a member, to greater activity. Upon one occasion, when a new movement against slavery was being discussed in the Yearly Meeting, and a trifling opposition was made, he arose and cried out: "Ethiopia shall soon stretch out her hands unto God."[8]

Among the more pretentious works against slavery were *A Short Account of that Part of Africa inhabited by the Negroes*, of which a second edition appeared in 1762, *A Caution and Warning to Great Brtiain and her Colonies on the Calamitous State of the Enslaved Negroes in the British Dominions*, published in 1767, and *An Historical Account of Guinea* . . . . Twenty years after publication of the *Caution and Warning*, the Yearly Meeting of London caused it to be distributed widely among the regular and dissenting clergy, officials of the realm, and the most important schools.

Benezet was impressed by the fact that men failed to be logical in their advocacy of freedom and equality. In 1767 he wrote:

At a time when the general rights and liberties of mankind, and the preservation of those valuable privileges transmitted to us from our ancestors, are become so much the subjects of universal consideration, can it be an enquiry indifferent to any, how many of those who distinguish themselves as the advocates of liberty remain insensible and inattentive to the treatment of thousands and tens of thousands of our fellow men, who, from motives of avarice and the inexorable decree of tyrant custom, are at this very time kept in the most deplorable state of slavery in many parts of the British dominions?[9]

In the *Account of Africa*, he concludes:

Upon the whole of what has been said it must appear to every honest, unprejudiced reader that the negroes are equally entitled to the common privileges of mankind-with the whites; that they have the same rational powers, the same natural affections and are as susceptible of pain and grief as they; that, therefore, the bringing and keeping them in bondage is an instance of oppression and injustice of the most grievous nature, such as is scarcely to be paralleled by any example in the present or former ages. Many of its woeful

---

[8]*Biographical Sketches of Friends*, 301.
[9]*Caution and Warning to Great Britain and her Colonies, in Views of American Slavery taken a Century Ago*, 29.

effects have already been expressed, but those which more particularly call for the notice and redress of the government arise from its inconsistency with everything that is just and humane, whence the worst effects naturally flow to the religion and morals of the people where it prevails.[10]

Concerning his experience as a teacher of the Negroes, Benezet stated:

I can with truth and sincerity declare that I have found amongst the Negroes as great variety of talents as among the like numbers of whites; and I am bold to assert that the notion, entertained by some, that the Blacks are inferior in their capacities, is a vulgar prejudice, founded on the pride or ignorance of their lordly masters, who have kept their slaves at such a distance as to be unable to form a right judgment of them.[11]

The same liberal sentiments characterized Benezet's view of the Indian natives.

Upon the whole, it is a matter of undoubted persuasion, with impartial people, who have been conversant with Indians, that if their dispositions and natural power are duly considered, they will be found to be equally with our own, capable of improvements in knowledge and virtue, and that the apparent difference between us and them, is chiefly owing to our different ways of life, and different ideas of what is necessary and desirable, and the advantage of education, which puts it in our power to gloss over our own conduct, however evil; and to set theirs, however defensible, in the most odious point of light.[12]

The philanthropy towards both Negro and Indian, that so characterized his whole life, was evident after death. His will provided that the residue of his small estate should be used:

to hire and employ a religious minded person or persons, to teach a number of negro, mulatto or Indian children, to read, write, arithmetic, plain accounts, needle work, etc., and it is my particular desire, founded on the experience I have had in that service, that in the choice of such tutor, special care may be had to prefer an industrious careful person, of true piety, who may be or become suitably qualified, who would undertake the service from a principle of charity, to one more highly learned, not equally disposed.[13]

Yearly Meeting's Attitude towards Slave Holding

The statements which embodied the sentiment of the superior meeting of the Society on the subject of Negro slavery, were all in harmony with individual views already discussed. These state-

---

[10]*A Short Account of Africa* in *Views of American Slavery*, 63.
[11]*Ibid.*, 25–6.   [12]*Some Observations on the Indian Natives*, 40.
[13]Vaux, *Memoirs of Benezet*, 135.

ments, issued from time to time, are indeed the crystallization of
the best thought on the subject.

As early as 1688 the *Christian Advices* stated that a paper was
presented by some German Friends concerning the lawfulness
and unlawfulness of buying and keeping of Negroes, but it was
judged not to be proper for the Yearly Meeting at that time to
give a "positive judgment" as it had so "general a relation to
many other parts . . ."

During the succeeding eight years the opinion of the meeting
became more crystallized and the following advice was given out in
1696:

> Whereas several papers have been read relating to the keeping and bringing
> in of negroes, which being duly considered, it is the advice of this meeting
> that Friends be careful not to encourage the bringing in of any more negroes,
> and that such that have negroes be careful of them, bring them to meetings or
> have meetings with them in their families and restrain them from loose and
> lewd living as much as in them lies, and from rambling abroad on first days
> "or other times."[14]

In 1712 the Philadelphia Yearly Meeting received a letter from
London Meeting concerning Negro slaves. In this, reference
was made to their earlier advices of 1696, notwithstanding which

> traders flocked in among us over whom we had no gospel authority, and such
> have increased and multiplied negroes amongst us, to the grief of divers
> Friends whom we are willing to ease if the way might open. . .

Since Negroes were more numerous in other provinces than here,
it was thought desirable to have an expression from the provinces.
Hence the epistle closed with a request for counsel from Philadelphia.[15] In 1714 the reply of Philadelphia Meeting adverted
to the law passed by the Quaker Colony laying a duty of £ 20
on each head imported "which Law the Queen was pleased to
disannul." Furthermore,

> we could heartily wish that a way might be found to stop bringing in more
> here, or at least that Friends may be less concerned in buying or selling of any
> that may be brought in and hope for your assistance with the government if
> any further law should be made discouraging the importation.

It seems that at this early date Friends in New Jersey and
Pennsylvania were clear of the practise only in part: many held
slaves but "we know not of any Friend amongst us that has any

---

[14]*Ms.* Christian Advices of Phila. Yearly Meeting, 171.   [15]*Ibid.*, 172.

hand or concern in bringing any out of their own country."[16]

In 1715 the lower meetings were advised that

If any Friends are concerned in the importation of Negroes, let them be dealt with, and advised to avoid that practice. . .and that all who have or keep Negroes do use and treat them with humanity. . .

Yet it is necessary to recognize in these early advices a very cautious attitude. The Yearly Meeting received numerous letters from lower meetings, which urged more drastic action than it attempted. Thus, in 1716, in answer to a vigorous proposal from Chester, the Yearly Meeting advised:

This meeting cannot see any better conclusion than what was the judgement of last meeting, and therefore do confirm the same—and. . . Friends . . . as may be, avoid buying such Negroes as shall hereafter be brought in, rather than offend any Friends who are against it. Yet this is only Caution and not Censure.[17]

The advice of 1719 was a little more specific:

Advised that none among us be concerned in the fetching or importing negroe slaves from their own country or elsewhere. . .treat them with humanity. . . make them acquainted with the principles of Truth and inculcate morality among them.

However, many years were to elapse before all this could be achieved. In 1730, the monthly meetings were directed to admonish and caution those who offended by the practice of purchasing those newly imported or to be imported. This advice was repeated year after year, and in 1737 the lower meetings were charged to send in an account to the Yearly Meeting. On the receipt of the forthcoming reports

Divers Friends. . .expressed their satisfaction in finding by the reports of the Quarterly Meetings that there is so little occasion of offense given by Friends concerning. . .encouraging the importing of negroes.[18]

This feeling of satisfaction, however, gave way, after nearly 20 years, to a recognition that the "number is of late increased amongst us." This realization brought forth a long pronouncement addressed to all quarterly metings. Essential portions of the advice are quoted:

. . .if we continually bear in mind the Royal Law of doing to others, as we would be done by, we shall never think of bereaving our fellow creatures of that valuable blessing, Liberty; nor endure to grow rich by their bondage. . .

---

[16]*Ibid.*, 173.   [17]*Ibid.*, 174.   [18]*Ibid.*, 176.

How can we, who have been concerned to publish the gospel of universal love and peace among mankind, be so inconsistent with ourselves as to purchase such who are prisoners of war. . .and thereby encourage this unchristian practice? And more especially, as many of these poor creatures are stolen away. . . .Do we consider that they are called, and sincerely desire that they may become Heirs with us in glory, and rejoice in the liberty of the sons of God, whilst we are withholding from them the common liberties of mankind? Or can the spirit of God, by which we have always professed to be led, be the author of those oppressive and unrighteous measures? Or do we not thereby manifest that temporal interest hath more influence on our conduct herein than the dictates of that merciful, Holy and unerring Guide?

And. . .you who by inheritance have slaves now in your families. . .consider them as souls committed to your trust whom the Lord will require at your hands. . .watch over them for good, instructing them in the Fear of God and the knowledge of the Gospel. . .and train them up, that. . .should (you) think it your duty to set them free they may be the more capable to make a proper use of their liberty. Finally, . . .we entreat you. . .seriously to weigh the cause of detaining them in bondage; if it be for your own private gain, or for any other motive than their good, its much to be feared that the Love of God. . .is not the prevailing principle in you and your hearts not sufficiently redeemed from the world. . .[19]

The last pointed statement obviously laid a firm basis upon which meetings might act, and disown those who still refused to manumit or properly care for their slaves. Action by local meetings was much more vigorous during the last half of this century.

In 1758 the meeting found a "unanimous concern prevailing to put a stop to the increase of the practice of importing, buying, selling or keeping slaves . . .," and approved of John Woolman, John Churchman, John Scarborough, John Sykes and Daniel Stanton, who were to visit Friends in all meetings who held slaves. It was also specifically stated that "the respective Monthly Meeting . . . should manifest their disunion" with such as refused to comply with the advices, after admonition had been given.[20] This was further emphasized in a committee report of 1774, and specific mention made of instruction:

and . . .where there are young ones, or others of suitable age that they excite the master. . .to give them sufficient instruction and learning in order to qualify them for the enjoyment of the liberty intended, and that they be instructed by themselves (the masters) or placed out to such masters and mistresses who will be careful of their religious education, to serve for such time, and no longer than is prescribed by law and custom for white people.[21]

---

[19]*Ibid.*, 177–181.   [20]*Ibid.*, 182–3.   [21]*Ibid.*, 186.

In spite of these measures it appears by the advice of 1776 that "many difficult and complicated cases" of Negro slaves still required attention, and it was therefore urged that "all such cases might well be submitted to the quarterly meetings where they subsist, whose advice and judgment should be observed . . ." In 1778 Friends were urged to

advise and assist them on all occasions particularly in promoting their instruction in the principles of the Christian religion and the pious education of their children

as also to advise them in respect to wordly concerns; and a year later the quarterly meetings were directed to encourage "a continued care for the instruction of these people in schools . . ."

By 1780 there were but "few remaining in bonds with any of our members" and most attention of the higher and lower meetings was given to their education, since, with freedom, came opportunity to profit by an education. In the local meetings it is evident that little difference was made between the poor child of Negroes and those of white parents.

The Negro Question in Local Meetings

In the following pages is set forth the activity of local meetings relative to the freedom and care of the Negroes. No attempt is made to deal with this question as fully as its importance well deserves, but sufficient material will be presented to indicate what the efforts were, and how nearly they measured up to the ideals held by leaders in the Society and expressed in the injunctions of the official meetings. In general, the records that have been found show there were efforts (1) to secure freedom (2) give religious education (3) advise them in material affairs and (4) to give an elementary school education such as was common at that time.

The official interest of the superior meeting in the welfare of the Negro was expressed in a query[22] relating to them, concerning which mention has already been made. Answers were made to the query by the monthly meetings and forwarded by the quarterly meetings to the Yearly Meeting.

In 1757 Burlington Quarter reported:

[22]In 1765 this was the 7th query.

One of our particular Meetings say they have no negroes among them, all clear of importing them for term of life. They are generally well fed and cloathed; some are taught to read and taken to meetings but others are taken little care of in these respects.[23]

Though from the above report the situation seems to have been fairly under control, it was necessary to remain vigilant. It was customary to deal with members in case they infringed upon the discipline of the society by dealing in slaves. A case of this kind appeared in 1761 when T. H. of Mt. Holly was reported to have purchased a Negro and certain Friends were named to speak to him and report to the next Meeting.[24] Similar action was taken concerning a member of Old Springfield in 1764.[25] Ten years later the Yearly Meeting urged still greater attention to the practice of individual members, in reply to which Burlington made the following minute:

> The Meeting taking under consideration the recommendation of last Yearly Meeting to extend further labor to such members among us who hold negroes in bondage, after deliberating thereon it was concluded for the present to recommend it to the several Monthly Meetings to enter on that service as they find the way open and to report at next Quarter how far they have proceeded.[26]

In response the monthly meetings appointed committees to deal "as wisdom and strength shall be afforded." A year later this committee of the Monthly Meeting at Burlington was urged to give "attention to these matters and proceed thereon according to the discipline."[27] In 1776 they reported that "as to those who hold Negroes we have the satisfaction to say that a considerable number have manumitted their Negroes by deeds duly executed" to take effect at the proper age and in the meantime taking care of their education.[28] ·The following report of the manumission committee was given in 1779.

> We of the committee for the manumisson of negroes do report that we have labored in this service since last year, but the number of three, then reported to be withheld from freedom, have since increased one by birth, yet we are not without a hope that some or all may be released in a little longer time and we

---

[23]Min. Burlington Q. Mtg., 29/VIII/1757.
[24]Min. Burlington Mo. Mtg., 4/V/1761.
[25]*Ibid.*, 1/X/1764.   [26]Min. Burlington Q. Mtg., 28/XI/1774.
[27]Min. Burlington Mo. Mtg., 6/III/1775.   [28]*Ibid.*, 5/VIII/1776.

desire still to attend thereto until the work is perfected or judgment is placed where it belongs.[29]

In 1780 the number of slaves held in this meeting had been reduced to one, under age, who, it was thought, would soon be set free. Furthermore, regarding

their instruction in schools and in the principles of the Christian religion do report that a degree of religious care has been taken; one meeting has also been appointed for them which, agreeable to an invitation given. . .the most of them attended and. . .we may express our having received the reward of satisfaction.[30]

By 1782 the committee was able to report:

The committee of the manumission of negroes reports that they have gone through that service and that there is now none remaining amongst us in bondage that they know of. They are therefore released from that appointment.[31]

Though freedom was secured there remained a great problem in their education. The intimate concern for the Negroes' education is in part evidenced by the fact that the committee on schools was often given charge of Negro affairs. Likewise the Yearly Meeting with the same breath usually spoke of education, and urged a concern for the Negroes. Especially was this true after manumission had in most places been secured and the greatest problem remaining was education. In 1788 Burlington appointed a school committee of nineteen "who are also desired to attend to the concern . . . of doing full justice to the Black People."[32] At the same time another committee of visitation was appointed:

The following Friends are appointed to join with Women Friends in a solid visit to the families of such Black people as are among us, and inquire into their situation and pursuits in life, administering to them such advice temporally and spiritually as may arise on their minds agreeable to the sense of the last Yearly Meeting, viz., Robert Grubb, Joseph Wetherill, Thomas Buzby, Joseph Buzby, Samuel Hedges, Asa Shinn, John Brown and Samuel Woolman, who are desired to meet and confer with the committee appointed in this case by our last Quarterly Meeting and make report. . .of their progress therein.

An early minute of Chesterfield Monthly Meeting indicates a hesitation to enforce the Christian principle for fear that contentions might arise:

Dear Friends. This Meeting having considered the proposal of some

---

[29]*Ibid.*, 2/VIII/1779.   [30]*Ibid.*, 7/VIII/1780.
[31]*Ibid.*, 7/I/1782.   [32]*Ibid.*, 1/XII/1788.

Friends to our last Quarterly Meeting to restrict Friends from purchasing negroes imported into these parts, it is the sense of this Meeting that as Friends both here and elsewhere have been in the practice of it for time past and many Friends differing in their opinions from others in that matter, we think restricting Friends at this time and bringing such as fall into the same thing under dealing as offenders, will not be convenient lest it create contention and uneasiness among them, which should be carefully avoided. We hope these Friends that are dissatisfied with such actings will not only be exemplary but in a Christian spirit persuade against a practice so contrary to the noble rule laid down in Holy Scriptures in doing to all as they would that they should do to us.[33]

Again, even as late as 1775, they recorded that several were "disposed to set their Negroes free, but most of those are discouraged from the apprehension of incumbrance which it might occasion to their outward estates and some few refuse at present."[34] In 1776 the committee reported:

We further add that the committee last year appointed and this year reappointed to the weighty service of visiting those who keep negroes in bondage report they have made some progress therein since last year and altho there appears too great a disregard to common justice and disposition to reject the Christian labor of their brethren in favor of that oppressed people in some whom they have not yet sufficiently discharged their duty to, and in others a small degree of compliance has appeared which gives encouragement to hope that further labor will be useful and a more satisfactory report be made to a future meeting.[35]

In 1778 the efforts to secure manumission at Chesterfield brought out seven refusals and testimonies were duly launched against those members.[36] A year thereafter the

Committee appointed by the Monthly Meeting to advise and assist those negroes and their children who have been restored to freedom, particularly in the instruction of the Christian religion and the pious education of their offspring have attended to that service and visited all such within the compass of this Monthly Meeting and advised them therein as way opened and we find there is but few of these people who attend our meetings having but little savor of true religion. They are generally ignorant as to reading and writing— both old and young, yet we hope there is an increasing care among Friends to advise and encourage such of our members who have the care of their young ones to be more attentive towards them in these necessary points and that on all occasions we show forth a Christian and benevolent spirit toward them.[37]

In spite of the drastic action, reported above in the expelling

---

[33]Min. Chesterfield Mo. Mtg., 6/VI/1730.   [34]*Ibid.*, 3/VIII/1775.
[35]*Ibid.*, 1/VIII/1776.   [36]*Ibid.*, 10/IX/1778.   [37]*Ibid.*, 5/VIII/1779.

of members, the meeting had still in 1786 to report that there were two cases of Negroes held in slavery and that more attention was needed for those set free. A year later they reported none held as slaves and a "care on the minds of Friends" regarding their education. In 1789, according to the Yearly Meeting's desire a committee was appointed to advise and assist them in temporal and spiritual affairs.

Upper Springfield reported in 1784 they were "clear of purchasing, disposing or of holding mankind as slaves, except some late instances . . ." and "there is some care taken for their education."[38] In 1795, "one minor held" but "education too much neglected, both as to religion and learning," was the essence of their report. By 1803 the situation had improved:

We know of no slaves amongst us and the few black people under our care appear to be well used, with some care for their religious education.[39]

Mount Holly Monthly Meeting in 1780 reported two slaves not manumitted, and that the meeting was interested in "discharging their duty with those Negroes that are manumitted."[40] Two years later they report

the releasement of our fellowmen from bondage is completed and their education has been in a good degree attended to, as well as justice done to those set free. . .

At the same time, the care of Negroes and schools was placed under a new committee:

Isaac Hilliard, Samuel Hilliard, Asa Shinn, William Lovet Smith and Thomas Gaskill are appointed to have the care of negroes that are set free and their education and the establishment of schools for the instruction of our children agreeable to the direction of the Yearly Meeting heretofore and in the present Extracts, and to report to our Meeting as soon as necessary.[41]

Following the urgent advices of the Yearly Meeting in 1754 and 1758, such members of Haddonfield Monthly Meeting as still held slaves were dealt with. In 1760, the minutes inform that:

J. W. appeared and declared that he did not know that the purchasing a negro was a breach of our discipline or he should not have done it—in confirmation thereof he hath set his hand to this minute in the meeting (J. W.)[42]

The next twenty years witnessed great changes. In 1771 a

---

[38] Min. U. S. Mo. Mtg., 4/VIII/1784.   [39] *Ibid.*, 9/II/1803.
[40] Min. Mt. Holly Mo. Mtg., 9/VIII/1780.   [41] *Ibid.*, 4/XII/1782.
[42] Min. Haddonfield Mo. Mtg., 14/IV/1760.

committee, appointed to visit such as still held Negroes reported there had been "good satisfaction to the visitors and, by what appeared, also to the visited."[43] The effect on "the visited" was more tangibly expressed in 1777 when the committee reported they had "gone thru the service of visiting those who have them and obtained manumission for 18."[44] They shortly announced the manumission of 28 more.

As was the general custom, at this time, religious meetings were established for Negroes, as described in the following minute:

This meeting from a desire to promote religion and virtue among the negroes of this neighborhood and from a sympathy with them, appoints a public meeting for worship to be held with that people at this house on the first day preceding our next Monthly Meeting to begin at 2 o'clock in the afternoon.[45]

The promotion of religious gatherings was followed immediately by a more adequate plan to raise funds for Negro education, in which connection a committee reported:

The committee appointed to consider the proper step to be taken for schooling of the children of Free Negroes, made report in writing which was approved in manner following.

The Yearly Meeting having long manifested a concern that the law of righteousness might more unitedly prevail among us, with regard of doing to others as we would they should do to us, and thereby abolish the unrighteous practice of holding our fellowmen in slavery; which concern has been blessed with success so that there are but few remaining slave holders among us; but as their education has been too generally neglected whereby they are disqualified for improving the advantage of freedom, these with other considerations induced the Monthly Meeting of Haddonfield to propose raising a fund to be applied in schooling of negro children; and we the subscribers being appointed to consider how this benevolent intention may, the most effectually be carried into execution do propose the sum of one hundred pounds be immediately raised by subscription, and that the Monthly Meeting should appoint a treasurer to receive said money or notes payable on demand, and the committee appointed, agreeable to the advice of last Yearly Meeting, should consist of two or more Friends in each Meeting and be distinguished by the name of the Committee for Negro affairs, and have the charge and laying out of said money for schooling negro children, buying books, or any other use necessary for their school education, and have stated meetings one in three months to confer with and assist each other in perfecting the object of their appointment and the treasurer to pay out said money agreeable to the direction of the committee, at any of the said meetings, for the purposes aforesaid; and he to keep fair accounts of all his receivings and disbursements and

---

[43]*Ibid.*, 9/IX/1771.   [44]*Ibid.*, 14/VII/1777.   [45]*Ibid.*, 11/I/1779.

lay them before the Monthly Meeting in the 8th month annually and at such other times as may be required by the said meeting; and it is our sense that the giving to this service ought to be a free will offering and that no Friend should be urged or persuaded to give; all which we submit to the Meeting.

Woodbury, 2nd mo. 15th 1779.

Solomon Lippincott
David Cooper
Thomas Redman, John Hopkins
Samuel Paul
James Whitehall, Jun.[46]

In accordance with the above proposal the meetings of Haddonfield, Woodbury and Upper Greenwich raised within three months the sum of £ 131/14/0.

By 1782 Haddonfield Monthly was able to report that "we have no negroes held in bondage . . ." But, though this was achieved, more attention was needed in other respects. Thereafter, frequent minutes inform us that "care has been extended to free Negroes, to advise and assist them in their temporal concerns," special Negro meetings were continued,[47] and assistance afforded respecting the education of their children.[48] Regarding education, the committee reported, in 1788, money was being raised and some had been applied to schooling of Negro children. From all available records it appears that Negro education was provided on the same basis as for other poor children, as indicated in the following extract:

The committee appointed reported they had paid some attention to schools, kept within the compass of this meeting to good satisfaction. One large school has been kept up at Haddonfield, and a number of black children have partaken of school learning with other poor children, from the fund provided for that purpose.[49]

At Evesham Monthly Meeting in 1771 Friends were appointed to visit those that kept slaves. After four years the situation was described as follows:

Those that hold slaves have been closely treated with and there appears only two men within the compass of Evesham, and 4 men and 3 women at Chester, that are of suitable age to be set at liberty, that are held in bondage, some of which there is a prospect of their being set at liberty.[50]

In 1780,

---

[46]*Ibid.*, 23/III/1779.
[47]These religious meetings were held in every locality.
[48]*Ibid.*, 12/IX/1785; 8/V/1786; and 10/XII/1787.
[49]*Ibid.*, 8/IX/1794.   [50]Min. Evesham Mo. Mtg., 7/IX/1775.

The committee in negro cases proposed to this Meeting the raising a sum of money in order for schooling the children of that people, which, after consideration was approved of; and the sum of £ 12 is agreed to be raised for that purpose, which the preparative meetings are desired to attend to and report to next meeting and said committee are desired to expedite the schooling of such children as soon as conveniency will admit.[51]

Provision was made for religious services as in other localities. In 1791 the committee on Negroes reported it had been "instrumental towards the enlargement of some of that people by manumission, admitting of others partaking of school learning, and the placing of others out apprentices."[52]

Similar reports were made in the northern and eastern Quaker settlements. Shrewsbury Quarterly Meeting noted in 1756:

For some time past Friends have neither bought nor imported negroes, but we fear some that have them do not fully discharge their duty to them in training them up in the principles of the Christian religion, some there is that is careful in the discharge of their duty in that respect.[53]

In 1769 they report themselves "clear of importing, but one Friend under dealing for buying,—a shortness we believe as to their education." Similar reports were made for several years. In 1773 it was necessary to deal with certain members for purchasing Negroes.

All the committee except one, appointed by the Quarterly Meeting held in the 8th month last, to assist the Monthly Meeting of Shrewsbury in a case, depending in the said Meeting relative of some Friends that had purchased negroes for a number of years, reported in writing that they had attended two Monthly Meetings on the occasion and that the said Meetings had solidly deliberated and considered the case and had agreed and concluded that those Friends who had purchased said negroes as aforesaid, had acted therein contrary to the rules of discipline established amongst Friends and were to be treated with on the occasion.[54]

Woodbridge, in 1775,

. . .agreed to report that we have enquired into their situation and we find that some of them are old and incapable of procuring a comfortable subsistence were they to be set free by their masters and that some are under age, and encouragement given that they should have learning and when of age that they should be manumitted and that there is one we judge proper for freedom whose master cannot be prevailed with to set him free.[55]

[51] *Ibid.*, 7/XII/1780.   [52] *Ibid.*, 9/XII/1791.
[53] Min. Shrewsbury Q. Mtg., 26/I/1756.   [54] *Ibid.*, 26/IV/1773.
[55] Min. Woodbridge Mo. Mtg., 19/IV/1775.

The number held as slaves at Rahway and Plainfield Monthly Meeting in 1803 had been reduced to two:

Rahway Preparative Meeting informs that Aaron Shotwell holds a black woman contrary to the rules of our discipline. This meeting agrees to refer the consideration thereof till next month. Also that Daniel Hurley had purchased a lad to serve till he became twenty-eight years of age, and has since sold him for the same term. Thomas Bills, John Moore Carpenter and Joseph Laing are appointed to treat with him on the occasion and report to next Meeting.[56]

The next year these two cases had been disposed of and the meeting reported "no slaves among us" and "care is taken of those who are set free and are necessarily under our care."[57]

In 1792 Isabel Hartshorne gave in her last will the sum of £ 200 "to be used for the schooling of poor children, particularly those of the blacks." This sum, it would seem, was never actually paid to the trustees until 1844.[58] Thereafter it was applied to Negro education, being used to sustain a colored school in Rahway. This colored school was apparently under the control of Friends, as a minute adds "The said trustees on the 31st of the 5th month 1872 gave up the colored school to the City of Rahway to be thereafter under its control." The amount of the legacy in 1873 was $852.08.[59]

In the Salem Quarter a report of 1756 stated that "none imported" but some "not so careful to train them up in the principles of the Christian religion as they ought."[60] A year later the same report is made, with the exception "that there has been one purchased since last Quarter." The purchaser was at once visited:

This Meeting appoints James Daniel and Joshua Thompson to treat with our Friend Samuel Mason concerning his purchasing a negro and endeavor to convince him of his error therein and report to next Meeting.[61]

The frequent urging of the Yearly Meeting seems to have been responsible, largely, for the movement towards a more liberal care of Negroes' education, described in this minute of 1778:

A concern having prevailed in the minds of many Friends for some years respecting the education of negro children, at least so far as to be capable of

---

[56]Min. Rahway and Plainfield Mo. Mtg., 20/IV/1803. Meeting known as Woodbridge until 1789.
[57]*Ibid.*, 19/I/1804.   [58]Amounting to $759.53 at that time.
[59]Min. Rahway Prep. Mtg. Women Friends, 13/III/1873.
[60]Min. Salem Mo. Mtg., 25/X/1756.   [61]*Ibid.*, 28/XI/1757.

reading the Scriptures and other writings and being now revived, it was proposed to this Meeting to raise a sum of money by subscription to be applied in
such a manner as Friends may think most conducive to the end intended and
it is recommended to each Preparative Meeting to enter into subscription for
that purpose and Mark Reeve, Samuel Lippincott, Edward Bradway and
Bartholomew Wyatt are appointed to take the necessary care in each Meeting
and report to next.[62]

Soon after, some of the committee reported that "from the
unanimity and liberality that appeared amongst Friends it is
likely a considerable sum may be raised that may be sufficient to
answer the purpose." Another committee was named to determine
how the money should be applied, and make report as follows:

We the committee appointed to consider in what manner the money now
raised for the education and schooling the negroes may be best applied, having
several times met and deliberately considered the subject matter, their distance
from each other and the difficulty of settling a school for them at present by
themselves do agree to report and advise that two or more Friends be appointed
in each Meeting to have the care and oversight of them and to provide schooling
and books for all such as they may think proper and pay for it out of the said
moneys without distinction of bond or free, and to have a care of their conduct
and morals, to advise and reprove as occasion may require, that so we may
demonstrate that we have their future good and present well being at heart.
Visiting such schools at suitable times to inspect their conduct and improvement and once a year render proper and full accounts of all moneys expended
and on whom, and what improvement they have made, unto such whom the
Meeting may appoint and that such a care and labor may not become burthen-
some such Friends as are appointed may be released on application and others
appointed in their room.[63]

In 1782, the following report was sent up to the Yearly Meeting:

Our care has been extended to our fellowmen who have been released from
bondage and a visit performed to them in their several habitations in order to
encourage them in a life of virtue and morality and assistance afforded them in
the schooling of their children.[64]

Reports, similar to the above, now became the general rule. In
1801 the minutes inform that "none are held in bondage" and
there "is an increasing concern for the religious and civil benefit
of the black people."[65] This interest was a continued one. In
1852 among items of the financial report we find that there was
$30.00 appropriated to pay teachers of the colored school.[66]

As has been found in all other localities, so in the vicinity of

---

[62]*Ibid.*, 29/VI/1778.   [63]*Ibid.*, 26/X/1778.   [64]*Ibid.*, 26/VIII/1782.
[65]*Ibid.*, 20/I/1801.   [66]*Ibid.*, 31/III/1852.

Salem, there were stated religious meetings appointed for the Negroes under the direction of prominent members of the Society. Concerning these they often write:

It appeared they were measurably sensible of the kindness extended towards them through Friends' care, by their respectful and affectionate conduct.

The attitude of the Quaker settlers of New Jersey and Pennsylvania towards the native Indians, forms another exception to the general truth quoted from Bryce at the beginning of this chapter. In the liberal, humble spirit of these settlers may not be found that "sense of scornful superiority" which resists the teachings of Christianity.

The basis for just dealing with the inferior peoples was laid in Chapters XXV and XXVI of *The Concessions and Agreements of West Jersey* the text of which follows:

That there may be a good understanding and friendly correspondence between the Proprietors, Freeholders, and Inhabitants of the said Province, and the Indian Natives thereof.

It is concluded and agreed, that if any of the Indian Natives within the said Province, shall or may do any wrong or injury to any of the Proprietors, Freeholders, or inhabitants in person, estate, or otherways howsoever, upon notice thereof, or complaint made to the Commissioners, or any two of them, they are to give notice to the Sachem or other chief person or persons, that hath authority over the said Indian Native or Natives, that Justice may be done, and satisfaction made to the person or persons offended, according to Law and Equity, and the nature and quality of the offence and injury done or committed.

And also in case any of the Proprietors, Freeholders or inhabitants shall any wise wrong or injure any of the Indian Natives there, in person, estate, or otherwise, the Commissioners are to take care upon complaint to them made, or any one of them, either by the Indian Natives or others, that justice be done to the Indian Natives, and plenary satisfaction made them according to the nature and quality of the offence and injury. And that in all trials wherein any of the said Indian Natives are concerned, the trial to be by six of the neighborhood, and six of the said Indian Natives, to be indifferently and impartially chosen by order of the Commissioners, and that the Commissioners use their endeavor to persuade the Natives to the like way of trial, when any of the Natives do any ways wrong or injure the said Proprietors, Freeholders, or inhabitants, that they choose six of the Natives and six of the freeholders or inhabitants, to judge of the wrong and injury done, and to proportion satisfaction accordingly.

It is agreed that when any land is to be taken up for settlements of towns, or otherways, before it be surveyed, the Commissioners or the major part of

them are to appoint some persons to go to the chief of the Natives concerned
in that land, so intended to be taken up, to acquaint the natives of their intention, and to give the Natives what present they shall agree upon, for their
good will or consent, and take a grant of the same in writing, under their hands
and seals, or some other public way used in those parts of the world; which
grant is to be registered in the public Register, allowing also the Natives (if
they please) a copy thereof, and that no person or persons, take up any land,
but by order from the Commissioners, for the time being.[67]

This was the basis of their dealings with the Natives, and so
successfully was it incorporated in practice, that no Indian war
filled the pages of New Jersey's history.   Thus, she was unique
among the "fires" of the white men.

Throughout the latter part of the seventeenth and most of the
eighteenth centuries most efforts for betterment of the Indians,
in a religious and educational way, were individual.   The works
of Chalkley, Story, Fox, Benezet, Savery, Richardson, Woolman,
and many others, emphasize the fact that they came and went
among the Indian Natives because of an individual "concern."
The sentiment of the society as a whole was favorable towards the
Indian, but it was generally believed that instruction of a practical
nature would be more efficacious than much exhortation.   The
advices of the Yearly Meeting on the subject of Indians are always
of very practical import.

Soon after the establishment of the Yearly Meeting at Philadelphia and Burlington the following advice regarding Indians was
sent out:

This Meeting doth unanimously agree and give as their judgment that it is
not consistent with the honor of truth for any that makes profession thereof, to
sell rum, or other strong liquors to the Indians, because they use them not to
moderation but to excess and drunkenness.[68]

The above advice was often repeated, and in 1687 it was directed
to be transcribed in every monthly meeting book "and every Friend
belonging to the said Meeting to subscribe the same."   It was also
added in 1719 that "to avoid giving them occasion of discontent
it is desired that Friends do not buy or sell Indian slaves."   Three
years later a minute informs that

it is yet too notorious that the same (advice) hath not been duly observed by
some persons and therefore it is become the weighty concern of this Meeting

[67]Signed in 1676-7.   N. J. ARCHIVES, First Series, I, 259-60.
[68]*Ms.* Advices of the Yearly Meeting, 102.

earnestly to recommend the said testimony to the strict observance of all Friends, and where any under our profession shall act contrary there unto, let them be speedily dealt with and censured for such their evil practice.[69]

This was repeated and spread throughout the meetings. In 1763 it was further advised, that Friends should not

purchase nor remove to settle such lands as have not been fairly and openly first purchased from the Indians by those persons who are, or may be fully authorized by the government to make such purchases. . .and that Monthly Meetings should urge a strict observance of this advice.

This was but a reiteration of the principle heretofore adhered to, as in the cases of the earliest settlements the land was first purchased from the Indian holders.

In the last decade of the eighteenth century the Yearly Meeting of Philadelphia became interested in practical efforts to relieve the situation of the Indians of the Six Nations, and to this work the lower meetings contributed. At a conference between the United States and the Six Nations at Canandaigua in New York, representatives of the Society of Friends were present upon request.[70] The Friends remained there some two months and, during their conference there was expressed a desire that Friends might send teachers to them.[71] This was accomplished and the work thus began was soon transferred to the direction of New York Yearly Meeting.

In 1798 several Friends went among the Senecas, in the Allegheny Valley near the southern boundary of New York, and began the mission work at Genesanguhta, which was later (1804) transferred to Tunesassah.[72] Here it was that a school for Indian boys was set up by Joseph Elkinton and one for the girls by Mary Nutt. The purchase of land, about 750 acres, and the establishing of saw and grist mills were necessary steps toward a practical as well as "literary" education. Such steps were expensive and it was to meet the expense that the Yearly Meeting called on local meetings for assistance.

All monthly meetings in the several Quarters of New Jersey

---

[69]*Ibid.*, 104.   [70]*Quaker Biographies*, 122.

[71]Some years before Cornplanter, Chief of the Senecas, had requested aid, and instruction from the Friends. See Woody: *Quaker Education in Pa.*, 263–4.

[72]Min. Phila. Yr. Mtg. Indian Committee, I, 189–90; also *Quaker Biographies*, 111–139, and Kelsey, *Friends and the Indians*, Ch. V.

responded readily to the request for assistance. The early minutes of a few of them, relating to the subject are given below. In 1795 Burlington minuted:

The important concern of the Yearly Meeting respecting the civilization and well being of the Indian Nations, as mentioned in the Extracts, gaining our solid attention, it was decided that two or more persons be appointed in each Preparative Meeting to raise subscriptions agreeably to the recommendation of the Yearly Meeting's Committee and forward the same to John Smith, who is desired to report the sum he may so receive and forward it to John Elliot, Treasurer of the said Committee. The following persons are appointed to the service—John Cox, Jr., John Smith, Robert Smith Jr., Joseph Buxby, Samuel Wills Jr., Solomon Thomas, Joshua Newbold, Cleayton Brown and Samuel Woolman.[73]

Upper Springfield Monthly Meeting acknowledged receipt of information relative to the Indians in 1795 and, at once appointed a committee "in order that that great and desirable work may be carried into effect."[74] A year later this meeting's report stated they had raised $295.75 for the "Indian Welfare." In similar manner, whenever requests were made collections were started and the work supported. The amounts were sometimes small, sometimes large. The smallest meetings took part. East Branch Preparative mentioned a subscription of $14.12½ for the Indians in 1806;[75] Medford Monthly sent $54.04 to their quarterly meeting for that purpose in 1806;[76] and Haddonfield, at the same time, sent in $138.00.[77] Salem, in 1795, noted the Yearly Meeting's rquest for aid, and appointed a committee to raise money:

A minute of the Quarterly Meeting being produced and read in the Meeting recommending to the attention of Friends that part of the Extracts relating to making some provision towards assisting the Indian natives in the civilization and the circular letter from the committee and some copies of letters from Indian Natives being read, the Meeting uniting therewith, William Carpenter and Clement Hall are appointed to hand the subscription round and amongst Friends to report to next Meeting.[78]

A few months thereafter,

The committee appointed to take subscriptions for the Indian Natives now reported that £ 92/12/6 has been collected and forwarded to the Treasurer for

---

[73]Min. Burlington Mo. Mtg., 7/XII/1795.
[74]Min. U. S. Mo. Mtg., 9/XII/1795.
[75]Min. East Branch Prep. Mtg., 20/III/1806.
[76]Min. Medford Mo. Mtg., 8/III/1806.
[77]Min. Haddonfield Mo. Mtg., 14/IV/1806.
[78]Min. Salem. Mo. Mtg., 30/XI/1795.

their benefit and that there is £ 56/15/0 now ready which is directed to be put into the hands of John Wistar to pay forward.[79]

The support of work among the Indians, though the missions were not in their midst, was thus generously assisted by Quaker meetings of New Jersey and continued even to the present day.

[79]*Ibid.*, 29/VIII/1796.

CHAPTER X

SCHOOL CONTROL AND ORGANIZATION

CENTRAL CONTROL

Schools were established by the Quaker organization as an adjunct to the church. The common aim of colonial elementary education emphasized the religious values to be derived from schools. The education of the Quakers was practical, moral and religious, above all else; a useful education for the life the individual must lead. As the meeting and its activity bulked large in the life of the member it was but natural that the meetings should control the school. This control of agencies, such as the church and the school, however, required some years to develop. The meetings grew up and schools were later created to help perfect their control of the institution over the individual. The most perfect crystallization of the educational efforts of the meeting came a full century after the first settlement of English Quakers in New Jersey. Nevertheless, the rising tide of interest in the question on the part of the superior meetings can be traced throughout that period.

The schools being created by the meetings, it is natural to find that their external control fell into its hands. Therefore an understanding of the meeting's organization is essential to a comprehension of school control. The system of meetings comprised four grades: (1) the yearly, (2) quarterly, (3) monthly, and (4) preparative or particular meetings. The relation of the Yearly to the lower meetings is represented schematically in the drawing on page 289.[1]

The functions of the Yearly Meeting were at first advisory and have continued so; but to the advisory functions there was added a more specific control. Often, as a result of the tendency towards centralization, advice of the Yearly Meeting was sent to the quarterly, and in turn, to monthly and preparative meetings. The

---

[1]Reproduced from Woody: *Early Quaker Education in Pennsylvania*, 18. For a more thorough discussion of the development of meetings and their relation to educational work, consult Chapter Two of the work cited.

actual establishment of schools, with a few exceptions, was accomplished by the monthly and the preparative meetings, through the agency of special trustees or school committees.

The London Yearly Meeting, established in 1672, began to urge the provision of "schoolmasters and mistresses who are faithful Friends to teach and instruct their children . . ." as early as 1690; and repeated the advice on many occasions thereafter. Similarly,

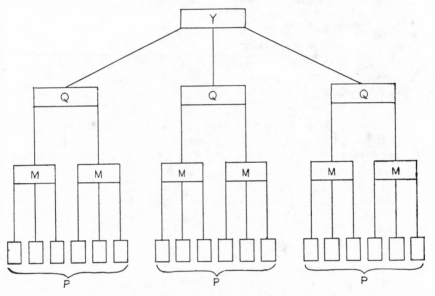

PLAN OF THE MEETING ORGANIZATION

"advices" were sent out by Philadelphia and Burlington Yearly Meeting, when it was established,[2] but its advices did not in any way act as a substitute for those of London. Thus Burlington in 1761 acknowledged the receipt of "forty of the Printed Yearly Meeting's Epistles of London," which were distributed to lower meetings and caused to be read in them.[3]

Upon receipt of the more urgent, and specific instruction from Philadelphia in 1778, a very evident concern is found in the

[2] For fuller discussion of the educational policy of the Quakers see Chapter Two.
[3] Min. Burlington Mo. Mtg., 7/XII/1761.

minutes of most of the lower meetings, yet in almost all there is an admission that they find the difficulties numerous, and the room for improvement quite large. The following comment from the records of Evesham Meeting is typical of the sentiment in many localities:

> The earnest advice of the Yearly Meeting respecting the education of youth and the establishment of schools under the direction of religious teachers, hath been measurably attended to, and it appears that the cause gradually gains the attention of many friends; and most of the schools are taught by members of the society, under the care of committees appointed to that service. Yet there is room for further weighty labor in that respect.[4]

It is not to be assumed from the above that initiative lay entirely in the Yearly Meeting. Its guidance was always sought, and its favorable decision in a matter was necessary for success of a movement, such as education; but, far more progressive attitudes were at times expressed by lower meetings. A case in point was Chester's urgent demands that a more definite stand be taken with regard to slave holding.[5] Likewise, on the subject of education, the following committee report of Salem evinces a very progressive attitude on several points.

> The committee appointed in the fifth month last on the subject of the religious guarded education of our children, both at home and at school, way has not opened to propose to the Quarterly Meeting any settled plan or step to be taken or pursued by this Meeting in relation to the establishment of schools; yet it is believed if friends in their different neighborhoods would keep sufficiently alive to the importance of this concern a more lively zeal will be manifested in the support of our primary schools—and that as Friends manifest a liberal disposition for the encouragement of these schools, teachers among the younger part of society of both sexes, will feel their minds engaged to enter into this noble and dignified calling of expanding the youthful mind and teaching the young idea how to shoot. And, in neighborhoods where friends are so circumstanced as not to be able to keep a school the whole of the year under well qualified male teachers, it is believed that competent female teachers might be obtained especially in the summer season, under whose religious feeling care, our children might be profitably instructed in school learning and their precious minds preserved in a good degree of innocency. The committee have felt particularly desirous that this part or view of the subject should claim the close attention of friends, everywhere being persuaded it would prove a blessing to the children not only of Friends but others. And it is also believed that if such schools were visited by committees of friends who felt a lively concern for

---

[4]Min. Evesham Mo. Mtg., 6/IX/1781.
[5]*Ms.* Christian and Brotherly Advices, pp. 195 and 198.

their improvement they would prove useful in supporting the dignity and order of the schools, a strength to the teachers, and afford encouragement to the children; and when female teachers are engaged that these committees be composed of both sexes. They would also recommend that Friends keep in view the advice of the Yearly Meeting that where Friends are so circumstanced as to be able to keep up a school or schools, that they manifest greater liberality towards well qualified teachers in the prices of tuition; also in furnishing such schools with proper books, maps, globes and other apparatus necessary for an improved state of instruction; thus way might be opened for children to be admitted into these schools who might be boarded at a reasonable price, and an opportuuity furnished them (as well as those within their limits) for a liberal education consistent with our profession; and thus give stability and permanency to such schools.

And it is further believed that if we were all more concerned to live up to the golden rule of doing unto others as we would they should do unto us, under like circumstances, and look around us, within the limits of our several meetings, children might be found among our members who are so circumstanced that it is difficult for them to come at such an education as would qualify them to be most useful to society; much good might be done by friends of sufficient ability and liberality in taking such into their families and giving them their board or otherwise contributing to their education.

Signed on behalf of the committee,

By David Cooper   Hannah Cooper
Thomas Shourds   Elizabeth T. Andrews[6]

Yet, united action was never accomplished without the leadership of the Yearly Meeting. It collected and disseminated information, aroused enthusiasm in the backward meeting, gave advice, helped select proper teachers when desired, made visitations, arbitrated exceptional cases,[7] and was generally ready to perform such duties as seemed needful from time to time. In 1839 it

---

[6]Min. Maurice River Mo. Mtg., Women Friends, (H), 13/XI/1834.

[7]One example of many appeals to the authority of the Yearly Meeting may be mentioned:

"The subject of setting apart a portion of the Fund left under the care of the Monthly Meeting, by the will of David Bacon, for school purposes, to assist in sustaining Friends school at Mullica Hill, having come before the meeting, and after a free discussion of the matter, it was thought best to apply to the Representative Committee for its advice in the case. . .The friends continued last month in charge of the matter, concerning the Bacon School Fund, report that they referred the subject to the subcommittee appointed by the Representative Committee who made a clear explanation. The report is accepted and directed to be recorded. And the Bacon School Fund directed to be annually apportioned amongst all pay schools under the care of Friends within the limits of the Monthly Meeting, agreeable to said report." Min. Pilesgrove Mo. Mtg., (H.), 28/VIII/1877 and 30/X/1877.

stated that "a lively interest was manifested for the welfare of the youth . . ." in the several quarterly meetings,[8] and urged

> that those who have received a liberal education might turn their minds towards the improvement of the condition of the ignorant and destitute by promoting schools for their instruction; that there may be none of any class to whom our influence can extend, without the means of obtaining at least the rudiments of education.[9]

In 1842, recognizing the difficulty experienced by local meetings in the country "in procuring for their children the opportunity of a guarded religious and literary education consistent with the principles and testimonies of our society . . .," a large committee was appointed to investigate conditions and to find ways "of affording efficient relief to Friends so circumstanced." This committee undertook to gather full information as to the status of meetings educationally, by means of a questionnaire, given below:[10]

Query 1st. What number of children of each sex is there belonging to your meeting of a suitable age to go to school, say between five and sixteen years old? State how many are in the way of receiving education; and how many are not; and the age and sex of the latter.

2nd. What number of them reside near enough together to attend conveniently at the same school; and how many are situated so far from the others as to render this impracticable?

3rd. Is there a school within your limits taught by a member and superintended by a committee of the Monthly or Preparative Meeting? If there is state the whole number of children who attend it, and what proportion of them are members; and what is the price charged for tuition.

4th. What school houses and school funds are there belonging to your meeting; and how are they situated and used.

5th. Does any school under the care of Friends within your limits receive aid from the public funds? If it does, state to what extent; and how far the school officers of the district or township consider it under their jurisdiction; and what account is rendered, and to whom of the disbursement of the money so received.

6th. Is there any school (except the Public District Schools) within your limits, taught by a member of our Society, which is not under the care of a committee of the Monthly or Preparative Meeting? If there is state what

---

[8]Extracts Phila. Yr. Mtg. Minutes (H.), 1839, pp. 5–6.   [9]*Ibid.*

[10]It should be mentioned, in this connection that the increased centralization of control in the Yearly Meeting in the latter part of the century, was due in part to the fact that the institution of public schools in Pennsylvania in 1834, and the withdrawing of public funds from church schools in 1866 in New Jersey, necessitated a more perfectly organized system that could offer effective competition. See also Chapter Thirteen.

branches are taught in it; and the price charged for tuition; and what number of Friends' children attend it.

7th. What Public or District schools are there within the limits of your Meeting; and what number of Friends' children attend them? State what proportion of the year those schools are kept open, the number of scholars usually in attendance, and the general character of the schools and of the teachers.

8th. What family schools are there among Friends of your Meeting; are they taught by members of the family or teachers hired for the purpose; do they receive other children than those of the family; and if so how many? State also whether the persons who teach them are Friends.

Any other information which may tend to elucidate the state of education within your Meeting is also solicited.[11]

In 1854 a similar list of 9 questions was answered by the quarterly meetings belonging to the Yearly Meeting of Hicksite Friends.[12] This was to secure additional information to that furnished by answers to the second annual query.

During the last quarter of the 19th century the Yearly Meeting resorted to visitation as a more effective means for maintaining a close relation with local schools, and a valuable supplement to written communication. Pilesgrove, in 1874, mentioned the arrival of a "portion of the Committee on Education from Philadelphia Yearly Meeting" and adjourned their meeting "to hold a conference with them."[13] In 1881 the Educational Committee's Report stated apropos of this point:

Feeling the continued importance of the concern entrusted to our care, and fully realizing the inestimable value to the youth of our Society of a truly guarded religious education, we have endeavored, during the past year to labor in the work as ability was afforded.

Small committees set apart for the purpose, have visited Friends in several neighborhoods, and earnestly urged them to gather the children within the fold of the Society, and surround them with the friendly atmosphere of Monthly and Preparative Meeting Schools under the care of religiously-concerned teachers, in membership with us. These visits have always been received in a spirit of kindness, and the appeals regarded with thoughtful consideration, ending in some places in the starting of new schools, or in the more general

---

[11]Copied from the Min. Burlington Mo. Mtg., 1842. These queries were answered by the local school committees of the Preparative and Monthly Meetings, and forwarded to the Yearly Meeting's committee. See no. 49, Burlington Prep. Mtg., School Trustees' Report at 142 N. 16th Street, Philadelphia.

[12]Min. Burlington Q. Mtg., (H.), 28/II/1854.

[13]Pilesgrove Mo. Mtg., (H.), 29/XII/1874.

and united support of those already in existence, but languishing for want of help; and where there has been no outward evidence of good resulting from the spread of the concern we have reason to believe it is owned by individual minds, who, by faithfulness, can promote its growth.

The difficulties at first encountered do not seem to diminish. Friends in their neighborhoods are often widely separated, other schools are numerous, good teachers are not always to be had, and many Friends, apparently well qualified to serve on School committees, do not seem willing to accept the service, and give the patient, intelligent care so needful to the proper success of a school.

The methods of instruction, the branches to be taught, what constitutes the proper qualifications of teachers, and how shall the schools perform the best work for the head, the hand and the heart of the rising generation, are subjects worthy not only of the attention and close study of School Committees, but of parents and guardians, who are encouraged to manifest their interest by frequent visits to the schools, and by giving their hearty support to rightly-concerned teachers, in their interesting but arduous work.

The subject of a General Superintendency over all our schools, by a thoroughly competent person, though not as yet fully united with by our Committee, continues from time to time to claim our attention, and press with great force upon many, who, in the visits made to several localities during the year, have seen where such service might be productive of much good.

We have expended during the year, in aid of schools $400, and for other expenses $17.98, making a total of $417.98.[14]

From general visitations, visitation by small special committees, and a general superintendent it was but a short step to entire control The Extracts for 1887 stated the Committee had supplied both permanent, special, and substitute teachers as occasion required, and that "in three instances, at the request or approval of monthly or preparative meetings, our committee . . . assumed the entire responsibility of the schools for the year, with the view of placing them on a firm basis . . .", with the view however, of "returning them again into the hands of the local committees . . ." when thus established. At this stage of development of the centralized control on the part of the Yearly Meeting one may well turn to an examination of the local control exercised by the trustees and school committees of the monthly and preparative meetings.[15]

LOCAL CONTROL

The local control of the school was in the hands of the monthly

---

[14]Extracts of Phila. Yr. Meeting (H.), 1881, pp. 9–11.
[15]Extracts Min. Phila. Yr. Mtg., (H.), 1887, 20–23.

or preparative meetings and it was accordingly known generally as a monthly or preparative meeting school. The actual task of looking after the school affairs, however, was given into the hands of school committees or trustees, who were responsible to the body that appointed them. This school committee became a most necessary factor as life increased in complexity; and especially, when the Yearly Meeting urged better schools in 1778 was it essential. Not only did the committee become the most important agent of control, but in some cases functions were specialized; some were to look after buildings and grounds; others, the visitation of schools, and hiring of teachers; while some committees, to judge from their reports, did little more than handle the financial matters for the meeting.

The committee was never anything more than the meeting's agent, which was directed to exercise certain powers. But, having performed its functions, it was bound to report results to the meeting for approval. Thus in 1791, "the report of the committee of schools" at Chesterfield,

being revived. . .the meeting. . .recommends the Preparative of Chesterfield they are hereby authorized to open a school. . .and make rules. . .for the government. . .of the institution, which rules and regulations shall always be inspected by the Monthly Meeting's committee for their approbation or disallowance. . .[16]

Voluminous illustrations could be cited to show this dependence of the trustees or committees upon meetings, but it is perhaps sufficient, in view of material presented elsewhere,[17] to quote the rules devised by Salem, late in the 19th century but which are quite representative, and show the limitations placed by the meeting on its school committee:

Rule 1st.   That the school shall be under the charge of 6 trustees, appointed annually by the Monthly Meeting whose duty it shall be to employ a teacher in such manner as they may think best for the benefit of the school.

Rule 2nd.   That the teacher so employed shall charge and collect the price per Quarter for each pupil as fixed upon by the trustees.

[16]Min. Chesterfield Mo. Mtg., 15/XII/1791.

[17]The account of educational activities of committees of various Meetings in Chapters Three, Four, Five and Six contains further evidence of dependence and limitation. It may be added, however, that committees always desired the approval of the meeting, and that treasurers' accounts were always carefully reviewed before they were released from service or named for another year. A minimum of dissatisfaction was the result.

Rule 3rd. That in case the trustees think it proper, to contract with the teacher, allowing him or her a stipulated price for each term, and if there should be a deficiency after collecting the price fixed upon for each pupil, the teacher may make out a bill for such deficiency, when, if signed by 4 trustees it may be presented to the treasurer of the Preparative Meeting for payment.

Rule 4th. The trustees should be careful to employ a teacher who is a member of the Society of Friends or a professor with them, having a good moral character who will use the plain language to the pupils. He or she should also be thoroly educated in the various branches and be well recommended.

Rule 5th. It will be required of the teacher to attend Mid-week Meeting with his or her pupils, having a guarded care over them while there, that their conduct may be orderly and the meeting not disturbed, that the object for so assembling may be realized.

Rule 6th. That the number of pupils instructed by one teacher shall not exceed 30, when an assistant may be employed as is the judgment of the trustees.

Rule 7th. That preference be given to children of Friends; if there should be more applicants than there are seats to accommodate. Parents and guardians of other children should be informed by the teacher, that they will be received only on condition that they comply with the rules of the school, a copy of which should be shown them.

Rule 8th. That the school be divided into terms of 55 days each; 2 sessions to be taught per day, having a recess in each, if thought proper of 15 minutes. Parents or guardians should be encouraged to send their children at the opening of each term and have them punctual in their attendance, as the charge will be by the term without loss of time, except in a clear evidence of sickness.

Rule 9th. The school should be visited by the trustees once a month at a stated time, and it is recommended that they call at other times when convenient; also that they attend jointly at the end of each term and have the teacher (review?) his or her pupils thoroly, and evidence to the trustees that they understand and can explain the various branches they have studied.

Rule 10th. That it be the duty of the teacher to enforce strict discipline in the school and preserve good order. Also to have a care over the school property that the desks be not defaced during recess and that each pupil replace damages of minor importance such as breaking windows, lights, etc. It is also enjoined upon him or her to have a guarded care over the morals of his pupils, to allow no corrupt unbecoming language used out of school whilst under his or her care, keeping those from the country as much as possible out of the streets of the town. It is also recommended that the teacher be absent from the house for as short a time as possible at noon, especially during the winter term.

Rule 11th. That the teacher keep a correct list of the children of Friends attending school each term and the length of time they attend as also all other children, to be furnished to the trustees for the information of the Monthly Meeting.

Rule 12th. That the above rules be posted in a conspicuous place in the school room to remain there and be observed until altered or otherwise directed by the Monthly Meeting.[18]

The school committee was apparently composed of members of unusual ability, whose judgment and integrity were held in high esteem. Often in the selection of a committee "on this interesting subject" the meeting employed such terms of appreciation as "solid," "weighty," "concerned," "suitable," and "of ripe judgment." As to the number composing a committee there was great irregularity, as no proper number was ever specified. There were committees of as few as three members, but others ran as high as ten, twenty, or thirty members. As a general rule, we may say that when an investigation was to be made or a concensus of opinion arrived at, a large committee was appointed; the committees actually in charge of local schools, however, usually numbered three to ten members.

In some localities these committees were composed of men and women; again, there was a men's committee and a women's committee. If a girls' school existed, or if a woman teacher was employed, at some time of the year, then the oversight of the actual school activity was placed in feminine hands. Thus in 1803 Burlington noted that,

The Trustees of the School desiring the company of some women to join them in visiting it, Margaret Smith, Martha Smith, Deborah Smith, Elizabeth Coleman, and Susanna Emlin are appointed for that purpose.[19]

Two volumes of their records, covering the period from 1800 to 1818 and 1828 to 1870, show that women were regularly chosen to visit the school with the men. The women made reports to their meeting, as did the men to theirs. In this instance their visitations occurred once each month. In 1802 the committee's report on schools at Evesham stated there were five of them in charge of trustees annually appointed, with whom, in some places women had usually joined; and "as some of their sex have engaged as teachers, which we have not visited, we think the care of them ought to rest on the Women's Meeting."[20]

---

[18]Min. Salem Mo. Mtg., (H.), 27/IX/1876.
[19]Min. Burlington Prep. Mtg. of Women Friends, 29/XII/1803.
[20]Min. Evesham Meeting, 5/III/1802; For prominent instances of women's comittees over schools see Alloway's Creek, Min. Greenwich Prep. Mtg. Women Friends, (H.), 22/VI/1836, and Min. Maurice River Mo. Mtg. Women Friends (H.), 1/II/1845; indeed women played an important role in school visitation, in every locality during the nineteenth century.

The duties delegated to committees to be performed covered a wide range, almost everything that had to be done for the school, except actually supporting it. The first duty in point of time, i. e., after schools came to have a permanent foundation, was to secure a lot of ground on which to build a schoolhouse, a master's house, or for a playground. In 1802 Evesham's committee lamented the fact that "The advice of the Yearly Meeting respecting making suitable accommodations for teachers, appears so little attended to, there is but one house erected for that purpose . . ." Yet they mention that they have provided five good school houses which are under trustees of the several Preparative Meetings.[21] In 1800 Upper Evesham Preparative instructed a committee definitely that it should secure a lot on which to build a master's dwelling.[22] All accounts for building houses, fences, and purchases of ground had to be reported to the meeting. Thus the committee at Upper Springfield, in 1793, after being reminded of the fact that no settlement had been made for building Friends' school house, were charged to bring in a report. They reported a few months later a total disbursement of £ 80/15/11.[23]

Not only did the trustees secure the building and lot, but in some cases it was specified they should provide the firewood, i. e., unless they could unload the job on the teacher.[24] On the whole it seems to have been a matter of small concern who should actually purchase fuel or other supplies. Numerous bills were presented by masters for purchases they had made for the school.[25] In one case the trustees agreed to get wood if the teacher would provide ink, quills, and paper and charge them to the pupils.[26] Repairs were made by the trustees, especially if of any considerable nature, but small tasks were frequently done by the master. Bills for repair work, no matter how insignificant the charge, were brought before the meeting.

---

[21]Min. Evesham Mo. Mtg., 5/III/1802.
[22]Min. U. E. Prep. Mtg., 3/XII/1800; More evidence, if desired, may be found in the activities of school committees described in Chapters Three. Four, Five, and Six.
[23]Min. U. S. Prep. Mtg., 25/VIII/1793.
[24]Min. East Branch School Trustees, 6/XI/1819. In 1820 the teacher was authorized to charge employers for the wood used at school at the rate of $4.50 per cord.
[25]See page 306.   [26]Min. U. S. School Trustees, 10/IV/1813.

The trustees "hired and fired" the teacher, but the last named function was not often exercised, or, at least the minutes mention few cases. This was due in part to the care with which the teacher was selected and also the fact that it was extremely hard to hold teachers a long time. If the teacher was at all capable of maintaining the "school in a good degree orderly" he was encouraged to remain. The agreement or contract was usually for one, two or three quarters, or for the summer term, often in the case of women teachers, and the tendency was to adhere to a rigid contract, though it was sometimes waived.[27] In securing a teacher advances were made, with equal propriety by trustees or by the teachers. T. Bennet, in 1791, informed a member of the committee he would engage "to teach a year, provided he could have 36 subscribed scholars."[28] At another time initiative was taken by the meeting, which entered the following minute:

The necessity of procuring a teacher for our school (which hath been some considerable time vacant) being now urged as a matter requiring speedy attention, Samuel Sykes and William Newbold are directed to write to those Friends of Philadelphia appointed to receive applications and inform them our situation and the probable salary we can give a suitable master.[29]

But the teacher once hired was by no means dictator of the school. Very frequently it was a part of his contract that he should follow a definite list of rules in the government of his school; the preparation of such list of rules was often performed by the school committee. The following rules were drawn up for the observance of the school at Evesham in 1792:

Articles agreed upon, and to be observed by the trustees, teachers, and employers, for the time being of Friends Schools within the compass of Evesham Monthly Meeting.

First. The teacher shall keep a book to enter employers names, the number of scholars, and time of entering.

Second. The hours of teaching shall be in the 11, 12, 1, 2 and 3rd months from half past eight to four, allowing 1 hour at noon, and the other months from eight to half past five, allowing two hours at noon.

Third. The teacher shall provide good firewood, paper, quills and ink. And once in each quarter assess every scholars proportion of the expense who use the same.

Fourth. The teacher shall suffer no scholar to continue in the school that hath any infectious distemper.

[27]More is said of contracts on page 302.
[28]Min. U. S. School Trustees, 30/XI/1791. [29]*Ibid.*, 15/II/1797.

Fifth. The teacher shall not dismiss any scholar without a sufficient cause, approved by the trustees, and if any employer from dissatisfaction incline to take away a child, the trustees are to be informed thereof that they may attend to the case.

Sixth. As the Scripture Language is most gramatic and consistent with plainness, it is desired that parents and guardians will unite in promoting the same in those they send, also to habit them in a decent plain dress becoming our religious professions and principles.

Seventh. And it is desired that the teacher will constantly bring with him all the scholars to our week-day meetings where the school house is within convenient distance.

Eighth. The teacher, if not engaged for a limited time shall not leave the school without giving the trustees three month's notice of his intention in writing, nor shall the trustees dismiss any teacher without giving him the same notice, except for a non-compliance with the Rules of The School, or a manifest deficiency in the duties of his station.

Ninth. When the teacher intends taking any time to himself, he shall give the children a clear timely notice thereof, and also let them know when to attend again.

Lastly, And it is desired that when the morning school ends, the teacher see that sobriety be observed by the scholars when at their dinner, spending the intermediate time between schools without rudeness.[30]

It was also a duty of the trustees to pay the school bills for poor children, and if necessary bring the care of the poor to the meeting before so doing. Account books contain numerous entries of expenditure for this purpose; indeed many of the funds established under the care of school trustees were described as being for the education of poor children. It often happened that after the meeting ceased to conduct a regular school of its own, its trustees paid for the education of poor children out of the old funds. In the following minute,

The treasurer informs he has paid Joshua Bullock two bills for the tuition of Joseph Cox's children, one in 3rd mo. 1838 and the other in 3rd mo. 1839—amounting to $7.56 which is now approved.—And the Trustees now order the Treasurer to pay the sum expended in fitting Elizabeth Cox for Westtown school amounting to $18.98.[31]

The trustees kept in touch with the schools' progress by means of visitations. The visits must have, at times, been a severe trial to a teacher. A report of 1790 says that,

In company with a large number of spectators the Trustees all attended the

---

[30]Min. Evesham Prep. Mtg. School Committee.
[31]Min. U. S. School Trustees, 10/IV/1840.

school to a good degree of satisfaction, finding considerable improvement in the order and regulation of the school as well as in the learning—had a seasonable opportunity with them before they separated—when some edifying council was given.[32]

However, there were extenuating circumstances. In 1788 this same committee reported that "six trustees atttended the school it being now agreed that we perform our visit to the school for the future on the fourth day in each month at 2 o'clock in the afternoon." Other reports stated they did not consider it wise to make a visit as a new teacher had just begun the school, or that the teacher had been there too short a time to allow a judgment to be made on the school's progress. Reports are generally too brief to give a real insight as to the methods of school work, but some mentioned that we "examined the copy books," "heard the children recite their lessons," "found the school in a good degree orderly," or "in a progressing way," and "some advancement is evident in their learning." Less frequently, the school was "not as orderly as could be desired" and we "formed such rules and regulations for the observation of the scholars as appeared to us most suitable."

But it must not be assumed that the trustees were at all times careful in the performance of their duty. On many occasions they frankly acknowledge remissness. Mickle, at Woodbury, recorded in his *Diary* that on a certain day of visitation not one trustee was present;[33] and at Upper Springfield they stated that "Whereas it has so happened that for some time past there has been but little attention paid to the school by us, it is thought expedient to renew our attention thereto . . ."[34]

TEACHERS

As a general rule teachers were secured from the locality of the school. Being well known to the members it was much easier to select one of sound moral character, and this qualification was chiefly desired. When there was no one available in the neighborhood, and no wandering master presented himself as a candidate, the committee had recourse to advertising, which was commonly

---

[32] *Ibid.*, 8/II/1790.   [33] Page 140.
[34] Min. U. S. Sch. Trustees, 30/XI/1791.

practiced by the middle of the 18th century. But few instances have been found, however, where this means was employed by Friends. In 1761, Joshua Thompson, a member of Friends in Elsinborough Township, advertised for a teacher, as follows, but it is not certain that he was acting either for the meeting or for a school committee:

> Notice is hereby given, that a schoolmaster is wanted in the Township of Elsinborough, in Salem County, and Western Division of New Jersey: One that can come well recommended, may meet with good Encouragement, by the Inhabitants of said Township, Signed on Behalf of myself and Neighbors.[35]
>
> Joshua Thompson.

Other instances occurred at Mt. Holly and Burlington, and later at Rahway. In 1875 they advertised:

> Wanted, a female teacher, a member of the Society of Friends for Rahway Preparative Meeting School, which is expected to open about the 1st of 9th month next. Apply ————.[36]

The desire of the superior meeting that schools should be on a permanent basis made it more necessary that teachers be bound by a rather definite agreement. After the beginning of the last quarter of the 18th century, contracts are generally mentioned, but it is not clear that there was always a written form—perhaps in many cases a contract was no more than a verbal agreement. In others, however, it was a written agreement, having terms clearly stated. In 1798 Upper Springfield recorded:

> As the time of our teacher is expired some time since, and a subscription paper set on foot by our direction, to obtain scholars for the year next ensuing being now returned with about twenty-six subscribed, it's concluded safe to hire him for one year, commencing on the seventh day of this present month at which time he opened school. The terms of the contract are: He to have thirty scholars made up at three pound per year counting both the subscription and all others that come. Then if the school fall short the deficiency to be made up out of the profits of the fund and if it exceeds 30 scholars the teacher to have the benefit provided the terms of the subscription is adhered to by him.[37]

Another reference to a binding contract is found in 1791 when Titus Bennett informed:

> that he had a prospect of leaving us at the end of his present engagement,

---

[35] *Pa. Gazette*, No. 1721, Dec. 17, 1761.
[36] Min. Rahway Prep. Mtg. Sch. Committee, 15/VII/1875.
[37] Min. U. S. Sch. Trustees, 16/V/1798.

but the school being small and he having some expectation of entering in another place to more advantage to his interest requests to be disengaged in three weeks, which will be upwards of two months short of the expiration of his time; after mature consideration it is fully agreed to leave him at his liberty.[38]

The above assures at least that a contract was so binding that a teacher desired to have his release formally agreed upon. This experience of having a teacher leave unexpectedly even though he was careful enough to ask a release, and another more questionable case, at length caused stipulation to be made that three month's notice of leaving or "firing" had to be given. A case that caused considerable trouble was recorded in 1804, as follows:

Information was communicated that we were likely to be deprived of our teacher in consequence of a letter of solicitation from a Friend or Friends of Philadelphia, who having drawn him there without our consent or knowledge have prevailed on him as he represents by pressing entreaty to enter into a positive contract to teach the school of black children there—which proceedings both of the Friend above alluded to and of our master, being altogether new, unexpected and really surprising to us, and in our view very unfriendly and disingenious. It is concluded and directed that the Clerk write on our behalf to said Friends acquainting them with our sentiments relative thereto, as now dictated—and to facilitate the business, it is judged sufficient that the letter be shown to Thomas Gaskill and if approved by him to be forwarded without delay.

A month later:

William Newbold reported at a special meeting that he had wrote and forwarded a letter to those Friends in Philadelphia in the manner directed at last meeting, a copy whereof he produced which was read and unitedly approved as suitable to the occasion—he further informs that after waiting some time and receiving no answer, he forwarded a note containing a request that they would favour us with one, but none still coming, Thomas Gaskill waited on one of the said Friends who informed him that they disapproved of the letter and had therefore concluded not to give us any answer; and at the same time manifested an entire disinclination to recede or withdraw from what they had done relative to drawing Charles Roberts from us, or to relinquish their claim upon him. After maturely considering the subject and the extraordinary part which these Friends appear to have acted from the beginning throughout it appears to us a matter, that in its effects and consequences is of great concernment and requiring our further attention. Therefore Thomas Gaskill, Thomas Sykes and William Newbold are appointed to go to Philadelphia as early as they can, and if they find on a further investigation of the business, that it cannot be adjusted on fair and equitable principles with the Friends themselves who have thus acted, they are to lodge a complaint with the over-

[38]*Ibid.*

seers of the Meetings whereof said Friends are members—That they had, as we conceived, clandestinely drawn our teacher from us—and they are also directed to pay such further attention to the business as they may judge needful.[39]

A month later a letter came from the overseers of the "Black School" that they had released Charles Roberts from his engagement. After this experience the trustees stipulated a three months' notice must be given before leaving.[40]

The schoolmaster of early times was occupied with many things besides school teaching. John Woolman learned tailoring. Many others tilled the land, carried on the trade of carpenter, or other "art" or "mystery." Sometimes their ability in other things was made clear in the contract between teacher and school committee.

The Yearly Meeting's suggestion that a house, garden, cows and so forth be supplied was in some cases carried out and opportunity offered for even renting more farm land of the committee. In 1834 Old Springfield Trustees contracted with Watson Pickering for 1 year, giving him the use of 2 lots containing 5 acres, more or less, and the buildings. He was to pay "$20 for the clover lot over the run, at the expiration of the year; the dwelling house etc. and lot containing 2 acres more or less belonging to the school to have gratis while he teaches the school . . ." It was specified he should "not remove hay, straw, grass, dung, ashes, soil or compost thereon, made during the said term."[41] The following is the contract with Franklin B. Haines, 1853:

This is to certify that we do hereby agree with Franklin B. Haines to teach the school belonging to Old Springfield Preparative Meeting on the following conditions viz.—said Haines is to have all the property belonging to said school (except 3 acres of land lying south of the run) rent free; and for the other 3 acres, south of the run, he is to pay the sum of $20 per acre, and is to farm all the land as the committee having said school in charge may from time to time direct, and said Haines is not to take off any hay, straw or manure except as much as he may bring on; and is to teach the school for .03 cents per scholar per day, (Mathematics, such as mensuration, surveying, and algebra also all fuel, stationery, etc., excepted) and in case of a change, each party is to give the other party three months notice.

Franklin B. Haines   Clayton Zelley

Daniel S. Zelley   Joseph Hancock[42]

William C. Hancock

---

[39] *Ibid.*, 22/II/1804, and 21/III/1804.
[40] For the text of this provision, see Art. 9, p. 108.
[41] Min. Old Springfield School Trustees, 5/III/1834.   [42] *Ibid.*, 21/IV/1853.

Not much need be said of the salaries paid. There was always great variation at different times and places. The usual rule was to make as "good terms" as possible. John Wright was paid $15 for four weeks and one day, to act as assistant to the master when the school was too full. In 1814 the trustees agreed to make up $360, if the school, by rates, should not yield that amount to the master. Moreover, the living could be eked out in various ways: one minute states that the "treasurer is directed to pay to the teacher four dollars for carpenter work he has done to the writing tables at the schoolhouses."[43] Moreover, it seems, strong argument could cause the trustees to raise a salary. Thus, on one occasion, Burlington stated that the trustees agreed to raise the salary to $150 as requested.

In Rahway, 1878, the salary paid was usually 400–500 dollars, but in one case, it was proposed that

> We would be willing to pay $500.00 and that, should the school so improve under her care, as to warrant it, we would give her the benefit to the extent of $600.00[44]

The salary might be guaranteed by the trustees, or it might not. The following minute made it clear that no guarantee was to be expected:

> The subject of the school under the care of the Meeting being under consideration it was united that the trustees should not be authorized to guarantee the teacher any fixed salary as heretofore, but in other respects to be continued as formerly, with the understanding that all the children accompany their teacher to our mid-week meetings.[45]

Women teachers were often obtained to teach in the summer, and were desirable because their service could be secured more cheaply than that of men. In 1825 Hannah Craft was to teach during the summer at "$1.75 per scholar for three months," but she was only secured after agreement had been made "to procure a female as teacher for 6 months, if it can be done on reasonable terms."[46] In 1832, Mary Craft was guaranteed 15 scholars at 2 dollars per quarter, deficit to be made good by trustees if the

---

[43]Min. U. S. Sch. Trustees, 20/X/1803.
[44]Min. Rahway Prep. Mtg. Sch. Com., 16/VII/1878.
[45]Min. Woodbury Prep. Mtg., (H.), 23/V/1878.
[46]Min. East Branch Sch. Trustees, 10/II/1825 and 11/VI/1825.

number of scholars was not found.[47] In 1877 Caroline Gibbons received $100 for teaching a 60 day term.[48]

The teachers' duties comprised many things besides teaching. Purchasing supplies of varied character seems to have been an important one. In 1808 the teacher at Upper Springfield presented the following bill to trustees which was approved and paid:

100 (marbles ?) 40 (hat pins ?) 1 (lb. ?) figs, 3 (lbs. ?) raisins	$ 1.44
Glass and putty, hooks and rings	.95½
Washing school house	1.10
Ciphering board and 8 pieces for (hat pins ?)	1.75
2 benches	6.00
2 (quarters ?) to subscription and entrance money	6.30
	$17.54½[49]

In 1813 a bill of $17.10 was presented for 2 dozen spelling books, 12 lights of glass, 2 lbs. of putty and glazing, 1 dozen ink stands, teaching, cash for chopping wood,[50] and also a stipulation that the teacher get "ink, quills, and paper and charge the cost to the pupils."[51] East Branch directed that their teacher charge the patrons for the wood used in his schoolhouse, at the rate of $4.50 per cord.[52]

In spite of all attempts to improve the conditions of living for teachers and thus retain them longer, there does not seem to have been any remarkable success. The teachers of Colonial days and the transition heeded the call of the *Wanderlust* with great readiness. Evesham stated in 1798 "the school has been kept up the most part of the year, under the tuition of several teachers to a good degree of satisfaction."[53] Thirty-five years later the yearly report stated:

the school has been taught nearly ever since our appointment, about 2 months by Benjamin M. Haines, and about 7 months by Hannah Gillingham, and at present by William R. Lippincott. . .[54]

In the case of Upper Greenwich we have a list of teachers from 1810 to 1865. In this list there are 28 teachers whose names appear in but one year; 10 whose names were given in two different

[47]*Ibid.*, 1832.   [48]Min. Woolwich Prep. Mtg., (H.),   15/IV/1880.
[49]Min. U. S. Sch. Trustees, 16/III/1808.
[50]*Ibid.*, 13/XII/1813.   [51]*Ibid.*, 31/IV/1813.
[52]Min. East Branch Sch. Trustees, 4/II/1820.
[53]Min. Evesham School Trustees, 9/VIII/1798.
[54]*Ibid.*, 2/I/1834.

years; 6 appeared three years; 2 appeared four, 1 appeared five; 1 appeared six; and 1 appeared ten years. This makes a total of 95 cases in 55 years. As the school year at this place was generally 3 quarters long we may estimate that the teachers mentioned one year probably served the school for a little over five months; those who were mentioned in two, three, four, five, six or ten years, served approximately two, three, four, five, six or ten times five months plus. The calculation, obviously cannot be more than an approximation and suggestive. For instance the terms of men and women were not usually equal; tho they varied much, where specific mention is made, the men seem to have taught in the winter from five to 6 months while the women taught summers for three or four months.[55]

[55]Upper Greenwich Prep. Mtg. Book for use of Schools, 1809-1874. For students of local history, the list of teachers will be of interest.

Date	Name	Date	Name
1810	George Mickle.	1831	Charles Brown.
1810	Mary Reeves.	1832	Wm. Thorn.
1811	Isaac Hinchman.	1833	Isaac Flitcraft.
1812	Samuel Barry.	1833	Mary A. Paul.
1812	William Mickle.	1834	Edward R. Bullock
1813	"	1835	"
1814	"		William Thorne
1815	"	1836	Thomas H. Bond
1816	"	1837	Wm. Haines
1816	Mary Thorne.		Elizabeth Pine
1816	Benjamin Shinn.	1838	"
1817	"		Wm. Brown
1818	Beulah P. Hancock.	1839	Sarah W. Brown
1819	Joseph Whitall.		Wm. Haines
1820	Isabella Paul.	1840	Sarah W. Brown
1820	Wm. Mickle.		John P. Brown
1821	James Haines.	1841	Sarah W. Brown
1821	Solomon W. Lewis.		John Haines
1822	Hannah Bacon.	1842	Charles Hankins
1823	Isabella Paul.		Wm. J. Doran
1823	Charles Brown.		John P. Brown
1824	Isabella Paul.	1843	Priscilla Haines
1824	Joseph Borton.		Joseph E. Haines
1825	Anna Haines.	1844	Burwood Moore
1825	Wm. E. Kay.	1845	"
1826	Anna Haines.	1846	Samuel Ogden
1826	Samuel Ogden.		Mary Moore
1827	Anna Haines.	1847	"
1827	Griffith Hinchman.		Joseph E. Haines
1829	Charles Brown.	1848	Burwood Moore
1829	Wm. Thorne.		Mary Moore
1830	"	1849	Elizabeth Warrington
1830	Daniel Bradshaw.		Charles Brown

There is no reason to believe that the above list does not fairly represent the tenure of teachers generally in the Quaker schools of the period. In every case in which data are available it is clear that "one term" was generally the longest acquaintance a teacher had with his job; the frequency of two, three or more terms is by no means great. At Upper Springfield, Titus Bennett taught probably four years between 1789 and 1795; Tucker Earl was mentioned in 1797 and 1799; Jonathan Mendenhall in 1800; Charles Roberts in 1803; Ethan Conley in 1804; Townsend Speakman, four years 1806 to 1809 inclusive; Charles Gaskill 1810; for 1811 and 1812 there were no minutes of the trustees. Samuel Gummere taught from 1813 to 1815 inclusive, at least; then for two years there were no minutes entered, though some meetings were probably held. In 1821 Wm. Sykes is mentioned as having been using the school for a time as teacher. Jane Harris is mentioned once in 1826, while Luisa Bennett taught terms in 1827, 1828 and 1829.[56]

With the exception of extremely few cases the character of these early teachers was above reproach. A few breeches of professional ethics have already been mentioned, but these do not appear to have been entirely the fault of the teachers. In one case, at least, the distant school committee was just as much to blame. In the other the school committee appeared entirely satisfied that the teacher should be at liberty to go where he could have a better school.

Two cases of immorality, serious enough to be taken into account by the meeting, appear on the records examined. In 1802, This meeting informed that——is charged with conducting himself in-

1850	Zillah Moore	1856	Elmira T. Ogden
	Burwood Moore		Benj. Heritage
1851	Priscilla P. Haines	1857	Elmira T. Ogden
1852	Burwood Moore		Benj. Heritage
	Priscilla P. Haines	1858	Benj. Heritage
	Edwin Craft		Anna Potts
1853	Zillah Moore	1859	"
	Augustus Sailer		Benjamin Heritage
1854	Emily Lewis	1860	Sarah Taylor
	Edwin Craft		Benjamin Heritage
1855	"	1861	Rachel Borton
	Eliza Gaunt		Benj. Heritage—continued
	Benjamin Heritage		teaching to 1865.

[56]Min. Trustees U. S. School.

decently toward a young woman in his school and also of sleeping in the time of his school, and he neglects clearing himself therefrom, on account of which charges he has been treated with by the overseers.[57]

Two months later a note explained that the charges were withdrawn and did not go to the monthly meeting (18/XI/1802) but in January 1803, "failing to clear himself before the meeting, of charges brought againt him some time past, a copy of the charges and this minute are to go to the Monthly Meeting."[58] Later in the century a teacher condemned his conduct before the meeting.

. . .do hereby, sincerely and honestly condemn my immoral conduct that has given rise to censure and reproach, during the past year . . .I do further agree with and promise the above trustees I will leave said school at any time during the year by their request, if this promise is not faithfully lived up to (Name.)[59]

The School

In the first period of school development in Quaker communities of New Jersey it was common to hold it in the meeting house, if no other building was ready for it. Vice versa it was just as common a practice to hold meeting in the schoolhouse. Burlington in 1756 permitted a school to be held in the upper meeting house; Mansfield Neck was allowed to hold meetings at the schoolhouse in 1761; and Friends at Upper Springfield held meetings, by permission of their Monthly Meeting, "at the School House nigh Shreve's Mount." In 1766 an additional meeting was permitted to convene at the "schoolhouse near William Bishop's." So far as cases are concerned, that came under the writer's observation, the number of permits to hold religious services in schoolhouses exceeded those permitting schools in houses of worship. However, the latter custom was commonly accepted.

Just what the earliest schoolhouses were like one cannot say with more precision than that they were usually of logs, but sometimes of stone, small, low, inadequately lighted, and heated. No comfortable desks or seats made the long school day more tolerable. In the second period that of educational expansion which began about 1778, there were many more substantial buildings erected. Some of these were of stone and brick, while many were ordinary frame

---

[57]East Branch Prep. Mtg., 23/IX/1802.   [58]*Ibid.*, 20/I/1803.
[59]Min. Old Springfield Sch. Trustees, 10/II/1855.

buildings; in shape they were generally rectangular, but also octagonal, and possibly hexagonal schools were built, though the writer has seen none of the latter. Most of those built just following the Revolution or in the early nineteenth century, which have come down to the present were of brick, brick and stone combined, and wood. Some in more recent years have been coated over with stucco. It is probable that the several photographs which illustrate the pages of this book do not fairly represent the schools of Quaker New Jersey in the nineteenth century, for, undoubtedly, only the best buildings have been preserved. In many of the smallest communities no building may now be found standing.

Within this simple house of brick, logs, or stone, the master or mistress presided over a number of boys and girls, sometimes as few as ten or as many as seventy or eighty. The winter school was under a master, generally, and was made up of older, bigger boys. The summer school was often specified as being for the "girls and little boys." This does not mean that "girls and little boys" were not schooled in the winter, but that big boys had to work in the summer.

To assist master or mistress in the control of the school no stone was left unturned, judging from the rules which were prepared for its government. These rules were usually drawn up by the school committee, thus setting the standard of conduct which they hoped to witness upon their regular visitations. The rigor of the regulations appear to harmonize with the severity of school architecture, and the lack of comfortable furnishing in the school itself. And, from the usual report of the school committee that "the school appeared to be kept in a good degree orderly" it may be surmised that the rules were strictly regarded. The following were drawn up for the school at Evesham about 1792.

Rules to be observed by the scholars in Friends' Schools within the compass of Evesham Monthly Meeting.

1st. Be at school at the hour appointed with your faces and hands washed and (heads combed).

2nd. With cheerfulness and attention observe the instructions of the teacher and always pay him due respect.

3rd. Study your lessons in silence, avoiding unnecessary conversation with each other, making your movements with ease, and as little noise as possible.

4th. Be not forward to divulge anything passed in school; mock not, or jeer your school fellows for being corrected; it is unkind and may happen to be your own case.

5th. Behave yourselves in a gentle obliging manner, becoming virtuous children, the boys to treat the girls with that respect and decency which is due to their sex, and the girls the boys with a becoming reserve and modesty.

6th. When you receive anything of another, observe to make some grateful return for the kindness done you, never returning injuries, but learning nobly to forgive, thus showing by examples how all ought to behave.

7th. If disputes at any time arise among you, ye are not to use provoking words, or blows, or give way to a sullen, revengeful temper, but refer the matter to be decided by the master.

8th. Carefully avoid speaking evil of any, treating aged persons with disrespect, jesting with those of weak abilities, making a mock of the lame, deformed, or those deprived of their senses. But behave yourselves modestly, civilly, and kindly to all.

9th. Not only avoid committing any indecent behaviour, or such amusements as are rude, dirty or dangerous yourselves, but shun the pernicious company and conversation of those who are accustomed thereto, especially the shameful and exceedingly sinful practices of lying and swearing. Considering you are always in His presence who made you, and notices all your words and actions.

10th. Be careful to observe true grammer, and Scripter plainness of speach, in using the singular number (as thee and thou) to a single person, and in every other respect, avoid such additions in your addresses to others as are inconsistent with truth. Plainness of apparel is also most consistent with our religious principles, it is therefore desired that you may be habited accordingly.

Lastly, And it is desired that you carefully avoid spending your time on first days in sport, or any way that tends to disturbance, but duly attend our religious meetings and when there, be still and sober; remembering the awfulness of the occasion that you are there met to worship the Divine being, who cannot be deceived and will not be mocked.[60]

In a few instances the trustees took special action regarding damage to property. In 1820 East Branch specified that:

such scholar or scholars as may or shall hereafter commit or do any damage to the school house either wilfully or carelessly, to repair to make good such damage at his or her own expense, or the expense of his or her parent or guardian, . . .and the teacher is requested to attend thereto from time to time.[61]

All of the records available, that deal in any way with details of the operation of the school seem to indicate that a great deal of attention was given to keeping the school clean. On this it is

[60]Min. Trustees of Evesham School.
[61]Min. East Branch Sch. Trustees, 6/III/1820.

impossible to write, save concerning a few schools. East Branch noted the purchase of pails, tub, and brushes; Mt. Holly paid Daniel Wills $2.26½ "for cleaning school house and some repairs and later entered an item of $.33 for a "dusting brush for school house."[62] Earlier Daniel Wills directed Samuel Carr, as follows:

> Thee will please to pay Mary Coom, or order, one dollar and twenty-five cents for scrubbing and cleaning the school house and charge the same to the school house.[63]

The Easton School purchased similar cleaning utensils, mentioned whitewashing the school (1827), and purchased curtains in 1857, which were evidently washable. In 1861 we find the item of "$1.62 to cash for cleaning school house and washing and ironing window curtains."[64]

Certain articles of equipment for the schools have been mentioned. It was sometimes purchased by trustees, but might be provided by the master, and then charged to the trustees. Upper Springfield's teacher in 1791 produced an account for "sundry repairs in the house and materials for the promotion of the school," which was laid before the preparative meeting for direction therein.[65]

The following items refer to the Mt. Holly Preparative Meeting School. In 1820, $4.13 was paid Daniel Wills "for Barrell on school house stove, 3.88, and stand 25c." J. J. Warner (1821) received .75 for "turning on (e) dozen inkstands." In 1796 a lock and staple was bought for the door, and a "light of glass" put in. A year later the windows were glazed for £ 1/5/6, and in 1801 the house was plastered at a cost of 11/3/4½.[66] Below is given a list

---

[62]Mt. Holly Prep. Mtg. School Fund Records, 1820 and 1822.
[63]*Ibid.*, 1817.
[64]Account Book of Easton School, 1861.
[65]Min. U. S. School Trustees, 13/VI/1791. Later items of expense shed some light; in 1793 "The Hearth and some parts of our school house wanting repair S. Skyes is appointed to get them done and make report of expense." . . .In 1806, "The teacher is authorized to get made two benches for the use of the school, to have a distinct seat for each scholar, in form of a stool." A bill of $9.28 was entered in 1808 for plastering the school. The teacher in 1813 was directed to get ink, quills and paper, charging them to the scholars, while the trustees promised to "find firewood." In 1819, the school having been discontinued for a time, it was proposed to dispose of "the maps, and gazateer belonging to the school." These were, however, retained until 1825.
[66]Mt. Holly Prep. Mtg. School Fund Records.

of articles purchased for the Easton School between 1827 and 1875.[67]

The length of the school term was variable in the extreme. In the case of Upper Greenwich, as before stated, it was generally about nine or ten months of the year,[68] but in other places they were not so regular. Eastbranch in 1824 mentions a school for six months while Rancocas speaks of holding school ten months in 1845. The "Brick School" at Chester was held three months in 1791 and 1804; four, nearly, in 1805; six, nearly, in 1806; eight, nearly, in 1808; four, nearly, in 1810; four, nearly, in 1818; nine in 1820; six in 1826; nine in 1827 and 1838; six in 1846; and ten, about, in 1862. "Moorestown School" was held six months in 1804; eight in 1805; nine in 1819; eleven in 1827; six in 1846; three in 1847; ten in 1853; and six in 1862.[69] No complete set of facts is available on this point but the above irregularities are probably representative.

Until the nineteenth century the Quaker institutions of learning were scarcely, if ever, called anything but "school;" in the school provision was made for girls and boys alike, but separate probably in a majority of cases. Thus, there were girls' schools and boys' schools. Likewise there was a winter and a summer school,

---

[67]*Easton School Account Book.*

Date	Items	
15/III/1827	Sweeping Brush	.62
30/III/1827	Cleaning school & whitewashing	1.00
	To putting in 2 lites of glass	.15
24/IV/1827	To cash paid for water pail	.37½
25/I/1828	To cash for 3 "Expositors"	.75
16/II/	To cash pd. for Inkstands for school	.31
3/XI/1828	·To cash pd.. Cornel (Cornwall?) Stevenson for map for school	5.00
	To cash for 6 lights of glass and putty and putting in	.47
	To repairing wrighting forms etc.	.25
	To one tin cup	∶10
1/V/1830	To drawing water and attendance at school house	.50
30/IV/1830	Cash pd. Cornel (Cornwall?) Stevenson for wood left at school house	3.82
1836	To making new legs to writing desk	.50
19/IV/1837	To making stove door	.37½
22/X/1839	To one lock on the school house door	.87½
22/XII/1853	Pd. for blackboard	.40
21/XI/1856	Pd. for a new stove for school house	16.00
4/XI/1857	Pd. for small table and curtains for school house	3.95
1/XII/1875	Pd. for a globe for school house	10.00

[68]Page 306f.   [69]Min. Chester Prep. Mtg.

recognized at least in the last quarter of the 18th century. But in the nineteenth century a number of terms became common even though the "learning" offered was the same. Such terms as "Boarding School," "family school," "Seminary," "Academy," "Select School," and "graded school" became common. The difference between some of them was only in name; and the latter is, in most cases, clear. The family school was commented on in 1834 by the Yearly Meeting as follows:

> There is a class of schools which has increased within a few years, that may be termed family schools, and are generally taught by females. They furnish useful employment for a number of young women, and are calculated to develop female intellect; their great utility is obvious and we believe much good would result from their being still further extended and encouraged.[70]

A "Boarding School" had been operated since 1799, at Westtown, and many others were patronized during the century. The term "Seminary" and "Academy" was at times applied to the same school. "Bacon Academy"[71] offered the most advanced course of any of the New Jersey schools. In 1854 the committee introduced co-education, uniting the

> male and female departments, formerly kept distinct, . . .under the superintendence of a female principal. . .suitable teachers to assist her. The school has been opened ten months of the year, attended by 102 pupils, 53 males and 49 females.[72]

In 1873 a committee was appointed at Salem to consider grading the schools and co-education. The next report of the school committee stated that:

> There is one graded school of the description queried after, with two teachers, whole number of pupils in attendance, 73. . . [73]

A graded system was established at Moorestown early in the last decade of the century.[74]

---

[70]Extracts, 1834, pp. 8–9.   [71]See pp. 155ff.
[72]Min. Pilesgrove Prep. Mtg. Women Frds., (H.), 20/IV/1854.
[73]Min. Salem Mo. Mtg., (H.), 30/IV/1873, and 25/II/1874.
[74]See page 224.

CHAPTER XI

CURRICULUM AND TEXTBOOKS

CURRICULUM

From the many references to a "guarded religious education" and injunctions against the reading of "pernicious books" and "heathenish authors," which appear in the records of the meetings and in the foregoing pages of this study, one is led to understand that the curriculum was always closely scrutinized and the books used in instruction carefully selected. This was for the purpose that the aim of a moral and religious education, according to Friends' standards, might be secured. A second guiding principle in selection of subjects and books was the belief in an essentially realistic education. "We are in pain to make them scholars, but not men," was Penn's criticism of current education. Quaker practice followed his suggestion by seeking to give a useful education, early showing a preference for scientific studies. Yet, in schools of higher grade the classic and modern languages were taught; but a careful selection of materials must have been always insisted upon. Penn deplored the fact that books had not been composed for youth, "by some curious and careful naturalists and also mechanics, in the Latin tongue, to be used in schools, that they might learn things with words . . ."[1] In this he represented distinctly the Realist point of view, and was far beyond actual school practice which, in the Colonial period, was limited to the four R's.

Though the question of teaching Latin hardly enters into a discussion of the *earlier* New Jersey schools, as they were elementary, the Quaker viewpoint may be mentioned, as the subject was taught in some schools of the 19th century. Haddonfield reported in 1865, "the usual branches continue to be taught as heretofore with the addition of Latin which has been studied by one class for

---

[1]*Reflections and Maxims*, 16; see also Chap. Two.

the last three months."[2] In a Latin text of elementary grade, published by a Friend in 1676, the preface stated that

Friends met and agreed together in language teaching to lay aside the heathenish books and the corrupt grammars taken out of them, and to set up the scriptures of truth, and what may be savory and good matter that may not corrupt childrens' minds.[3]

From this and other strictures we may safely assume that, wherever taught, Latin and Greek were limited in scope

Efforts were continually made, especially in the Colonial period when books were extremely scarce, to provide books of religious and doctrinal character, not only for use in the schools, which is sometimes specified, but for distribution among members. Such distribution was free in case of poor members. In 1772, Woodbridge stated:

There are divers who have not Friends' Books, one of which has no Bible and they think a Bible should be procured for that Friend and That this Meeting should procure for such Friends, Penn's Rise and Progress of the People Called Quakers, Barclay's Catechism, a Treatise Entitled, Reasons for not Paying Tythes, Richard Davis' Journal, Alice Halls Legacy, Harmony of Mankind by John Woolman and (of) these there should be Six of each sort. Jos. Shotwell Jr. is desired to Purchase and Deliver them to said Committee for said purpose. The further consideration of report is Referred to next Meeting.[4]

Burlington, in 1776, received a large collection of books, mostly for mature minds, and ordered that they "be spread among poor friends and such others who manifest a desire to be instructed in our religious principles . . ."[5] Similarly, action was taken in 1813 to provide Bibles for members in need of them:

The subject respecting the procurement of Bibles for the use of such of our members as may not be furnished with them being brought into view it is thought best to make an addition to the Committee formerly appointed: accordingly Stephen Pike and Samuel Emlen are named to the service.[6]

The reason for distributing books may be found in the minutes of every Quaker meeting. If books of authorized character were

[2]Min. Haddonfield Mo. Mtg., 13/II/1865; tradition has it that Day taught Latin, Greek and Hebrew at Haddonfield. The records (1803) make specific reference to the fact that Latin and French "are or may be taught."
[3]Moon's Master's Thesis on Early Quaker Education in New Jersey, 11. Teachers College, Columbia University.
[4]Min. Woodbury Mo. Mtg., 15/I/1772.
[5]Min. Burlington Q. Mtg., 25/XI/1776.   *[6]Ibid.*, 1/VI/1813.

not available it was impossible to answer the third query as the discipline of the society desired it should be. The following extract is typical of the answers of meetings. The restraint from "pernicious books" was made possible by supplying a large number of approved character.[7]

We believe Friends are in a good degree careful to bring up those under their direction in plainness of speech, behavior and apparel: in the frequent reading of the scriptures: and to restrain them from pernicious books and the corrupt conversation of the world.[8]

Not only were books distributed by the meetings, but subscriptions were made from time to time to provide for their publication. It is useless to catalog the well-nigh numberless instances of this practice, but space may be given to a few. In 1774 Chesterfield received proposals from the Meeting for Sufferings for "promoting subscriptions for John Woolman's *Journal;*[9] in 1790 Burlington urged subscriptions for publishing Gough's *History of our Religious Society* and that preparative meetings buy several sets to be loaned to poor members; further, that subscriptions be made "for the Bible printing by Isaac Collins."[10] Upper Springfield in 1797 reported subscriptions had been taken for Job Scott's *Journal*, and a year later, that they subscribed for the *Journal* of George Fox and the *Memoirs of the Life of Catharine Phillip*.[11] These are sufficient to indicate the manner in which publication of "approved books" was supported.

The revival of educational activity after 1778 is evidenced in the comments on books for schools, which became much more numerous. Efforts were made to supply school books in the same manner as religious literature for adults was provided. Regarding books for schools, Woodbridge wrote in 1789:

Our Meeting for sufferings being informed that a new impression of Robert Barclay's Catechism is wanted and enquired after in divers places and that the introduction thereof into our schools and families may be instructively useful to the youth have directed the reprinting a number of them for the service of Friends within the compass of our Yearly Meeting.

. . .that the Monthly Meetings would appoint suitable friends for a proper

<hr/>

[7]For lists of books supplied at various times, see pages 336ff.
[8]Min. Great Egg Harbor -Mo. Mtg., 6/III/1820.
[9]Min. Chesterfield Mo. Mtg., 2/VI/1774.
[10]Min. Burlington Q. Mtg., 29/XI/1790.
[11]Min. Upper Springfield Mo. Mtg., 7/VI/1797 and 4/IV/1798.

A

C A T E C H I S M

AND

CONFESSION of FAITH,

APPROVED OF AND AGREED UNTO,

BY THE

GENERAL ASSEMBLY

OF THE

PATRIARCHS, PROPHETS and APOSTLES,
CHRIST HIMSELF *Chief Speaker*

IN AND AMONG THEM.

Which containeth a true and faithful Account of the Principles and Doctrines, which are moſt ſurely belieued by the Churches of Chriſt in GREAT BRITAIN and IRELAND, who are reproachfully called by the Name of QUAKERS; yet are found in the one Faith with the Primitive Church and Saints, as is moſt clearly demonſtrated by ſome plain Scripture Teſtimonies, (without conſequences or Commentaries) which are here collected, and inſerted by way of Anſwer to a few weighty, yet eaſy and familiar Queſtions, fitted as well for the wiſeth and largeſt, as for the weakeſt and loweſt Capacities.

TO WHICH IS ADDED

An EXPOSTULATION with, and APPEAL to, all
other PROFESSORS.

BY ROBERT BARCLAY.

Search the Scriptures, (or, ye ſearch the Scriptures,) for in them ye think ye have eternal Life, and they are they which teſtify of me. And ye will not come unto me, that ye might have Life. John v, 39. 40.

P H I L A D E L P H I A :

PRINTED BY JOSEPH JAMES, IN CHESTNUT-STREET.
M.DCC.LXXXVIII

TITLE PAGE OF BARCLAY'S CATECHISM

distribution of them particularly to the schools under the care of Preparative or other Meetings enjoining the tutors to have them read at seasonable times by such of the children in classes who have made due advancement in their learning. . . [12]

The lack of suitable school books was relieved in 1793 by the Meeting for Sufferings. Evesham informed that:

In consideration of the great want of suitable books for the use of the schools in our Society the Meeting for sufferings had, for that purpose, directed a selection and impression of Wm. Penn's Reflections & Maxims, relating to the conduct of human life, and 29 volumes were now received from the Monthly Meeting, being our proportion, which were divided between Evesham, Cropwell and Pine Grove Schools. . .Note Cropwell has but nine books, the others have ten each.[13]

In the same year, Mt. Holly stated:

Thirty-one books printed for the use of schools was produced to the meeting, which were put into the care of the school committee.[14]

Some meetings felt advantage would result from greater uniformity in books used and that they should have the approval of the school trustees. Evesham Monthly Meeting stated in 1801 that:

Some of our number have visited the schools established by this Meeting, several of which are in an improving state, and we believe it would conduce much to their advantage if the trustees or teacher of each school would keep an assortment of schoolbooks from the interest arising on the funds, or otherwise; and that no employer may introduce any book into our schools which is not of the same kind, without the approbation of the trustees, that the master may have the advantage of fixing his whole school in proper classes, which we think would much forward the children's improvement.[15]

The question of more uniform books came before the Yearly Meeting in a report made in 1845, and a special committee was appointed to see what might be done. The report makes clear that the purposes of uniformity are chiefly (1) to get rid of certain objectionable books, and (2) to make a change from one school to another less harmful to the pupil. The report follows:

The attention of the committee has been directed to the mixed character and great variety of school books in use. As it was thought important to obtain more minute information on the subject, than was then in our possession

---

[12]Note from minute of Mtg. for Sufferings, copied from Woodbridge Mo. Mtg. Min., 21/V/1789.
[13]Min. Evesham Prep. Mtg., 7/II/1793.
[14]Min. Mt. Holly Mo. Mtg., 10/I/1793.
[15]Min. Evesham Mo. Mtg., 10/IV/1801.

INTRODUCTION
TO THE ENGLISH READER

PART I.
PIECES IN PROSE.

CHAPTER I.
SELECT SENTENCES AND PARAGRAPHS.

SECTION I.

TO be good is to be happy.

Vice soon or late, brings misery.

We were not made for ourselves only.

A good person has a tender concern for the happiness of others.

Modesty is one of the chief ornaments of youth.

Deceit discovers a little mind.

Cultivate the love of truth.

No confidence can be placed in those who are in the habit of lying.

Neglect no opportunity of doing good.

Idleness is the parent of vice and misery.

Cleanliness promotes health of body and delicacy of mind.

The real wants of nature are soon satisfied.

A contented mind is an inestimable treasure.

Deliberate before you promise.

Boast not of the favours you bestow.

Merit the approbation of the wise and good.

It is a great blessing to have pious and virtuous parents.

The most secret acts of goodness are seen and approved by the Almighty.

SECTION II.

OUR reputation, virtue, and happiness, greatly depend on the choice of our companions.

B2

MURRAY'S "INTRODUCTION", EDITION OF 1828

several queries relating thereto were addressed to the teachers of schools to which Friends' children are sent. Replies were received from ninety of these schools which confirm the reports received last year, and include the class books used in teaching, as well as the reading books.

The want in the different departments of education of standard works of such excellence as to insure their general adoption, is much to be regretted; as it renders the change from one school to another, in which other books and other modes of teaching are in use, a temporary and often a permanent disadvantage to a child. Arithmetic, for example, is taught from 20 different books and geography from 14, and so on, in most of the branches taught.

It is much to be desired that this evil should be remedied, and if means could be devised to secure the cooperation of teachers in bringing into general use in our schools the same system of elementary books, either selected from those now in use, or prepared under the direction of Friends by competent authors, it would greatly accelerate the progress of the pupils in learning, especially in those higher and larger institutions, such as Westtown, to which many of the children of these primary schools are ultimately sent. Most of the positively objectionable works are found under the head of reading books or history, the former of which often contain, with other objectionable matter, extracts from dramatic writers, and books of fiction, thereby promoting a taste for that hurtful description of reading; and the books of history abounding with accounts of warlike achievements which are calculated to produce a very injurious effect on the susceptible minds of youth, and powerfully to cherish the corrupt propensities of the natural man.

Although it appears as if no adequate remedy could be applied until reading books are prepared, adapted to the safe instruction of Friends children, yet as there are many in use which contain comparatively little objectionable matter, and some (such as Lindley Murray's Compilations) which may be safely recommended, it is very important that teachers and such Friends as have the care of schools, should be careful to procure only works which are known to be of that character.[16]

The result of this movement was the establishment of central book supply houses by both branches of the Society of Friends. It is but another phase of the tendency towards centralization.[17] In 1843 the Friends at 15th and Race Streets proposed the "appointment of a standing committee to encourage the establishment of libraries in Monthly or Preparative Meetings" and recommended the appointment of members in local meetings to ascertain "wants in relation to books and to correspond with the standing com-

---

[16]Extracts Yr. Mtg. Min. (O.), 1845, pp. 2–3.
[17]The Tract Association of Friends at 304 Arch Street, Philadelphia, was established in 1816, and the Textbook Association in 1866. The central depository, "on the east side of Mulberry Street" was established about 1844.— Min. of the Mtg. for Sufferings, 15/III/1844.

CONTENTS.

PART I.

PIECES IN PROSE.

CHAPTER I.

G 2

FROM MURRAY'S "ENGLISH READER" PUBLISHED IN 1808

mittee of the Yearly Meeting."[18] This central book supply was created at an early date; books were obtained from it for schools and when a school was closed, they might be returned to be sold.[19]

As above stated, the elementary curriculum was made up of the four R's, and we may well add, with emphasis on Religion. The scarcity of comment on subjects of instruction makes it impossible to describe with certainty when additions were made generally. The East Branch School trustees stated, in 1820, they had examined the "various branches of learning and their writing books and order . . ."; in 1825 they mentioned writing, "several books of arithmetic," spelling, reading, reciting, etc.; a similar report was made in 1831:

All attended and heard the scholars in their spelling, reading, etc., examined their writing and cyphering books—it being the first visit paid to the school by us since it has been under the tuition of the present teacher, Thomas Warren. Any remarks as to improvement at this time could hardly be expected. Edward Taylor, Jr.[20]

At Evesham in 1801 the committee expressed the belief that girls' schools "should be conducted in the summer, when men teachers discontinue," and "a female as usher in steady schools . . . who might teach needlework and obviate the necessity of going to other schools to learn that art."[21]

It is difficult to determine from any one statement in the minutes just what was taught. For instance, in the case of Woodstown, later in the century, (1852) there were mentioned "reading, writing, arithmetic, grammar, geography, botany, physiology, philosophy, history, and drawing . . ." in the female department and to these were added "chemistry and the higher branches of mathematics" for the boys' department. These subjects do not seem unusual for a school that was called "academy" and at other times "Seminary;" but they certainly were more than a "common school" education. . Yet, in another report, the trustees stated: "the usual branches pertaining to a common school education have been taught," and again "most of the branches pertaining to a common school education, together with mathematics and drawing have

18Extracts Yr. Mtg. Min., (H.) 1843, 9–10.
19Min. Woolwich Prep. Mtg., (H.), A letter to the School Committee, 1883.
20Min. East Branch School Trustees, 6/V/1820; 5/III/1825; and 8/I/1831.
21P. 189.

been taught."[22] There can be little doubt, however, that the term "common school education" was used rather loosely and that more than that was provided. The school about the end of the century, stated as its purpose,

> . . .a thoroughly practical education to all desiring to finish their scholastic course near home; also to prepare students intending to take a course in college. The instructors will endeavor to arouse in the minds of the pupils a desire to gain a thorough education for the good it will be to them, and with this end in view, the best individual results can be obtained. Independent thinking is especially encouraged. . .

The school, at this date, comprised kindergarten, intermediate department, and the high school, and granted a diploma, a feature just established, which admitted the holder to Swarthmore College.[23]

The above curriculum had much that indicated harmony with the ideal of Realistic education, but thorough-going realism developed slowly so far as general practice was concerned. Early in the century, thirty years before Spencer's views of education had attracted public attention, Jonathan Dymond had laid his strictures on the classics, so far as moral education was concerned, and expressed preference for an education of the people that should inculcate "the love and habits of inquiry," believing, in general, that "science is preferable to literature, the knowledge of things to the knowledge of words." The purpose of education is social for, "as the education of a people prevents political evil, it effects political good. Despotic rulers well know that knowledge is inimical to their power."[24]

During the nineteenth century science began to occupy a greater place in practice, as Realists had long declared it should. In 1814 the teacher of the little school at Upper Springfield recommended the introduction of geography, and as the house was not sufficiently roomy for hanging maps, etc. it was decided necessary to make an addition of about ten feet at the end of it.[25] Maps were purchased

---

[22]Min. Pilesgrove Mo. Mtg., (H.), 29/IV/1851; Min. Pilesgrove Prep. Mtg. of Women Friends, (H.) 21/IV/1852 and 20/IV/1854.
[23]Descriptive catalogs of Bacon Academy for 1894–95 and 1896–97, kindly furnished the writer by Annie E. Pancoast, Woodstown, N. J.
[24]Dymond: *Essays on the Principles of Morality*, Chapter on Education of the People.
[25]P. 108.

PART II.

EXERCISES IN ORTHOGRAPHY.

CHAPTER I.

Containing instances of false Orthography, arranged under the respective Rules.

RULE I.

Monosyllables ending with f, l, *or* s, *preceded by a single vowel, double the final consonant; as* staff, mill, pass, *&c. The only exceptions are, of, if, as, is, has, was, yes, his, this, us, and thus.* See Gram. 19edit. p. 37.

It is no great merit to spel properly; but a great defect to do it incorrectly.

Jacob worshiped his Creator, leaning on the top of his staf.

We may place too little, as well as too much stres upon dreams.

Our manners should be neither gros, nor excessively refined.

RULE II.

Monosyllables ending with any consonant but f, l, *or* s, *and preceded by a single vowel, never double the final consonant; excepting only,* add, ebb, butt, egg, odd, err, inn, bunn, purr, *and* buzz.

FROM MURRAY'S "ENGLISH EXERCISES" (1813)

FROM HART'S "CLASS BOOK OF PROSE" (1845)

for Burlington school in 1822–3,[26] and, as above noted, Bacon Academy was emphasizing a scientific course in 1851. It probably did so from the time of its founding, ten years earlier. In the meeting's school at Old Springfield, Franklin Haines was employed to teach mathematics, such as mensuration, surveying and algebra.[27] At Upper Greenwich in 1857 "a series of apparatus for illustrating the higher branches was purchased for the use of the school." The Library Association, founded 1834, had at this time 500 volumes.[28] The following minute from Chester Orthodox Friends, 1883, describes some assistance given to encourage science teaching.

. . .Thru the efforts of the teachers and the kind cooperation of some friends interested in the school, funds were raised to purchase a human skeleton, and a manikin and they were placed in the school. . .and suitable closets constructed to preserve them; there has also been received and placed in the school a valuable collection of fossils, minerals, shells, etc., gifts from our former principal teacher Edward Forsythe, and a citizen of Moorestown, all of which are thought to be material aids to instruction in physiology and natural science; and good use has been made by the teachers of the chemical and philosophical apparatus in possession of the school. . .[29]

In 1885 Chester recorded that "several instructive lectures on scientific subjects were delivered in the school building during the past year."[30] These scientific lectures in local schools were part of a program undertaken by the Yearly Meeting, concerning which it stated in 1887,

The advantages to pupils of having the many truths found in their studies in Physics, Chemistry, etc., properly illustrated with suitable apparatus, are apparent, and for this purpose lectures on scientific and other subjects to the number of eighty-one, have been delivered at stated times during the year to schools desiring them.[31]

The reports of the several meetings, shown in previous chapters, indicate that a considerable number from New Jersey schools finished or continued their education at Westtown Boarding School, Pennsylvania.

Regarding science instruction at Westtown in 1846 it was stated,

In the departments of mathematical science, Natural Philosophy, Astronomy

---

[26]P. 64. [27]Miscellaneous papers of Old Springfield Prep. Mtg., 1853.
[28]*Ms.* History of Upper Greenwich Mtg. by William Haines, in hands of Wm. Borden, Mickleton, N. J.
[29]Min. Chester Mo. Mtg., (O), 3/VII/1883. [30]*Ibid.*, 7/II/1885.
[31]Extracts of Yr. Mtg. Mins., (H.), 1887, 20–23.

and other studies, the pupils acquitted themselves in a very creditable manner; and we believe there are few seminaries in our country, which afford better opportunities for acquiring a knowledge of the useful branches of education.[32]

In 1858 the course was described as follows:

The same course is pursued as has heretofore been the case; embracing all the branches of a good English education, with instruction in the Greek and Latin languages, and lectures during the winter season; and the progress made by the pupils is as great as could reasonably be expected. The usual instruction in the Christian principles and testimonies of Friends, is also given.[33]

In 1862,

The course of studies, and the number of teachers employed are the same as last year. As heretofore, at stated periods, portions of the Holy Scriptures, Barclay's Catechism or Bevan's View, are committed to memory by the pupils; and the Bible and other religious books are frequently read to them when assembled in the collecting rooms. A thorough knowledge of those branches of an English education, which are of daily practical utility being very important, particular care is taken to give instruction in them, with probably as much success as at any other school. Lectures have been delivered the past session on Natural Philosophy, Chemistry, and Natural History; and 50 boys and 12 girls have studied Latin, and 15 boys have given some attention to Greek.[34]

Ten years later the scientific and classical courses were combined in one, Latin and Greek being assigned as optional studies so that "those whose time is limited, may complete a Scientific Course as heretofore and obtain a corresponding certificate."[35]

TEXTBOOKS

It is almost impossible at the present day to reconstruct the entire curriculum or the list of textbooks used in schools a hundred or more years ago. But a beginning can be made that is very suggestive of the atmosphere of the class room so far as that is reflected in the books used. In the frequent warning against "reading pernicious books" is found the guide in the selection of books for class use. The following list of textbooks is made up from items contained in minutes of School Trustees, Committees, and Meetings in New Jersey between 1788 and 1869, which specified that the books were for the use of schools. It is probably incomplete.

---

[32]Extracts Yr. Mtg. Min., (O), 7-8.
[33]*Ibid.*, 1858, 4.   [34]*Ibid.*, 1862, 11.   [35]*Ibid.*, 1872, 23-4.

10   CONTENTS.

FROM MURRAY'S "ENGLISH GRAMMAR" (1826)

INDEX.

FROM THE "SELECT READER" NUMBER III, PUBLISHED BY
THE TRACT ASSOCIATION OF FRIENDS

American First Class Book.
American Practical Catechism.
Barclay's Catechism.
Bibles.
Books on common things.
Comley's Spelling Book.
Cowper's "Task."
Expositors.
Greenleaf's Arithmetic.
Lessons for Youth.
The Monitor.
Maps (Wall Maps, presumably).
Murray's English Reader, Introduction, Sequel, Grammar abridged.
Oeconomy of Human Life.
Penn's Reflections and Maxims, and Advice to His Children.
Pike's Arithmetic.
"Reading Books."
Scripture Lessons.
Select Reader (a series of readers (at least 4 in the series), published
    by the Tract Association of Friends at Philadelphia.)
Spelling books.
Testaments.

The books were frequently sent out by the superior meetings and distributed to the schools by the local school committee. In some schools the trustees controlled the books, making purchases and reselling to the pupils.[36]

Besides these books there were others which we would expect, were used in the schools, though no specific reference is made to them in the meetings' minutes that remain. Such were Benezet's *First Book for Children* (1778), S. M. Day's *Pronouncing Spelling Book*, (1811), *Art of Spelling facilitated for the use of schools* (1804), and *Lessons in Reading* (1804), Fox's *Introduction for Right Spelling* (1762), and Woolman's *First Book for Children*, (1769). The preference for books by Friends would certainly have caused these to have been considered in making a selection. A copy of Murray's *English Exercises* (1813), Evans' *Examples of Youthful Piety* (1830), Hart's *Classbook of Prose* (1845), Cotton Mather's *Essays to do Good*, addressed to all Christians whether in public or private capacities, and Beecher's *Suggestions Respecting Improvements in Education* (1829), doubtless for the use of teachers, were found in

---

[36]Min. of Trustees of Easton School Fund, 1861, 70.

SEQUEL

TO

THE ENGLISH READER:

OR,

ELEGANT SELECTIONS

IN PROSE AND POETRY.

DESIGNED TO IMPROVE

THE HIGHEST CLASS OF LEARNERS IN READING;

TO ESTABLISH

A TASTE FOR JUST AND ACCURATE COMPOSITION;

AND TO PROMOTE

THE INTERESTS OF PIETY AND VIRTUE.

BY LINDLEY MURRAY,

*Author of an "English Grammar adapted to the different
Classes of Learners," &c.*

STEREOTYPED BY L. JOHNSON. PHILADELPHIA.

Philadelphia:

PRINTED AND PUBLISHED BY S. PROBASCO,

1831.

TITLE PAGE OF A FAVORITE TEXTBOOK
IN FRIENDS' SCHOOLS

EXAMPLES

OF

YOUTHFUL PIETY.

ELIZABETH C. SECOR was born at New Rochelle in the State of New York, in the first month, 1814.

In very early life she manifested an uncommon gravity and seriousness in her deportment, was scrupulously careful not to do anything which she thought wrong, and was remarkably cleanly and neat in her person and habits. Towards her parents, she evinced a tender and affectionate attachment, cheerfully obeying all their commands, and avoiding whatever she apprehended would give them uneasiness.

When about two years and a half old, she desired her uncle to read in the Bible for her; he accordingly read the narrative of Abraham's offering up his son Isaac, at which she was greatly affected, and requested him to read no more, as she could not help crying.

Some friends intending to have a religious opportunity in the family, she appeared anxious for the time to arrive; sat with becoming gravity while it continued, and expressed a wish that they might have more such seasons, saying, "I had no idea that we should have such a good meeting."

It was her wish to attend religious meetings, but the delicate state of her health mostly prevented her from

FROM THOMAS EVANS' "EXAMPLES" PUBLISHED IN 1830

A N

A P O L O G Y

F O R   T H E

True Chriſtian Divinity:

B E I N G   A N

EXPLANATION and VINDICATION

O F   T H E

PRINCIPLES and DOCTRINES

OF THE PEOPLE CALLED

Q U A K E R S.

Written in LATIN and ENGLISH
By R O B E R T   B A R C L A Y,
And ſince tranſlated into HIGH DUTCH, LOW DUTCH, FRENCH
and SPANISH, for the Information of Strangers.

PHILADELPHIA:
PRINTED BY JOSEPH JAMES, IN
CHESNUT STREET
M.DCC.LXXXIX

TITLE PAGE OF BARCLAY'S "APOLOGY"

an old cupboard of the school room at Woodbury.   Some of the books are inscribed "Friends Female School at Woodbury."

Adult education was assured by a supply of religious and doc-

CATALOGUE OF BOOKS IN WOODBURY MEETING

trinal books, which were sent out either to be sold, or distributed free to those who could not buy.   Libraries were established in some places, with a book committee and librarian to loan books and see that they were returned. Such libraries were mentioned at Woodbury, (1789), Alloways Creek (1845), Little Egg Harbor (1844), Upper Greenwich (1834), Woolwich (1860), Chesterfield (1870), Upper Springfield (1838). Libraries were not mentioned at all meetings but it seems that books were sent to all alike and distributed as above indicated. One meeting, Upper Greenwich, was said to have 500 volumes under the care of its Library association.[37]

In some of the libraries it appears that great care was taken of the books. Several catalogs of the books at Woodbury[38] and other places were made and those in charge urged to keep them in order. Modern librarians would not be expected to show more persistence in following delinquent borrowers of books than did Samuel Mickle of Woodbury. In a letter to a Friend at Evesham he wrote in March, 1824:

If when our Friend Esther Ballenger may be at Evesham, she will enquire for Samuel Inskeep, and get Barclay's *Apology*, which he hath had in posession perhaps 25 years or more, she will greatly oblige the Preparative Meeting of Woodbury and particularly

S. Mickle.[39]

The character of the collections of books, whether a formal library association was formed or not, may be seen from the list below, made up from about seventy sources.[40]

---

[37]*Ms. Hist. of U. G. Mtg.* No list of the 500 titles is available.
[38]Facsimile of such a catalogue of 1802 is shown on page 335.
[39]Letter in a package of papers in School House Cupboard, Woodbury, N. J.
[40]A Kiss for a Blow.
A short examination whether War is lawful for a Christian.
Account of Joseph Harris.
Adam's Atlas.
Adam's Geography.
Advices.
Advice against Swearing.
Africans, books on the status of the oppressed.
Alexander Ascate's "Books."
Ancient Christian's principle or Rule of Life.
Anarchy of the Ranters.
Andrews, Edward, Life of.
Anecdotes of Gamblers.
Arnold's "Wheat" (?) and Learning to Think.
Barclay, R. Apology.
　　　　Catechism.
　　　　Church Government.
Barclay, J., Letters.

Benezet, A., Account of Friends bound with Penn's Tender Counsel.
Brief Account of the Rise and Settlement of Friends in Pennsylvania.
"Writings" and "Books on Slavekeeping."
Besse's Sufferings of Friends.
Biography of Scholars.
Blain's Lectures.
Bordhead, Charles, Memoirs.
Book for Boys.
Bownas, Samuel, Journal.
Brooks, M., Silent Waiting.
Byerd, Ann. (No work named.)
Chandler's Works.
Christ's Gracious Invitation.
Christian Instruction.
Christian Memento.
Christianity and Infidelity contrasted.
Classbook of Nature.
Cockburn's Review.
Collection of Memorials.
Colley's Apology for Silent Waiting.
Comb's Moral Philosophy.
Comley's Reader.
Speller.
Consideration on the use of the Production of Slavery.
Cowper's Task.
Crisp, Stephen, Epistle concerning the Present and Succeeding Times.
Crook, John, (No work mentioned).
Daboll's Arithmetic.
Daughters of Britain.
Davis, Richard, "Life" and "Journal."
Dell, William, "Small books wrote by."
Discipline books.
Distinction of Jerusalem.
Doctrines of Baptism.
Douglass, F., Narrative.
Drunkard's Looking Glass.
Dymond's Essays.
Early Impressions.
Edmonson's Journal.
Emblem of Nature.
Epistles addressed to the Youth of Norwich.
Evans' Journal.
Exhortation to the Inhabitants of South Carolina.
Experienced Living, The.
Extracts from Pennington.
Farmer's Instruction.
Fay, Samuel, and Shipway, Ann, Short Account of.
Fenelon's Pious Reflection—Faithfulness in Little Things.
Floral Emblems.
Flowers for Children.
Follen, G. L. Facts and Considerations relating to War, Hymns, Songs, and Fables.
Follen, Ruth, Memoirs.
Fox, G., Works—Journal.
Friends' Family.
Friends' Miscellany.
Fruits of Solitude.

Fuller's Catechism and "Writings."
Geography, Modern.
Gleanor, The.
Gough's History.
Griscom, Animal Magnetism and Physiology.
Grover, William, Selections.
Grub, Sarah, Journal.
Hall, D., Compassionate Call to such as have gone out from the Unity of Friends.
Haldane, Catherine, Life of.
Heaven, The way to.
Heavenly Pilot.
Hersey's Treatise.
Hicks', Sermons.
History of Mary Watson and Jane Mortimer.
Holmes, B. Serious Call in Christian Love.
     "Books."
Hour I live in, The.
Hymns. (Sent gratuitously for use of the Sunday School of Woodbury.)
Imitations of Christ.
Improving Stories for the Young.
Indian's Speech in Answer to a Sermon.
Janney's Life of Penn.
     Conversation.
Jefferies, John, Serious Address to the Church of England.
Judge, Hugh (No work named).
Kersey's Narrative.
Knapp's Female Biography.
Letters from a man of color.
Literatus, Ancient and Modern, by the Author of Peter Parley.
Little Jane.
Little Sins.
London Epistles.
McDonnell, Memoirs.
Mentor, The.
Michener's Retrospect of Quakerism.
"Missalaneys."
Mite in the Treasury, A.
Mothers of England.
Music, Essay on.
Narrative of Peter and John Hay.
Nature and Efficacy of the Cross of Christ.
Natural History, A.
Natural History of Animals.
Naturalist on Books.
New England Judged.
Ocean Work.
On Prayer.
Pamphlets, collected by A. Benezet.
Pamphlets of Memorials.
Pamphlet on Scripture Help.
Parley's Columbus and Tales about Africa.
Parlor Book, The.
Paul, Marco, Adventure in Maine.
Peace and War.
Penn, William, No Cross No Crown.
     Rise and Progress of Quakers.
     "Writings."

Penn, Barclay and Pike. Treatises on Fundamental Principles and Doctrines of the People Called Quakers.
Pennington, Isaac, Memoirs .
Works—Select Essays
Penny Magazine ("nearly torn up").
People of Color, Testimonies and views on improving.
Phillips, Catherine, Memoirs.
Phipps, Original and Present State of Man.
On Christian Baptism
Piety Promoted.
Power of Religion.
Present for Children at School, A.
Price, Phillip and Rachel, Memoirs of.
Primitive Christianity.
Proceedings of the Joint Committee.
Reason for the necessity of Silent Waiting.
Recket's and Gough's Journal.
Reflections on Christian Temper and Character.
Religious Duties.
Religious Tracts for the Descendants of Africa.
Richardson, John, Journal.
Life of.
Rush, Extracts from his Enquiry into the effects of Ardent Spirits.
Rutty, Thomas, Rise and Progress of Friends in Ireland.
School of Good Manners.
Scott, Job, Journal.
Scott, Samuel, Diary.
Select Anecdotes.
Seneca Indians, A pamphlet on.
Seneca Indians, Further illustration of case of.
Sewell's History of the Quakers.
Shotwell, Mary, Some expressions of.
Slavery, Address on, to the Society of Friends.
Smith, Martha, Letters.
Spirits, address to Public on the use of ardent.
Spaulding, John, Convincement.
Stanton, Daniel, Journal.
Striking instance of influence of Divine Grace on the mind.
Sumner's Oration.
Teacher's Gift.
The Great Audit.
The two Lambs.
Thoughts on ye importance of Religion.
Time and Eternity.
True way of Turning to God.
Turford, Hugh, Grounds of a Holy Life.
Twilight Conversation.
Union Questions.
Universality and Efficacy of Divine Grace.
Vindication of the Religious Society Called Quakers.
Well Spent Day.
West, Moses "Books,"
Witty, G., Farewell Address.
Wood, Margaret, Journal.
Wooman, J., Works.
Yearly Meeting Extracts.
Young Chemist.
Youthful Piety.

CHAPTER XII

SCHOOL SUPPORT

A people has as good schools as it is willing to support. The difficulty of securing good teachers is often incident to the fact that they are not well paid. This fact was early realized in the Quaker schools of New Jersey, but for a long time no decided efforts were made to secure more certain and larger salaries. The uncertainty of pay (in full) was often as strong a deterrant to the teacher's enthusiasm as the small salary itself.

During the latter part of the eighteenth century a movement was set afoot to secure more unified action in the financial affairs of schools. Advices of general nature were first sent by the Yearly Meeting to the lower ones; these advices gradually became more definite in character and specific plans for school foundations were drawn up.

During the entire period covered by this study the support of schools was accomplished by some of the following methods, or variations of them: (1) subscriptions, (2) money distributed from central stocks, (3) legacies and donations, (4) portion of state school fund received, (5) fees, (6) loans, usually arranged for in case of urgent need, and for a short period, and (7) income from investments. Some space will be devoted to each of these methods in the above order. Little, however, need be said of some of them as they are self-explanatory. The legacy or donation depended on the generosity of an individual, largely; fees or rates were a commonly accepted mode of support at that time; and loans were accomplished then as now, only in case of emergency, and with more or less difficulty. These three methods fail to show any growth of united action or conviction on the part of the religious body with regard to education. In the establishment of permanent funds by subscription, however, may be seen a crystallized sentiment favoring schools of enduring character.

In 1750 the Philadelphia Yearly Meeting advised that

. . .the most likely means to induce such persons (i. e. of moral character,

340

and sufficient erudition) to undertake the business will be to have some certain income fixed, in consideration of which they should be obliged to teach so many children on behalf of each monthly meeting, as said monthly meeting might judge adequate to the salary and that no person should receive the benefit of the salary without the appointment of the said meeting.[1]

The above was transmitted to the various meetings but no school funds of this character were then established. Such advice was repeated often in the next twenty-five years, until the committee on education in 1777, with Anthony Benezet's influence, urged still more strongly that action be taken. The concern for education which followed 1777 is reflected in the many provisions made by meetings for establishing schools with permanent funds so that the poor might be educated free of cost, the master well paid, and supplied with such comforts of life that he would be induced to render a longer term of service. The efforts of some of these meetings will be presented here as briefly as possible. As space does not allow presentation of the steps taken by all meetings to establish funds, it may be stated that between 1780 and 1800 efforts were made in almost all Quaker communities to establish such funds. Some of these were monthly meeting school funds, others were distinctly under the preparative meetings. Exception should be made of Great Egg Harbor and Little Egg Harbor, where, it seems, practically no efforts were put forth at this early time. The educational efforts and accomplishments of the various meetings, however, are presented in other chapters[2] though without particular attention to support of schools, and will not be necessary here.

In 1790 Salem Monthly Meeting received the report of a special committee on the advisability of creating a school fund according to the plan offered by the Yearly Meeting. They reported they "had not seen their way clear to adopt the recommended plan . . ." and were continued to report to a future meeting.[3] About a year thereafter, "a plan for raising a fund for shooling poor children" was proposed, and adopted by the meeting, in these terms:

1st. That nine Trustees and a Treasurer be annually appointed to have the care and management of the said fund, who are to be called and known by the name of the Trustees and Treasurer of the School Fund of the Monthly Meet-

---

[1]*Ms.* Advices, 250.   [2]See chapters Three, Four, Five and Six.
[3]Min. Salem Mo. Mtg., 30/VIII/1790.

ing of Salem and are now appointed Trustees and Treasurer for the ensuing year.

2nd. Bills or notes to be taken for the money subscribed in the name of the Treasurer of the school fund of the Monthly Meeting of Salem for the time being at six percent. interest, the principal not to be called for during the subscriber's lifetime and residence in this Monthly Meeting, but may at any time be paid.

3rd. The Treasurer shall provide a book wherein he shall enter a list of said bills or notes, children's names, schooled out of the said fund, with full and clear entries of all moneys received and expended, etc.

4th. The interest arising shall be strictly applied to the schooling poor children and to no other purpose but by direction of the Monthly Meeting to be drawn by an order from the Trustees or a majority of them who are enjoined to meet every three months or oftener as they may find occasion.

5th. The treasurer and trustees shall lay their accounts and proceedings before the Monthly Meeting in the fifth month annually or a committee appointed for that purpose, and the appointment of Trustees and Treasurer shall be in the sixth month following, and the interest always paid in the first month yearly.

6th. The Treasurer shall call in all sums falling into the hands of Executors or Administrators, and such who remove their residence to another Monthly Meeting, and put that, or other parts of the principal as may be paid in, out again in safe hands by the advice and direction of the Trustees or a majority of them.

7th. No part of the principal shall at any time be made use of except by direction of the Monthly Meeting for the purpose of raising an annuity.[4]

In 1794, due to the division in Salem Monthly Meeting, it was agreed that six trustees would be sufficient in the future. In 1796 the treasurer reported that £ 6/8/6 had been expended for schooling poor children. "Poor children" seems at all times to have included black as well as white ones; occasionally it is stated, as for example in 1798, that a certain sum was spent for schooling black children.[5] Likewise in 1801, £ 14/4/10 was expended "in schooling poor white and black children."[6] The sums thus spent varied from year to year. This may be seen from the following table, made up from minutes of the monthly meeting for the years mentioned. It is understood the fund is still in existence.

Date.	Spent for Schooling poor Children		Amt. of Fund.
1804	£ 22/3/9	remains	£ 37/1/6
1810	£ 27/3/9	"	32/0/6

[4]*Ibid.*, 31/X/1791.   [5]*Ibid.*, 28/V/1798; 16/4 was spent on one child.
[6]*Ibid.*, 25/V/1801.

1813	$42.61			$663.76
1815	27.63½			656.67
1816	37.46			771.85
1817	40.33½			771.70
1822	40.66			779.65
1823	52.75			820.26
1824	84.23			818.90
1825	99.90			862.91
1826	104.24			843.86
1829				861.92
1832				934.48½
1833	4.87½	to erect house	300.50	842.36
1850	30.00 (to teacher of colored school)			
1852	30.00	(ditto)		
1854	79.33½			
1855	61.42			

The following report of the trustees of the fund in 1854 will give a fair idea of their financial concerns.

Since our last statement was presented we have
received of interest $84.80
    Rent from farm due 25th-3rd month 1853   60.00

Amounting to $144.80
    And have expended in payment of school bills (Not con-
fined to Friends children) $79.33½
For materials for fencing on farm   12.90
Balance due our Treasurer, last report.   1.06
    Amounting together to   ———   93.29½
    Leaving a balance in our treasury (3rd month, 25th)
of $51.50½

The farm is again rented for $60.00, and the amount of the fund from which our income is derived is $700.00, of this $200 has recently been paid in which it is desirable again to place at interest.[7]

In the case of Salem it was customary to have a report of the school trustees each year. These reports almost invariably dealt with finance, more than the actual activities or progress of schools in which they were concerned. After making their annual report the committeee was usually released and a new one appointed for the succeeding year. This custom was followed fairly closely in

---

[7]*Ibid.*, 29/III/1854.

other meetings, though some give greater attention to the school itself.

In 1790 Haddonfield Quarterly Meeting drew up a plan for raising funds, according to that proposed by the Yearly Meeting, and similar in some respects to that of Salem quoted above. The full text of Haddonfield's plan is given in Chapter Six.[8] In 1791, they stated there is "a fund established in this meeting the income whereof to be applied to the care of poor white and black children, and some attention paid to the schooling such children . . ."[9] By 1798 the value of this fund had risen to £ 239/18/0, plus £ 5/7/3¾, the interest in the hands of the treasurer.[10] In 1800 the total value was £ 700/0/1.[11]

In 1803 the school treasurer spent £ 36/8/4 for books and schooling poor children, while in 1814, $155.75 was spent for "schooling poor white and black children."[12] In 1837 the fund schooled 18 children, most of them for six months. None of these were members of the society.[13] In 1841, $198.30 was expended for education of poor without the circle of membership.[14] Though never as large as some of the funds, it was very considerable for the time. In 1855, without the difficulty of a loan, the trustees paid $1,781.41 for building a dwelling house for the teacher, and expended $78.49 for the regular schooling of the poor.[15]

A preparative meeting school fund was begun at East Branch in 1800, when Wm. Satterthwaite, Jr., Elijah Field and Samuel Craft were appointed to "prepare an instrument in writing for the regulation of said fund" and asked to report to next meeting.[16] Two months thereafter, the instrument was produced, read and agreed to, and Samuel Craft made treasurer to "collect and dispose of all the moneys given or in any wise belonging to this fund, as he may be directed by a majority of the trustees." Other trustees were named and directed

to keep fair minutes of all their proceedings in a book provided for that purpose which those now appointed shall procure and they shall report to this meeting from time to time as occasion may require and whenever it shall appear to this

[8]Page 167.   [9]Min. Haddonfield Mo. Mtg., 12/IX/1791; see p. 168.
[10]*Ibid.*, 12/III/1798.   [11]*Ibid.*, 13/I/1800.
[12]*Ibid.*, 14/II/1803 and 14/II/1814.   [13]*Ibid.*, 13/II/1837.
[14]*Ibid.*, 8/II/1841.   [15]*Ibid.*, 12/II/1855.
[16]Min. East Branch Prep. Mtg., 27/VIII/1800.

meeting necessary for to appoint either Treasurer or Trustees or both, those already appointed shall deliver up all the moneys that they have in hand, together with all the books, parchment, and papers in any wise belonging to this institution to their successors in office which successors shall observe and attend in all their proceedings to what is here prescribed.[17]

The instrument above mentioned was drawn on parchment and subscriptions to the amount of £ 68/15/0 were entered thereon by the end of 1800. As elsewhere mentioned cooperation among the meetings was strongly emphasized. Accordingly, since East Branch had earlier contributed to a school fund at Chesterfield, they now requested help from that meeting in particular, a committee being named to suggest to them "whether it might not be right for them in some way to contribute something towards advancing ours at this place . . ."[18] Chesterfield replied by naming a committee "to endeavor to receive subscriptions from their members . . ." and these subscriptions were entered on the back of the parchment noted above, under the following statement:

We the subscribers, members of Chesterfield Preparative Meeting in New Jersey, do hereby severally for ourselves, and our heirs, promise to pay on demand and in specie unto Samuel Craft, Treasurer of Friends School Fund at the Preparative Meeting called Robins, or to his successor or successors in office, the sum of money severally by us subscribed against our names with interest therefore after the rate of five pounds for the hundred by the year, which money so subscribed by us shall be deemed to be a part of the within school fund, for to be disposed of by the Trustees of the said fund in the way and for the purposes therein expressed and not otherwise.[19]

A new subscription was agreed upon in 1804. By 1810 the fund amounted to $550.11; in 1823, $683.40; 1826, $771.17, "of which sum there is of permanent stock $493.29, leaving the neat sum of interest accrued to stock of $277.88;" 1830, $870.60; and in 1833, $911.65.[20]

Upper Springfield Preparative Meeting in 1792 undertook the establishment of a fund as follows:

The promotion of a permanent fund for the use of Friends school at this place agreeable to the repeated and pressing advices of the Yearly Meeting on a solid foundation, coming now before this meeting, and the sentiment of

---

[17]*Ibid.*, 29/X/1800.   [18]*Ibid.*, 27/V/1801.   [19]*Ibid.*, 26/VIII/1801.
[20]*Ibid.*, for the dates mentioned; Minutes of the trustees of East Branch School from 1819 to 1838, are extant—deposited at 142 N. 16th Street, Philadelphia; in 1849 the fund amounted to $1,277.07, Min. Chesterfield Mo. Mtg., 8/V/1849.

divers Friends being had thereon, it is agreed that the Clerk of this meeting procure a subscription (drawn on parchment) for that purpose, and produce it at our next Preparative Meeting, the expense thereof to be paid out of this meeting's stock.[21]

In 1793 a further minute stated:

A subscription drawn on parchment for the purpose of establishing a permanent fund for the support or benefit of the school at this place being produced at a former meeting was subscribed to by a few Friends, but was not dated at that time; the meeting now thinks it best and unites that the said subscription be dated on this day—(to wit, the sixteenth of the first month, one thousand seven hundred and ninety-three.)[22]

The fund at Upper Springfield outdid most of the preparative meeting funds and many of those established by monthly meetings. In 1835 a report stated that the total value of it was $3,196.02, mostly invested in bonds and mortgages.[23]

Chesterfield minutes of 1793 informed that a fund of "several hundred pounds" was made up, and Joseph Lawrie and Wm. Abbott were appointed to receive the subscriptions as well as the central stock distributed to them by the quarterly meeting for the purposes of education.[24] In connection with their fund, the following memorandum of the account of Robert White is interesting, showing as it does the uselessness of paper:

1796 Dr. Robert White—in account 1796–1803.

		£	S	D
10th mo. 18th, To his subscription to the School Fund		25	0	0
10th mo. 18th				
1800 To three years interest due, 5th mo. 14th, 1800		3	15	0
10th mo. 18th, 1801 To one year's interest on his subscription		1	5	0
10th mo. 18th, 1802 "		1	5	0
10th mo. 18th, 1803 "		1	5	0
10th mo. 18th, "		1	5	0

£ 33 15 0[25]

By 1828 the fund at Chesterfield Preparative Meeting amounted to $3655.38; 1829, $3841.97; 1830, $4036.26; 1832, $4116.18; 1839, $5316.37½; and in 1841, $5521.59.[26]

---

[21]Min. U. S. Prep. Mtg., 18/VII/1792. [22]*Ibid.*, 1793.
[23]Minutes Trustees of U. S. Friends' School, 29/X/1835.
[24]Min. Chesterfield Mo. Mtg., 7/V/1793.
[25]Loose papers in volume "D" of original *Ms.* Minutes of Chesterfield, on Trenton Meeting House, Trenton, N. J.
[26]Min. Chesterfield Prep. Mtg., for the years named.

Evesham Monthly Meeting in 1790 adopted the plan proposed by Haddonfield Quarterly Meeting, referred to above.[27]

Pilesgrove Monthly Meeting drew up a plan for raising an educational fund in 1794.[28] According to the following minute,

John Barnes, Samuel Ogden, Elihu Pedrick, Benjamin Moore, and Isaac Eldridge (were) appointed trustees of the school fund and Jacob Davis Treasurer thereof.[29]

The fund was valued at $341.32 in 1819, and continued to be small. The success of the school, however, was assured by the large gift of David Bacon[30] which was used to found the "Bacon Academy."

In 1783 the Monthly Meeting at Woodbridge proposed the raising of a fund for a school at Rahway.[31] Many other cases might be cited here, but would be superfluous for our purpose. A sufficient number of localities have been mentioned to indicate the very general sweep of the movement, the unity of purpose, the manner in which funds were established, and the service they rendered.

The foregoing pages refer to the individual efforts made by local meetings to establish funds for the support of schools in their midst. Another phase of school support by subscription should also be touched upon, though the school in question was not located in New Jersey. It did, however, provide educational opportunities for many of New Jersey's citizens, after 1799.

The school at Westtown, Pennsylvania, was established in 1799, after a long campaign in its favor, by the leadership of the Yearly Meeting and the loyal cooperation of all lower units. This support of a central school is evidence of a greater unity of activity that had been developing during the last half of the eighteenth century. The occasions when support of the Westtown school was urged most strongly on the lower meetings were (1) just prior to the school's establishment, (2) about 1800, when an effort was made to clear off a debt of $4000, (3) about 1812, in order to increase the pay of teachers and, again for the same purpose in 1834, and (4) at times when special obligations had to be incurred in order to provide buildings adequate to the needs of schools and masters, such as in 1850. In an examination of the available records of all

---

[27]For a description of school development in Evesham Mo. Mtg., see Chapter Six, p. 181; see also Min. Evesham Mo. Mtg., 9/VII/1790.
[28]For text of this plan see page 152.
[29]Min. Pilesgrove Mo. Mtg., 20/XI/1794. [30]See page 155. [31]p. 46,

meetings in New Jersey no case was found in which the meeting failed to raise money to assist the new central school. Some meetings that had no local school directly under their charge, paid the quota assigned them by superior meetings to secure the welfare of one at a distance. Yet there was no compulsion used to secure the cooperation of members. The minute concerning the collection of money for the purpose was usually stated " . . . to receive subscriptions from such of our members as feel disposed to contribute thereto . . ."[32] or "to open subscription papers for that purpose and offer to the members generally."[33]

Haddonfield's minute on the subject in 1797, gives a fair picture of the cooperative spirit with which they entered upon the undertaking:

> Divers friends of the committee appointed by our last Quarterly Meeting to unite with and afford assistance to the Monthly Meetings, on the subject of the Boarding School as recommended by the Yearly Meeting, attended this meeting and the subject being now opened, the Minutes of the Yearly Meeting and report of the committee to that Meeting read, it is recommended to the Preparative Meetings to open a subscription to forward the design of the instituting of a boarding school; and that they produce their subscriptions to this meeting.[34]

A few months later Haddonfield Preparative had raised £ 39/18/9, while Newton Preparative contributed £ 15.[35]

FUNDS FROM CENTRAL "STOCK"

The use of "stocks," established for particular purposes, was early recommended by George Fox and became a regular practice of the religious society. Thus there were stocks or funds for the relief of the poor, relief of the Negroes, relief of Indians, for putting out apprentices, and so on. The funds might be either central or local, or both. Thus, a local meeting had a stock for the poor, but it also contributed towards a "general stock." This "general" or central stock might be used to relieve a situation which a local meeting was not able to meet. As a rule the support of schools was by local funds, as has been seen in the foregoing pages. There were, however, central funds made up for special purposes, for instance creating the Boarding School at Westtown, and to this

[32]Min. U. S. Mo. Mtg., 7/XII/1796.   [33]*Ibid.*, 6/VII/1803.
[34]Min. Haddonfield Mo. Mtg., 9/I/1797.   [35]*Ibid.*, 11/IX/1797.
[36]Min. Burlington School Committee, 1792.

central fund all meetings contributed. Again, there were cases in which surplus funds were divided by the superior meeting and distributed for a particular purpose to those of lesser rank, as the following extracts illustrate. In 1792, Burlington stated:

Please to pay to the Monthly Meeting of Upper Springfield seventy-one pounds, seven shillings and three pence ½ being the said meeting's share of the surplus of the stock to be distributed for the use of schools in the several Preparative Meetings where funds are or may be established agreeable to the direction of the Quarterly Meeting. Signed on behalf of committee. . . [26]

Later the same meeting, through its school committee informed:

Please to pay to the monthly meeting of Little Egg Harbor nineteen pounds, thirteen shillings and nine pence, it being their quota of the surplus of the stock of the Quarterly Meeting for the express purpose of promoting schools by the establishment of funds within the same Monthly Meeting.[37]

Chesterfield, in the following minute, acknowledged receipt of her part of the fund distributed:

The Friends appointed to receive this meeting's quota arizen from the Quarterly Meeting's stock for the use of the fund of Friend's schools to the amount of £ 63..19..8½ reported they have received it.[38]

Likewise, Upper Springfield in the same year:

Upper Springfield Preparative Meeting received 20/16/3½ as their part of a division made by Burlington Quarterly Meeting, this sum was directed to be added to their subscription for the schools.[39]

The distribution to which these minutes of meetings of Burlington Quarter refer was rather unusual,—certainly not a general practise at that time. In the late 19th century, however, with a still greater degree of centralization, a central educational fund, and a central educational committee, the expenditures made for local schools by the Yearly Meeting were more common, and some schools could not have operated without this assistance. Thus, for example, Woolwich Preparative Meeting, in 1876 received $200 from the central source for the use of their school; that amount was to be used for salaries, books, furniture, and building.[40]

The expenditures of the central authorities in charge of education in Philadelphia Yearly Meeting, in both branches of the society, amounted to $2,587.99 in 1890.[41]

---

[37]*Ibid.*, 1794. [38]Min. Chesterfield Mo. Mtg., 6/VIII/1793.
[39]Min. U. S. Prep. Mtg., 20/III/1793.
[40]From a loose leaf report of the Treasurer of Woolwich School Committee, in the minute books of the Preparative Meeting, 15/IV/1880.
[41]Yearly Meeting Extracts, Orthodox and Hicksite.

LEGACIES AND DONATIONS

Individual philanthropy was strongly encouraged among the members of the early society of Friends, and one of the objects of it was education. Friends were, from the beginning of their organization, urged to make the proper disposition of their property during days of health and to "lend to the Lord, who will repay." Following this injunction we are not surprised to find numerous bequests, some large for the times, some small, made for the benefit of the schools, the poor, Indians, and Negroes. The following extract is representative of the meeting's warning to those who are rich, that they do good with their wealth:

Warn those that are rich in this world that they apply not the blessings of God to the indulging their appetites in pleasure and vanity; but that they be ready to do good, and to communicate to the relief of those who are in necessity. The principal, if not only, satisfaction a man of truly Christian disposition can have, in affluence, and the increase of the things of this world, must arise from the greater advantages and opportunities put into his hands of doing good therewith. But, alas, it is most melancholy to observe, that the very superfluities of apparel of one person might sometimes be sufficient to cloathe the nakedness of several fellow creatures.[42]

To keep before the minds of members the propriety of disposing of property, the following query was early adopted:

Are Friends careful to settle their affairs and make their wills in time of health?[43]

Pursuing the advices so often given, many members disposed of part of their goods for the support of schools. The following extracts are representative of the various bequests made for that purpose.

In 1791, the sum of £ 20, bequeathed by Ann Tomlinson "to any purpose desired by the Meeting," was added to the fund for "schooling poor Friends' children."[44] Six years later, the will of Sarah Hopkins being read, it was found that she gave " . . . fifty pounds to be put into the fund of Haddonfield Meeting for the purpose of schooling poor children .. ." and the treasurer was directed to receive it.[45] Similarly, a minute of the same meeting,

---

[42]Epistles of London Yearly Mtg., 1681–1817. (1818), 253.
[43]Michener: *Retrospect,* 256; from the list of queries approved in 1743.
[44]Min. Haddonfield Mo. Mtg., 10/I/1791.
[45]*Ibid.,* 8/V/1797.

in 1799 mentions a legacy of £ 50 given by Joseph Sloan for "schooling poor children of any color . . ."[46]

Legacies not left for specific purposes frequently found their way into the school fund as the following minute indicates:

And as it doth not appear that the said money was given for any specific purpose the Meeting after deliberate consideration feeling desirous in gratitude to the memory of the giver to dispose of it in a way that may be of lasting benefit doth unitedly agree that the said money be added to our school fund, and that it shall be deemed as a part of the permanent stock thereof and disposed of by the Trustees appointed by this Meeting to the care of our school fund in the same way and manner as subscriptions given for the advancement of said fund, and not otherwise, and the said money is at present to be lodged with the Treasurer to said fund.[47]

In 1806 William Wilkins and Sarah Wilkins deeded to Joseph Haines, Obadiah Engle, John Engle and John Borton, ground for the benefit of Easton School and other religious purposes of Friends and no other use whatsoever.[48]   There is also a deed giving title to land for the use of Easton School under Lower Evesham Preparative Meeting in 1847, but whether this ground was a gift or not, is not evident.[49]   Easton School was also benefitted by the legacy left by Samuel Shute, in 1823:

Item. I order and direct my executors to pay to the Treasurer of Easton School of Friends, or to his successor in office, the further sum of five hundred dollars, to be put out at interest, on good security, the proceeds whereof to be applied at the discression of the trustees, of said school, for the time being, for the education of Friends children and others in lowish circumstances; within its limits. 2nd mo. 5th, 1825. Obadiah Engle has received the above five hundred dollars.[50]

The following bequest of £ 25 was made to Rancocas School in 1820 by Hannah Buzby:

First, after payment of my just debts and incidental charges, I give and bequeath to my executors and to the survivors, or survivor of them, the sum of £ 25 to be paid over by them, as soon after my decease as convenient, to the treasurer of Friends School at Rancocus, or to his successor in office for the time

---

[46] *Ibid.*, 14/X/1799.
[47] The amount of the above was £4/15/7½; Min. East Branch Prep. Mtg., 19/VI/1806.
[48] Min. Evesham Mo. Mtg., 5/II/1808.
[49] Min. Evesham Prep. Mtg., (H.); the deed bears date of 15/IV/1847, and is in the vault at 15th & Race Streets, Philadelphia.
[50] Easton School Fund Minutes, 1823, 1.

being, duly appointed by the trustees of the said school, to be applied by the said trustees to and for the benefit of the same, and to no other purpose.[51]

In the same year, George Dilwyn gave £ 20 for the same school:

I give and bequeath to my said executors and the survivors of them in trust, £ 20 to be invested in the fund of the school under the care of the Preparative Meeting of Friends in Rancocus.   George Haines, Treasurer of the school fund is appointed to receive from the executors of George Dilwyn, deceased, the legacy left. . .and give his receipt on behalf of the Meeting.[52]

In 1821 the trustees of Upper Springfield School mentioned ¼ acre of land, bequeathed by George O'Neal for the benefit of the school.[53] This land remained a part of the permanent foundation and the income from its lease was regularly applied to education.

Other benefactions, to select certain notable cases, were made by David Bacon and Samuel Nicholson.   About 1840 David Bacon provided in section 13 of his will, that a certain sum of money and the residue of his estate, after paying other bequests, should be given for education.   This was stated later to amount to $5,956.   The sum was used to further Bacon Academy at Woodstown, which was one of the best schools supported by Friends in New Jersey in the middle nineteenth century.[54]   Another prominent school was that at Haddonfield which was benefitted by a bequest of Samuel Nicholson in 1880:

. . .I propose to donate the sum of one thousand dollars to the meeting for the purpose of promoting the guarded education of the children of its members in schools under the care of Friends.[55]

PUBLIC SCHOOL FUND

A very material amount of support of Friends' schools prior to 1867 was derived from the public school fund of the State, after it was established.   Just how valuable this income was it is difficult to say, but it was certainly regarded by some schools as a great assistance.   Moreover, when the use of the public funds was cut off by law there were protests made.   The questions were: can the state levy a tax, and yet withhold support, and can the state support, and yet exercise no control over, the institution it

[51]Min. Rancocas Prep. Mtg. 30/III/1820; in vault at 15th & Race Sts., Phila.
[52]*Ibid.*, 28/IX/1820.   [53]Min. U. S. School Trustees, 7/III/1821.
[54]See p. 154.   [55]Min. Haddonfield Mo. Mtg., 13/XI/1880.

supports. A phase of this difficult question that arose is presented in Chapter Thirteen.

From the very meagre school reports that are now available, dealing with the finances of these early Quaker schools, the writer has taken the items relating to aid received from the state fund. The reports extant relate to but few schools, but others, if found, would unquestionably present similar items of money received from the state fund.

The following table shows items of school money received by Easton School between 1831 and 1854:[56]

Date	Memoranda	Amount
1831	Received on state school fund for Margaret Joyce	$ .48
	Received on state school fund for O. Boston	.48
	Received on state school fund for Joseph Lippincott	.48
1832	Received on state school fund	$ 1.22
1833	To a balance on the state school fund	12.66
1836	Received of the township school committee	14.95
1846	Received from state school fund	18.43
1847	Received of the state school fund	20.99
1848	Received of the state school fund summer term	11.35
	Received of the state school fund winter term	.29
	Later	10.55
1854[57]	Received of state school fund balance on bills	.08

The following report made by the treasurer of East Branch Preparative Meeting School in 1838, also bears upon the question of state funds:

I received of Richard Mount township collector, eighteen dollars and fifty-one cents of the publick's money applied to promote the schooling of children that being Stony Brook School's and district No. 1 proportion thereof, which money has been applied by the Trustees of said school as follows, to wit: first I paid Mary Ann Taylor who taught said school six months beginning in 4th month and 10th month 1838, on account of deficiency of scholars the sum of eight dollars $ 8.00

1839—26th of 3rd month, I paid Isaac Craft who taught said school this winter, on account of deficiency of scholars the remaining balance of said money in my hands, to wit, ten dollars fifty one cents 10.51

$18.51

Samuel Craft[58]

---

[56]Collected from the pages of the Accounts of the Easton School Trustees.
[57]After 1854 no further receipts are mentioned.
[58]Min. East Branch School Trustees, 1838.

The treasurer of the school fund of Upper Greenwich (Mickleton, N. J.) registered the following item:

Public School money received during the year 1854—$155.00, wholly used for the purposes of education.[59]

The Minutes of Old Springfield show that the treasurer in 1850 acknowledged $1.68 "borrowed from township to pay Asa Foster's bill."[60] Other items were "8/VII/1864 to Cash paid Daniel Zelley out of township money—$9.75;" "22/VII/1864 to cash paid Anna M. Baker per order out of Township money $61.72," and, 18/V/1864, "Received of Benjamin R. Lamb, School Superintendent of township money, $88.06."[61] The school at Woodbury also received assistance from the state fund. In 1858 we find an item of $100 received from that source.[62]

FEES

Fees or rates levied on each scholar, unless he or she were too poor to afford it, were a most common source of income to the early teachers, and continued so in the nineteenth century, though in some cases a regular salary was guaranteed. The teacher was not only allowed to charge so much per child; it was also a part of his function to collect it. Often he was unable to collect and there was a deficit. On such occasions he might suffer the loss, or ask the trustees of the school to make it good. The latter were also called upon to make good a deficiency resulting from too small a number of scholars. Thus in 1838 and 1839 Samuel Craft paid Mary Ann Taylor and Isaac Craft $10.51 and $8.00 respectively for "deficiency of scholars."[63]

The following minute describes the function of the school trustees, and points out that they paid the teacher two dollars per scholar for three months:

Edward Taylor, Ezekiel Combs, Samuel Bunting and Edward Taylor Jr. attended and after examining the writing books and hearing the scholars in their different branches of learning and observing the order of said school, we are united in saying that the same appeared to us satisfactory. This being the first visit paid since the commencement of the present teacher (Betsy Watson) whose services began the 16th of last month, agreeably to the following agree-

[59]Prep. Mtg. Book for use of Schools, Upper Greenwich.
[60]Miscellaneous Papers of Old Springfield Prep. Mtg., dated 19/I/1850.
[61]*Ibid.*, 1864.   [62]See p. 147.   [63]Min. East Branch School Trustees.

ment made with us, that is, we engaged her 18 scholars at two dollars per scholar, for three months, and if there was more to pay her in the same proportion for half a year—and we to collect the money for her quarterly.[64]

In 1853 Franklin B. Haines was employed by trustees of Old Springfield. Among other items of his contract we find that he was "to teach the school for three cents per scholar per day." He was also to teach mathematics, mensuration, surveying and algebra but these subjects did not come within the three cent limit.

Much variation is found in amounts paid for rates, depending sometimes on the quality of the master. Records on this point, however, are not at all as full as desirable.

After public funds were withdrawn as a means of support, many of the church schools languished, or even became defunct. Some became public schools. Others continued in competition with the publicly supported institutions. In this competition we find evident two necessities recognized by the private school: (1) to make themselves as good or better than the public institution, and (2) to keep tuition low enough to compete successfully with it. The extract below indicates partially the effect of competition:

. . .The price for tuition appears to be as high as it is prudent to ask; for the competition of public schools and others is such as to make it difficult for us to fill our own, even at present rates. . . [65]

LOANS

Due to the success of the subscription method, the large number of bequests given for schools, and the common reliance on fees to pay a teacher, it was only in rare cases that loans were resorted to as the only way out of difficulty. In fact money seems even to have been loaned by the school trustees, on long term loans at "good security." The money loaned out or invested "safely" was that which accrued through subscription funds, legacies, and so on. As evidence that loans were used occasionally to serve the school it may be cited that Salem in 1880 recorded an item of seventy-five dollars "borrowed" for that purpose;[66] and a similar instance at Woodstown[67] in 1896 described in this minute:

John G. Borton in behalf of the trustees of Bacon School asked the consent

---

[64]*Ibid.*, 1821. [65]Min. Chester Mo. Mtg., (O), 8/VII/1890.
[66]Min. Salem Mo. Mtg., (O), 31/III/1880. [67]Pilesgrove Meeting.

of this meeting to borrow a sum not to exceed $300 to meet their running expenses, stating at the end of school year, if nothing appears unforeseen they would be able to liquidate all debts. Request granted after being duly considered.[68]

INCOME FROM INVESTMENTS AND PROPERTIES

Income from investments in property, sale of property, and interest on funds loaned, played a considerable part in the support of schools. Income from property disposed of was often added to the school fund. A case in point was that of East Branch Meeting which in 1802 was informed by Samuel Craft:

that in consequence of the order given him at our last meeting, he has received of Samuel Middleton the sum of six pounds, eight shillings, and six pence, it being our full dividend of the moneys arising from the sale of the old Meeting house at Crosswicks in Chesterfield, which moneys agreeable to the minute of our Monthly Meeting is to be considered as a part of our school fund and to be disposed of or applied in the same way as the subscription thereunto is directed, to be disposed of. The clerk is directed to furnish the Trustees of the school fund with a copy of this minute in order for them to transcribe it in their book. The Clerk produced a number of addressed and subjoined forms of a bequest from the school committee to this meeting, which is directed to be distributed among our members.[69]

After the emphasis of 1778, on the necessity of permanent houses grounds, etc., for the school, had begun to take effect, there may be noted many properties secured for schools. Sometimes only enough land was secured, suitable for the house and playground, but some contained enough acres to occupy a part of the teacher's time in agriculture. Such was the intention of the Yearly Meeting.

This land was sometimes given to the teacher, free of rent, as a part of his salary, so he might make a better living; in other cases, and these more frequent, he was allowed to rent the school land for a consideration mentioned in his contract. Thus Old Springfield in 1829 rented Joseph Kimble two lots of land at fifty-four dollars a year. In this agreement it was specified that a certain number of acres were to be tilled, that he was *not* to remove any straw, grass, dung, ashes, soil, or compost, but might have two tons of hay.[70] In 1834 an agreement was made between the

[68]Min. Pilesgrove Mo. Mtg., (H.), 1/XII/1896.
[69]Min. East Branch Prep. Mtg., 23/XII/1802.
[70]Miscellaneous Papers of Old Springfield.

trustees and Watson Pickering for two lots containing five acres, more or less, and buildings. The latter was to pay "$20 for the clover lot 'over the run,' at the expiration of the year; the dwelling house etc. and lot containing two acres more or less belonging to the school to have gratis while he teaches the school . . ."[71]   In 1853 the teacher, Franklin B. Haines, was allowed to have

all the property belonging to said school (except three acres of land lying south of the run) rent free; and for the other three acres of land laying south of the run he is to pay the sum of $20 per acre and is to farm all the land as the committee. . .may direct. . . [72]

Again in 1866 the trustees note an item of sixty dollars received from Daniel Kimble as rent from the school property.[73]

Salem Meeting may be mentioned as another instance in which a rent income of 90 dollars a year is recorded to the school's credit.[74] At an earlier date, 1850, the farm in Penn's Neck was rented for sixty dollars per year.[75]

---

[71]*Ibid.*, 5/III/1834.
[72]*Ibid.*, 21/IV/1853.
[73]*Ibid.*, 27/III/1866.
[74]Income from a farm.   See for a particular year, Min. Salem Mo. Mtg., (O), 1/IV/1885.
[75]*Ibid.*, 27/III/1850.

CHAPTER XIII

TRANSITION TO STATE SCHOOLS

PUBLIC SCHOOL LAWS

In the adoption of her state constitution in 1776, New Jersey made no provision relating to education. Herein she was neither alone, nor unfaithful to tradition established in the colony. For during Colonial days, with the exception of legislation for special schools, nothing was accomplished. Reliance was placed upon private institutions. However, early in the nineteenth century, (1816) an effort was made to begin a state school fund, by providing an annual appropriation of $15,000 to be invested in six per cent United States bonds.[1] Changes in the constitution of this fund were made from time to time. In 1820 townships were empowered to levy a tax for educational ends, but excepting in 1830–1831, money so raised was used solely to educate "such poor children as are paupers belonging to said township and the children of such poor parents resident in said township as are, or shall be, in the judgment of said committee, unable to pay for schooling the same."[2]

The law of 1829 attempted the establishment of a complete system, authorizing an annual appropriation of $20,000 from the income of the school fund, (or, if such source was not sufficient, to draw upon the treasurer to make up the deficiency), and distribution to counties on the basis of tax paid by the county. Townships were authorized to determine "by the vote of the town meeting so assembled, whether or not any additional amount shall be raised by said township by tax or otherwise, for the same object." Provision was made for the election of a township school committee and three district trustees to have immediate care of the school. Teachers were to be licensed by the township committee. The law of 1829, however, had little effect as the essential sections, four,

---

[1]LAWS OF N. J., 1816, 21; 1817, 26.
[2]*Ibid.*, 1820, 125–6; 1830, 120; 1831, 146.

five, six, and nine, were repealed in 1830.[3] By the enactment of 1830, schools already established were given a measure of security in the assurance that "they shall remain unaltered if a majority of the inhabitants shall so elect." The law of 1831 was a more decided victory for the advocates of church schools. By it the acts of 1829 and 1830 were both repealed, though certain of their provisions were re-incorporated. Twenty thousand dollars was appropriated for school support, and apportioned according to taxes paid; townships were privileged to raise additional amounts; but the greatest opportunity given to church schools lay in the provision:

That it shall and may be lawful for the patrons, supporters, or proprietors of the several common schools in the respective townships of this state to organize their respective schools, if not already so organized, by the appointment of a board of trustees in such form and manner, and consisting of such number as they may deem proper; and it shall be the duty of any board of trustees so organized to transmit to the school committee of their respective townships a certificate of· their organization, whereupon every such school shall be recognized by the said committee, as being entitled to an apportionment of the money assigned to such township by the respective boards of chosen freeholders from the appropriation of the school fund of this state and also of such sum or sums of money as may be raised by the said townships. . . [4]

A law, less reactionary in tone, was passed in 1838, granting an appropriation of thirty thousand dollars to schools and making licensing of teachers optional. Support of education was not limited to paupers, and the township was allowed to raise additional funds if desired. The essential contention of the friends of church schools was admitted, however, and section 12 provided:

That where the patrons or proprietors of any school already organized and established under the care of any religious society or denomination of Christians. whose church discipline provides for the establishment of schools, and the appointment of trustees, are unwilling to relinquish such school and become subject to all the provisions of this act, it shall be the duty of the trustees of such school to transmit to the school committee of their respective townships a certificate of their organization, together with a list of the children of such patrons and proprietors between the ages of five and sixteen years who are capable of attending school; whereupon every such school shall be entitled to receive its just and rateable proportion of the money assigned to said township out of the income of the school fund, and of such additional sum as may be raised or apportioned by said township for the support of public

---

[3]*Ibid.*, 1829, 105–108.   [4]*Ibid.*, 1831, 146.

schools; which apportionment shall be made by the school committee of the respective townships and a copy thereof filed with the township collector, whose duty it shall be to pay to the trustees of said school their just proportion of such money for the use and benefit of said school.[5]

The above section was retained in the more pretentious law of 1846, which provided for state supervision, made licensing of teachers obligatory, and required that the local township tax be double the amount received from the state school fund.[6]

But dissatisfaction and "misunderstanding" soon developed, regarding section 12 especially. That there was "considerable misunderstanding" became evident, in a very definite manner, as early as 1847. In his report for that year the Superintendent of Public Schools stated:

. . .objections have also been made to the uncertain wording of the 12th section. I have always entertained the opinion that the said section had reference exclusively to the schools of Friends, whose church discipline alone of all the religious denominations, provides for the establishment of schools and appointment of trustees."

Others however interpreted it differently. Another question arose as to whether under section 13 it was the town superintendent's duty to visit the school of a religious society which was receiving state money. On the interpretation, which had been authorized that they be not subject to visitation the superintendent wrote:

Here I cannot agree, even with the high authority, who has sanctioned a different course. The 13th section makes it the duty of the town superintendent to visit every school in said township. . .And makes no exception of any kind; nor are those schools exempted by section 12, whilst the evident intention and spirit of the law is that supervision should be extended over all the schools receiving public money. If such is not its intention, it should be more plainly expressed.[7]

The superintendent, in another place, attempted to make clear that his attitude was not one of hostility to any particular church organization:

. . .Let it not, however, be understood that I object to the privileges of the Society of Friends, for in no section of our state is more attention paid to education than in the districts occupied by them; but as a principle it is wrong that any preference should be given to the members of any one society over another.[8]

Considerable time elapsed before the law was "more plainly ex-

---

[5]*Ibid.*, 1838, 249–50.   [6]*Ibid.*, 1846, 164–70.
[7]ANN. REPORTS SUPT. P. S., 1847, 25–6.   [8]*Ibid.*, 1847, 24.

pressed." In the meantime the "misunderstanding" of its interpretation grew apace. In 1864 the superintendent's condemnation of section 12 was more severe:

. . .I have been appealed to by town superintendents asking if they were authorized by law to require the trustees of religious schools, established and organized in accordance with the provision of section 12. . .to open the ed schools to the inspection of the superintendents. In other cases I have been requested to notify the trustees of religious schools that their teachers should become subject to the yearly examination, or else the said trustees should forfeit their portion of the public money. I have been further asked to do that respecting these schools which I am not authorized to do. Complaints concerning them have been numerous, and I have had appeal cases which have been extremely difficult of solution. I have observed also that there is a disposition among members of certain religious organizations to avail themselves in every possible manner of the privileges extended by the section of the law referred to; and this year, for the first time, demands have been made by the trustees of several religious schools upon town superintendents for a portion of the school money. It is probably true, in a few instances, that these schools were organized and in actual operation prior to April 17th, 1846, yet the proof of their organization is hardly as conclusive as it should be to warrant me in rendering a decision favorable to the parties who have appealed. In all these cases, I have advised the parties to let the cases go to the courts for adjudication. Whether or not the church discipline of the religious organizations, of which the parties who have appealed to me are members, provdes for the establishment and maintenance of schools, is a matter for the courts and not for me to decide.

In view of the complications arising, concerning religious schools, and the manifest injustice of appropriating public monies to aid in the advancement of denominational interests, I would most respectfully and earnestly recommend that section 12. . .be repealed.[9]

The culmination of developments was reached in 1866, when, as the legislators recited, because of "considerable misunderstanding in regard to the meaning . . . the same (Section 12) is hereby repealed."[10] This action was followed by a movement to secure the reenactment and a conference assembled at Camden in December and memorialized the following legislature to that effect.[11] This memorial was acknowledged by the Senate in formal fashion:

Mr. Wurts presented a memorial from the Monthly Meeting of the religious Society of Friends held at Camden, 12th month Tenth, 1866, relative to the public school law. On motion of Mr. Wurts said memorial was laid on the

[9]*Ibid.*, 1864, 31–2.
[10]LAWS OF NEW JERSEY, 1866, 971.
[11]See page 367.

table and ordered to be printed for the use of the Senate.   It was read by the secretary Tuesday, Feb. 12th, but no action.[12]

THE QUESTION

An established institution yields ground grudgingly to a competing newcomer.   Men are prone to believe one thing is good because it *is*; and another bad because it *is not*.   The problem of yielding always raises questions.   The proposal that private church schools should give way to state supported institutions raised, among others, question as to: (1) the possibility of continuing moral and religious instruction not under church control; (2) possible evil results from mixed associations in public schools; (3) the justice of taxing citizens who already supported good schools in their communities, and (4) relating particularly to the law of 1866, the justice of withdrawing public support from the church school.[13]   It seems that all the questions raised might be placed under one or the other of these heads.   Loyalty to the Society and its traditions dictated the answers in many cases.

In 1834 the Yearly Meeting commented on the public schools as follows:

. . .The present most common methods of instruction in public schools, are generally admitted to be defective, so that many parents object to sending their children to them; alleging that from the manner in which the hours of relaxation from study are most usually spent, or from some other cause, many manifest a strong disinclination, after leaving school again to engage in manual labor employments. . .[14]

In 1845, the same source informed through a committee's report that in a Pennsylvania county (it may well be pointed out in this connection that the earliest opposition was aroused by the public school law of Pennsylvania in 1834) the parents are "unable to pursue any other course, especially with their younger children, than to send them to the common neighborhood or district schools although many Friends who do so seem aware that they are subjecting them to associations of a very hurtful tendency."[15]

One effect of public schools on the church school was inevitable. In localities such as that mentioned above, the parents sent children

---

[12]SENATE JOURNAL, 1867, 168 and 178.   [13]See page 360.
[14]Yr. Mtg. Extracts, 1834, (H)., 5–10.
[15]Extracts Yearly Mtg. Minutes, 1845, 3–4.

to the former and thus strengthened it. After public schools began to be established, but few meetings were able to report that they did not have any children attending them. Some kept such a tendency to a minimum, reporting but one or two children "who go to a common school," but others, Burlington for instance, had trouble in keeping a school open. Glover, the teacher in 1843, objected that the trustees, while promising him a hundred and fifty dollars, had only paid that amount for one year and had then cut his pay to one hundred dollars. He urged them to make good the one hundred and fifty dollars promised, asking whether "it may not be a subject worthy of the consideration of the trustees whether or not anything can be done to increase the interest of our school."

On the cause of the lapse of "interest" in his school, he says: "The decrease in my school has been caused by the establishment of the public school."[16]

The educational committee of the Yearly Meeting (Hicksite), in 1852, stated that of "4500 children requiring school education, only 998 were taught in schools under the care of the society . . ." and that "2600 (these figures it must be remembered refer to both New Jersey and Pennsylvania meetings) of these children attend public schools, thus showing an amount of encouragement on the part of Friends to the public school system, which must materially influence the prosperity of the schools of Friends, as contemplated by the discipline."[17]

The decrease in Friends' schools and the increasing tendency on the part of members, in out of the way districts, especially, to send their children to public schools, caused a greater effort to be made by the Yearly Meeting to arouse local meetings to action. For, as they stated:

the operation of the public school law has very materially increased these difficulties, and is likely to continue a very serious obstacle to the proper education of our youth, unless Friends are willing to set aside the pecuniary considerations which are alleged as the reason for accepting its provisions.[18]

The statements made in connection with the problem in Pennsylvania described New Jersey's situation as well:

. . .In many sections of the country there are no other than the district schools to which Friends can conveniently send their children. In sections

[16]See page 67. [17]Yr. Mtg. Extracts, (H.), 1852, 13–15.
[18]Yr. Mtg. Extracts, (O), 1845, 4–6.

where there is a sufficient number of children to form a school Friends allege that they are obliged to pay the school tax, and they give way to the idea that they cannot afford to pay it and for the schooling of their children also. Hence they have been induced to convert schools under the care of the preparative meetings into district schools, greatly, we fear, to the disadvantage of their children. We cannot doubt, that if Friends were impressed with a just sense of what appears to us to be the unavoidable injury which must result to the children from the mixed associations of such schools, and the difficulty which must be experienced in bringing them up in conformity with our religious profession and discipline while they are subject to such influences, there would be a greater willingness on the part of some to make the needful pecuniary sacrifices to insure the more guarded education of the youth.[19]

The answer of the Yearly Meeting to the subordinates' objection to supporting two systems of schools, suggests that "we ought not to hesitate at making the sacrifice, however great it may be . . .," but pay the tax and redouble efforts in the establishment of family schools, select schools, preparative meeting schools, or other agencies. The text of these suggestions follows:

. . .Although the number of families has increased since the last report, the principal causes of embarrassment continue unabated. Over one of these,—the scattered situation of our members,—we have no control. The difficulties which have arisen from the operation of the public school law, are not of this character; and if we act in relation thereto, on the principles which have always guided the society in similar cases, we shall not hesitate about the course we ought to pursue. Friends have always paid the tax levied for the support of the poor without complaining of the double burden thus imposed upon them, of assisting to maintain the poor not of our own Society, while at the same time we support our own without calling upon the public for aid; For we have always regarded the assistance given to our own poor members as the performance of a religious duty. If then, the religious and guarded education of our children, so as to train them up in the knowledge of our doctrines and the practice of our testimonies, is a duty not less incumbent than the support of our poor, we ought not to hesitate at making the sacrifice however great it may be, which is necessary to accomplish it. Many of the difficulties which seem to oppose the attempt, would, we are persuaded, lessen, and even disappear, before a resolute and persevering effort. In those cases in which select schools cannot be supported, schools conducted under the charge of suitable committees, in conformity with our principles and testimonies, would in all probability be resorted to by our sober neighbors, and thus become the means of sustaining and upholding our religious principles.

The whole subject deserves the earnest and continued attention of Friends; and we believe, that as they dwell under a sense of the obligations due to the Society, and to their children, they will be enabled to find some way of avoiding

[19]*Ibid.*

the manifold evils of the mixed associations, inevitable in the public district schools. In some places, this religious concern would lead to the establishment of schools, select, or otherwise, under the care of meetings; in others to the employment of teachers in families, or by a few families combining together; in other cases it will lead, and in some measure qualify members of a family to undertake themselves the instruction. In all cases, the awakening of a religious concern, faithfully to discharge, our duty to the rising generation will, of itself, greatly diminish the seeming difficulties of the undertaking, and bring with it its own rewards, in the increased prosperity and brightness of our religious society.[20]

The beginning of the movement toward state education, and the passing of laws to secure it, almost coincided with the division in the Society of Friends. Both of the events greatly influenced the tendency to centralize control over education; centralize control in order to stand firm against the foe from without and restrain tendencies to follow strange doctrines within. In 1845 the Educational committee expressed its views on the benefit of a centralized educational fund as follows:

It was stated in a former report to the Yearly Meeting that there are considerable funds set apart for the purposes of education in different districts, chiefly in the city of Philadelphia, and in Burlington, and Haddonfield Quarterly Meetings. The usefulness of these funds is in many cases much lessened by the strictness of the limits within which they are confined. Some of them have been raised by preparative meetings for the exclusive use of the members; and it has in certain instances happened that the fund has been allowed to accumulate, and the decrease in the number of the members of the meeting has left Friends without any objects on which to expend the interest; so that no small portion of these funds throughout the Yearly Meeting is lying almost idle, while the Society is suffering for want of means to educate its children.

It is well worthy the consideration of Friends, whether similar trusts should hereafter be so narrowly restricted whether it would not in all cases be advisible to make the larger bodies in the Society the trustees of the funds, with directions to appropriate it for the benefit of the nearest meetings needing it, in case the particular locality intended to be benefitted in the first place, should not require the assistance.

The committee again press upon the meeting, and upon Friends generally, the importance of creating a fund for the general purpose of education, and they repeat their conviction that as their ability to aid meetings, by procuring and distributing suitable books, and in the establishment of schools, depends greatly upon the possession of such a fund, their labors must, without it, fall very far short of what is called for by the wants of Friends in various places.[21]

---

[20]*Ibid.*   [21]*Ibid.*

THE ANSWER

In the foregoing pages, the analysis of the problem by the Yearly Meeting, in one way, suggested what the answer would be. These suggestions, however, were only partial answers. Many localities did, indeed, seek to follow its directions and maintain church schools of one kind or another. The complete solution is often a compromise, and so it was in this case. The most urgent inducements, to a compromise, it seems, were financial. As the yearly report mentioned, " . . . Friends allege that they are obliged to pay the school tax, and they give way to the idea that they cannot afford to pay it and for the schooling of their children also." Moreover, the New Jersey law made the way of compromise easy, by allowing church schools to receive public school funds until 1866. The schools' acceptance of state funds was one step towards their conversion into public schools. Having received state funds, for a long period of years, a number of the Quaker schools capitulated completely in the few years following 1866 and became thus the foundation of public institutions.

Few of the old school account books are now available, but most of those that have been found in New Jersey show entries of money received from the state school fund. The record of the Old Springfield School Trustees shows in 1850 $1.68, "borrowed from tp. to pay Asa Foster's bill," in 1864, "cash paid Daniel Zelley out of township money, $9.75," and "Cash paid Anna M. Barker per order out of tp. money, $61.72," and also "received of Benjamin R. Lamb, school superintendent of township money $88.06."[22] Other cases, notably Woodbury, Easton School, and Upper Evesham may be mentioned. Only one reference was found in the case of the last named, but the school account book if still extant would probably reveal more. In 1845, the school trustees reported the school was kept open " . . . nearly all the year past, and taught by members a part of the time . . . and we have received our portion of the school money from the township and apportioned it amongst the scholars as we thought most advisable."[23] Elsewhere in this

---

[22] *Misc. Papers of Old Springfield.*
[23] Min. U. E. Prep. Mtg., (H), 27/II/1845.

work is quoted a list of items from the treasurer's account book of Easton School.[24]

The repeal of section 12 of the school law in 1866 withdrew state funds as a means of support for schools controlled by religious bodies. A voice of protest was raised immediately against this action, and a conference called to meet in Camden in December of that year. Each monthly meeting was asked to send representatives. The following minute from Salem Meeting (Hicksite) describes the purpose:

A paper was received from Woodbury Monthly Meeting of Friends dated 10th month 29th, 1866, requesting that Salem Monthly should appoint one or more Friends to meet in conference with other Friends that may be appointed to meet in Friends Meeting House in Camden on 2nd day, 10th of 12th month next, to consult and decide upon what measures shall be taken to establish Friends in their just rights to the public school funds; which an act of the last legislature deprived them of Andrew Griscom, Thomas T. Hilliard, and David Pettit are appointed to meet with the proposed conference of Friends to be held in Camden at the time appointed.[25]

Three months later another monthly meeting's committee reported the results of the conference in the following minute:

The committee appointed in the 10th month last to attend the conference at Camden, in regard to the school law, report that they all attended and had an interesting meeting, and were united in memorializing the legislature on the subject of reenacting the 12th section of the school law.[26]

The above metioned memorial was unsuccessful in so far as getting a reenactment of section 12 was concerned; and the way was now prepared for the next step in the transformation of schools. This final period of transition in which numerous Quaker schools became extinct and others became public in name and fact reaches to the present time. It may be well to notice the cases of certain of these schools that passed into public control.

The earliest example that has been noted was that of Penn's Neck, where the school was turned over to the public in 1855.[27] A similar change in Mansfield Township, school district Number Three, is described in the following minute:

At the time appointed all of the committee convened together with about

---

[24]See page 197.   [25]Min. Salem Mo. Mtg., 31/X/1866.
[26]Min. Pilesgrove Mo. Mtg., (H), 1/I/1867; this conference appears to have been conducted entirely by the Hicksite Friends.
[27]See page 162.

ten adult male residents of the vicinity, when a full explanation of the powers of the committee and the situation of the property was made by reading the foregoing minute report, and memorandum, and also by a free and full interchange of sentiment. Whereupon it was agreed and assented to by the committee on one hand, by the trustees of the school district number three of Mansfield township on the other, that so far as they are concerned, the said subscription money amounting to $65.00 shall within thirty days from this time be paid to Empson Haines.

And that the said meeting house shall be used for educational purposes by the residents of this vicinity, as heretofore, and without any additional charge, subject to the regulation and restrictions as set forth in the report aforesaid dated 11th month, 5th, 1855. And also that no use be made of the said house inconsistent with the testimonies and principles of the religious society of Friends.

And further, that the said house will be delivered up on six months notice to the said committee or their successors, or the said Monthly Meeting of Burlington, in good repair whenever they may demand the same, with the understanding that if the occupancy thereof for the purposes aforesaid has not been equivalent to the money subscribed as aforesaid, then the said committee, their successors, or the said Monthly Meeting will return such amount as justice and equity may require.

It being represented to the committee that certain alteration in the seats, forms, and in the house would be needed for the better accommodation of a school, Empson Haines was appointed to give attention to the subject, and make such alterations for school purposes as in his opinion may be needed, provided the school district furnish him the necessary funds, with the understanding that the district may remove such improvements in case they abandon or leave the house.

And provided also that the fixtures, benches, and so forth belonging to the house at the time be restored in as good condition as they are now in.[28]

The following minute regarding the "Bacon Academy" at Woodstown describes how the meeting still retained "entire control of the school," yet was able to "receive its proportion of public money . . ." until the passage of the law in 1866.

On again resuming the consideration of the case of the Bacon School the committee reporting that the district trustees of the school situated in the same district, are willing to rent the Bacon School House, and allow it to receive its proportion of public money and our meeting still have the entire control of the school. After free expression thereon the report of the committee was adopted.[29]

In the case of Chesterfield Preparative Meeting School, in

---

[28]Min. Burlington Mo. Mtg., (H.), 2/II/1857.
[29]Min. Pilesgrove Mo. Mtg., (H.), 25/IX/1866.

April, 1866, the trustees were "instructed to ascertain what is the best disposition they can make with our school house for the ensuing year . . .," and two months later it was reported "rented . . . to the public trustees for one year, beginning 4th month, first, 1866."[30] A minute, three years later, indicated that the school was still controlled "subject to the direction of the meeting trustees."

> The schoolhouse has been rented to the district trustees for the present year for the sum of $100, payable quarterly, subject to the same rules and regulations that governed the school when Friends had charge of the same. The district trustees subject to the direction of the meeting trustees.[31]

At Salem, in 1872, the public school trustees sought to lease the Friends' school, but a committee of fourteen, having considered it reported "way did not open for leasing the house and grounds for a public school, and the applicants were so notified."[32] The continuance as a Friends' School, and without state aid was not without reason. It was, in 1872, composed of "male, female, and primary departments," and had 126 students enrolled. The popularity of the school declined, however. In 1900 there were 47 students and in 1905 it was discontinued as a Friends' School.[33]

Concerning the school in Delaware Township, Haddonfield reported in 1874:

> The committee appointed to enquire into the situation of the school property in Delaware township (late Waterford) belonging to this preparative meeting report that they have been to the premises and examined it. There are nearly two and a half acres of land upon which a small frame school house and also a dwelling house are erected; the schoolhouse is rented to the public school district for twenty dollars per annum and the dwelling house to a tenant for $25. There are no Friends' children now attending the school and but few Friends residing in that vicinity. Both the houses need new roofs and the fences around the land are in poor condition.

The deed for this school property was made in 1787. The report closed with a suggestion that since the district school now provided an education for all others, and but few Friends resided in the neighborhood the property should be disposed of and the money used to school Friends' children when necessary.[34]

---

[30]Min. Chesterfield Mo. Mtg., (H.), 26/IV/1866 and 28/VI/1866.
[31]Min. Chesterfield Prep. Mtg., 25/III/1869.
[32]Min. Salem Mo. Mtg., (H.), 29/V/1872 and 26/VI/1872.
[33]See page 131. [34]Min. Haddonfield Prep. Mtg., 4/II/1874.

In 1887,

The trustees of the public school in Woodbury, desiring to rent Friends' Female School on Delaware street, this meeting authorized the trustees of that school to act in the matter as in their judgment seems best.[35]

In 1889 the rent of the school house was entered as $25.[36] After 1890 there was no item of rent entered, nor was it continued as a Friends' school.

UPPER GREENWICH FRIENDS' SCHOOL NOW OCCUPIED BY DISTRICT SCHOOL

One other instance of this transformation may be mentioned, one of the twentieth century. At Upper Greenwich Meeting, in 1908, the school opened with ten scholars, but increased later to fourteen. This was the last year it was conducted as a Friends' School. In 1910,

The matter was discussed at some length, put to vote and carried that we lease the property for one school year, at a compensation of fifteen dollars. The secretary was ordered to notify the board of education to that effect.[37]

A minute of 1912 showed that the school property was rented to the district trustees year by year.[38]

---

[35]Min. Woodbury Prep. Mtg., (H.), 24/III/1887.   [36]*Ibid.*, 24/I/1889.
[37]Min. U. G. Prep. Mtg., (H.), 6/VIII/1910.
[38]Mr. Wm. Borden, Mickleton, N. J., informs that this practice is still continued.

CHAPTER XIV

IN CONCLUSION

Contrary to the statement that "from the first New Jersey was in advance of every American State in education" it is evident that but little was accomplished during the earlier years, and that mostly through individuals or individual congregations. Where New England elements dominated, efforts were made to create the town school system. In the four large Quaker centers, Salem, Burlington, Shrewsbury and Haddonfield, educational activity became dependent upon their local meetings. In 1682, however, education was encouraged by act of legislature, when the Island of Matinicunk was granted to Burlington for "educational purposes" forever. From the beginning the Quakers devoted themselves to elementary education, but did not encourage higher institutions of learning. The English government, on the other hand, after a time sought to encourage projects of higher, but neglected elementary education. Its educational policy is further shown in the instructions to Cornbury on the "inconvenience that may arise by the liberty of printing" and, in 1757, in the instruction that no one be allowed to keep school in the "Province of New Jersey without your license first obtained." The constitution of 1776 made no provision for education, leaving it entirely in private hands; in this period of Independence, Quaker Schools increased greatly in number, and a more uniform organization and centralization was perfected.

Educational developments in New Jersey were at all times in accord with the Pietistic, Realistic, and Philanthropic viewpoints, expressed by such leaders as Fox, Penn, Benezet, Woolman, Tuke, Griffith, Phipps, Bellers, Budd and others. All believed in a "guarded religious education," which was to be secured through many prohibitions, and carefully limited associations. Nevertheless, we find the children of other denominations, and of Negroes, often attended the Friends' schools. It was always stipulated, however, that they demean themselves "according to the rules of the school." Official advices of the Yearly and local meetings always emphasized the idea of a guarded religious education, according to the interpretation of Quaker leaders.

Regarding classical learning "they acknowledge the understanding of Languages, especially of Hebrew, Greek and Latin formerly was, and still is very useful yet . . . not . . . necessary to make a minister . . ." As colleges in that day were largely ecclesiastical in character and purpose, Quakers did not encourage them. Languages, for realistic ends, and "to answer the just desires of those that desire to read them, and for other very good reasons, as maintaining commerce and understanding among divers nations by these common languages . . ." were thought worthy of cultivation. There can be little doubt, however, that to some members, opposition to classics and colleges on the basis of being nonessential or even harmful for the training of ministers, became coextensive with opposition to them generally.

Quaker policy in the 19th century endorsed greater centralization in the control of schools, but continued an emphasis on "a guarded religious education." The movement for more "real" studies in the curriculum, and the idea of "manual labor institutions" both found support among Friends. Nevertheless, the number of their schools declined, and many that were maintained were attended largely by other denominations. After the middle of the century, many of them declined while others became partially or wholly public schools.

In the great Philanthropic Movement in Education the Quakers played a prominent role. Leaders such as Bellers, Budd, Woolman, Fox, Benezet and Penn viewed it as a "reproach to religion and government" that poverty on the one hand and excessive luxury on the other should be allowed to exist. With their pious sentiments the meetings concurred officially as early as 1695 and desired that "care be taken, that poor Friends' children may freely partake of such education, in order to apprenticeship." Members, "endowed with plenty of outward substance," were frequently urged to contribute to philanthropic projects, especially education. The minutes of the local meetings invariably point out that care was taken for the maintenance of the poor, and funds were raised for the education of their children.   Probably the most prominent philanthropic organization was the Friendly Institution of Burlington (1796); but each preparative, monthly, and quarterly meeting had its poor fund and took care of those in need of assistance.

In their dealings with the Indian and Negro in the new colony, the Quakers sought to exemplify the doctrines of Christianity. Not only did they aim to avoid dissension by provision for proper purchase of land from the Indians and fair trial of those implicated in wrongdoing, but also made attempts to encourage their education.   As for the Negroes, the first effort was, necessarily, to secure freedom for those held as slaves, and to discourage the importation and purchase of others.   The movement was gradual, beginning in the late 17th century and becoming decidedly effective between 1750 and 1780.   At the latter date there were but "few remaining in bonds with any of our members."   From this time on, the education of the Negro became a grave concern for he now stood in need of it.   Religious education was offered in special meetings held for Negroes and in conferences with them; Friends were on various occasions appointed to advise with manumitted Negroes as to "their temporal affairs;" and their school education came under the care of the school committee, though in some cases special committees were named.   In face of their best efforts the minutes often admit failure, or partial failure, as there is "a shortness we believe as to their education," and "education too much neglected."   But efforts were apparently never-ceasing, and while there is frequent admission of room for improvement, there is always "some care taken for their education." As a rule it appears that Negro children were educated on the same basis as children of the poor.   Special funds existed for their education in many places.

In accord with English law and practice, the Quaker colonists of New Jersey provided for education through apprenticeship. Fox, in 1669, advised the "putting out poor children to trades" and Philadelphia Yearly Meeting advised putting out children as apprentices to such as are members of Friends; and the fifth query was instituted to ascertain whether children were placed among Friends or not.   Certificates were given to those members who were apprenticed to trades at a distance from their home meeting.

After 1774 this was necessary to fulfill the letter of the law. If parents or guardians failed to take steps to put out children at the proper time, the meeting took the affair into its hands; likewise at a second marriage, the meeting sought to safeguard the rights of children by the first marriage.

Education of Colonial days existed primarily for religious ends. The school was an auxiliary of the church and the curriculum reflected this religious purpose. It is but natural, then, to find the Quaker schools controlled by the religious organization, which consisted of Yearly, quarterly, monthly and preparative or particular meetings. The functions of the first two were advisory, and to an extent supervisory, and directive. They helped to unify sentiment and action, to collect information, and to formulate programs, through the labors of educational committees. The great movement for better schools and more uniformity and centralization, about 1778, was successful largely because of the influence of superior meetings whose vigilance stimulated lower meetings to action. Individual schools of New Jersey were either under a school committee of the monthly or preparative meeting. These school committees sought to provide school lots, playgrounds, houses, masters' homes, occasionally land for tillage by the school master, a master of "solid" qualities, or mistress as the case might be, rules for school government, the necessary equipment of the schoolhouse, and the opportunities for education of poor and Negro children. One committee did not always suffice. Sometimes there were school fund committees apart from those who actually had charge of immediate school affairs. The committee was at all times the meeting's agent and made regular reports to that body. It was composed of men, women, or a combination of both sexes, usually determined according to the nature of the school and the sex of the teacher. The summer school, under a woman teacher frequently, was visited by a committee of women.

Teachers, as a rule, came from the local district, though some came from distant cities. Tenure, save in a few unusual cases, was brief and salaries slender, so it was natural that the teacher should continue to be also a farmer, blacksmith, carpenter or tailor. Contracts seem to have been generally used. With a very few exceptions the character of masters seems to have been above reproach. The school year varied greatly in length: some were open three and some eleven months, but the majority, probably, six or seven. Girls and boys attended, but apparently, separately for the most part. Girls and little boys had their best opportunities in the spring and summer when older boys had to do farm work.

Schools were generally elementary in character, but a few such as Westtown Boarding School in Pennsylvania, Bacon Academy at Woodstown, the Moorestown Academy and High School in the 19th century, gave attention to secondary school subjects. Advanced studies also found a place in many schools due to an unusual master or mistress who was capable of teaching a language or higher mathematics. After completing the regular elementary school of the meeting the youth either went to Westtown Boarding School —in Pennsylvania—, attended private schools, many of which existed under Quaker tutors in New Jersey, or else continued his studies no further.

Support of schools, at first very haphazard and dependent on local desire, became more uniform in the latter part of the 18th century. At one time or another the following methods, or a combination of them, were used to maintain schools: (1) subscription, (2) money distributed from central stock, (3) legacies and donations, (4) state school fund, (5) fees, (6) loans, and (7) income from investments. After 1778 most meetings established permanent school funds, some of which increased to the amount of several thousand dollars. These funds were managed by special committees, usually, appointed by the meeting, and bound by definite regulations drawn up by it. A remarkable degree of cooperation obtained between meetings in the establishment of these school funds, as also in the creation of those for relief of the poor, Negroes, and the education of Indians.

If, besides the religious note in the curriculum, we can detect another, it is unquestionably a realistic one. "We are in pain to make them scholars, but not men" was Penn's terse judgment of current practice. Practice seems to have followed his suggestion in a preference for scientific subjects. Classic and modern languages were taught, but, keeping in mind the stern prohibition against the heathenish books, gods, and goddesses, we must believe that such study was limited for the most part to "what may be savory and good matter that may not corrupt children's minds."

While the curriculum of the elementary school, in most cases, could not have been more than religion, reading, writing, and ciphering, some specific references are made to spelling, history, geography, mathematics, "such as mensuration, surveying, and algebra," in the first quarter and middle of the 19th century. Needle work for girls was mentioned at Evesham in 1801.

The Westtown Boarding School curriculum at its founding in 1799 seems to have been elementary in character, spelling, reading, writing, arithmetic, and bookkeeping being specified as the subjects to be taught. In the first half of the century the following subjects were gradually added: Mathematics, Arithmetic, Writing, French, Reading, Latin, Grammar, Sewing, Surveying, Trigonometry, Conic Sections, Astronomy, Chemistry, Physiology, Psychology, and Greek. In the latter part of the century emphasis was placed upon mathematical science, natural philosophy and astronomy, chemistry and natural history. There was also "instruction in the Greek and Latin languages." In 1862 the report states "50 boys and 12 girls have studied Latin, and 15 boys have given some attention to Greek."

In the Bacon Academy, 1852, girls were taught "reading, writing, arithmetic, grammar, geography, botany, physiology, philosophy, history, and drawing," and to these were added "chemistry and the higher branches of mathematics for the boys." A charming "old, old lady" admits the subjects in the female department were as formidable as they appear on paper.

A study of all available records of the four centers, Shrewsbury, Burlington, Haddonfield and Salem, reveals the fact that schools of elementary character were set up in practically all local communities by the close of the eighteenth century. Some, however, were not continuously in operation, due to lack of teachers, or scattered membership, and the consequent difficulty of supporting a school. Against all obstacles, however, there was steady advancement in point of numbers and popularity from 1778 until the influence of the public school movement was felt. A gradual decline then took place, due to the fact that (1) many members sent children to public schools because they were better situated, (2) many preferred the public school because it was free, (3) others did not wish to support a church school and pay for a public one at the same time, and (4) there was a dissension among the Quakers themselves which divided their strength and purpose, educationally. In a majority of cases, after 1827, there was an attempt to maintain two schools where before there had been but one. This period of division among Friends coincided with the movement for state free schools. Allegiance to the church school, on the part of many, was transferred to the state institution. A few of the old foundations, however, still remain and have large enrollments.

The transition was gradual, and accomplished, apparently, with little bitterness and less genuine opposition. The state free school movement may be said to have begun in 1816 when the school fund was created and reached its fulfillment in 1866. Definite provision was made in 1846 that schools, established by religious bodies whose discipline provided for the establishment of schools, should receive aid from state funds. Rivalries and jealousies flamed up and many difficult and embarrassing questions came before the State Superintendent of Schools. So difficult was the administration of the law, and especially section 12, that the superintendent in 1866 recommended the repeal of the latter, which was accomplished.

An official step was taken by the Monthly Meeting at Camden, and participated in by a number of others, to secure the reenactment of Section 12, but the effort was ineffectual. Though the transformation of some Quaker schools into public ones has been noted before 1866, the changes were more rapid and numerous after that date. Some properties were sold, and others rented to public school authorities. In some cases, apparently, Quaker control continued in fact for a number of years after the schools were technically public institutions.

Viewing the whole period of growth and decline of these schools, in connection with modern state education, it is apparent that the privately established schools, which were so widespread, rendered a great service to education in a day when no more universal institution had entered the field. The idea of extended education was primarily based upon religious philanthropy; it yielded, necessarily, to a broader conception of education for all, dependent not upon charity but the common wealth of society.

BIBLIOGRAPHY

Manuscript Material

Sources

(Note: (H.) refers to Hicksite and (O.) to Orthodox Friends' records.)

Allegheny Reservation, Account of Schools on the Sixth Month, 1872.

Alloway's Creek Preparative Meeting Minutes, 1783–1900. Two Volumes (H.) Friends Meeting House, Woodstown, N. J.

Alloway's Creek Preparative Meeting, Women's Minutes, 1841–1884. Four volumes. (H.) 15th and Race Streets, Philadelphia.

Ancocus Preparative Meeting, Miscellaneous Papers. (H.) 15th and Race Streets, Philadelphia.

Ancocus Preparative Meeting, Women's Minutes, 1853–1882. (H.) 15th and Race Streets, Philadelphia.

Ancocus Preparative Meeting Minutes, 1799–1881. (H.) Two volumes. 15th and Race Streets, Philadelphia.

Bacon, David. Papers relating to his Estate. Meeting House, Woodstown, N. J.

Bordentown Preparative Meeting Minutes, 1860–1878. (H.) Meeting House, Trenton, New Jersey.

Bordentown Preparative Meeting, Women's Minutes, 1804–1827. Two Volumes. 142 N. 16th Street, Philadelphia.

Burlington Preparative Meeting, Women's Minutes, 1800–1818 and 1828–1837. Two Volumes. 142 N. 16th Street, Philadelphia.

Burlington Preparative Meeting School Committee Minutes, 1822–1870. 142 N. 16th Street, Philadelphia.

Burlington Monthly Meeting Minutes, 1678–1850. Nine Volumes. 142 N. 16th Street, Philadelphia.

Burlington Quarterly Meeting Minutes, 1686–1898, excepting 1767–1770. Three Volumes. 142 N. 16th Street, Philadelphia.

Burlington Quarterly Meeting Minutes, 1827–1880. (H.) Meeting House, Mt. Holly, N. J. Minutes, 1880–1917, at home of F. S. Zelley, Mt. Holly, N. J.

Burlington Monthly Meeting Minutes, 1828–1922. Three Volumes. (H.) F. S. Zelley, Mt. Holly, N. J.

Burlington Monthly Meeting, Miscellaneous Papers. 15th and Race Streets, Philadelphia.

Burlington Monthly Meeting, Women's Minutes, 1828–1885. Two Volumes. (H.) 15th and Race Streets, Philadelphia.

Burlington Quarterly Meeting, Women's Minutes, 1827–1889. (H.) 15th and Race Streets, Philadelphia.

Cape May Preparative Meeting Minutes, 1797–1817. (H.) 15th and Race Streets, Philadelphia.

Catalog of Books belonging to Woodbury Preparative Meeting in 1802. In cupboard at Woodbury School.

Cheney, Eliza A. Report of the Boarding School at Tunesassa, from 5th month 2nd, 1874–3rd month 13th, 1875.

Chester Preparative Meeting Minutes, 1785–1889. Three Volumes. 302 Arch Street, Philadelphia.

Chester Preparative Meeting, Treasurer's Accounts, 1761–1848. 302 Arch Street, Philadelphia.

Chester Monthly Meeting Minutes, 1827–1898. Two Volumes. 302 Arch Street, Philadelphia.

Chester Monthly Meeting Minutes, 1804–1912. Three Volumes. (H.) Meeting House, Moorestown, N. J.

Chester Monthly Meeting, Women's Minutes, 1827–1900. Two Volumes. (H.) Meeting House, Moorestown, N. J.

Chester Preparative Meeting Minutes, 1827–1857. (H.) Meeting House, Moorestown, N. J.

Chester Monthly Meeting, Account Book, 1829–1889. (H.) Meeting House, Moorestown, N. J.

Chesterfield Monthly Meeting Minutes, 1684–1896. Seven Volumes. (H.) Meeting House, Trenton, N. J.

Chesterfield Preparative Meeting, Women's Minutes, 1838–1878. (H.) Meeting House, Trenton, N. J.

Chesterfield Preparative Meeting Minutes, 1809–1883. Three Volumes. (H.) Meeting House, Trenton, N. J.

Chesterfield Preparative Meeting, Women's Minutes, 1846–1897. Three Volumes. (H.) Meeting House, Moorestown, N. J.

Chesterfield Monthly Meeting Minutes (Copies), 1684–1793 and 1797–1852. Eight Volumes. 142 North 16th Street, Philadelphia.

Chesterfield Preparative Meeting Minutes, 1827–1841. Two Volumes. 142 North 16th Street, Philadelphia.

Collection of Christian and Brotherly Advices, compiled from minutes of the Yearly Meeting, 1762.

Cropwell Preparative Meeting Minutes, 1794–1836. 302 Arch Street, Philadelphia.

Dearborn, Henry (Secretary of War) Letter to Henry Drinker concerning Indian Education. 5th month 22nd, 1801.

East Branch (Robins) Preparative Meeting Minutes, 1828–1858. (H.) Meeting House, Trenton, N. J.

East Branch (Robins) Preparative Meeting Minutes, 1800–1813; 1822–1833. Six Volumes. 142 North 16th Street, Philadelphia.

East Branch School Fund, Trustees Minutes, 1819–1838. 142 North 16th Street, Philadelphia.

Eastlack, Sarah. Report to the Indian Committee of Philadelphia Yearly Meeting, Tunesassa, 4th month 6th, 1851.

Easton Preparative Meeting Minutes, 1810–1879. Two Volumes. 302 Arch Street, Philadelphia.

Easton School, Treasurer's Account Book, 1824–1900, though irregular. 302 Arch Street, Philadelphia.

Educational Committee of the Yearly Meeting, Minutes of. 15th and Race Streets, Philadelphia.

Elkinton, Joseph. Letter to Halliday Jackson on Indian education. Tunesassa, 12th month 3rd, 1820.

Evesham Monthly Meeting Minutes, 1827–1884. (H.) 15th and Race Streets, Philadelphia.

Evesham Monthly Meeting, Women's Minutes, 1828–1884. (H.) 15th and Race Streets, Philadelphia.

Evesham Preparative Meeting Minutes, 1854–1884. (H.) 15th and Race Streets, Philadelphia.

Evesham Preparative Meeting, Women's Minutes, 1847–1884. (H.) 15th and Race Streets, Philadelphia.

Evesham Monthly Meeting Minutes, 1760–1908. Six Volumes. 302 Arch Street, Philadelphia.

Evesham Preparative Meeting Minutes, 1761–1836. Two Volumes. 302 Arch Street, Philadelphia.

Evesham School, Trustees' Minutes, 1795–1840. 302 Arch Street, Philadelphia.

Great Egg Harbor and Cape May Monthly Meeting, 1726–1843. Two Volumes, 302 Arch Street, Philadelphia.

Greenwich Monthly Meeting Minutes, 1827–1914. Two Volumes. (H.) Meeting House, Woodstown, N. J.

Greenwich Monthly Meeting, Women's Minutes, 1884–1892. (H.) 15th and Race Streets, Philadelphia. Minutes 1827–1884, Meeting House, Woodstown, N. J.

Greenwich Preparative Meeting, Women's Minutes, 1804–1884. (H.) 15th and Race Streets, Philadelphia.

Greenwich Monthly Meeting Minutes, 1784–1893. Four Volumes. 142 North 16th Street, Philadelphia.

Greenwich Preparative Meeting, Women's Minutes, 1807–1884. Three Volumes. 142 North 16th Street, Philadelphia.

Haddonfield Quarterly Meeting Minutes, 1827–1916. Two Volumes. (H.) 15th and Race Streets, Philadelphia.

Haddonfield Quarterly Meeting, Women's Minutes, 1827–1896. (H.) 15th and Race Streets, Philadelphia.

Haddonfield Quarterly Meeting Minutes, 1697–1919. Five Volumes. 302 Arch Street, Philadelphia.

Haddonfield Monthly Meeting Minutes, 1710–1897. Eight Volumes. 302 Arch Street, Philadelphia.

Haddonfield Preparative Meeting Minutes, 1820–1913. Eight Volumes. 302 Arch Street, Philadelphia.

Hardwick Preparative Meeting, Women's Minutes, 1834–1852. Rutherford Place, New York City.

Hardwick and Randolph Monthly Meeting, Women's Minutes, 1840–1849. Rutherford Place, New York City.

Hardwick and Randolph Monthly Meeting Minutes, 1795–1855. Rutherford Place, New York City.

Little Egg Harbor Monthly Meeting Minutes, 1715–1762; 1784–1881. Four Volumes. Also miscellaneous papers. 142 North 16th Street, Philadelphia.

Little Egg Harbor Preparative Meeting Minutes, 1805–1842. 142 North 16th Street, Philadelphia.

Mansfield Preparative Meeting Minutes, 1818–1845. 142 North 16th Street, Philadelphia.

Mansfield School Fund, Treasurer's Account Book, 1797–1858; also Parchment roll of subscribers to the School in 1782. 142 North 16th Street, Philadelphia.

Maurice River Preparative Meeting, Minutes of Ministers and Elders. (H.) 15th and Race Streets, Philadelphia.

Maurice River Preparative Meeting, Women's Minutes, 1809–1830. (H.) 15th and Race Streets, Philadelphia.

Maurice River Monthly Meeting, Women's Minutes, 1833–1854. (H.) 15th and Race Streets, Philadelphia.

Maurice River Monthly Meeting Minutes, 1804–1823. 15th and Race Streets, Philadelphia.

Mendham (Randolph) Preparative Meeting Minutes, 1790–1826. Rutherford Place, New York City.

Minutes of the Meeting for Sufferings, 1756—. Ten Volumes. 302 Arch Street, Philadelphia.

Moon, A. W. Early Quaker Education in New Jersey. (Master's Thesis, Columbia University, 1904.)

Moorestown School Book, Accounts, 1834–1854. (H.) Mrs. H. Herr, 601 E. Main Street, Moorestown, N. J.

Mount Preparative Meeting Minutes, 1808–1850. (H.) 15th and Race Streets, Philadelphia; 1850–1870, Meeting House, Mt. Holly, N. J.

Mount Preparative Meeting, Women's Minutes, 1824–1844. (H.) Meeting House, Mt. Holly, N. J.; 1844–1850. (H.) 15th and Race Streets, Philadelphia.

Mount Preparative Meeting, Account Book, 1797–1870. (H.) 15th and Race Strets, Philadelphia.

Mt. Holly Preparative Meeting, School Fund Records, 1793–1881. Three Volumes. (H.) 15th and Race Streets, Philadelphia.

Mt. Holly Preparative Meeting Minutes, 1816–1850. (H.) Meeting House, Mt. Holly, N. J.

Mt. Holly Preparative Meeting, Women's Minutes, 1797–1811; 1865–1880. (H.) Meeting House, Mt. Holly, N. J.

Mt. Holly Monthly Meeting, Account Book, 1777–1878. (H.) Meeting House, Mt. Holly, N. J.

Mt. Holly Monthly Meeting Minutes, 1776–1903. Four Volumes. (H.) Meeting House, Mt. Holly, N. J.

Mt. Holly Monthly Meeting, Women's Minutes, 1776–1880. Three Volumes. (H.) Meeting House, Mt. Holly, N. J.

Mt. Holly Monthly Meeting Minutes, 1776–1793; and 1827–1828. 142 North 16th Street, Philadelphia.

Mt. Holly, Early Settlement of. Richard C. Shreve. H. S. P., Philadelphia.

Newton Preparative Meeting Minutes, 1828–1838 and 1847–1913. Three Volumes. (H.) Office of Howard Cooper, 106 Market Street, Camden, N. J.

Newton Preparative Meeting, Women's Minutes, 1845–1903. Six Volumes. (H.) Office of Howard Cooper, 106 Market Street, Camden, N. J.

Old Springfield Preparative Meeting Minutes, 1835–1851. (H.) 15th and Race Streets, Philadelphia.

Old Springfield Preparative Meeting, Miscellaneous Papers. 15th and Race Streets, Philadelphia.

Old Springfield Preparative Meeting, School Fund Book, 1849–1872. 15th and Race Streets, Philadelphia.

Penn's Neck Preparative Meeting, Women's Minutes, 1842–1867. (H.) 15th and Race Streets, Philadelphia.

Philadelphia Yearly Meeting Minutes. (H.) 15th and Race Streets, Philadelphia.

Philadelphia Yearly Meeting Minutes, 1681–1908. 302 Arch Street, Philadelphia.

Pilesgrove Monthly Meeting, Deeds and Miscellaneous Papers belonging to Meeting House, Woodstown, N. J.

Pilesgrove, Book of Records for Legacies and Investments. Meeting House, Woodstown, N. J.

Pilesgrove Preparative Meeting, Women's Minutes, 1851–1886. Two Volumes. (H.) Meeting House, Woodstown, N. J.

Pilesgrove Preparative Meeting Minutes, 1860–1901. (H.) Meeting House, Woodstown, N. J.

Pilesgrove Monthly Meeting, Women's Minutes, 1794–1822; 1827–1893. Three Volumes. (H.) Meeting House, Woodstown, N. J.

Pilesgrove Monthly Meeting Minutes, 1794–1904. Four Volumes. (H.) Meeting House, Woodstown, N. J.

Pilesgrove Monthly Meeting Minutes, 1827–1830. 142 North 16th Street, Philadelphia.

Plainfield Preparative Meeting, Women's Minutes, 1841–1893. Three Volumes. (H.) Meeting House, Plainfield, N. J.

Plainfield Preparative Meeting Minutes, 1879–1904. 142 North 16th Street, Philadelphia.

Plainfield Preparative Meeting, Women's Minutes, 1834–1861. 142 North 16th Street, Philadelphia.

Quakertown, earlier Bethlehem and Kingwood, Monthly Meeting Minutes, 1744–1905. First National Bank, Newtown, Pa.

Quakertown Monthly Meeting, Women's Minutes, 1744–1885. First National Bank, Newtown, Pa.

Rahway Preparative Meeting Minutes, 1845–1878. (H.) Meeting House, Plainfield, N. J.

Rahway Preparative Meeting Minutes, 1884–1910. 142 North 16th Street, Philadelphia.

Rahway and Plainfield Monthly Meeting, Miscellaneous Papers of. 142 North 16th Street, Philadelphia.

Rahway and Plainfield Monthly Meeting, Women's Minutes, 1848–1865; 1872–1875; 1879–1903. 142 North 16th Street, Philadelphia.

Rahway Preparative Meeting, Women's Minutes, 1838–1878. Two Volumes. 142 North 16th Street, Philadelphia.

Rahway and Plainfield Monthly Meeting Minutes, 1802–1910. Two Volumes. 142 North 16th Street, Philadelphia.

Rahway and Plainfield Monthly Meeting, Book of Accounts, 1802–1869. Meeting House, Plainfield, N. J.

Rahway Preparative Meeting School Committee's Minutes, 1875–1885. In box of miscellaneous material, 142 North 16th Street, Philadelphia.

Rahway and Plainfield Monthly Meeting, Women's Minutes, 1828–1893. Four Volumes. (H.) Meeting House, Plainfield, N. J.

Rahway and Plainfield Monthly Meeting Minutes, 1771–1781; 1784–1789; 1796–1799; 1827–1829. Rutherford Place, New York City.

Rancocas. (see Ancocus).

Representative Committee, Minutes of, 1827–1898. (H.) 15th and Race Streets, Philadelphia.

Salem Quarterly Meeting Minutes, 1827–1904. Two Volumes. (H.) Meeting House, Woodstown, N. J.

Salem Quarterly Meeting, Women's Minutes, 1827–1901. Three Volumes. (H.) Meeting House, Woodstown, N. J.

Salem Monthly Meeting Minutes, 1676–1900. Six Volumes. (H.) Meeting House, Salem, N. J.

Salem Monthly Meeting, Women's Minutes, 1828–1855 and 1895–1901. Four Volumes. (H.) Meeting House, Salem, N. J.

Salem Preparative Meeting, Women's Minutes, 1828–1850. Two Volumes. (H.) Meeting House, Salem, N. J.

Salem Monthly Meeting Minutes, 1676–1854. Six Volumes. 142 North 16th Street, Philadelphia; 1855— Clayton Wistar, Salem, N. J.

Shrewsbury Monthly Meeting Minutes, 1757–1786; 1828–1854. Two Volumes. 142 North 16th Street, Philadelphia.

Shrewsbury Monthly Meeting Minutes, 1732–1756; 1786–1904. Five Volumes. (H.) Rutherford Place, New York City.

Shrewsbury Monthly Meeting, Women's Minutes, 1680–1732; 1738–1816. Two Volumes. 142 North 16th Street, Philadelphia.

Shrewsbury Monthly Meeting School Fund. Five small volumes. 1790–1810. Rutherford Place, New York City.

Shrewsbury, Deeds for School Property of the Monthly Meeting, 1802. Rutherford Place, New York City.

Shrewsbury Monthly Meeting, Women's Minutes, 1680-1816. Two volumes. 142 North 16th Street, Philadelphia.

Shrewsbury and Rahway Quarterly Meeting, Women's Minutes, 1841–1893. Two Volumes. (H.) Meeting House, Plainfield, N. J.

Shrewsbury and Rahway Quarterly Meeting Minutes, 1705–1857. Three Volumes. 142 North 16th Street, Philadelphia.

Shrewsbury Quarterly Meeting Minutes, 1828–1921. (H.) Charles Trafford, Manasquan, N. J.

Stiles, Amos. Day Book, 1812–1821. Moorestown, N. J. H. S. P., Philadelphia.

Stony Brook Preparative Meeting Minutes, 1826–1878. Three Volumes. 142 North 16th Street, Philadelphia.

Taylor, Jacob and Thomas, Jonathan. Recommendation to the Indian Committee on Indian Education. Oneida, 11th month 4th, 1797.

Trenton Preparative Meeting, Women's Minutes, 1813–1878. Two Volumes. (H.) Meeting House, Trenton, N. J.

Trenton, Preparative Meeting Minutes, 1827–1900. Three Volumes. (H.) Meeting House, Trenton, N. J.

Trenton Preparative Meeting Minutes, 1816–1881. Two Volumes. 142 North 16th Street, Philadelphia.

Upper Evesham Preparative Meeting, Women's Minutes, 1828–1891. (H.) 15th and Race Streets, Philadelphia.

Upper Evesham Preparative Meeting Minutes, 1828–1862. (H.) 15th and Race Streets, Philadelphia.

Upper Evesham Monthly Meeting Minutes, 1828–1878. (H.) 15th and Race Streets, Philadelphia.

Upper Evesham Monthly Meeting, Women's Minutes, 1828–1896. (H.) 15th and Race Streets, Philadelphia.

Upper Evesham Monthly Meeting Minutes, 1794–1871. Three Volumes. 302 Arch Street, Philadelphia.

Upper Evesham Preparative Meeting Minutes, 1783–1842. Two Volumes. 302 Arch Street, Philadelphia.

Upper Greenwich School Minute Books, 1894–1921. Two Volumes. (H.) Herbert Brown, Mickleton, N. J.

Upper Greenwich Preparative Meeting Book for the use of Schools, 1809–1874. (H.) William Borden, Mickleton, N. J.

Upper Greenwich School Minutes, 1874–1884. William Borden, Mickleton, N. J.

Upper Greenwich Meeting, History of, by Wm. Haines. Wm. Borden, Mickleton, N. J.

Upper Greenwich Preparative Meeting Minutes, 1872–1904. (H.) Meeting House, Woodstown, N. J.; 1904— Wm. Borden, Mickleton, N. J.

Upper Penn's Neck Preparative Meeting Minutes, 1796–1867. (H.) 15th and Race Streets, Philadelphia.

Upper Springfield Monthly Meeting, Women's Minutes, 1806–1812. 15th and Race Streets, Philadelphia.

Upper Springfield Monthly Meeting Minutes, 1828–1857. (H.) 15th and Race Streets; 1857— in care of Martha E. Gibbs, Columbus, N. J.

Upper Springfield School Trustees' Proceedings, 1788–1849. 142 North 16th Street, Philadelphia.

Upper Springfield Monthly Meeting Minutes, 1783–1905. Four Volumes. 142 North 16th Street, Philadelphia.

Upper Springfield Preparative Meeting Minutes, 1789–1844. Two volumes. 142 North 16th Street, Philadelphia.

Vincenttown Preparative Meeting Minutes 1830–1855. (H.) 15th and Race Strets, Philadelphia.

Westfield Preparative Meeting Minutes, 1827–1857. 302 Arch Street, Philadelphia.

Westfield Preparative Meeting, Women's Minutes, 1827–1911. Three Volumes. (H.) Meeting House, Moorestown, N. J.

Westfield Preparative Meeting, School Trustees' Minutes, 1885–1902. (H.) Meeting House, Moorestown, N. J.

Westfield Preparative Meeting Minutes, 1897–1916. (H.) Meeting House, Moorestown, N. J.

Woodbridge Monthly Meeting Minutes, 1686–1905. (Called Rahway and Plainfield after 1788). Ten Volumes. Meeting House, Plainfield, N. J.

Woodbury Preparative Meeting, Women's Minutes, 1828–1893. Three Volumes. (H.) 15th and Race Streets, Philadelphia.

Woodbury Preparative Meeting Minutes, 1828–1890. Two Volumes. (H.) 15th and Race Streets, Philadelphia.

Woodbury, Minutes and Proceedings relating to the establishment of the School Fund, 1790. Warner Underwood, Woodbury, N. J.

Woodbury Monthly Meeting Minutes, 1808–1897. Four Volumes. (H.) Meeting House, Woodstown, N. J.

Woodbury Monthly Meeting, Women's Minutes, 1827–1893. Two Volumes. (H.) Meeting House, Woodstown, N. J.

Woolwich Preparative Meeting, Women's Minutes, 1834–1884. Three Volumes. (H.) 15th and Race Streets, Philadelphia.

Woolwich Preparative Meeting Minutes, 1835–1884. (H.) 15th and Race Streets, Philadelphia.

PRINTED MATERIAL

Source and Secondary

Ackworth School, Rules of. London, 1790.

Acrelius, Israel. A History of New Sweden . . . Translated by W. M. Reynolds. Philadelphia, 1874.

Allen, W. O. B. and McClure, E.　History of the Society for Promoting Christian Knowledge, 1698–1898.　London, 1898.

Allinson, Samuel.　Acts of the General Assembly of the Province of New Jersey, 1702–1776.　Burlington, 1776.

American Slavery, Views of, Taken a century ago.　By Anthony Benezet and John Wesley.　Philadelphia, 1858.

Andrews, B. A.　Historical Sketches of Greenwich on the Old Cohansey.　Vineland, N. J., 1905.

Annual Reports of the Superintendent of Public Instruction of New Jersey, 1847–1911; combined with Annual Reports of State Board of Education, 1867–1911.

Apgar, E. A.　History of the New Jersey School System.　In Report of New Jersey State Board of Education, 1879, pp. 33–62.

Appendix to the Extracts from the Minutes and Advices of London Yearly Meeting.　London, 1792.

Archives of the State of New Jersey.　By W. A. Whitehead and others.　1st Series, documents relating to Colonial History, 1631–1800.　28 Volumes.　Newark, 1880–1918.

Barber, J. W. and Howe, Henry.　Historical Collections of the State of New Jersey.　Newark, 1857.

Barclay, Robert.　Apology.　Philadelphia, 1789.
　　　　　　　　　Catechism and Confession of Faith.　Philadelphia, 1788.

Beecher, Catherine E.　Suggestions respecting Improvements in Education.　Hartford, 1829.

Bellers, John.　Proposals for raising a College of Industry . . .　London, 1696.
　　　　　Epistle to the Quarterly Meeting of London and Middlesex, 1718.

Benezet, Anthony.　First Book for Children.　1778.
　　　　　Some observations on the Situation, Disposition and Character of the Indian Natives of this Continent.　Philadelphia, 1784.
　　　　　Observations on the enslaving, importing and purchasing of Negroes . . . Germantown, 1760.

Bevans, John.　Brief View of Doctrines . . . professed by Friends.　Philadelphia, 1843.

Biddle, Owen.　A plan for a school . . . for Pennsylvania and New Jersey.　Philadelphia, 1790.

Biographical Sketches and Anecdotes of Members of the Religious Society of Friends.　Philadelphia: Tract Association of Friends, 1870.

Brief remarks on . . . a guarded and religious education.　Bristol, 1820.

British and Foreign School Society Report.　London, 1814.

Brown, Henry A.　The Settlement of Burlington.　Burlington, 1878.

Bryce, James.　The Relations of the Advanced and the Backward Races of Mankind.　The Romanes Lectures, 1902.　Clarendon Press, 1903.

Budd, Thomas.　Good Order Established in Pennsylvania and New Jersey.　Philadelphia, 1685.

Bunting, Morgan.　A List of Records of the Meetings constituting the Yearly Meeting at 15th and Race Streets, Philadelphia.　Philadelphia, 1906.

Carpenter, W. H. and Arthur, T. S. (Editors.) History of New Jersey from its earliest settlement to the Present Time. Philadelphia, 1853.

Carter, B. F. Woodbury and Vicinity. Woodbury, 1873.

Catalogue of Books and Rules of the Woodbury Library Company, instituted 1794. Philadelphia, 1815.

Catalogue of Books belonging to the Library Company of Burlington. Burlington, 1807.

Chalkley, Thomas. A collection of the Works of . . . in two parts. Philadelphia, 1749.

Clement, John. First Emigrant Settlers in Newton Township. Camden, 1877.

Clews, Elsie W. Educational Legislation and Administration of the Colonial Governments. Columbia University, Ph.D. Thesis. New York, 1899.

Cockburn, James. Review. Philadelphia, 1829.

Comly, John. A New Spelling Book, adapted to the different classes of Pupils . . . Philadelphia, 1827.

Constitution and By-Laws of the Haddonfield Library Company . . . Catalog of books. Philadelphia, 1805.

Cooper, H. M. Historical Sketch of Camden. Camden, 1909.
Historical Sketch of Newton Meeting.

Crawford, Charles. Observations upon Negro Slavery. Philadelphia, 1784.

Crouch, William. *Posthuma Christiana;* or a Collection of some of his papers. London, 1712.

Cubberley, E. P. The History of Education. Boston, 1920.

Cushing, Thomas, and Sheppard, C. E. History of the Counties of Gloucester, Salem and Cumberland. Philadelphia, 1883.

Darby, Abiah. Useful Instruction for Children. London, 1819.

Day, Stephen Munson. The Art of Spelling Facilitated. Philadelphia, 1804.
Lessons in Reading; Being Select Passages from the Scriptures . . . Philadelphia, 1804.

Dewees, W. W. History of Westtown Boarding School. Philadelphia, 1884.

Discipline, books of. 1831, 1856, 1888, 1894. (H.)

Dymond, Jonathan. Essays on the Principles of Morality. Philadelphia, 1896.

Education of Children, Some advices in the Yearly Meeting Epistle, 1709, Concerning the . . . For Friends to put into Practice. London, 1710.

Education of Youth, Some necessary remarks on the, Anonymous. No date. 302 Arch Street, Philadelphia.

Ellis, Franklin. History of Monmouth County, N. J. Philadelphia, 1885.

Elmer, Lucius Q. C. History of the Early Settlement and Progress of Cumberland County. Bridgeton, 1869.
The Constitution and Government of the Province and State of New Jersey. In Collections of the N. J. Hist. Soc. Vol. VII. Newark, 1872.

Epistles from London Yearly Meeting, 1681–1817. London, 1818.

Evans, Thomas. Examples of Youthful Piety. Philadelphia, 1830.

Extracts from Yearly Meeting Minutes, 142 N. 16th Street, Philadelphia.

Extracts from Minutes of Yearly Meeting held at 15th and Race Streets, Philadelphia, 1827–1895, Six Volumes.

Fox, George.   A Warning to all teachers of Children which are called School-masters and Mistresses and to parents . . .   London, 1657.

   To all Schoolmasters, Priests and Teachers, and Magistrates that be Christians.   London, 1660.

   Journal.   Two Volumes.   London, 1852.

   A Primer for the Schollers and Doctors of Europe.   London, 1659.

Friend, The, A Religious and Literary Journal.   Philadelphia.

Friends' Library.   Ten Volumes.   Philadelphia, 1837.

Friends' Intelligencer.   Seventy-nine Vols.   Philadelphia, 1844—.

Friends' Miscellany.   Edited by John and Isaac Comly.   Twelve volumes. Philadelphia, 1831–1839.

Friendly Institution of Burlington, one Hundredth Anniversary of the Found-ing of.   Burlington, 1896.

Fry, John.   Essay on Conduct and Education.   Bristol, 1776.

Gordon, Thomas F.   The History of New Jersey.   Trenton, 1834.

Graves, F. P.   A History of Education, Three Vols.   Macmillan: New York.

Grubb, Sarah and Woolman, John.   Extracts on Education.   Bristol, 1820.

Gummere, Amelia M.   Friends in Burlington.   Philadelphia, 1884.

   The Journal and Essays of John Woolman,   New York.   1922.

Haddonfield, The Two Hundredth Anniversary of the Settlement, 1713–1913. Published at Haddonfield, N. J.

Hageman, John F.   History of Princeton and its Institutions.   Philadelphia, 1879.

Hallowell, Benjamin.   Autobiography.   Philadelphia, 1883.

Hart, John S.   Class Book of Prose.   Philadelphia, 1845.

Hatfield, E. F.   History of Elizabeth, N. J.   New York, 1868.

Hazard, Samuel.   The Register of Pennsylvania, Vol. VII, Philadelphia, 1831.

Hood, John.   Index to the Laws of New Jersey.   Trenton, 1877.

Indian Tribes . . . in East and West Jersey and Pennsylvania, Account of the Conduct of the Religious Society of Friends towards.   Published by the Aborigines Committee of the Meeting for Sufferings.   London, 1844.

Indians, A brief Sketch of the effort of the Religious Society of Friends to Promote the Civilization and Improvement of the.   Philadelphia, 1879.

Jerseyman, The.   A Quarterly Magazine of Local History.   Two Volumes 1891–1905.   Flemington, N. J.

Johnson, R. G.   An Historical Account of the First Settlement of Salem in West Jersey by John Fenwick, Esq.   Philadelphia, 1839.

Kalm, Peter.   Travels into North America.   Three Volumes.   First Volume, Warrington, 1770; Second and third volumes, London, 1771.

Kemp, W. W.   Support of Schools in Colonial New York by the Society for the Promotion of the Gospel in Foreign Parts.   New York, 1913.

Kelsey, R. W.   Friends and the Indians, 1655–1917.   Philadelphia: Ex-ecutive Committee of Friends on Indian Affairs, 1917.

Kilpatrick, W. H. The Dutch Schools of New Netherlands and Colonial New York, Washington, 1912.

Kite, N., Smith, D. B., and Scattergood, Joseph. A statistical inquiry into the condition of the People of Color . . . Philadelphia, 1849.

Lancaster, Joseph. Improvements in Education as it respects the Industrious Classes of the Community . . . London, 1805.

A letter to John Foster . . . London, 1805.

Leaming, Aaron and Spicer, Jacob. The Grants, Concessions, and Original Constitution of the Province of New Jersey. Philadelphia, n. d.

Lee, F. B. New Jersey as a Colony and as a State . . . Four Volumes. New York, 1902.

Maclean, John. History of the College of New Jersey. Philadelphia, 1877.

Mandeville, Bernard de. Fable of the Bees; also an Essay on Charity and Charity Schools. London, 1723.

Mather, Cotton. Essays to do Good. A new edition by George Burde. Johnstown, 1815.

Mayo, A. D. Historical Sketches of New Jersey Schools. (In Reports of U. S. Commissioner of Education, 1895–6, Vol. I, 247–55; 1897–98, Vol. I, 465–72.

Michener, Ezra. Retrospect of Early Quakerism. Philadelphia, 1860.

Mickle, Isaac. Reminiscences of Old Gloucester . . . Philadelphia, 1845.

Monro, George. Extracts from an Essay on Christian Education, London, 1768.

Monroe, Paul. A Textbook in the History of Education. New York, 1905.

Moore, J. W. Records of the Kingwood Monthly Meeting of Friends, Flemington, 1900.

Mulford, Isaac S. Civil and Political History of New Jersey. Camden, 1848.

Murray, David. History of Education in New Jersey. Washington, 1899.

Murray, Lindley. Compendium of Religious Faith and Practice designed for Young Persons of the Society of Friends. New York, 1817.

English Exercises. Baltimore, 1813.

Biographical Sketch of Henry Tuke, Burlington, 1816.

Introduction to the English Reader. Philadelphia, 1828.

Sequel to the English Reader: or Elegant Selections in Prose and Poetry. Philadelphia, 1831.

The English Reader. Philadelphia, 1808.

Abridgement of Murray's English Grammar. Philadelphia, 1807.

NEWARK TOWN RECORDS. Collections of the N. J. Historical Society. Vol. VI. Newark, 1864.

NEW JERSEY ARCHIVES, First Series. Twenty-eight Vols. Newark, 1880–1899.

NEW JERSEY HISTORICAL SOCIETY COLLECTOINS. Newark and New York, 1846–1916.

NEW JERSEY, LAWS OF, FROM 1800. Trenton, New Jersey.

NEW JERSEY HISTORICAL SOCIETY, PROCEEDINGS OF. Six Volumes. Newark, 1845–1852.

Observations Relating to the Establishment of Schools. 10th month 2nd, 1778. Signed by Anthony Benezet and Isaac Zane and laid before the Yearly Meeting for consideration.

Parrish, Edward. An Essay on Education in the Society of Friends. Philadelphia, 1866.

Pattern of Christian Education (Benezet's copy). Germantown, 1756.

Patterson, William. Laws of the State of New Jersey. Newark, 1800.

Penn, William. Extracts from the Advice to his Children. London, 1819.
    Letter to his Wife and Children. Bound in a volume of Friends' Tracts. London, 1822.
    Reflections and Maxims. Philadelphia, 1901.

Pennington, Isaac. Works. Four Volumes. London, 1784.

Pennsylvania Gazette. Miscellaneous numbers.

Phipps, Joseph. Original and present State of Man. . . . Trenton, 1793.

Prescribed course of Study of Friends School for Indian Children. n. p., n. d.

Prowell, George R. History of Camden County, N. J. Philadelphia, 1886.

Purdy, James C. Moorestown, Old and New. Moorestown, 1886

Quaker Biographies. Five Volumes. Philadelphia, 1912.

Raum, John O. History of New Jersey from its earliest settlement to the present time. Two Volumes. Philadelphia, 1877.
    History of the City of Trenton. Trenton, 1871.

Rules of Discipline of Philadelphia Yearly Meeting. Philadelphia, 1806.

Salter, Edwin. A History of Monmouth and Ocean Counties . . . Bayone, 1890.

Schools for Black People and their Descendants, established by the Religious Society of Friends in 1770, A brief sketch of the. Philadelphia, 1867.

Select Reader, No. III. Published by the Tract Association of Friends, Philadelphia. n. d.

Sharpless, Isaac. Quaker Ideals of Education. (THE FRIEND, Volume 88, 328.)

Shotwell, A. M. Annals of our Colonial Ancestors. n. p., 1895.

Shourds, Thomas. History and Genealogy of Fenwick's Colony. Bridgeton, 1876.

Smith, Samuel. History of Nova Caesaria or New Jersey . . . Trenton, 1877.
    Some Advice to teachers. Dublin, 1794.

STATUTES OF THE REALM. Ten Volumes. London, 1810–1828.

Stevens, L. T. History of Cape May County. Cape May City, 1897.

Stewart, Frank H. Notes on Old Gloucester County, New Jersey. Published by the New Jersey Society of Pennsylvania, Camden, 1917.

Stillwell, J. E. The Quaker Records of Shrewsbury, New Jersey. (in Middletown, N. J. Town Book of old Middletown.) n. p., n. d.

Sypher, J. R. and Apgar, E. A. History of New Jersey . . . Philadelphia, 1870.

Tanner, Edwin P. The Province of New Jersey, 1664–1738. New York, 1908.

Thomas, A. C. and Thomas, R. H. History of the Society of Friends in America. Philadelphia, 1905.

Thomas, Gabriel. An Historical and Geographical account of the Province and country of Pennsylvania and West New Jersey in America. London, 1698.

Tracts on Moral and Religious Subjects. London, 1823 and 1824.

Tuke, Henry. Works. 4 Vols. York, 1815.

Tuke, James H. The Common and Free Schools of the United States of America. 1846.

Vaux, Roberts. Memoirs of the Life of Anthony Benezet. Philadelphia, 1817.

VOTES AND PROCEEDINGS OF THE GENERAL ASSEMBLY OF THE PROVINCE OF NEW JERSEY. 1745–1775.

Whitehead, W. A. East New Jersey under the Proprietary Governments, Newark, 1875.
    Contributions to the Early History of Perth Amboy and adjoining County . . . New York, 1856.

Wilson, Peter. Acts of the General Assembly of New Jersey, 1776–1783. Trenton, 1784.

Woodstown Almanac and Yearbook. First National Bank, Woodstown, New Jersey.

Woodward, E. M. and Hageman, J. F. History of Burlington and Mercer Counties . . . Philadelphia, 1883.

Woody, Thomas. Early Quaker Education in Pennsylvania. New York, 1920.

Woolman, John. Works. Philadelphia, 1806.
    First Book for Children, 1769.
    Considerations on keeping Negroes. Philadelphia, 1762.

INDEX

INDEX OF NAMES